AMERICAN EDUCATION

Its Men

Ideas

and

Institutions

Advisory Editor

Lawrence A. Cremin
Frederick A. P. Barnard Professor of Education
Teachers College, Columbia University

The Development of High-School Curricula in the North Central States from 1860 to 1918

John Elbert Stout

ARNO PRESS & THE NEW YORK TIMES
*New York * 1969*

Reprint edition 1969 by Arno Press, Inc.

*

Library of Congress Catalog Card No. 77-89240

*

Manufactured in the United States of America

Editorial Note

AMERICAN EDUCATION: *Its Men, Institutions and Ideas* presents selected works of thought and scholarship that have long been out of print or otherwise unavailable. Inevitably, such works will include particular ideas and doctrines that have been outmoded or superseded by more recent research. Nevertheless, all retain their place in the literature, having influenced educational thought and practice in their own time and having provided the basis for subsequent scholarship.

Lawrence A. Cremin
Teachers College

The Development of High-School Curricula in the North Central States from 1860 to 1918

The Development of High-School Curricula in the North Central States from 1860 to 1918

By
JOHN ELBERT STOUT

THE UNIVERSITY OF CHICAGO
CHICAGO, ILLINOIS

Published June, 1921

PREFACE

The purpose of this study is to trace the development of high-school curricula in the North Central states from 1860 to 1900. An introductory chapter presents a brief account of the early high schools. It furnishes a background for a treatment of the development of curricula in the geographical area indicated in the title.

The monograph is divided into three Parts. Parts I and II are devoted to the period 1860–1900. Part III covers the period 1900–1918. Part I contains a treatment of subjects and their organization into curricula. Part II is devoted to the subject matter of the various fields and subjects. Part III deals with subjects and subject matter, a chapter being devoted to each.

A few authorities are cited but tabulations and discussions are for the most part based upon data secured from original sources. These sources are chiefly published courses of study and textbooks. Some of the material was made available for use by the libraries of the University of Chicago, the University of Illinois, Oberlin College, and Cornell College. A considerable portion of it, however, was widely scattered, particularly the published courses of study, and had to be collected from the schools throughout the area.

In selecting curricula for purposes of display and tabulation, an effort was made to secure those which would fairly represent prevailing practices. Small schools have somewhat less proportional representation than medium size and large ones for the reason that copies of curricula used in the small school have in many cases not been preserved. Textbooks for reference have been selected on the basis of their general use as shown by lists displayed in published courses of study.

For purposes of tabulation, the period 1860–1900 has been divided into eight units of five years each. In Part III two units were selected, 1906–1910 and 1911–1918. This has been done to determine as accurately as possible the dates at which significant changes took place.

In the treatment of subjects, organization of curricula and subject matter, the facts are presented as revealed by the sources consulted. No attempt has been made to give connected accounts of particular schools. Peculiarities of individual schools have been noted but conclusions deal with general practices and tendencies.

J. E. S.

TABLE OF CONTENTS

INTRODUCTION

PART I. DEVELOPMENT IN SUBJECTS AND IN CURRICULA ORGANIZATION

CHAPTER PAGE

studies. Subjects offered not included at present in high-school curricula. Some schools offered little work in English. Wide range in science. Prevalence of short courses. Fewer subjects and longer time devoted to each was the later practice. Social studies received less attention than at present time. Increased attention to the field toward the close. Range of work in foreign language changed little. Little work offered in commercial subjects. Increased attention in a few schools after 1890. Miscellaneous subjects relatively numerous in the earlier years. Rapid decline after 1870. Manual training offered in a few schools after 1890.

VI. CONSTANTS AND VARIABLES 71

Table X. Mathematics, English and science were constants. Social studies a constant after 1870. Increase in number of schools offering foreign language. Algebra and geometry constants. Arithmetic next in importance. Trigonometry declines. Analytics and Calculus disappear after 1885. Literature is a constant after 1885. Grammar a variable and declined in importance. Status of composition uncertain. Some increase of attention given to it. Rhetoric ranked next to literature. Little change evident. Physics practically a constant. Physiology ranked second, followed by botany. Physical geography and chemistry have equal rank. Astronomy and geology decline in importance. Status of European history not easily determined. Probably a constant throughout. United States history increases in importance. Same true of civics. Political economy gains, though relatively unimportant. Latin gains and is practically a constant at the close. Greek unimportant and declines. German remains unchanged while French declines. Bookkeeping only commercial subject of importance until 1890.

VII. VARIATIONS IN TIME DEVOTED TO FIELDS AND SUBJECTS 80

Tables XI–XVIII show variations in time devoted to fields. Table XIX show time in years devoted to each field. Tables XX–XXVII show time in years devoted to each subject. Lack of uniformity in time devoted to fields. Wide range shown. Lack of standardization. Little change in average time devoted to mathematics. Small increase in time devoted to arithmetic. Considerable increase in algebra. Some increase in geometry. Increase of one year in English. Little change in grammar, composition, or rhetoric. Time devoted to literature increased nearly one year. Time devoted to science remained practically unchanged. Increase in time devoted to physics. Only slight changes in the other sciences. Time devoted to the social subjects increased approximately one year. Little change except in European history. Uncertainty concerning time devoted to foreign language owing to lack of exact data. Probably little change in time devoted to the field. Increase in time devoted to the commercial subjects near the close. Required subjects and electives. Algebra and geometry required subjects. English not required in all the earlier classical

INTRODUCTION

CHAPTER I

THE EARLY HIGH-SCHOOL MOVEMENT

The English Classical School was established in Boston in 1821. Later it was called the English High School. This school was the first of the type of schools which constitutes the chief means of secondary education in this country[1] and it no doubt exercised considerable influence upon the high schools established subsequently in Massachusetts and elsewhere. It is therefore thought desirable to set forth the aim which dominated this school and to trace in some detail the early development of the curriculum.

It should not be understood that the plan of the Boston school was followed in detail. The fact is, it was not.[2] But this school led in a movement which resulted in public secondary education, and its aim became one of the two outstanding aims dominating the high schools since that time.[3]

At a meeting of the School Committee of Boston in October, 1820, a resolution was introduced relating to the establishment of an English Classical School. The resolution was referred to a subcommittee which reported favorably for the establishment of such a school, and the report was adopted by the School Committee. In January, 1821, a town meeting was held at which the plan was approved with only three dissenting votes. The report of the subcommittee is set forth in E. E. Brown's well-known work.

The mode of education now adopted, and the branches of knowledge taught at our English grammar schools, are not sufficiently extensive nor otherwise calculated to bring the powers of the mind into operation to qualify youth to fill usefully and respectably many of those stations, both public and private, in which he may be placed. A parent who wishes to give a child an education that shall fit him for active life, and shall serve as a foundation for eminence in his profession, whether Mercantile or Mechanical, is under the necessity of giving him a different education from any which our public schools can now furnish. Hence, many children are separated from their parents and sent to private

[1] In 1915 there were 11,674 public and 2,248 private secondary schools. (*Report United State Commissioner of Education*, 1916, II, 447.)

[2] Cf. pp. 20-42; also Appendix, Tables A–H.

[3] Cf. pp. 6, 10, 13, 14; also Tables I and XXVIII.

academies in this vicinity to acquire that instruction which cannot be obtained at the public seminaries. Thus, many parents who contribute largely to the support of these institutions are subjected to heavy expense for the same object in other towns.[1]

The committee, for these and many other weighty considerations that might be offered, and in order to render the present system of public education more nearly perfect, are of the opinion that an additional school is required. They therefore recommend the founding of a Seminary which shall be called the English Classical School, and submit the following as a general outline of a plan for its organization and of the courses of studies to be pursued.[2]

In the report of the School Committee, "Regulations of the School Committee of the City of Boston,"[3] is found the following:

This school is situated in Derne Street. It has been instituted, at the publick expense, with the express design of furnishing the young men of this city, who are not intended for a collegiate course of study and who have derived the usual advantages of the other publick schools, with the means of completing a good English education, to fit them for active life, or qualify them for eminence in private or publick stations. Here are enjoyed, especially, the best instructions in the elements of Mathematicks and Natural Philosophy, with their application to the Sciences and Arts, in Grammar, Rhetorick, and Belles-Lettres, in Moral Philosophy and in History, Natural and Civil. This establishment is furnished with a very valuable mathematical and philosophical apparatus for the purposes of experiment and illustration.

"In addition to the common Regulations Sect. 2 Chap. 1 the following are required to be observed in this school:

1. No boy shall be admitted, as a member of the English High School, under the age of 12.

2. Boys shall be examined for admission into this school only once a year, viz., on the Friday and Saturday following the semiannual visitation and exhibition of the school in August.

3. Candidates for examination shall produce from the masters of the schools they last attended, certificates of good character and presumed qualifications for admission into this school. It shall, however, be the duty of the master of it, to institute a personal examination of them in Reading, Writing, English Grammar, Geography and Arithmetick as far as Proportion, including a general view of Vulgar and Decimal Fractions, in all of which they must be found well versed, in order to be admitted. The lads, who produce the certificates granted them for their merit, as in Sect. 2, Chap. 2, Reg. 16 shall be exempted from examinations accordingly. (This refers to the "two boys most distinguished for their improvement and good behavior" who were admitted without examination.)

4. The school shall be devided into three classes; and such sections of these shall be formed as the good of the school shall from time to time demand. Each class shall have their appropriate studies assigned them, corresponding to the

[1] Brown, E. E., *The Making of Our Middle Schools; An Account of the Development of Secondary Education in the United States*, 1902, pp. 298-300.

[2] *Ibid.*, pp. 300-1.

[3] Report of 1823, pp. 23-26.

intellectual progress of the institution; and to every class and section of the same the matter shall be required to give a due proportion of his personal attention.

5. Individuals shall be advanced in these classes according to their scholarship and no faster; and none shall be permitted to remain members of the school longer than three years to complete their course.

6. The classes or sections shall be required to pursue their respective branches of study not less than one week, without mixture, except where occasional exercises, as writing, reading, declamation, composition, &c, may be advantageously introduced as a relief to the pupils.

7. Particular reviews of each class or section shall be instituted, once a week, and general reviews once a quarter by the several instructors, in their appropriate departments.

8. The branches of learning and authors, to which the several classes shall, at present, be required to attend, are as follows: 3d or lowest Class. No. 1. *Intellectual and Written Arithmetick*, by Colburn and Lacroix. 2. *Ancient and Modern Geography*, by Worcester. 3. *General History*, by Tyler; *History of the United States*, by Grimshaw. 4. *Elements of Arts and Sciences*, by Blair. 5. Reading, Grammar and Declamation. 6. Book-keeping by Single and Double Entry. 7. Sacred Geography.

2d Class. No. 1, 2, 3, 4, 5, 6, 7 Continued, and No. 8 Algebra, by dictation . . . and Euler. 9. Rhetorick and Composition . . . Blair's *Lecture* abridged. 10. *Geometry*, by Legendre. 11. Natural Philosophy. 12. *Natural Theology*, by Poley.

1st. Class. No. 5, 8, 9, 10, 11, 12 Continued, and No. 13, Chronology. 14. *Moral Philosophy*, by Poley, 15. Forensicks. 16. Criticisms on English Authors. 17. Practical Mathematicks, Comprehending Navigation, Surveying, Mensuration, Astronomical Calculations, &c, together with the Construction and Use of Mathematical Instruments. 20. A course of Experimental Lectures on the various branches of Natural Philsophy. 21. *Evidences of Christianity*, by Poley.

9. For every accession of forty pupils to the whole number in this school an additional assistant shall be allowed the master, that is, there shall be at least one instructor for every forty pupils.

This course of study remained unchanged, with the following exceptions, up to 1852: In 1829[1] the following "studies are allowed if the masters think proper to introduce them": Smellie's *Philosophy of History*, chemistry, intellectual philosophy, linear drawing, and logic. In 1836[2] trigonometry, French, and constitution of the United States were added.

In 1852 a four-year course was provided instead of a three, with the following course of study:

Class 3. 1. Review of preparatory Studies using the text books authorized in the Grammar and Writing Schools of the City. 2. Ancient Geography. 3. Worcester's *General History*. 4. Sherwin's *Algebra*. 5. French Language. 6. Drawing.

[1] Report of 1829, p. 19.
[2] Report of 1836, p. 19.

Class 2. 1. Sherwin's *Algebra*, continued. 2. French Language, continued. 3. Drawing, continued. 4. Legendre's *Geometry*. 5. Bookkeeping. 6. Blair's *Rhetoric*. 7. Constitution of the United States. 8. Trigonometry, with its application to Surveying, Navigation, Mensuration, Astronomical Calculations &c. 9. Poley's *Evidences of Christianity*—a Monday-morning lesson.

Class 1. Trigonometry, with its applications &c continued. 2. Poley's *Evidences*, continued—a Monday-morning lesson. 3. Drawing, continued. 4. Astronomy. 5. Natural Philosophy. 6. Moral Philosophy. 7. Political Economy. 8. Natural Theology. 9. Cleveland's *Compendium of English Literature*. 10. French, continued, or the Spanish language may be commenced by such pupils, as in the judgment of the master have acquired a competent knowledge of the French.

For the pupils who remain at the school the fourth year, the course of studies shall be as follows: 1. Astronomy. 2. Intellectual Philosophy. 3. Omitted in Report. 4. Logic. 5. Spanish. 6. Geology. 7. Mechanics, Engineering and the higher Mathematics with some option.

Sect. 9. The several classes shall also have exercises in English Composition and Declamation. The instructors shall pay particular attention to the penmanship of the pupils, and give constantly such instruction in Spelling, Reading and English Grammar as they may deem to be necessary to make the pupils perfect in these fundamental branches of a good education.[1]

This course of study as given above remained without important change and "The Regulations Relating to the English High School" were practically unmodified up to 1860. As pointed out above, a fourth year was added to the course and boys were permitted to remain in the school four years instead of three.

The regulations and course of study of the Latin Grammar School[2] indicate a very different purpose for this school. Its avowed object was to prepare for the University[3] and the course of study[4] consisted (except for arithmetic, algebra, geometry, and trigonometry) of Latin, Greek, and subjects closely allied. Boys were admitted at nine years of age,[5] and it required five years[6] to complete the course.

In the Report of 1827, are given the regulations relating to the high school for girls and the course of study. The course was one year in length. No girl was admitted before the age of fourteen nor after sixteen. The purpose of the school is not stated. The course of study was as follows:

1. Reading, Pierpont's *First Class Book*. 2. Spelling, Walker's *Dictionary*, abridged; Boston Stereotype Edition. 3. English Grammar, Murray's Abridg-

[1] Report of 1852, pp. 39-40.

[2] Report of 1823, pp. 26-30.

[3] *Ibid.*, p. 26.

[4] *Ibid.*, p. 28.

[5] *Ibid.*, p. 27.

[6] *Ibid.*, p. 27.

ment; Collin's Stereotype Edition. 4. Rhetoric, Blair's *Lectures*, abridged; Greene's *Edition*. 5. Composition. 6. Modern Geography, by Worcester. 7. Ancient Geography. 8. The drawing of Maps. 9. Mental Arithmetic, Colburn's *First Lessons*. 10. Written Arithmetic, Colburn's *Sequel*. 11. Practical Geometry. 12. Natural Philosophy, Blake's Edition of the *Conversations*. 13. Bookkeeping, by Single Entry. 14. History of the United States, by Goodrich.[1]

No mention of this school is made in subsequent reports.

The early reports of the School Committee of Lowell, Massachusetts, contain very meager information concerning the high school. In the Report of 1839 is found the following:

One of the strongest arguments in favor of placing it (the high school) at once on the most permanent and respectable basis, is that it may draw to its halls, the children of all classes: that it may be the place where rich and the poor may meet together; where the wall of partition which now seems raised between them, may be removed; where the kindlier feelings between the children of these classes may be begotten; where the indigent may be excited to emulate the cleanliness, decorum and mental improvement of those in better circumstances; and where the children of our wealthier citizens will have an opportunity of witnessing and sympathizing, more than they now do, in the wants and privations of their fellows of the same age; where both insensibly forget the distinction which difference of circumstances would otherwise have drawn between them and where all feel the conscious dignity of receiving their instruction as a *right*, to which as the children of citizens they are entitled and which cannot be denied them.[2]

In the Report of 1840 the following statement is made:

The influence of this school is felt as an incentive to exertion through all the public schools in the city. Its object is to place within reach of the poorest citizen such means of preparing his children for college, or for giving instruction, or for any branch of active business, as the richest shall be glad to avail themselves of, for their own children. This object has been thus far realized. More needs not to be said to commend this institution to the especial sympathy and favor of the people.[3]

Again in the Report of 1843 we find:

Of our High school little need be said. It has so far become an object of pride and affection with our citizens, that it may be said to be constantly under their eye; and there is therefore the less necessity that the Committee should call the public attention to it.

It has entirely superseded all private schools in our City, and all necessity for them. No class of our citizens is excluded from its benefits, and none certainly can have any inducement to deprive themselves of its advantages, by sending their children to seek higher, or more thorough instruction elsewhere.[4]

[1] Report of 1827, pp. 22-23.
[2] Report of 1839, pp. 4-5.
[3] Report of 1840, pp. 6-7.
[4] Report of 1843, p. 5.

It is probable that the course of study was not very well worked out from the following statement found in the Report of 1851:

There are two modes in which a High School may be organized and conducted. One is, that of an exact and prescribed course of study, limited to a term of three, four or five years, (generally three) with annual admission, and a corresponding course of study for each year. The other is no prescribed course; but in its place an authorized list of studies, left to the option of the pupil, with entire freedom of admission or absence each term.

The former is now adopted by every other important High School in Massachusetts, including that of Lawrence; Lowell is left almost in the exclusive advocacy of the latter. Is our practise founded in wisdom, sanctioned by experience, or enforced by an inevitable necessity?[1]

It is evident that Lowell soon fell into line in adopting the plan found in other high schools. In the Report of 1852 courses of study for both the male and female departments are given in detail. The English course for the male department was as follows:

ENGLISH COURSE[2] FOR MALE DEPARTMENT

First Term	Second Term	Third Term
	FIRST YEAR	
English Grammar and Parsing	English Grammar and Parsing	Natural Philosophy
Physiology	Physiology and General History	General History
Arithmetic	Arithmetic	Algebra
	SECOND YEAR	
Natural Philosophy	Chemistry	Chemistry
Useful Arts	Useful Arts, Natural History	Natural History
Algebra	Algebra	Geometry
	THIRD YEAR	
Astronomy	Astronomy	Intellectual Philosophy
Physical Geography	Political Economy	Rhetoric
Geometry	Trigonometry	Surveying or Review

The English course offered in the female department differed but very little from that of the male department. The classical course was the same in both departments and was as follows:

CLASSICAL COURSE IN BOTH DEPARTMENTS

First Term	Second Term	Third Term
	FIRST YEAR	
Latin Lessons	Latin Reader	Latin Reader

[1] Report of 1851, p. 50.
[2] Report of 1852, p. 9.

	SECOND YEAR	
Caesar	Caesar	Caesar
	THIRD YEAR	
Virgil and Greek Reader	Virgil and Greek Reader	Virgil and Greek Reader
	FOURTH YEAR	
Cicero and Greek Reader	Cicero and Greek Reader	Review

Whether students in the classical department carried studies in addition to those listed is not made clear.

It will be seen that the purpose of the Lowell High School was to fit for college as well as for the practical duties of life. In this respect it differed from that of the English Classical School of Boston.

The Report of 1857[1] contains revised courses of study. The word "Department" has now been dropped and "Courses of Study" substituted. An English course of three years and a classical course of four years are maintained. A study of these courses makes it clear that the purpose remains the same, viz., the English course to fit for the practical duties of life, and the classical course to fit for higher institutions.

The number of years required to complete the course of study offered by the Springfield, Massachusetts, High School is not given in the earliest report in which the high school is mentioned—that of 1852. In this report it is stated that three departments were maintained—the department of common English branches, one of higher English and mathematical branches, and a third course called the classical department. The following subjects were taught, the number following each indicating the number of pupils pursuing the subject:[2]

Greek, 4	Natural Philosophy, 48
French, 31	Bookkeeping, 33
Latin, 98	Algebra, 90
Arithmetic, 60	Mensuration, 15
Grammar, 58	Surveying
Geography, 64	Botany, 16
History of United States, 67	Watts, 6
Parker's *Exercises*, 50	Geometry, 20
Physiology, 10	Meteorology, 36

All are required to attend regularly to Orthography, Reading and Composition, and all in the male department to declamation. Singing is a daily exercise.

[1] Report of 1857, p. 37.
[2] Report of 1852, p. 10.

In the Report of 1855[1] the list of subjects taught is given, and it differs from that of 1852 in the following particulars: Parker's *Exercises*, mensuration, and surveying were dropped; ancient and modern history, chemistry, rhetoric, astronomy, geology, natural theology, and United States constitution were added. In 1858 two departments were maintained—English and classical. No information is given concerning the requirements of either course. The statement is made that the English course requires three years to complete it, and provides that certain studies may be pursued during the fourth year. No ancient languages were offered in this course.

A high school was established in New Haven, Connecticut, in May, 1859.[2] No information is given in this report, nor in the reports of 1860, 1861, or 1862 concerning the course of study. In the Report of 1863, the following subjects are listed:[3]

Arithmetic
Bookkeeping
Algebra
Geometry
Trigonometry
Mensuration
Surveying
Navigation
English Language and Literature
Reading and Declamation
Spelling and Defining
Composition
French
German
Latin
Greek
Rhetoric
Logic
Mental and Moral Philosophy
History
Political Philosophy
Constitution of United States
Physical Geography
Natural Philosophy
Chemistry
Astronomy
Philosophy
Botany
Geology

The early reports of Baltimore, Maryland, contain no reference to a high school, the first definite information concerning a course of study being found in the Report of 1851. In this Report the following high school course of study is given:[4]

FIRST YEAR	SECOND YEAR
Ancient and Modern History	Ancient and Modern History
Grammar	Composition
Geography	Ancient Geography

[1] Report of 1855, p. 37.
[2] *Annual Report of Board of Education*, 1859, p. 31.
[3] Report of 1863, p. 18.
[4] Report of 1851, p. 20.

Arithmetic
Bookkeeping
Algebra
Geometry
Natural Philosophy
Physiology
Ancient & Modern Languages
Writing
Drawing
Music

Arithmetic
Geometry
Astronomy and Globes
Bookkeeping
Mensuration
Natural Philosophy
Physiology
Ancient and Modern Languages
Writing
Linear and Perspective Drawing
Mechanical Drawing
Music

THIRD YEAR

Ancient and Modern History
Composition
Elocution
Rhetoric
Trigonometry
Surveying
Bookkeeping
Chemistry with lectures
Natural Philosophy
Astronomy
Physiology
Moral Philosophy
Ancient and Modern Languages
Writing

FOURTH YEAR

Composition
Declamation
Rhetoric
Logic
History
Bookkeeping
Analytic Geometry
Engineering with the use of instruments of surveying and leveling
Dialling
Practical Astronomy
Descriptive Geometry
Navigation
Calculus
Conic Sections
Natural Philosophy
Chemistry
Writing
Drawing
Mineralogy
Physiology
Constitution of Maryland
Political Economy
Ancient and Modern Languages

As early as 1855 there was a high school established for girls and the course of study is given in the report of that year.[1] The course of study of the Central High School in this city is given in the Report of 1860. The course was as follows, the number following each subject indicating the number of recitations per week:[2]

[1] Report of 1855, p. 63.
[2] Report of 1860, p. 164.

FIRST YEAR	SECOND YEAR
Latin, 3	United States History, 1
United States History, 1	Bookkeeping, 3
Greek, 3	Reviews, 3
German, 3	German, 3
French, 2	French, 2
Analytical Geometry and Calculus, 3	Analytical Geometry and Calculus, 3
Astronomy, 1	Astronomy, 1
Chemistry, 3	Chemistry, 3
Physiology, 1	Physiology, 1
Rhetoric and Elocution, 2	Rhetoric and Elocution, 2
Mental and Moral Philosophy, 3	Mental and Moral Philosophy, 3

THIRD YEAR	FOURTH YEAR
Greek, 3	German, 4
Latin, 3	French, 4
German, 3	History, 2
French, 3	Surveying, 3
History, 2	Astronomy, 2
Surveying, 3	Bookkeeping, 3
Astronomy, 2	Vocal Music, 1
Natural Philosophy, 4	Natural Philosophy, 4
Bookkeeping, 1	Composition and Declamation, 2
Composition and Declamation, 2	Mensuration, 3
	Geometry, 4
	Physiology, 4

The Philadelphia High School was established in 1837.[1] In the report of the following year is contained the following:

Since that period (referring to the last Report) a building admirably adapted to its intended uses has been completed on the east of Penn Square, near the mint of the United States, professors in various branches of classical, English Belle-Lettes, mathematical, astronomical and physical science appointed, the school opened, and an adequate number of pupils after due and strict examination have been admitted. Lectures are delivered on natural history, comparative anatomy, botany, chemistry, mineralogy and geology. The French, German, and Spanish languages will be added as classes are formed.

The vast advantages of such an establishment to the pupils of this school. to the best interests of geographical, nautical, and astronomical science, and to the enviable distinction of our noble commonwealth are too obvious to need comment here.[2]

In the report of the acting high-school principal, 1840, the following information is given concerning the course of study:

Three courses were contemplated as follows: Principal Course, Classical Course, and English Course. The Principal Course offered the following range

[1] *Annual Report of the Controllers of the Public Schools of the City of Philadelphia*, 1837, pp. 5-6.

[2] Report of 1838, pp. 8–9.

of subjects: English Belles-Lettres and History; French; Morals; Mathematics; Natural Philosophy and Geography; Natural History; Drawing and Writing.

Pupils in the Classical Course substituted classics for French and those in the English Course substituted English and Mathematics for French.[1]

An analysis of the rather broad designations used above reveals the following:

English Belles-Lettres and History consisted of the following: European and United States History; Rhetoric Etymological exercises; Analysis of sentences with reference to grammar and rhetoric, and of words with reference to etymological composition, declamation, etc.

The Department of Moral and Mental Science consisted of oral lessons on morals; and the Constitution of Pennsylvania.

The Department of Mathematics included Algebra; Arithmetic; Geometry; Plane Trignonometry; Geography; Natural Philosophy; and Mechanics.

The Department of Natural History included the following: General principles of special Physics; Bony, Muscular, Vascular and Nervous systems, etc.; Evidences of design; Application to the Ordinary cases of bodily injuries.[2]

The subjects offered and the time devoted to each[3] are shown in the Report of 1845:

Moral, Mental and Political Science.—Political Economy 1, Mental Philosophy 1, Moral Philosophy 1, Constitution of Pennsylvania ½, Constitution of the United States ½, Belles-Lettres and History, Guizot's *History of Civilization* ½, Schlagel's *History of Literature* 1, Whateley's *Logic* ½, Whateley's *Rhetoric* ½, Robertson's *Charles V* ½, Goldsmith's *History of Rome* ½, Composition and Rhetorical Analysis ½, White's *Elements of General History* ½, History of Greece ½, History of England ½, History of the United States ½, Oswald's *Etymology* 2.

Ancient and Modern Languages.—Greek 2, Latin 4, Spanish 1, and apparently 1 year of French.

Languages and Extra English.—Chemistry 1, Natural Philosophy 1, Historical Narrations ½, Etymology 2, Mathematics and Astronomy, Algebra, Geometry, Trigonometry, Analytical Geometry, Calculus, Navigation, Mensuration, Anatomy, Physiology and Natural History, Anatomy and Physiology (lectures) 3, Zoölogy, Hygiene (lectures ½, Domestic Medicine and Surgery (lectures) ½, Natural Philosophy and Chemistry (lectures) 1½.

Drawing, Writing, and Bookkeeping.—Bookkeeping was offered two and a half years. The other work consisted of what was called Drawing and Plain and Ornamental Writing. The drawing was from solid objects and patterns.[4]

This course remained without material changes up to 1860 as is shown by the high-school course on pages 142–43 of the report of that year.

[1] Report of the Acting High-School Principal, 1840, pp. 18-26.
[2] *Ibid.*, pp. 31-34.
[3] The figures indicate years or fractions of a year.
[4] Report of 1845, pp. 79-80.

An analysis of the course of the Boston school, 1823, shows the following range of subjects in the various fields:

Mathematics: Arithmetic, Algebra, Geometry, and "Practical Mathematicks." (Since this included surveying, navigation, etc., trigonometry was no doubt taught.)

English: Reading, Grammar, Declamation, Rhetoric, Composition, Criticism of English Authors.

Science: Natural Philosophy, A course of Experimental Lectures on the various branches of Natural Philosophy, Elements of Arts and Sciences, Ancient and Modern Geography.

Social Studies: General History, United States History.

Commercial Subjects: Bookkeeping.

Miscellaneous: Sacred Geography, Blair's *Lectures*, abridged, Natural Theology, Chronology, Moral Philosophy, Forensicks, *Evidences of Christianity.*

The course of study for 1852 which remained without important change to 1860, gives evidence of the same aim as that of 1823. A fourth year was made optional. A somewhat wider range of subjects was offered and a few subjects discontinued. Those added are indicated below and those in parentheses have been discontinued.

A review of preparatory studies is required:

Mathematics: Mechanics, Engineering and "higher mathematics with some option." (Arithmetic.)[1]

English: (Criticism of Authors.) *Compending English Literature.* (Grammar.)[1]

Science: Astronomy, Geology, (Modern Geography.)[1]

Social studies: Constitution of United States. (United States History.)[1]

Commercial subjects: No change.

Foreign language: French or Spanish.

Miscellaneous: Drawing, Political Economy, Intellectual Philosophy, Logic (Sacred Geography), (Chronology), (Forensicks).

The aim of this school remained unchanged as shown by the foregoing analysis. The absence of ancient language and the emphasis upon the so-called English subjects is conclusive proof that no attempt was made to prepare for higher institutions. Boston maintained another type of secondary school, the Latin Grammar School[2] for this purpose.[3] Its curriculum[4] was almost exclusively classical, no attempt being made to perform the function of the other type of school.

An analysis of the English courses of study in other high schools will reveal the same general facts as those revealed by an analysis

[1] Included in the preparatory studies.

[2] Report of 1823, pp. 26-30.

[3] *Ibid.*, p. 26.

[4] *Ibid.*, p. 28.

of the English Classical School. There was lack of uniformity with regard to range of subjects—some offered three and others four years of work—but the aim, that of fitting for active life, was the same.

A comparison of the course of study of Springfield, Massachusetts,[1] 1852 with that of Baltimore, Maryland,[2] 1851 shows clearly the wider range of work offered by the latter school.

SPRINGFIELD	BALTIMORE
Mathematics:	
Algebra	Arithmetic
Arithmetic	Algebra
Geometry	Geometry
Mensuration	Mensuration
Surveying	Trigonometry
	Surveying
	Analytic Geometry
	Engineering
	Descriptive Geometry
	Navigation
	Calculus
	Conic Sections
English:	
Orthography	Grammar
Reading	Composition
Composition	Elocution
Grammar	Rhetoric
Parker's *Exercises*	Declamation
Science:	
Geography	Geography
Physiology	Astronomy
Natural Philosophy	Natural Philosophy
Botany	Chemistry
Meteorology	Physiology
	Mineralogy
Social Studies:	
United States History	Ancient and Modern History
	History
	Political Economy
	Constitution of Maryland
Commercial Subjects:	
Bookkeeping	Bookkeeping

[1] Report of 1852, p. 10.
[2] Report of 1851, p. 20.

Miscellaneous:	
Watts[1]	Ancient Geography
	Drawing
	Linear and Perspective Drawing
	Mechanical Drawing
	Moral Philosophy
	Logic
	Dialling

It will be seen that the Baltimore school offered a much wider range of subjects particularly in mathematics, in the social studies, and in the miscellaneous subjects. The Lowell school[2] offered a range of subjects similar to that of Springfield, while the course in the Philadelphia school[3] was similar to that of Baltimore.

Other high schools undertook to perform the functions of both types of Boston schools, that of preparing for higher institutions and also for the practical duties of life. The twofold aim of the Lowell high school is made clear in the Reports of 1840[4] and 1843[5] and also in the courses of study for 1852[6] and 1857.[7]

The schools of Springfield, Massachusetts,[8] New Haven, Connecticut,[9] Baltimore, Maryland,[10] and Philadelphia, Pennsylvania,[11] carried out both educational aims in a single type of school.

In summary, the following conclusions may be drawn:

1. The aims of these high schools (Boston excepted) were to fit for higher institutions and also to prepare for the active duties of life. These two aims are revealed both in the stated purposes of the schools and in their curricula.

2. The curricula constituted a wide range of subjects and included several subjects now found only in college curricula.[12] Examples of these are intellectual philosophy, moral philosophy, theology, evidences of Christianity, logic, calculus, analytics, surveying, navigation, and engineering.

[1] Probably intellectual or moral philosophy.

[2] Report of 1852, p. 9.

[3] *Ibid.*

[4] Report of 1840, pp. 6-7.

[5] Report of 1843, p. 5.

[6] Report of 1849, p. 9.

[7] Report of 1847, p. 10.

[8] Report of 1852, p. 10, and Report of 1853, p. 37.

[9] Report of 1859, p. 31.

[10] Report of 1851, p. 20.

[11] Report of 1837, pp. 8-9, and Report of 1840, pp. 18-26.

[12] Some high schools in the North Central states offered these subjects as is shown by reference to Appendix, Table A.

3. While these schools were all influenced by the same controlling aims, there was lack of uniformity in length of course, subjects offered, and in the organization of the curricula. These were, however, only minor differences, and the broad lines along which high-school education would develop were determined by these early schools.

PART I

DEVELOPMENT IN SUBJECTS AND IN CURRICULA ORGANIZATION

CHAPTER II

SIMILARITY IN GENERAL PLAN AND LACK OF UNIFORMITY IN DETAILS OF CURRICULA

The public secondary-school movement extended westward, and schools of this type were established prior to 1860. Dexter places the number in the North Central States[1] at 45 in 1860, and the whole number at 108.[2] Cleveland, Ohio, established a high school in 1846, Cincinnati, Ohio, in 1847, and Toledo, Ohio, in 1849.[3] A movement to establish a high school was inaugurated in St. Louis, Missouri, as early as 1843, but the school was not authorized until 1853.[4] The need of such a school was urged in Chicago, Illinois, in 1846, but it was not established until 1856.[5] Racine, Wisconsin, established a high school in 1852,[6] Dubuque, Iowa, prior to 1858,[7] and Columbus, Indiana, in 1859.[8] Burlington, Iowa, did not authorize a high school until 1863, but high-school subjects were taught as early as 1853.[9] In connection with the union-school movement in Michigan, high schools were established at Adrian, Ann Arbor, Coldwater, Grand Rapids, Jonesville, and Ypsilanti as early as 1857.[10]

It is evident that the high-school movement was well under way by 1860. It is also clear, as shown by the courses of study, that the aim of the English Classical School (Boston) was recognized by all these schools, and the twofold aim of the Lowell school was general.[11] To what extent the western schools were directly influenced by the eastern is not clear although there is some evidence of such influ-

[1] Iowa, Illinois, Indiana, Kansas, Michigan, Minnesota, Missouri, Nebraska, North Dakota, Ohio, South Dakota, and Wisconsin.

[2] Dexter, E. G., *A History of Education in the United States*, 1904, p. 173.

[3] *Ibid.*, p. 171.

[4] *Annual Report St. Louis Schools*, 1867, pp. 108-09.

[5] *Annual School Report*, 1867, pp. 50-51.

[6] *Columbian History Racine Public Schools*, p. 9.

[7] *Annual School Report*, 1876, p. 65.

[8] *Education in Indiana*, p. 272.

[9] *Report of Board of Education*, 1902, p. 60.

[10] *Report Superintendent of Public Instruction*, 1855-56-57, pp. 440-41, 449, 465, 476.

[11] Cf. Appendix, Table A and Table II.

ence.[1] Similar social and educational needs and ideals in the two sections would account for similarity of educational aims and organizations, and this is clearly revealed both by the stated purposes of the schools and by their courses of study. A comparative study of Table A and the courses of study set forth in chapter I will reveal the points of similarity between the curricula of the eastern and western schools. This comparison also shows a lack of uniformity that would not be expected if the western schools had adopted, without modification, the courses of study of the eastern schools.

An analysis of two courses of study[2] reveals the similarity in general plan and also the lack of uniformity in details.[3]

BALTIMORE, MARYLAND, 1851[4]	COLUMBUS, OHIO, 1851[5]
MATHEMATICS[6]	
Arithmetic	Arithmetic
Algebra	Algebra
Geometry	Geometry
Trigonometry	Trigonometry
Mensuration	Mensuration
Surveying	Surveying
Navigation	Navigation
Engineering	Engineering
(Analytics) (Calculus)	(Higher Algebra)
(Conic Sections)	(Higher Geometry)
(Dialling)	
(Descriptive Geometry)	
ENGLISH	
Grammar	Grammar
Composition	Composition
Rhetoric	Rhetoric
Declamations	Declamations
(Elocution)	(Higher Grammar)
	(Word Analysis)
	(Synthetical Analysis)
	(Reading)
	(Rhetorical Reading)
	(History of Literature)
	(Elements of Criticism)
	(Study of Poetry)
FOREIGN LANGUAGES	
Ancient and (Modern)	Latin
Languages	Greek

[1] *Columbian History of Racine Public Schools*, 1893, p. 9.
[2] *History of Education in Iowa*, 1915, III, 174.
[3] Each course four years in length.
[4] *Annual School Report*, 1851, p. 20.
[5] *Annual School Report*, 1851, p. 33.
[6] Subjects in parentheses not offered in the other school.

SCIENCE	
Physiology	Physiology
Natural Philosophy	Natural Philosophy
Astronomy	Astronomy
Chemistry	Chemistry
(Mineralogy)	(Physical Geography)
(Geography)	(Botany)
	(Geology)
SOCIAL STUDIES	
(Ancient) and Modern History	Modern History
Political Economy	Political Economy
Constitution of Maryland	Constitution of Ohio
(History)	(United States History)
	(Chronology)
	(Philosophy of History)
	(Laws of Nations)
	(History of Civilization)
	(Constitution of United States)
COMMERCIAL SUBJECTS	
Bookkeeping	Elements of Bookkeeping
	Double Entry Bookkeeping
	(Business Forms)
MISCELLANEOUS SUBJECTS	
Moral Philosophy	Moral Science
Drawing	Drawing
Music	Music
(Linear and Perspective Drawing)	(Evidences of Christianity)
(Mechanical Drawing)	(Logic)

As further illustration of lack of uniformity, Cleveland, Ohio, offered a three-year course in 1852 with a more limited range of subjects than offered by either Baltimore, Maryland, or Columbus, Ohio.[1] No foreign language was offered which indicates that the school did not attempt to prepare for higher institutions, and mathematics was not taught beyond trigonometry. A four-year course was offered by Dubuque, Iowa, in 1856 with no foreign language.[2] Two years later it was reduced to three years, and Latin, Greek, German, and French were provided, all of which were optional except Latin.[3]

[1] *Annual School Report*, 1852, p. 23.
[2] Aurner, C. R., *History of Education in Iowa*, 1915, III, 281-82.
[3] *Ibid.*, pp. 282-84.

The representative courses of study given in full and the various tables will show in detail the marked lack of uniformity and also the characteristics common to high-school curricula for the period included in this study. For purposes of convenience and clearness in analyses and interpretations, the entire period of forty years is divided into periods of five years each.

Tables A, B, C, D, E, F, G, H, I, and J, in the Appendix, show the number of courses and names of towns and cities for each period, the length of the courses offered, the subjects offered, and length of time devoted to each subject and field. Bibliography of material used is given under separate title with the general bibliography at the close.

Table I shows the number of courses offered by each school for the several periods and indicates the various descriptive titles used.

Tables II–IX show the number of schools for each period offering the subjects, and Table X indicates in percentages the number of schools offering each subject.

Tables XI–XVIII indicate the differences in total time devoted to the fields by the several schools in each period. Table XIX shows the maxima, minima, modes, and averages in time devoted to each field for each period, and Tables XX–XXVII indicate the same for the various subjects.

The tables will be found on the following pages: Table I, 46-50; Tables II–IX, 62–68; Table X, 71–74; Tables XI–XVIII, 80–90; Table XIX, 90–91; Tables XX–XXVII, 92–99. Interpretations follow the tables in each case.

CHAPTER III

REPRESENTATIVE COURSES OF STUDY

The courses set out in the following pages were selected as typical for the several periods. In most cases they are reproductions of the printed forms found in school reports cited in the footnotes. In some instances where parallel courses are offered, all are not given in detail.[1] Analyses, comments, and interpretations will be found in succeeding chapters.

ANN ARBOR, MICHIGAN, 1859[2]

FIRST YEAR

Davies' *Elementary Algebra*
Green's *English Analysis*
Davies' *University Arithmetic*
Willson's *United States History*
Lambert's *Physiology*

SECOND YEAR

Wells' *Natural Philosophy*
Quackenbough's *Rhetoric and Exercises*
Willson's *General History*
Davies' *Legendre's Geometry*
Warren's *Physical Geography*
Trigonometry and Surveying

THIRD YEAR

Davies' *Higher Algebra*
Wayland's *Intellectual Philosophy and Moral Science*
Wells's *Chemistry*
Kane's *Elements of Criticism*
Gray's *Botany*

Bookkeeping (optional) any year in the Course. Reading and Spelling required daily during the whole Course. Declamation and Composition semi-monthly. Two years of French and one year of German offered.

The instruction in the Classical Department is confined to the Latin and Greek classics, and such other studies as are requisite to prepare young men for the University.

In addition to Latin and Greek the following subjects are offered in the Classical Department:

English Analysis	Modern Geography
University Arithmetic	History of Rome
Higher Algebra	Ancient Geography

[1] Cf. pp. 20, 28, 30, 31, 32, 35, 40, 41.

[2] Report Superintendent Public Instruction, Michigan, 1860, pp. 244-45.

MADISON, WISCONSIN, 1863[1]

First Term	Second Term	Third Term
	FIRST YEAR	
Higher Arithmetic	Higher Arithmetic	Higher Arithmetic
United States History	Elementary Algebra	Elementary Algebra
English Analysis	English Analysis and Parsing	Botany and Vegetable Physiology
	SECOND YEAR	
Higher Algebra	Higher Algebra	Higher Algebra
Physical Geography	Physical Geography	Botany
Physiology	Physiology	Bookkeeping
Analysis of Words	English Literature	English Literature
	THIRD YEAR	
Geometry	Geometry	Geometry
Natural Philosophy	Natural Philosophy	Rhetoric
Rhetoric	Rhetoric	Geology
Ancient History	Ancient History	
	FOURTH YEAR	
Mental Philosophy	Mental Philosophy	Butler's *Analogy*
Chemistry	Chemistry	Logic
Astronomy	Moral Science	Political Economy

Exercises in Declamation and Composition weekly throughout the Course. Latin may be substituted for other courses during the four years and Greek during the last year year by those preparing for college.

CINCINNATI, OHIO, 1862[2]

Five recitations per week unless otherwise indicated by figures after subjects.

First Session	Second Session
FIRST YEAR	
Algebra	Algebra
German or French, 4	German or French, 4
English Classics and Rhetoric, 3	English Classics and Rhetoric, 3
Higher Arithmetic, 2	Higher Arithmetic, 2
SECOND YEAR	
Latin	Latin
Geometry	Geometry
German or French, 4	German or French, 4
Ancient History, 4	Medieval History, 4
English Classics and Composition, 1	English Classics and Composition, 1
THIRD YEAR	
Algebra	Trigonometry or Greek
Greek	Latin
Latin	Natural Philosophy or Greek, 4

[1] *Annual School Report*, 1863, pp. 22-23.
[2] *Thirty-third Annual Report Common Schools of Cincinnati*, 1862, pp. 70-71.

German or French, 4	German or French, 4
Modern History, 4	English Classics and Composition, 1
English Classics or Composition, 1	

FOURTH YEAR

Latin	Latin
Chemistry or Greek	Chemistry or Greek
Natural Philosophy or Greek, 4	Astronomy
Review of Algebra and Geometry, 2	Constitution of United States, 1
Surveying (for boys), 3	

Instead of Latin in the second year, those making such choice may take a course of Commercial Forms and Bookkeeping, five lessons per week. Beginning with the third year original addresses and essays will be required once in three weeks to the end of the course. Vocal Music throughout the course.

LEAVENWORTH, KANSAS, 1867[1]

High School Course of Study

FRESHMAN YEAR

First Term	Second Term	Third Term
Higher Arithmetic	Higher Arithmetic	Outlines of History
English Analysis	Outlines of History	Botany
Anatomy	Anatomy	Physical Geography
	Physical Geography	

Latin, German, French and Spanish are optional.

SOPHOMORE YEAR

Algebra	Algebra	Algebra
Natural Philosophy	Natural Philosophy	Botany
Political Economy	Meteorology	Constitution and Science of Government.

Latin, German, French and Spanish are optional.

JUNIOR YEAR

Geometry	Geometry	Chemistry
Chemistry	Chemistry	Trigonometry
Rhetoric	English Literature	Rhetoric
		English Literature
		Reviews

Latin, German, French and Spanish are optional.

SENIOR YEAR

Astronomy	Moral Philosophy	Bookkeeping
Intellectual Philosophy	Mensuration and Surveying	Intellectual Philosophy
Trigonometry	Logic	Moral Philosophy
		Geology
		Reviews

[1] *Report of Superintendent of Schools*, 1867, pp. 43-44.

Latin, German, French, and Spanish are optional. Composition and Declamation weekly throughout the entire course. Physical exercises daily. Reading and writing twice a week.

JACKSONVILLE, ILLINOIS, 1869[1]

English and Classical Course

FIRST YEAR

First Term	Second Term	Third Term
Arithmetic	The same, except Greek is added	English Language
Grammar		Algebra
Algebra		Caesar
Natural Philosophy		Greek
Latin		Ancient History

SECOND YEAR

First Term	Second Term	Third Term
Ancient History	Ancient History	Intellectual Philosophy
Geometry	Geometry	Geometry
Bookkeeping	Virgil	Botany
Physiology	Bookkeeping	Science of Government
Caesar	Physiology	Virgil
Greek	Greek	Greek

THIRD YEAR

First Term	Second Term	Third Term
Rhetoric	Rhetoric	Intellectual Physiology
Astronomy	Astronomy	Moral Philosophy
Chemistry	Chemistry	Botany
Geology	Geology	Zoölogy
Cicero's *De Senectute*	Greek	Cicero
Anabasis	Cicero's *De Senectute*	Greek

Reading, spelling, declamation, and composition continued throughout the entire course.

Normal Course

FIRST YEAR

First Term	Second Term	Third Term
Arithmetic	Geography	Grammar
Methods of Instruction	Economics	Spelling
Inventive Drawing	School Organization	Penmanship
Physiology	Mechanical Drawing	Physical Geography

SECOND YEAR

First Term	Second Term	Third Term
School Discipline	Algebra	Mental Philosophy
Mental Arithmetic	Natural History	Astronomy
Object Lessons	Physiology	Science of Government
Music	Reading	School Registration

[1] *Report of Superintendent of Schools to Board of Education*, 1869, p. 50.

WATERLOO, IOWA, 1870[1]

First Term	Second Term	Third Term
FIRST YEAR		
History or Latin	History or Latin	History or Latin
Algebra	Algebra	Algebra
Higher Arithmetic or Bookkeeping	Higher Arithmetic or Bookkeeping	Higher Arithmetic or Bookkeeping
SECOND YEAR		
Latin or German	Latin or German	Latin or German
Geometry	Geometry	Trigonometry
Physiology	Physiology	Natural Philosophy
THIRD YEAR		
Latin or German	Latin or German	Latin or German
Astronomy	German	German
Rhetoric	Mental Philosophy	Moral Philosophy
	Rhetoric	Logic

Penmanship, Declamation, and composition throughout the course.

CINCINNATI, OHIO, 1872[2]

First Session	Second Session
GRADE D	
Latin	Latin
College Latin	College Latin
German	German
Algebra	Algebra
Anatomy, Physiology and Hygiene, 2	Anatomy, Physiology and Hygiene, 2
History, 4	History, 4
Composition, 1	Composition, 1
Elocution, 1	Elocution, 1
Drawing, 1	Freehand Drawing, 1
GRADE C	
Latin	Latin
College Latin	College Latin
Greek	Greek
French	French
German	German
Algebra, 4	English Grammar, 4
History, 4	Composition, 1
Composition, 1	Elocution, 1
Elocution, 1	Freehand Drawing, 1
Freehand Drawing, 1	
GRADE B	
Latin	Latin, 4
College Latin	College Latin

[1] *Rules and Regulations*, 1870, p. 19.

[2] *Annual School Report*, 1872-73, pp. 291-94. Figures after subjects indicate number of recitations per week. Five recitations per week unless otherwise indicated.

Greek
French, 4
German, 4
Geometry
English Literature, 3
Natural Philosophy, 4
Elocution, 1
Drawing, 1

Greek
French, 4
German, 4
Geometry and Plane and Spherical Trigonometry
Natural Philosophy, 4
Botany, 3
English Literature, 3
Composition, 1
Elocution, 1
Drawing, 1

GRADE A

First Session

Latin, 3
College Latin
Greek
French, 3
Astronomy, completed, 4
Chemistry, 4
Natural History, 1
Mental Philosophy, 1
Constitution of United States, 1
Bookkeeping, 2
English Literature, 3
Composition, 1
Drawing, 1

Second Session

Latin, 3
College Latin
Greek
French, 3
Plane Surveying, 3
Chemistry, 4
Mental Philosophy, 1
Geology, 3
Natural History, 1
English Literature, 3
Composition, 1
Drawing, 1

Pupils in the Grades A, B, and C may, under the direction of the principal, select from the studies of their respective grades an amount of work equal to fifteen recitations per week exclusive of Composition, Reading, and Declamation. In the latter branch all pupils shall have one lesson every two weeks.

MADISON, WISCONSIN, 1872[1]

FIRST YEAR

First Term	Second Term	Third Term
Grammar Algebra Physical Geography Latin	The same with Physiology added	Composition Algebra Physiology Latin

SECOND YEAR

First Term	Second Term	Third Term
Natural History Geometry General History Latin	The same with Botany added	The same with Natural History added.

THIRD YEAR

First Term	Second Term	Third Term
Philosophy Higher Arithmetic Rhetoric Latin	Philosophy Higher Arithmetic History of England Latin	Civil Government Sentential Analysis History of England Latin

[1] Annual School Report, 1872, p. 32.

Greek and German will be optional studies, and any student taking either of these languages will be excused from one of the English studies. Compositions, Declamations, Music, Drawing, and Reading throughout the course.

CHICAGO, ILLINOIS, 1872[1]

First Term	Second Term	Third Term
FIRST YEAR		
Algebra Physical Geography Latin	Algebra Physical Geography Latin	Algebra Physical Geography and Physiology Latin
SECOND YEAR		
Geometry Natural History Latin General History Greek (optional)	Geometry Natural History and Botany Latin General History Greek (optional)	Same as second
THIRD YEAR		
Trigonometry Mechanics Latin, French, or German English Literature Greek	Astronomy Physics Latin, French, or German English Literature Greek	Astronomy Physics and Mechanics Latin, French, or German English Literature Greek
FOURTH YEAR		
Mental Science Chemistry Latin, French, or German Civil Government Greek	Mental Sciences Bookkeeping Latin, French, or German Geology Political Economy	Mental Sciences Bookkeeping Latin, French, or German Political Economy Greek

Composition, drawing, and reading throughout the courses. Those in preparation for college who desire it, can omit the English branches, except the requisite mathematics, and complete the course in three years.

COLUMBUS, OHIO, 1878[2]

FIRST YEAR

Algebra, English, Latin or German.

SECOND YEAR

First Term	Second Term	Third Term
Geometry Ancient History or Greek Latin or German	Geometry Ancient History or Greek Latin or German	Geometry Physiology or Greek Latin or German

[1] *Annual Report Board of Education*, 1872, p. 220.
[2] *Annual Report Board of Education*, 1878.

THIRD YEAR

Chemistry	Chemistry	Trigonometry
Rhetoric or Greek	Rhetoric or Greek	Rhetoric or Greek
Latin or German	Latin or German	Latin or German
	SENIOR YEAR	
Physics	Physics	Arithmetic (review)
English Literature	English Literature	English Grammar (Review)
Latin or German	Latin or German	Astronomy

MISCELLANEOUS EXERCISES

Senior Class—Weekly lectures in Political Economy.
Junior Class—Weekly lessons in Civil Government (7 months).
Junior Class—Weekly lessons in Botany (6 months).
Second Class—Weekly lectures in Physics.
All Classes—Music twice a week, and Drawing twice a week.
All Classes—Rhetorical Exercises once each week.

OSKALOOSA, IOWA, 1876[1]

SUB-JUNIOR YEAR

First Term	Second Term	Third Term
Algebra	Algebra	Algebra
Physiology	Physiology	Natural Philosophy
English Grammar	English Grammar	English Composition
Latin—Beginner's Book	Latin—Beginner's Book and Reader	Latin Reader
	JUNIOR YEAR	
Algebra	Geometry	Geometry
Natural Philosophy	Physical Geography	Physical Geography
Outlines of History	Outlines of History	Outlines or History
Latin Reader	Caesar	Caesar
	SENIOR YEAR	
Geometry	Review Algebra	Review Arithmetic
Zoölogy	Botany	Botany
Rhetoric	Rhetoric	Constitution of United States
Caesar	Virgil	Virgil

Spelling during entire course. Literary exercises monthly.

SPRINGFIELD, ILLINOIS, 1880[2]

ENGLISH COURSE

FIRST YEAR

First Term	Second Term	Third Term
Algebra General History Physiology Lessons in English Composition	Same	Same

[1] *Rules and Regulations, Courses of Study*, 1876, p. 17.
[2] *Annual Report Superintendent Public Schools*, 1880, pp. 72-73.

	SECOND YEAR	
Algebra	Geometry	Same
Bookkeeping	Physical Geography	
United States Constitution	Botany	
Rhetoric	Rhetoric	
	THIRD YEAR	
Geometry	Trigonometry	Same
Political Economy	Natural History	
Natural Philosophy	Natural Philosophy	
English Literature	English Literature	
	FOURTH YEAR	
Geology	Mathematics (reviewed)	Mathematics (reviewed)
Astronomy	Chemistry	Science (reviewed)
Chemistry	English (reviewed)	English (reviewed)
English		

Declamation and Composition throughout the course.

CLASSICAL COURSE

FIRST YEAR: Substitute Latin or German for Physiology.

SECOND YEAR: Substitute Latin and Greek for Bookkeeping, United States Constitution and Science.

THIRD YEAR: Substitute Virgil or German and Greek for Political Economy and Science.

FOURTH YEAR: Substitute:

First Term: Livy or German, Ancient Geography for Science.
Second Term: Horace or German, and Homer for Science.
Third Term: Same.

AUBURN, INDIANA, 1882[1]

First Term	Second Term	Third Term
	GRADE ONE	
Reading	Arithmetic	Arithmetic
Spelling	Grammar	Grammar
Writing	History	Geography
Arithmetic	Reading	Reading
Grammar	Spelling and Writing, continued	Spelling and Writing, continued
History		
	GRADE TWO	
Arithmetic	Physiology	Algebra
Grammar	Algebra	Physical Geography
Physiology	Bookkeeping	Latin
	GRADE THREE	
Algebra	Algebra	General History
Physical Geography	General History	Geometry
Latin	Latin	Latin
	GRADE FOUR	
Geometry	Chemistry	Chemistry
Philosophy	Philosophy	Civil Government
Caesar	Caesar	Virgil

[1] *Rules and Regulations of the Public Schools*, 1882-83, pp. 9-10.

ST. LOUIS MISSOURI, 1881[1]

FIRST YEAR

Latin, Arithmetic, Physiology or German, Rhetoricals 3, Drawing 2.

SECOND YEAR

Algebra, Natural Philosophy, Latin, German or Greek, or History of Art or Mechanical Drawing, Rhetoricals 3, Drawing 2.

THIRD YEAR

Greek or Bookkeeping or Mechanical Drawing; Latin or German or French; General History; Chemistry 2; Rhetoricals 3; Geometry 2.

FOURTH YEAR

History of English Literature, Shakespeare and Constitution of United States; Latin or French or German; Zoölogy and Geology or Greek or Laboratory Chemistry or Mental Philosophy or Trigonometry; Rhetoricals 2.

The boys in the Senior class are required to take 2 of the 6 studies under 4. Music throughout the course.

MILWAUKEE, WISCONSIN, 1884[2]

ENGLISH-SCIENCE COURSE

First Term	Second Term	Third Term
	FIRST YEAR	
Algebra Grammar and Composition Etymology	Same	Algebra Arithmetic Physiology
	SECOND YEAR	
Geometry General History Biology	Same	Trigonometry General History Rhetoric
	THIRD YEAR	
Physics English History English Literature	Physics English Literature United States Constitution	Physics Physiology Political Economy
	FOURTH YEAR	
Chemistry Astronomy English Classics	Chemistry Mental Science English Classics	Geology Mental Science American Classics

Theme writing throughout the last three years. German or French elective for English History or Political Science in the third year, or for Mental Science and Astronomy in the fourth year.

GERMAN-ENGLISH COURSE

FIRST YEAR

Substitute German for Etymology, Latin, and Physiology.

[1] *Annual Report President of Board of Education*, pp. 293-96.

[2] *Annual Report School Board*, 1884, p. 54.

SECOND YEAR

Substitute German for General History.

THIRD YEAR

Substitute German for English History, United States Constitution, and Political Economy.

MILWAUKEE, WISCONSIN, 1884

German-English Course

FOURTH YEAR

First Term	Second Term	Third Term
Chemistry	Chemistry	Geology
English History	Civil and Literary History	Political Economy
German	United States Constitution	German
Civil and Literary History	German	Civil and Literary History

General History elective for mathematics in the second year.

Latin-English Course

FIRST YEAR		
Algebra	Algebra	Algebra
English Composition	English Grammar	Physiology
Latin Grammar	Latin Lessons	Latin Grammar Lessons
SECOND YEAR		
Geometry	Same	Trigonometry
Biology		Rhetoric
Caesar		Cicero
THIRD YEAR		
Physics	Same	Physics
English Literature		Physiology
Cicero		Virgil
FOURTH YEAR		
English History	Civil Government	Roman History
English Classics	English Classics	Two elective studies
Virgil	Eclogs	

German or French elective for English Literature, Physiology, and English Classics of the third and fourth years for those desiring to prepare for College.

SANDUSKY, OHIO, 1889[1]

Regular Course

FIRST YEAR

Fall Term	Winter Term	Spring Term
Latin or German	Latin or German	Latin or German
Physiology	Civil Government	Physical Geography
Algebra	Algebra	Algebra

[1] *Annual Report Board of Education*, 1889, pp. 80-82.

Arithmetic, 1 Bookkeeping, 1 Drawing, 1	Arithmetic, 1 Bookkeeping, 1 Drawing, 1	Arithmetic, 1 Bookkeeping, 1 Drawing, 1
	SECOND YEAR	
Latin or German Geometry Physics Arithmetic, 1 Drawing, 1	Latin or German Geometry Physics, 4 weeks Chemistry, 8 Arithmetic, 1 Drawing, 1	Latin or German Geometry or Trigonometry Chemistry Arithmetic, 1 Drawing, 1
	THIRD YEAR	
Latin or German Rhetoric Geology Drawing, 1	Latin or German Astronomy Rhetoric, 4 weeks English History, 8 Drawing, 1	Latin or German English History Botany Drawing, 1
	FOURTH YEAR	
Latin or German English Literature Roman History or Bookkeeping	Latin or German English Literature or English Grammar Greek History or Natural Philosophy Drawing, 1	Latin or German, 2 Algebra, 2 Arithmetic, 2 History of Mental Philosophy, 4 Essays, 2

Elocution, Composition, and Music throughout the course. Four recitations per week except where otherwise stated.

English Course

FIRST YEAR: same as General Course, except English substituted for Latin or German.

SECOND YEAR: American History substituted for Latin or German, or General History substituted.

THIRD YEAR: History or Bookkeeping, Commercial Law, and Reviews substituted for Latin or German.

No Fourth Year offered in the English Course.

COLUMBUS, OHIO, 1889[1]

General Literary Course

FIRST YEAR

First Half Year	Second Half Year
Algebra Latin or German English	Algebra Latin or German Physiology and Hygiene
SECOND YEAR	
Plane Geometry Latin or German Ancient History and English	Algebra Latin or German Mediaeval and Modern History and English

[1] *Annual Report Board of Education*, 1889, pp. 322–23.

THIRD YEAR

Latin or German	Latin or German
Chemistry	Chemistry and Trigonometry
Geometry	Botany and English
English	United States Constitution

FOURTH YEAR

Latin or German	English Literature
English Literature	Physics
Physics	Arithmetic and English Grammar
	Astronomy

English Course

FIRST YEAR

Substitutes English Composition, one year, and Botany one-half year for Latin or German.

SECOND YEAR

Substitutes Physical Geography and Civil Government for Latin or German.

THIRD YEAR

Substitutes Rhetoric and Composition for Latin or German. Also substitutes Physics, one-half year, for Trigonometry and Chemistry.

FOURTH YEAR

First Half	Second Half
United States History	English Literature
English Literature	Chemistry
Chemistry	Arithmetic and English Grammar
Astronomy (optional)	Astronomy

COLUMBUS, OHIO, 1889[1]

Business Course

FIRST YEAR

First Term	Second Term
Algebra	Algebra
Phonography and Penmanship	Phonography and Penmanship
English	Physical Geography and Hygiene

SECOND YEAR

Mental and Written Arithmetic	Arithmetic
Phonography and Penmanship	English
Physical Geography	Phonography and Penmanship
	Civil Government

[1] *Annual Report of Board of Education*, 1889, pp. 322-23.

THIRD YEAR

Bookkeeping and Practice in Phonography	Bookkeeping and Practice in Phonography
Geometry and Chemistry	Geometry and Chemistry
	English and Trigonometry

FOURTH YEAR

General History	English Literature
English Literature	Physics
Reviews	Reviews
Physics	Astronomy

SPRINGFIELD, ILLINOIS, 1890[1]

Four different courses are provided: English, German-English, Latin-English and Classical. These courses are not printed separately, however, and are made up of certain required studies and electives. The subjects, the names of which are italicized, are required.

Course of Study

Fall Term	Winter Term	Spring Term
	FIRST YEAR	
English	*English*	*English*
Algebra	*Algebra*	*Algebra*
Zoölogy	Zoölogy, Bookkeeping	Bookkeeping
Latin or German	Latin or German	Latin or German
Historical Reading	*Historical Reading*	*Historical Reading*
	SECOND YEAR	
English	*English*	*English*
Geometry	*Geometry*	*Geometry*
Physical Geography	Botany	Botany
Latin or German	Latin or German	Latin or German
Historical Reading	*Historical Reading*	*Historical Reading*
	THIRD YEAR	
English	*English*	*English*
Arithmetic	Algebra	Geometry
Natural Philosophy	Natural Philosophy	Natural Philosophy
Latin, Greek, or German	Latin, Greek, or German	Latin, Greek, or German
Historical Reading	*Historical Reading*	*Physiology*
	FOURTH YEAR	
English	*English*	*English*
Chemistry	Chemistry	Chemistry
Astronomy	Astronomy, Geology	Geology
Latin, Greek, or German	Latin, Greek, or German	Latin, Greek, or German
Trigonometry	Political Economy	Political Economy
Historical Reading	*Civil Government*	*Civil Government*

Industrial Drawing, Composition, and Rhetorical Exercises through the course.

[1] *Annual Report Public Schools*, 1890, p. 54.

MORRISON, ILLINOIS, 1888[1]

First Term	Second Term	Third Term
	FIRST YEAR	
Algebra	Algebra	Algebra
Grammar	Grammar	Rhetoric
United States History	United States History	Bookkeeping
Dictation Work	Reading	
	SECOND YEAR	
Arithmetic	Arithmetic	Botany
Rhetoric	English Literature	English and American Literature
Chemistry	Natural Philosophy	Natural Philosophy
	THIRD YEAR	
Geometry	Geometry	Trigonometry
Zoölogy	Geology	Physiology
Ancient History	Ancient History	Civil Government
	Drawing	Astronomy

Latin is optional two years. Declamations and recitations continue throughout the entire course.

ATTICA, INDIANA, 1895[2]

The High School Course

First Semester	Second Semester
FIRST YEAR	
Commercial Arithmetic	Bookkeeping and Business Practice
Elementary Latin	Elementary Latin
Physiology	Zoölogy
English—3 recitations in Literature, and 2 in Composition	English—same as first semester
SECOND YEAR	
Algebra	Algebra
Latin	Latin
Zoölogy	Botany
General History—4 times a week	History and English—same as first semester
Composition—1 day per week	
THIRD YEAR	
Algebra	Algebra
Latin	Latin
Physics	Chemistry
English Authors—3 days per week	English—same as first semester
Composition—2 days per week	

[1] Report of Public Schools, 1888, p. 13.
[2] *Report and Manual*, 1895, p. 45.

FOURTH YEAR

Geometry	Geometry
Latin	Latin
Civics	Social Science
American Literature—3 days per week	English—same as first semester
Composition—2 days per week	

EVANSTON TOWNSHIP HIGH SCHOOL, 1894[1]

Classical Course

FIRST YEAR

First Term	Second Term	Third Term
Latin	Latin	Latin
Physical Geography 15 weeks	English History, 23 weeks	Physiology
English	Physiology	

Drawing through the year.

SECOND YEAR

Caesar	Caesar	Caesar
Algebra	Algebra	Civics
Ancient History	Greek	Greek

English alternating with drawing.

THIRD YEAR

Geometry	Geometry	Arithmetic or solid Geometry
Cicero	Cicero	Cicero
Greek	Greek	Greek

FOURTH YEAR

Virgil, Greek, Physics, French, or German throughout the year.

Latin-Scientific Course

First year is the same as the Classical Course.

Second year Zoölogy and Botany instead of Ancient History and Greek.

Third year General History instead of Greek.

Fourth year English Literature instead of Greek.

Modern-Language Course

This is the same as the Latin-Scientific Course except that German takes the place of Latin after the first year and French is required during the Senior Year.

English Course

First-year Bookkeeping and Arithmetic instead of Latin.

Second-year Rhetoric and Civics instead of Latin.

Third-year Plane and Solid Geometry, Chemistry, Political Economy, Astronomy.

Fourth-year Physics, General History and English Literature.

[1] Four-page pamphlet.

CHICAGO, ILLINOIS, 1894[1]

Six Years' College Preparatory Course

SIXTH CLASS—FIRST YEAR

Latin, 5
English, 4
Arithmetic and Geometry, 4
American History, 4
Penmanship and Drawing, 2
Physiology and Hygiene, 1
German, 1

FIFTH CLASS—SECOND YEAR

Latin, 5
English, 4
Algebra and Geometry, 4
English and American History, 3
Drawing, 2
German or French, 2

FOURTH CLASS—THIRD YEAR

Latin, 4
English, 4
Algebra and Geometry, 4 until March, 1
Arithmetic with applications of Geometry, 4; after March, 1
Botany, 4, ½ year
Elements of Chemistry, 4, ½ year
Drawing, 2

THIRD CLASS—FOURTH YEAR

Latin, 4
English including Mythology, 4
French or German, 2
Greek, 3
Plane Geometry, 4
Drawing, 2
Elements of Geology, 1

SECOND CLASS—FIFTH YEAR

Latin, 4
English, 2
Greek, 4
French or German, 2
Grecian and Roman History, 4
Plane Trigonometry and Review Algebra, 4
Drawing, 1

FIRST CLASS—SIXTH YEAR

Latin, 5
French or German, 2
Greek, 4
English, 2
English, German, French, and American History, 3
Physics, 4

CHICAGO, ILLINOIS, 1895[2]

COURSE OF STUDY, ENGLISH HIGH AND MANUAL TRAINING SCHOOL

Academic

FIRST YEAR

First Term	Second Term	Third Term
Algebra, 4	Algebra, 4	Algebra, 4

[1] *Annual Report Board of Education*, 1895, p. 321.
[2] *Annual Report Board of Education*, 1895, pp. 319-20.

Biology (Zoölogy), 4 Rhetoric and Composition, 4 Manual Training Mechanical Drawing, 4 Freehand Drawing, 1 Joinery and Wood-turning, 10 Lectures on wood	Biology (Zoölogy and Botany), 4 Rhetoric and Composition, 4 Mechanical Drawing, 4 Freehand Drawing, 1 Cabinet Work and Bench Work, 10 Lectures on wood	Biology (Botany), 4 Rhetoric and Composition, 4 Mechanical Drawing, 4 Freehand Drawing, 1 Pattern Work, 10 Lectures on wood
	SECOND YEAR	
Geometry, 3 Physics, 3 General History, 3 English or French, 3 Book Reviews Mechanical Drawing, 4 Freehand Drawing, 1 Foundry and Blacksmith Work, 10 Lectures on iron	Geometry, 3 Physics, 3 General History, 3 Book Reviews, 3 Mechanical Drawing, 4 Freehand Drawing, 1 English or French, 3 Foundry and Blacksmith Work, 10 Lectures on iron	Geometry, 3 Physics, 3 General History, 3 English or French, 3 Book Reviews Mechanical Drawing, 4 Freehand Drawing, 1 Foundry and Blacksmith Work, 10 Lectures on iron
	THIRD YEAR	
Solid Geometry or Shorthand, 3 Civil Government, 3 Chemistry, 3 English or French, 3 Book Reviews Mechanical or Architect Drawing, 4 Freehand Drawing, 1 Machine Shopwork: Chipping, filing, and fitting, 10	Trigonometry or Bookkeeping, 3 Shorthand, continued and typewriting commenced Political Economy, 3 English or French, 3 Chemistry, 3 Book Reviews Mechanical or Architect Drawing, 3 Freehand Drawing, 1 Machine Shopwork: Use of lathes and planer, 10 Lectures on machinery and its work	Higher Algebra or Typewriting, 3 Political Economy, 3 English or French, 3 Chemistry Book Reviews Mechanical or Architect Drawing, 4 Freehand Drawing Machine Shopwork: Use of milling machine, 10 Lectures on machinery and its work

WILMETTE, ILLINOIS, 1898[1]

FIRST YEAR

Scudder's *Latin Lessons*
Geikie's *Physiology*
Lockwood's *Rhetoric*
Montogomery's *English History*
Beren's *Mythology*

[1] *Course of Study*, 1898, p. 13.

SECOND YEAR

Kelsey's *Caesar*
Wells's *Algebra*
Boyer's *Biology*
Bergen's *Botany*
Slections from Literature

THIRD YEAR

Kelsey's *Cicero*
Wentworth's *Geometry*
Myer's *General History*
English Classics

COLUMBUS, OHIO, 1897[1]

General Literary Course

Unless otherwise indicated, five recitations per week.

FIRST YEAR

English, 4
Physical Geography, 4
Latin or German
Algebra, 4
Arithmetic, 1
Drawing, 2

SECOND YEAR

English, 4
Ancient History, 4
Latin or German
Algebra and Geometry

THIRD YEAR

English, 4
French and English History, 4
Latin or German, 4

ONE ELECTIVE

Solid Geometry
Advanced Algebra and Plane Trigonometry, 4
Physiology and Botany, 4
Chemistry, 4
French, 4
Greek, 4
Latin
German

FOURTH YEAR

English Essays, 1
United States History and Civics, 4
Latin or German, 4

ONE ELECTIVE

Physics, 4
Greek, 4
German, 5
French, 4
Latin, 5

COLUMBUS, OHIO, 1897

English and Commercial Course

FIRST YEAR

English, 4
Arithmetic
Civil Government
Physical and Commercial Geography, 4
Drawing, 2

SECOND YEAR

English, 4
Bookkeeping, 4

[1] *Annual Report Board of Education*, 1897, pp. 228-29.

TWO ELECTIVES

Phonography	Algebra
German	General History, 4
Latin	

THIRD YEAR

English, 4	Business Methods, 4

TWO ELECTIVES

Phonography	Algebra and Geometry
German	General History, 4
Latin	

FOURTH YEAR

English, 4
Business Methods, Commercial and Legal Forms, 4
History and Civics, 4

ONE ELECTIVE

Phonography, 4	Solid Geometry, Advanced Algebra, and Trigonometry, 4
German, 4	Chemistry, 4
Latin, 4	Physics, 4

JAMESTOWN, OHIO, 1896[1]

FIRST YEAR

First Semester	Second Semester
Algebra	Algebra
English, 3	English, 2
Physics, 2	Botany, 3
Latin, 5	Caesar, 5

Drawing once a week throughout the year.

SECOND YEAR

Algebra, 2	Plane Geometry, 3
Plane Geometry, 3	English, 2
English, 2	General History, 3
General History, 3	Caesar
Caesar	

THIRD YEAR

Solid Geometry	English, 2
English, 2	Physics, 3
Physics, 3	Bookkeeping
Cicero	Cicero

FOURTH YEAR

Physical Geography, 3	Physical Geography, 2
Arithmetic, 2	United States History, 3
Civil Government	Arithmetic, 3
Virgil	Grammar, 2
	Virgil

[1] *Rules and Regulations*, 1896, pp. 19-20.

APPLETON, WISCONSIN, 1900[1]

Modern Classical Course

First Term	Second Term	Third Term
	FIRST YEAR	
Algebra	Algebra	Algebra
Ancient History	Ancient History and French History	French History
Latin	Latin	Latin
English Composition, 2	English Composition, 2	English Composition, 2
Expression, 2	Expression, 2	Expression, 2
	SECOND YEAR	
English History	English History and Constitution	Constitution
Geology and Physical Geography	Geology and Botany	Botany
Caesar and Latin Composition	Caesar, 3	Caesar, 3
	Latin Composition, 2	Latin Composition, 2
Literary Reading, 3	Literary Reading, 3	Literary Reading, 3
Expression, 2	Expression, 2	Expression, 2
	THIRD YEAR	
Geometry	Geometry	Geometry
German	German	German
Cicero, 4	Cicero, 4	Cicero, 4
Latin Composition, 1	Latin Composition, 1	Latin Composition, 1
Literary Reading, 3	Literary Reading, 3	Literary Reading, 3
Expression, 2	Expression, 2	Expression, 2
	FOURTH YEAR	
Physics	Physics	Physics
German	German	German
Virgil	Virgil	Virgil
Expression, 1	Expression, 1	Theory and Art of Teaching
Reviews, 3	Reviews, 3	

German Course

FIRST YEAR

Substitute German for Latin.

SECOND YEAR

Substitute German for Latin and Physiology for Geology.

THIRD YEAR

Substitute Geology and Chemistry for Latin.

FOURTH YEAR

Substitute Literature, and Political Economy, Psychology and Pedagogy for German and Latin.

APPLETON, WISCONSIN, 1900

English Course

FIRST YEAR

Substitute English for Latin.

[1] *Catalog*, 1900, pp. 54-61.

SECOND YEAR

Substitute Rhetoric and Composition for Latin and Physiology for Geology.

THIRD YEAR

Omit Library Reading and substitute Geology and Chemistry for German and Literature for Latin.

FOURTH YEAR

Same as German Course.

Commercial Course

FIRST YEAR

Substitute Bookkeeping for Latin.

SECOND YEAR

Substitute English for Science and Shorthand and Typewriting for Latin.

THIRD YEAR

Substitute Physiology and Commercial Arithmetic for German and Shorthand and Typewriting for Latin.

FOURTH YEAR

Substitute Shorthand and Typewriting for Latin and Political Economy, Commercial Law and Pedagogy for German.

APPLETON, WISCONSIN, 1900

Manual Training Course

FIRST YEAR

First Semester

Algebra
Ancient History
Drawing:
- *a*) Notes on Experimental Geometry, 3
- *b*) Geometrical Solution of Problems with Draughting Instruments, 2

Shopwork, 10:
- *a*) Instruction in Construction, care, and use of Bench Tools
- *b*) Joinery
- *c*) Instruction and Practice in putting Bench Tools in order.

Composition and Expression as in other courses

Second Semester

Algebra
French History
Drawing:
- *a*) Block and Freehand Lettering
- *b*) Shade Lining
- *c*) Tracing, Blue Printing and Mounting Prints (9 weeks)
- *d*) Freehand Drawing (from models)
- *e*) Dimension Sketches, for Mechanical Drawings (from models), (9 weeks)

Shopwork, 10:
- *a*) Joinery, 12
- *b*) Wood Carving, (6 weeks)

Composition and Expression as in other courses

The shopwork includes a finished article—such as a stand, table grille, which shall be, as far as possible, the product of the pupil's work.

SECOND YEAR

English History
Physiology
Drawing:
- a) Mechanical Drawing (from Copy)
- b) Tracing and Blue-Printing from each drawing

Shopwork:
- a) Lathe-work in wood (hand tools)

Literary Reading and Expression same as other courses

Civil Government
Botany
Drawing:
- a) Mechanical Drawing (from models)
- b) Tracing and Blue Printing from each drawing
- c) Notes on Pattern Making Molding and Casting, 3

Shopwork:
- a) Pattern Making
- b) Molding
- c) Casting (in brass, zinc and Plaster of Paris)

Literary Reading and Expression same as other courses

APPLETON, WISCONSIN, 1900

Manual Training Course

THIRD YEAR

First Semester

Geometry
Geology and Physical Geography
Drawing:
- a) Pattern and Machine Drawing (designing)

Shopwork
- a) Pattern Making
- b) Molding
- c) Casting (in brass, zinc and Plaster of Paris)

Literary Reading and Expression same as other courses

Second Semester

Geometry
Chemistry
Drawing:
- a) Elementary Mechanism
- b) Notes on Forging, Welding and Tool Making, 3

Shop-work
- a) Forging (in iron and steal)
- b) Welding
- c) Case Hardening
- d) Hardening and Tempering Steel

Literary Reading and Expression same as other courses

FOURTH YEAR

Physics
Literature
Drawing:
Orthographic Projection
Shopwork:
Bench Work in metals (6 weeks)
Machine Work in metals, 12
Expression, 1; Reviews, 3

Physics
Literature
Drawing:
Perspective Projection, (9 weeks)
Shopwork:
Machine Work in metals
Machine Finishing, Polishing, and Grinding
Expression, 1; Reviews, 3

Lack of uniformity in subjects offered is revealed by the Courses found on 20–42. The following is an analysis of six of these with respect to subjects included. Subjects placed in parentheses are not offered in both schools. Others are common to both.

MADISON, WISCONSIN, 1862[1]	CINCINNATI, OHIO, 1862[2]
MATHEMATICS	
Arithmetic	Arithmetic
Elementary Algebra	Algebra
(Higher Algebra)	Geometry
Geometry	(Trigonometry)
ENGLISH	
(Grammar and Analysis)	(Composition)
(Work Analysis)	Rhetoric
Rhetoric	Literature
Literature	
SCIENCE	
(Botany)	Natural Philosophy
(Physiology)	Chemistry
(Physical Geography)	Astronomy
(Geology)	
Natural Philosophy	
Chemistry	
Astronomy	
SOCIAL STUDIES	
(United States History)	(Mediaeval History)
(Political Economy)	(Modern History)
Ancient History	(Constitution United States)
	Ancient History
FOREIGN LANGUAGE	
Latin	Latin
Greek	Greek
	(German)
	(French)
COMMERCIAL SUBJECTS	
	(Bookkeeping)
	(Commercial Forms)
MISCELLANEOUS SUBJECTS	
(Mental Philosophy)	
(Moral Philosophy)	
(Butler's *Analogy*)	
(Logic)	

[1] *Annual School Report*, 1863, pp. 22-23.
[2] *Report of Common Schools of Cincinnati, Ohio*, 1862, pp. 70-71.

AUBURN, INDIANA, 1882[1]	MILWAUKEE, WISCONSIN, 1884[2]
MATHEMATICS	
Arithmetic	Arithmetic
Algebra	Algebra
Geometry	Geometry
	(Trigonometry)
ENGLISH	
(Reading)	Grammar
(Spelling)	(Rhetoric)
(Writing)	(Literature)[3]
Grammar	(Classics)
SCIENCE	
Physiology	Physiology
Natural Philosophy	Physics
Chemistry	Chemistry
(Physical Geography)	(Astronomy)
	(Biology)
	(Geology)
SOCIAL STUDIES	
(United States History)	General History
General History	Civil Government
Civil Government	(English History)
	(Roman History)
	(Civil and Literary History)
	(United States Constitution)
FOREIGN LANGUAGE	
Latin	Latin
	(German)
	(French)
COMMERCIAL SUBJECTS	
(Bookkeeping)	

JAMESTOWN, OHIO, 1897[4]	APPLETON, WISCONSIN, 1900[5]
MATHEMATICS	
(Arithmetic)	Algebra
Algebra	Geometry
Geometry	
ENGLISH	
English, 1½ years	English, 3 years
SCIENCE	
Physiology	Physiology
Physical Geography	Physical Geography
Botany	Botany
Physics	Physics
	(Chemistry)
	(Geology)

[1] *Rules and Regulations of the Public Schools*, 1882-83, pp. 9-10.
[2] *Annual Report School Board*, 1884, p. 54.
[3] Probably History of English Literature.
[4] *Rules and Regulations*, pp. 19-20.
[5] *Catalog of the Public Schools*, pp. 54-61.

SOCIAL STUDIES[1]

(General History)	(Ancient History)
(United States History)	(English History)
(Civil Government)	(French History)
	(Political Economy)
	(Constitution)
FOREIGN LANGUAGE	
Latin	Latin
	(German)
COMMERCIAL SUBJECTS	
Bookkeeping	(Bookkeeping)
	(Short Hand)
	(Typewriting)
	(Commercial Law)
	(Commercial Arithmetic)
MISCELLANEOUS SUBJECTS	
	(Pedagogy) (Psychology)
	(Manual Training, 4 years)

The foregoing courses selected for analysis were chosen from the following periods: 1860–65, 1881–85, and 1896–1900. A comparative study of courses chosen from the other periods reveals the same wide range of difference in subjects offered. Even greater difference is found in connection with some of the courses. For example, a comparison of Wilmette, Illinois, 1898,[2] and Columbus, Ohio, 1897, and Waterloo, Iowa, 1870,[3] and Cincinnati, Ohio, 1872, makes this clear. It is also evident that neither locality nor population, except within very broad limits, were determining factors.

It will be observed that there was more uniformity in the field of mathematics than in other fields. This became increasingly so as the practice of offering higher mathematics, quite common in 1860, gradually declined to the close of the century. In the other fields marked lack of uniformity prevailed. Some allowance should be made for confusion in terminology in English and the social studies, but even when this is done, the practice in different schools varied widely both in amount of work offered and in the subjects as well. As would be expected, commercial and miscellaneous subjects manifest the least degree of uniformity. Details relating to each school are given in the Appendix, Tables A–H. For details concerning the number of schools offering each subject and for summaries, see Tables II–IX and X.

[1] It is very probable that lack of uniformity appears to be greater than it really was on account of confusion in terminology.

[2] Cf. pp. 37-38.

[3] Cf. pp. 24-25.

CHAPTER IV

NUMBER OF COURSES OFFERED; TITLES AND ORGANIZATION

1. NUMBER AND TITLES OF COURSES

TABLE I

The following table gives a summary of the number of courses offered by the various schools in each period and shows the designations of the courses.

1.—TWENTY SCHOOLS, 1860–65

Number of Courses	Number of Schools
1	12
2	6
3	2

Designation of Courses	Number of Schools
Classical	7
English and Classical	1
English	2
General	3
Latin-English	1
Regular	1
Normal	2

2.—TWENTY SCHOOLS, 1866–70

Number of Courses	Number of Schools
1	10
2	9
4	1

Designation of Courses	Number of Schools
Classical	8
English	3
English and Latin	2
English and German	1
General	3

3.—TWENTY SCHOOLS, 1871–75

Number of Courses	Number of Schools
1	9
2	9
3	1
5	1

Designation of Courses	Number of Schools
Classical	8
College Preparatory	2
Commercial-English	1
English	5
English-German	1

English-Latin	1
Latin	1
General	5
Scientific	1

4.—TWENTY-FIVE SCHOOLS, 1876-80

Number of Courses	Number of Schools
1	17
2	4
3	3
4	1

Designation of Courses	Number of Schools
Classical	4
Commercial	1
Commercial-English	1
English	2
General	3
Latin-Scientific	1
Modern Classical	1
Preparatory	1
Preparatory-English	1
Scientific	2
Scientific-Engineering	1
Technological	1

5.—TWENTY-FIVE SCHOOLS, 1881–85

Number of Courses	Number of Schools
3	14
2	5
3	4
4	2

Designation of Courses	Number of Schools
Ancient Classical	1
Classical	6
English	4
English-Science	1
General	2
German	1
German-English	2
Latin	4
Latin-English	2
Latin-German	1
Latin-Scientific	1
Modern Classical	1
Modern Language	1

6.—THIRTY-FIVE SCHOOLS, 1886–90

Number of Courses	Number of Schools
1	20
2	7
3	5

Number of Courses	Number of Schools
4	1
5	2

Designation of Courses	Number of Schools
Academic	1
Ancient Classical	1
Business	1
Commercial	1
Commercial-English	1
Classical	5
English	9
French-English	1
General	3
General-Literary	1
General Science	1
German	3
German-English	1
Latin	5
Latin-English	1
Latin-German	1
Modern Classical	3
Normal	1
Preparatory-English	1
Regular	1

7.—SIXTY SCHOOLS, 1891–95

Number of Courses	Number of Schools
1	28
2	13
3	9
4	5
5	3
6	2

Designation of Courses	Number of Schools
Business	4
Commercial	2
Classical	9
College Preparatory	1
English	20
English and French	1
English and German	1
English-Scientific	4
English-German	1
German	4
German-English	1
General Science	3
General	1
German-Scientific	1
Latin	17
Latin-English	3

Latin-German	4
Latin-Scientific	4
Latin-Greek	1
Literary and Science	1
Modern Classical	3
Modern Language	3
Normal	1
Preparatory	1
Practical	1
Science	2
Scientific	6

8.—SIXTY SCHOOLS, 1896–1900

Number of Courses	Number of Schools
1	25
2	12
3	12
4	8
6	2
7	1

Designation of Courses	Number of Schools
Ancient Classical	1
Business	2
College Preparatory	1
Commercial	6
Complete Commercial	1
Shorter Commercial	1
Classical	12
English	1
English-Science	24
English-Scientific	3
English-Latin	1
English-Commercial	3
English-German	2
Engineering	1
French-English	1
General	3
General Literary	1
General Science	3
German	3
German-English	3
German-Scientific	1
Literary	1
Language	1
Latin	16
Latin-Science	1
Latin-Scientific	3
Latin-English	3
Latin-German	3

Modern-Classical	1
Manual Training for Boys	1
Manual Training for Girls	1
Natural Science	1
Preparatory	1
Philosophical	1
Science	2
Scientific	7

2. CURRICULA ORGANIZATION

The courses of study shown on pages 20–42 and Table I show that the criteria used in curricula organization were of the same generalized sort as prevailed in the early schools discussed in chapter I. Two purposes of high-school instruction are indicated: that of preparing for college, and that of preparing for life. The absence of definite standards for the organization of curricula for the latter purpose is very evident. Those designed to prepare for higher institutions, particularly in the earlier years, offered a very narrow range of subjects determined, apparently, wholly by entrance requirements.[1] As requirements changed, these courses changed, and the tendency to include in them subjects not required for entrance is more marked as time goes on.[2]

In the case of non-preparatory college courses, there is no apparent demand or complex of demands sufficiently clear in purpose or definite in influence to secure any sort of uniformity in length of course, organization, or subjects offered. The only exception to this is found in the comparatively few business or commercial, normal and manual training courses. The latter do not appear until near the close of the period, and even then are rare. The normal courses were usually only one or two years in length, emphasizing the common branches and devoting some attention to pedagogy[3] and less frequently to psychology. They recognized rather vaguely a demand for the training of teachers, although the attempt to meet the demand was meager and they reveal clearly that the purpose was to prepare for teachers' examinations rather than for the actual work of teaching. At best they offered nothing more than was provided by other courses designated by the use of other titles. For example, Madison, Wisconsin, offered four courses in 1883 having the titles, Ancient Classical, Modern Classical, Science,

[1] Cf. p. 20.
[2] Cf. pp. 23 and 28.
[3] Cf. p. 23.

and English and each of these offered pedagogy and reviews of the common branches.

Toward the close of the century a few schools offered courses providing a considerable range of commercial subjects,[1] but the rule was a short course providing a very meager offering of commercial subjects. Even in the four-year commercial courses, as will be observed by reference to pages 32 and 41, the offering of commercial subjects was limited. In the former, none were offered in the last year, and in the latter, none the first half of the first year, and in third and fourth years, part of the work was elective.

For the most part, courses bearing such titles as Business or Commercial were not essentially different from other courses which included a meager offering of commercial subjects except that they usually provided only one or two years of work. Until the last years of the nineteenth century, industrial and commercial demands had very little influence in determining the character of high-school curricula. On the whole it is very clear that only educational ideals of the most generalized sort determined differentiation in curricula except for those students who were preparing for higher institutions.

Further confusion is added by the fact that many courses undertook to perform both functions—that of preparing for college and preparing for life. These were always almost identical in that they provided the college entrance subjects, but frequently differed widely in the other subjects included.[2] There are no apparent well-defined standards for determining electives. In many of the courses, subjects which may be substituted for college-entrance subjects are not indicated. For example, in the course on page 21, Latin and Greek may be substituted for other subjects, but the substitutions allowed are not indicated. On page 22, we find the statement that Latin, German, French, and Spanish are optional. It is probable that optional means elective, but there is no indication of what subjects are to be displaced. In the course on page 24, it is almost certain that several electives are provided, but there is no hint with regard to what these are. These are but examples of the confusion which one finds in a study of these courses.

As has been pointed out, many of the schools offered nominally only one course. Table I reveals that a maximum of three-fifths

[1] Cf. pp. 31 and 38.
[2] Cf. pp. 21, 22, 23, 24, 31, 33.

(1860–65) and a minimum of five-twelfths (1896–1900) of the schools provided a single course. This does not mean, of course, that no electives were provided and that all the students pursued the same subjects. On the contrary, it is very probable that single courses usually provided electives.[1] It is not possible to state the proportion of such courses with any degree of accuracy since it is not clear in some cases whether each student carried three, four, or more subjects.[2] The general rule, no doubt, was four subjects reciting five times per week as a maximum, and in case a course provided more than this number, electives were offered. In some cases the same rule did not hold throughout the course.[3] It is also true that five recitations per week in each subject was not the universal practice.[4] Neither was the minimum number of recitations per week always twenty when four or more subjects were carried by each student. In some cases[5] it seems certain that more than twenty recitations were required, and in others[6] this was probably true. In other cases where four subjects was the minimum less than twenty recitations per week was the rule.[7]

The plan of parallel courses rather than that of single courses with electives in vogue in the early high schools continued in favor to the close of the century. The tendency to multiply both courses and titles is apparent. In the period 1860–65, the average number of courses for schools offering more than one was two and one-fourth, and seven different titles were used. The average for the period 1896–1900 was three and one-sixth courses and thirty-six titles were employed. The proportion of single courses, as has been pointed out, decreased during this same period from three-fifths to five-twelfths. In spite of the tendency to multiply both courses and titles, there was little gain with respect either to clearly defined educational aims or to definite use of titles. It is probably true that the rapid growth of the high-school movement and the constantly increasing enrollment resulted in this multiplication in an attempt to meet the demands of the various classes of students enrolled. The demands, however, were evidently not sufficiently

[1] Courses given on pp. 24, 25, 26, 28, and 37 are examples of single courses with electives Those found on pp. 25, 27, 28, 34, and 36 apparently provided no electives.

[2] Cf. pp. 20, 22, 23, 26.

[3] Cf. pp. 21, 22, 28, 34.

[4] Cf. pp. 21, 24, 30.

[5] Cf. pp. 29, 33, 36.

[6] Cf. p. 36.

[7] Cf. p. 38.

specific to indicate the needs of these different classes. At any rate, both titles and courses lack evidence of such demands being met, if they were made known to those responsible for curricula making.

A few titles furnish rather definite information concerning purpose and content of courses. This is true, for example, of the college preparatory courses having such titles as Preparatory, College Preparatory, and Classical. On the whole, however, titles furnish very little information concerning either purpose or content. Such titles as General, Regular, and the like, furnish no clue concerning what was offered or what was left out. Greek was not included but there was a lack of uniformity in regard to other foreign languages.[1] In the earlier years the two purposes of the school were made clear by the use of the terms "Classical Department" and "English Department" or "General Department." The former term indicated a comparatively narrow range of subjects including always Latin and Greek and the purpose was to prepare for college. The latter terms signified the absence of ancient language and indicated a wider range of subjects including frequently the modern languages.[2]

The word "English" as applied to departments or courses was used in the broad sense to indicate all subjects except Latin and Greek and retained this general meaning even after a multiplication of titles became an established practice. The more restricted use of the term, as now employed, was very rare prior to 1880,[3] and even after this use became well established, English courses did not necessarily offer any more work in English than did the courses having other titles. For example, Springfield, Illinois, offered the same work in English in both the classical and English courses.[4] The difference is found in the substitution of science and mathematics in the latter for Latin or German, and Greek in the former. The same is true as regards English in two courses, one classical and the other English offered by Shenandoah, Iowa, except that one-half year of etymology is substituted in the latter for Latin.[5] The other subjects substituted are science, social studies, and

[1] *Annual Report of the Public Schools*, Jacksonville, Illinois, 1878, p. 76, and *Second Annual Report of Trustees of the Lakeview (Illinois) High Schools*, 1876, pp. 14-15.

[2] *Annual Report Board of Education*, Detroit, Michigan, 1863, p. 63, and *Annual Report Public Schools*, Danville, Illinois, 1871, pp. 26-27.

[3] Cf. Table X.

[4] *Annual Report of the Public Schools*, Springfield, Illinois, 1887, pp. 56-57.

[5] *Rules and Regulations: Public Schools*, Shenandoah, Iowa, 1894-95, p. 23.

bookkeeping. The only difference between the Latin and English courses offered by Lincoln, Nebraska, is that the latter offered no Latin and substituted bookkeeping, science, and the social studies.[1] Except for bookkeeping, however, the substitutions were not the same. It is true, of course, that English courses offered more work in English as time went on, but this was also true of other courses. The foregoing examples will, however, serve to illustrate the general sense in which the term continued to be used. The frequent use of the term as a course title, either alone or in combination, is revealed in Table I. This seems to be very clear evidence of the survival and persistence of the educational ideal which gave rise to the English Classical School of Boston, later called the English High School.[2]

This loose distinction between an English education and a classical education is further illustrated by the absence or infrequent use of titles indicating the presence in courses of other subjects. No course titles found in Table I indicate that the social studies were offered, although Tables II–IX show the relatively large number of schools offering these subjects, and Table XVIII indicates the comparatively large amount of time devoted to this field as compared with other subjects from which course titles are derived. Science is not recognized at all in course titles in the earlier years, and at no time is the recognition commensurate with the importance of this field. The infrequency of the use of the word "Science" or its derivatives is shown in Table I. It is particularly noticeable until after 1890, and then some such hyphenated title as English-Scientific, Latin-Scientific, and the like is commonly used.

The term "Science" or "Scientific"[3] when used as course titles is no more reliable from the standpoint of determining the purpose or content of the course than is the term "English." The former terms were even less definite than the latter since they did not indicate the exclusion of ancient language. On the whole, however, these titles were justified since the courses so named usually offered a considerable amount of science. In the later years, these courses frequently included modern language, particularly German.

Hyphenated titles such as Latin-English, Latin-Scientific, English-German, Latin-German, and the like, wholly absent in the earlier years, became relatively common by 1880. They invariably

[1] *General Regulations*, Lincoln, Nebraska, High School, 1893, p. 15.

[2] Cf. chap. i., pp. 2-3.

[3] The word "science" or "scientific" is used alone in only twenty out of approximately three hundred and twenty course titles.

offered the subjects indicated in the titles but not infrequently different titles stood for practically the same subjects. Other titles such as General-Literary and Philosophical gave no clue concerning what subjects were offered since nothing peculiarly literary or philosophical is discoverable in the courses so named.

It has been pointed out that course titles are deceiving and that distinctions between courses were often attempted where differences were negligible. In spite of this, however, it is evident that there was a growing consciousness that the generalized ideals determining the character of non-preparatory courses needed to be broken up into more specific ones. The introduction of commercial, normal, and industrial subjects, and also the use of titles indicating the presence of these subjects, is an evidence of this. But progress was very slow and differentiation of courses continued without much recognition being given to commercial and industrial demands. The superintendent of the Chicago schools in 1866 urged the importance of a reorganization of the course of study in order to meet the "demands of the community."[1] He commends the German Realschule but specific recommendations are lacking except that he urges the teaching of drawing. Evidence is not lacking that there was serious opposition on the part of school officials to the introduction of industrial courses into the high schools. As late as 1886, the president of the Chicago board in his report says:

> During the last few years the tendency has been too much toward the practical. The ideal has been thrown aside and everything is being measured by gold and silver standards. Educators even are being whirled down the stream and education is being measured by value in dollars and cents.[2]

He insists that the board has acted contrary to the spirit of the law and contends that the purpose of the school is to give a "foundation for an education" which is interfered with by an attempt to prepare for specific vocations. He further says that there is no place where the line can be drawn since it is "just as much the purpose of the public school to educate the surgeon as it is to educate the carpenter."

The high school frequently referred to as the "people's school" was not so to any important extent as far as commercial and industrial courses were concerned until after the close of the nineteenth century. Preparation for specific vocations was left to private

[1] *Annual Report of Board of Education*, 1866, pp. 46-51.
[2] *Ibid.*, 1886, pp. 18-19.

schools such as commercial or business colleges, which were relatively numerous, and to the few manual training schools founded and maintained by private enterprise. The foundations, however, were laid in the high schools for the development of commercial and industrial education so marked in recent years.

3. ORDER IN WHICH SUBJECTS APPEAR IN THE CURRICULA

The order in which subjects appear in curricula is important for two reasons. First, it determines the character of education for those who drop out of school before graduation; and secondly, it determines the organization from the standpoint of sequence of courses.

An interpretation of the courses used in Table I shows the following for the several periods:

Mathematics.—As would be expected, the following sequence obtained: arithmetic, algebra, geometry, and trigonometry. The exception to this order is furnished by arithmetic and algebra. These two subjects were frequently offered simultaneously in the first year; in a few cases the former followed the latter immediately, and in about an equal number of cases it was offered after geometry. The tendency to place it immediately following algebra, increased toward the close. When it followed geometry, it was usually designated as a review subject.[1]

Algebra was usually begun in the first year and rarely after the second. Geometry invariably followed algebra and was in turn followed by trigonometry and other higher mathematics.

English.—The usual order in this field was grammar, composition, rhetoric, and literature. The first named was rarely offered in any year except the first. Like arithmetic it is sometimes found as a review subject in the last year, but less frequently.[2] Composition is not easily classified. In the earlier years it was frequently listed in a footnote along with other general exercises.[3] Classification is also made difficult by the fact that the mention of composition was frequently in connection with other English subjects. Three stages are quite well marked in this particular. In the early periods it was associated with grammar, later with rhetoric, and finally with literature. When not thus associated, however, it was rarely placed in any year except the first.

[1] Cf. pp. 26-27.
[2] Cf. p. 26.
[3] Cf. pp. 20, 21, 22, 23, 24, 25, 26, 27, 30.

Rhetoric was found in all years of the course, but most frequently in the second and third with the former leading. The latter is particularly true of three-year courses. After about 1880 it is found more frequently in the first year which is probably owing to its association with composition.

Literature, offered under various titles, was confined largely to the third and fourth years until about 1890. In fact, during the period 1891–95 it was offered after the second year in more than 70 per cent of the schools. In the next five-year period this percentage had decreased to 60. Exact data are not easily available for any of the subjects in this field after the use of the term "English" as it is now employed, came into use. It is clear, however, that the use of literature as a source for composition work resulted after 1890 in its more frequent introduction into the earlier years of the course.

Science.—The science subjects fall into two fairly well defined groups, those commonly found in the earlier years and those in the later years of the course. Physiology, physical geography, botany, and zoölogy belong to the first group, and physics, chemistry, geology, and astronomy to the second. While botany and zoölogy belong to the first group, these subjects show a greater tendency toward distribution over all the years than is the case in the other science subjects. This is particularly true of zoölogy.

Physiology[1] was a first-year subject with a few schools offering it in the second year. It is rarely found after the second year. This condition was relatively permanent.

Physical Geography[2] belongs largely to the first two years with the emphasis rather decidedly upon the first year except for the periods 1886–90 and 1891–95. In the former, the ratio in favor of the second year was 4 to 3, and in the latter, the frequency of occurrence for the two years was equal. During the earlier periods it is not found at all in the last year, but toward the close there are a few cases in which it is offered in this year.

Botany is found most frequently in the second year. The first year stands next in importance with the third year following closely. The fourth year is never represented by more than 5 per cent of the schools, and this percentage occurs in the period 1891–95. In two periods, 1871–75 and 1881–85, it was not offered in the fourth year

[1] Offered in the first year in 70 per cent of the schools.

[2] Offered in the first year in 50 per cent of the schools; in the second year in 30 per cent.

and in the remaining periods by not more than one or two schools. This distribution of the subject holds throughout the forty years.

Zoölogy, as has been pointed out, is not so easily classified in respect to frequency of occurrence as other sciences. It follows botany more closely than it does any other subject in its field, but not closely enough to indicate any general practice of correlating these subjects until after 1890. On the whole, distribution between the first and second years is fairly equal, followed by the third year in point of frequency. The fourth year also has considerable representation as compared with botany. For example, in the period 1891–95, while botany is represented in this year by about 5 per cent of the schools, zoölogy is represented by about 20 per cent.

Physics is found in all years but most frequently in the third. It very rarely appears in the first year and is found in the second year to some extent in the case of three-year courses. In the case of four-year courses not offering chemistry, physics is usually offered in the fourth year. If both are offered, the latter usually preceded the former although there were exceptions amounting to about 20 per cent of the schools in 1860–65. Thereafter the percentage fell off rapidly until 1885, after which it increased somewhat amounting to approximately 15 per cent in 1896–1900.

Chemistry is rather distinctly a last-year subject, the exception being chiefly in the cases when it preceded physics referred to above. It seems never to have been offered in the first year and very rarely in the second, even in the case of three-year courses.

Geology was generally offered in the last year, the third year standing next in point of frequency. The percentage of frequency for the second year ranges from 0 to approximately 20 per cent and there is apparently no permanent tendency in regard to the second year. Only two cases were found in which the subject was offered in the first year.

Astronomy follows geology somewhat closely, the percentage of schools offering it in the last year being large. Like geology, the third is next in point of frequency in less ratio, while the cases in which it is offered in either the first or second years are almost negligible.

The place in a course assigned to a science subject, with the exception of physics and chemistry, seems to have been determined largely by administrative convenience. As has been pointed out, when physics and chemistry were both offered the former usually preceded, and it is not likely that the sequence was merely a matter of administrative convenience. Some correlation was no doubt attempted and secured. The two subjects most frequently making up a year's work are physiology and physical geography.[1] There seems to be no reason for this except that of administrative convenience. One would expect that botany and zoölogy would be found in the same year since each was usually offered for one-third or one-half year; but such is not the rule. There seems to have been no general attempt at correlation except in the few schools offering biology. Neither geology nor astronomy follow any rule in their relations to other sciences in the course.

The Social Studies.—European history, taught under various titles, is found in all years of the course although rarely in the last year. The second year is highest in point of frequency. This is followed by the third year until after 1895 when the first year takes second place.

Aside from the fact that ancient, medieval, and modern history were taught in the logical order, there is no apparent attempt at correlation. These subjects usually constituted a one-year course based upon some textbook such as Swinton's *Outlines*, Barnes's *General History*, or Meyer's *General History*. English history seems to have been placed in the course with no reference to United States history or other European history.

United States history was almost exclusively a first-year subject until after 1885, and the emphasis upon that year continued to the close. After 1890 a considerable number of schools offered the subject in the last year, and when offered in that year, it was usually designated as a review subject. In 1896–1900 more schools offered it in the last year than in any other.

As has been said, there was no apparent correlation between this subject and other history subjects. On the whole, the same can be said of it and civics. This is made clear in at least two ways. In the first place, civics under various titles, was offered in more schools in every period than was United States history, the ratio by periods being as follows: 8:7, 4:1, 5:2, 3:1, 2:1, 2:1, and 2:1. A study of the courses also reveals that the relative positions in the courses occupied by the two subjects make it improbable that any general attempt at correlation was made at least until after 1890.

[1] Cf. pp. 22, 25, 26, 28, 30, 35.

For example, civics is found but once in the first year until after 1876, while during the same period, United States history was rarely offered in any other than the first year.

Little more need be said concerning civics. Except for the first three periods referred to and the period 1891–95, when it was offered the first year in approximately 40 per cent of the schools, it was fairly well distributed over the entire course. As has been said, it is rather clear that some general attempt at correlation with United States history was made after 1890.

Political economy was offered in comparatively few schools, the ratio of the subject to civics being as follows for the several periods: 3:4, 1:4, 1:6, 1:5, 3:8, 2:7, and 2:5. It is never found in the first year and rarely in the second. For the whole period covered by the study, the ratio of the fourth year to the third is 3:7. In the earlier years it is clear that no attempt was made to correlate the subject with civics, but after 1890 there seems to have been some correlation attempted.

Foreign Language.—Since the rule in Latin was to offer three years in a three-year course and four years in a four-year course, the schools offering beginning Latin in the first year are in an overwhelming majority. If but two years were offered in either a three- or four-year course, then the subject was begun in the second and third years respectively. Caesar almost invariably followed the first year. The usual order after Caesar was Cicero and then Virgil, although the latter occasionally preceded the former. What has been said of beginning Latin is also true in general of other foreign languages. If, for example, but two years of German or French were offered in a four-year course it was begun in the third year. The number of schools after 1890 having beginning German in the third year is relatively large, being approximately 50 per cent.

Commercial Subjects.—Bookkeeping was a first- and second-year subject, with the former leading. It was rarely offered after the second year until after 1890 when some increase is noticed.

Miscellaneous Subjects.—Mental philosophy, moral philosophy, and logic are almost invariably found in the last years of the course. The first named usually preceded the second while logic seems to have had no relation to the other two.

Pedagogy and psychology were also last-year subjects. No order of procedure is discernible, sometimes one being offered first and sometimes the other.

4. UNITS OF TIME IN ORGANIZATION

The plan of three terms to the year prevailed generally to the close of the century.[1] A few schools from the very beginning used the semester plan[2] and the comparative number had increased somewhat by 1900. A still less number offered no subject for less than one year, and in such cases some subjects had less than five recitation periods per week.[3] In one school the year was divided into quarters resulting in a majority of half-year subjects, and in a few cases in which but a single quarter was devoted to a subject.

The semester plan, as has been said, grew somewhat in favor toward the close of the century, and the increasing practice of devoting at least a half-year to a subject pointed very definitely to a giving-way of the three-term plan. For example, a school would preserve the old plan but would offer one subject during the fall term and the first half of the winter term, this being followed by another subject during the last half of the winter term and the spring term.

Tables XX–XXVIII, showing the maximum and minimum time devoted to subjects, indicate clearly the prevalence of the three-term plan. The number of schools, however, adhering to the three-term plan always exceeded the number indicated by the tables because of the practice referred to in the preceding paragraph.

The following tables, III–X, constitute an analysis of Tables A–H from the standpoint of number of schools offering the various subjects. In Tables II, III, IV, and V, twenty schools are represented, twenty-five in Table VI, thirty in Table VII, and forty in Tables VIII and IX.

[1] Cf. chap. iii.
[2] Cf. pp. 21, 24.
[3] Cf. pp. 36, 38, 39.

CHAPTER V

SUBJECTS INCLUDED IN CURRICULA

The following tables are summaries from Tables A–H, in Appendix, inclusive and show the range of subjects and also the number of schools offering the various subjects.[1]

TABLE II

TWENTY SCHOOLS, 1860–65

Mathematics	English	Science
Arithmetic, 17	Grammar, 12	Physiology, 17
Algebra, 18	English Analysis, 11	Physical Geography, 17
Geometry, 19	Word Analysis, 4	Natural Philosophy, 20
Trigonometry, 12	Reading, 6	Physics, 1
Analytics, 2	Composition, 11[2]	Chemistry, 17
Surveying, 8	Rhetoric, 18	Geology, 14
Engineering, 3	English Literature, 6	Astronomy, 14
	Literature, 1	Botany, 14
	Classics, 1	Natural History, 5
	Elements of Criticism, 4	Zoölogy, 4
	Elocution, 1	Geography, 2
	English, 1	

Social Studies	Foreign Language	Miscellaneous Subjects
Ancient History, 8	Latin, 16	Mental Philosophy, 12
Medieval History, 3	Greek, 7	Moral Philosophy, 11
Modern History, 6	German, 7	Logic, 5
United States History, 3	French, 4	Psychology, 2
English History, 3		Evidences of Christianity, 2
General History, 3	Commercial Subjects	Ancient Geography, 2
Universal History, 2		Butler's *Analogy*, 1
Science of Government, ment, 3	Bookkeeping, 3	Domestic Science, 2
United States Constitution, 8	Business Forms, 1	Natural Theology, 2
Political Economy, 4		
History, 2		
History of Civilization, 1		

[1] The number of subjects, particularly in English and the social studies, is increased somewhat by lack of uniformity in terminology.

[2] Composition was actually taught in more schools than is indicated in this and the following tables. It is not included in the count because it did not appear as a regular subject, but was listed in the footnotes as one of the general exercises. More detailed explanation will be found in Part II.

TABLE III

TWENTY SCHOOLS, 1866–70

Mathematics	English	Science
Arithmetic, 12	Grammar, 9	Physiology, 15
Algebra, 20	Analysis, 8	Physical Geography, 14
Geometry, 20	Reading, 7	Natural Philosophy, 20
Trigonometry, 14	Composition, 8	Physics, 1
Calculus, 1	Rhetoric, 15	Mechanics, 1
Analytics, 1	Etymology, 1	Chemistry, 16
Surveying, 4	English Language, 1	Astronomy, 18
Engineering, 1	English Literature, 13	Geology, 12
	American Literature, 2	Botany, 15
	History of English Literature, 1	Zoölogy, 4
	Elocution, 2	Natural History, 6
		Mineralogy, 1
		Meteorology, 1
		Geography, 5

Social Studies	Foreign Language	Miscellaneous Subjects
Ancient History, 8	Latin, 17	Mental Philosophy, 15
Modern History, 2	Greek, 13	Moral Philosophy, 9
General History, 9	German, 11	Logic, 2
United States History, 4	French, 6	Drawing, 2
English History, 2		Classical Antiquities, 2
History, 4		Evidence of Christianity, 1
Science of Government, 2	**Commercial Subjects**	Ancient Geography, 2
Civil Government, 8	Bookkeeping, 12	Pedagogy, 2
United States Constitution, 4		
Political Economy, 6		
Political Science, 1		
Chronology, 1		

TABLE IV

TWENTY SCHOOLS, 1871–75

Mathematics	English	Science
Arithmetic, 12	Grammar, 8	Physiology, 17
Algebra, 20	Analysis, 7	Physical Geography, 15
Geometry, 20	Reading, 1	Natural Philosophy, 14
Trigonometry, 15	Composition, 12	Physics, 4
Analytics, 1	Rhetoric, 17	Mechanics, 3
Surveying, 4	English Literature, 18	Electricity, 1
Navigation, 1	American Literature, 2	Light and Heat, 1
Calculus, 1	History of English Literature, 1	
Spherical Geometry, 1		

English Language, 1
Etymology, 2
Elocution, 2

Natural Science, 1
Chemistry, 18
Botany, 17
Zoölogy, 8
Natural History, 4
Geology, 17
Astronomy, 16
Geography, 2
Mineralogy, 1

Social Studies

Ancient History, 4
Medieval History, 1
Modern Histoy, 3
United States History, 5
General History, 11
Universal History, 1
Outlines of History, 1
History, 4
Science of Government, 3
Civil Government, 7
United States Constitution, 5
State Constitution, 1
Political Science, 1
Political Economy, 5

Foreign Language

Latin, 18
Greek, 10
German, 13
French, 12

Commercial Subjects

Bookkeeping, 10
Commercial Law, 1

Miscellaneous Subjects

Mental Philosophy, 10
Moral Philosophy, 5
Logic, 2
Classical Antiquities, 1
Ancient Geography, 2
Biblical Antiquities, 1
Manual of Fine Arts, 1
Pedagogy, 1
Art, 1
Drawing, 2
Evidences of Christianity, 2

TABLE V

TWENTY SCHOOLS, 1876–80

Mathematics

Arithmetic, 14
Algebra, 20
Geometry, 20
Trigonometry, 11
Analytics, 1
Mensuration, 1
Surveying, 2
Plane Geometry, 3
Solid Geometry, 1

English

Grammar, 6
Analysis, 5
Word Analysis, 1
Reading, 2
English Language, 2
Composition, 12
Rhetoric, 14
English Literature, 14
History of English Literature, 2
Elements of Criticism, 1
Elocution, 1

Science

Physiology, 19
Physical Geography 13
Natural Philosophy, 16
Physics, 5
Mechanics, 1
Chemistry, 13
Geology, 10
Astronomy, 13
Botany, 17
Zoölogy, 9
Natural History, 6
Natural Science, 1
Meteorology, 1
Geography, 2

Social Studies

Ancient History, 6
Medieval History, 1
Modern History, 3
United States History, 5
English History, 5
General History, 10
Universal History, 1
Outlines of History, 2
History 3
History of Michigan, 1
Science of Government, 3
Civil Government, 8
United States Constitution, 4
Political Economy, 3
Parliamentary Rules, 1

Foreign Language

Latin, 15
Greek, 8
German, 12
French, 3

Commercial Subjects

Bookkeeping, 10
Business Forms, 1
Commercial Arithmetic, 1

Miscellaneous Subjects

Mental Philosophy, 8
Moral Philosophy, 4
Logic, 1
Classical Antiquities, 1
Manual Art, 1
Drawing, 1

TABLE VI

TWENTY-FIVE SCHOOLS, 1881–85

Mathematics

Arithmetic, 22
Algebra, 25
Geometry, 25
Trigonometry, 10
Surveying, 3

English

Grammar, 13
Analysis, 6
Word Analysis, 3
Reading, 6
Composition, 9
Rhetoric, 21
Etymology, 1
Elocution, 4
English Literature, 18
American Literature, 3
History of English Literature, 1
History of American Literature, 1
Literature, 4
Classics, 8
English, 1

Science

Physiology, 23
Physical Geography, 17
Natural Philosophy, 18
Physics, 7
Chemistry, 20
Geology, 14
Botany, 18
Zoölogy, 10
Natural History, 3
Astronomy, 12
Geography, 2
Biology, 1

Social Studies

Ancient History, 5
Medieval History, 1
Modern History, 1
United States History, 8
English History, 8
General History, 18
History, 5
History of Civilization, 1
Science of Government, 2

Foreign Language

Latin, 23
Greek, 5
German, 12
French, 5

Commercial Subjects

Bookkeeping, 17
Business Forms, 1
Commercial Arithmetic,

Miscellaneous Subjects

Mental Philosophy, 6
Moral Philosophy, 3
Logic, 1
Drawing, 1
Pedagogy, 1

Civil Government, 15
United States Constitution, 4
Political Economy, 8

TABLE VII

THIRTY SCHOOLS, 1886–90

Mathematics

Arithmetic, 25
Algebra, 30
Geometry, 26
Plane Geometry, 6
Solid Geometry, 5
Trigonometry, 11
Surveying, 2

English

Grammar, 20
Analysis, 4
Word Analysis, 5
Reading, 9
Composition, 13
Rhetoric, 25
English Literature, 21
American Literature, 6
Literature, 6
Classics, 1
Orthography, 1
Etymology, 1
Elocution, 2
First Year English, 8
Second Year English, 8
Third Year English, 7
Fourth Year English, 1

Science

Physiology, 26
Physical Geography, 27
Natural Philosophy, 11
Physics, 19
Chemistry, 18
Geology, 19
Botany, 29
Zoölogy, 19
Astronomy, 17
Geography, 6
Entomology, 1

Social Studies

Ancient History, 10
Medieval History, 5
Modern History, 5
United States History, 16
English History, 13
French History, 1
General History, 17
Science of Government, 1
Civil Government, 23
United States Constitution, 6
State Constitution, 2
Civics, 1
Political Economy, 11
Historical Reading, 1

Foreign Language

Latin, 25
Greek, 4
German, 14
French, 3

Commercial Subjects

Bookkeeping, 24
Business Forms, 1
Commercial Arithmetic, 1
Business Arithmetic, 1
Commercial Law, 3
Phonography, 1

Miscellaneous Subjects

Mental Philosophy, 6
Moral Philosophy, 3
Drawing, 5
Theory and Art of Teaching, 5
Psychology and Pedagogy, 2
Manual Training, 2

TABLE VIII

FORTY SCHOOLS, 1891–95

Mathematics

Arithmetic, 28
Algebra, 40
Geometry, 33

English

Grammar, 14
Analysis, 1
Word Analysis, 4

Science

Physiology, 32
Physical Geography, 29

Plane Geometry, 6
Solid Geometry, 7
Trigonometry, 8
Mensuration, 1

Reading, 1
Composition, 21
Rhetoric, 27
English Literature, 21
American Literature, 9
Literature, 13
Classics, 10
Etymology, 2
Orthography, 1
Elocution, 3
First Year English, 13
Second Year English, 9
Third Year English, 6
Fourth Year English, 3

Natural Philosophy, 5
Physics, 35
Chemistry, 28
Geology, 19
Botany, 33
Zoölogy, 15
Biology, 2
Astronomy, 20
Geography, 2
Meteorology, 1

Social Studies

Ancient History, 13
Modern History, 1
United States History, 15
English History, 14
French History, 2
General History, 25
Outlines of History, 1
Political History, 5
Historical Readings, 1
Current Events, 1
Social Science, 1
United States and State Constitutions, 1
United States Civil Government, 1
State Civil Government, 1
Civil Government, 25
Civics, 7
Political Economy, 11

Foreign Language

Latin, 38
Greek, 7
German, 21
French, 5
Spanish, 1

Commercial Subjects

Bookkeeping, 19
Business Forms, 2
Commercial Arithmetic, 3
Business Arithmetic, 3
Commercial Law, 5
Commercial Geography, 1
Business Practice, 1
Stenography, 3
Typewriting, 1

Miscellaneous Subjects

Mental Philosophy, 3
Psychology, 7
Pedagogy, 8
Ethics, 1
Drawing, 3
Manual Training, 2

TABLE IX

FORTY SCHOOLS, 1896–1900

Mathematics

Arithmetic, 28
Algebra, 40
Geometry, 29
Plane Geometry, 12
Solid Geometry, 9
Trigonometry, 9

English

Grammar, 14
Analysis, 1
Word Analysis, 5
Reading, 4
Composition, 17
Rhetoric, 25
English Literature, 15
American Literature

Science

Physiology, 28
Physical Geography, 30
Natural Philosophy, 1
Physics, 37
Chemistry, 26
Geology, 9
Botany, 33

Literature, 14
Authors, 1
Classics, 5
History of English Literature, 2
Orthography, 2
First Year English, 17
Second Year English, 14
Third Year English, 11
Fourth Year English, 5

Zoölogy, 18
Biology, 4
Astronomy, 11
Natural History, 1
Geography, 2
Physiography, 1

Social Studies

Ancient History, 15
Medieval History, 2
Modern History, 3
United States History, 18
English History, 20
French History, 4
General History, 26
Economic History, 1
History, 2
United States Constitution, 2
State Constitution, 1
Civil Government, 24
Civics, 10
American Politics, 1
Social Science, 1
Political Economy, 16

Foreign Language

Latin, 39
Greek, 10
German, 23
French, 4

Commercial Subjects

Bookkeeping, 29
Business Forms, 4
Commercial Arithmetic, 8
Commercial Law, 9
Commercial Geography, 3
Business Correspondence, 1
Banking, 1
Stenography, 5
Phonography, 1
Typewriting, 5

Miscellaneous Subjects

Mental Philosophy, 1
Moral Philosophy, 1
Psychology, 9
Ethics, 2
Pedagogy, 6
Drawing, 6
Domestic Science, 1
Manual Training, 1

The wide range of subjects offered in the early courses of study, particularly in certain fields, is shown in Tables II–IX. This does not mean, of course, that a majority of schools offered all the subjects listed. On the contrary, only a few schools offered the wide range. Tables A–H, Appendix, show the marked difference in this particular among the schools. These tables also indicate the constants and variables in the curricula.

In some fields, the number of subjects is not as large as the tables indicate because of lack of uniformity in terminology. This is particularly true of English and the social studies. For example, grammar, analysis, and sentential analysis do not necessarily indicate different types of subject-matter. The same is true of reading, classics, and literature. Civics, civil government, and science of government are examples in the field of social studies. Another example in this same field is the various titles used in European history. Mensuration and conic sections in mathematics, and mechanics, meteorology, mineralogy, magnetism, heat and light, and electricity in science are further examples.

The wide range of subjects is not, however, wholly accounted for by a multiplication of terms. Some of the schools actually offered a comparatively wide range of subjects, including some which are not found at all in present secondary curricula. In mathematics, in addition to the subjects now included in high-school curricula, trigonometry was much more common than at the present time, and analytics, calculus, surveying, and navigation, which were offered in a few of the earlier schools, practically disappeared after 1880.

In the case of English the opposite is true. Some schools offered very little in this field and the practice was common in the early years even in the large schools to omit English in the classical courses. On the whole, the range of work provided was comparatively narrow until about 1885, except in a few of the larger schools.

Science is one of the fields in which a wide range of subjects was offered. The general practice was to offer short courses in several science subjects rather than longer courses in two or three subjects. This was particularly true in the earlier periods, while toward the close the practice was more general to offer fewer subjects with no diminution of time devoted to the field.

The social studies, like English, received less attention in a majority of schools than at the present time. Here, again, as in English, the range of work increased somewhat in the larger schools and the number of schools offering the wider range of subjects increased as time went on.[1]

The range of work in the foreign languages differed very little throughout the forty years. Except for the elimination of advanced subject-matter offered in Latin by a few of the earlier schools, the work in the foreign languages remained practically unchanged.

In the commercial field, except for bookkeeping, little was offered until near the close of the century. Judged from the standpoint of the narrow range of work and the comparatively large

[1] Courses of study after 1900 show that the increase of amount of work in English continues until four years of work becomes the standard. The same tendency is also shown in the social studies although less marked. See Part III.

percentage of schools offering no commercial work, it is very clear that on the whole high schools provided very little in the way of commercial education.

The miscellaneous subjects were relatively numerous in the earlier years. Some of these received considerable attention while others were offered in but few curricula as shown by the tables. Mental and moral philosophy, being offered in more than half the schools in 1860, headed the list in point of frequency, and logic was next to these in importance. Other subjects such as evidences of Christianity, ancient geography, biblical antiquities, classical antiquities, Butler's *Analogy*, natural theology, ethics, and art were each offered in a few schools prior to 1880. Drawing was offered in a few schools in all the periods. Psychology was offered in 1860 and then dropped out until 1890. Pedagogy was included in the list in all except two periods. Domestic science was found in two schools in 1860 and in one in 1900. Manual training was just beginning to receive attention at the close and, like domestic science, its development belongs to the present century.

In the following chapter, Table X shows a further analysis of Tables II–IX, dealing especially with constants and variables.

CHAPTER VI

CONSTANTS AND VARIABLES

Table X indicates the percentage of schools offering the different subjects in the various fields for the several periods. This table does not, of course, represent with absolute accuracy the comparative percentages of schools offering the subjects because the same schools do not enter into all the computations. It does, however, make clear that some subjects were relatively constant while others were variable in different degrees, and it also shows tendencies of subjects to increase or decrease in importance.

TABLE X

PERCENTAGE OF SCHOOLS OFFERING THE DIFFERENT SUBJECTS FOR THE SEVERAL PERIODS

Subjects	1860–65	1866–70	1871–75	1876–80	1881–85	1886–90	1891–95	1896–1900
Mathematics—								
Arithmetic	85	60	60	70	88	83	70	65
Algebra	90	100	100	100	100	100	100	100
Plane Geometry	.....	.....	.....	.....	.....	20	15	25
Solid Geometry	.....	.....	.....	.....	.....	17	17½	22½
Geometry	95	100	100	100	100	80	82½	72½
Trigonometry	60	70	75	75	40	36	20	22½
Analytics	10	5	5	5	.....	.....	.....	.....
Surveying	40	20	20	10	12	6	.....	.....
Engineering	10	5	.....	.....	.....	.....	.....	.....
Mensuration	.....	.....	.....	5	.....	.....	2½	.....
Calculus	.....	5	5	.....	.....	.....	.....	.....
Navigation	.....	.....	5	.....	.....	.....	.....	.....
Spherical Geometry	.....	.....	5	.....	.....	.....	.....	.....
English—								
Grammar	60	45	40	30	52	66	35	35
Analysis	55	40	35	25	24	15	2½	2½
Word Analysis	20	.....	.....	5	12	17	10	12
Reading	30	35	5	10	24	30	2½	10
Composition	55	40	60	60	36	42	52½	42
Rhetoric	90	75	85	85	84	83	67½	62½
English Literature	30	65	90	70	72	70	52½	37½
American Literature	.....	10	10	15	12	20	22½	15
Literature	5	.....	.....	.....	16	20	32½	35

TABLE X—*Continued*

PERCENTAGE OF SCHOOLS OFFERING THE DIFFERENT SUBJECTS FOR THE SEVERAL PERIODS

Subjects	1860–65	1866–70	1871–75	1876–80	1881–85	1886–90	1891–95	1896–1900
Classics	5	.....	.....	.....	32	3	25	15
Elements of Criticism	20	.....	.....	5	.....	.....	.....	.....
Orthography	.....	.....	.....	.....	.....	3	.....	5
Orthoepy	.....	.....	.....	.....	.....	.....	.....	.....
Elocution	5	10	10	5	16	6	.....	.....
English	.....	.....	.....	.....	4	.....	.....	.....
First Year English	.....	.....	.....	.....	.....	26	32½	42½
Second Year English	.....	.....	.....	.....	.....	26	22½	35
Third Year English	.....	.....	.....	.....	.....	23	15	27½
Fourth Year English	.....	.....	.....	.....	.....	3	7½	15
History of English Literature	5	5	5	10	4	.....	.....	.....
English Language	.....	5	5	10	.....	.....	.....	.....
Science—								
Physiology	85	75	85	95	92	87	80	70
Physical Geography	90	65	75	65	68	90	72½	75
Natural Philosophy	100	100	70	80	72	36	12½	.....
Physics	5	5	20	25	28	64	87½	95
Chemistry	85	80	90	65	60	72½	65	.....
Geology	70	60	85	50	56	64	47½	22½
Astronomy	70	90	80	65	48	57	50	27½
Botany	70	75	85	85	72	97	82½	82½
Zoölogy	20	20	40	45	40	64	37½	42½
Biology	.....	.....	.....	.....	4	.....	.....	10
Natural History*	25	30	20	30	12	.....	5	2½
Geography	10	25	10	10	8	20	.....	5
Mineralogy	.....	5	.....	.....	.....	.....	5	.....
Meteorology	.....	5	.....	5	.....	.....	.....	.....
Mechanics	.....	5	15	5	.....	.....	.....	.....
Electricity	.....	.....	5	.....	.....	.....	.....	.....
Natural Science	.....	.....	5	.....	.....	.....	.....	.....
Physiography	.....	.....	.....	.....	.....	.....	.....	2½
Light and Heat	.....	.....	5	.....	.....	.....	.....	.....
Social Studies—								
Ancient History	40	40	20	30	20	33	32½	37½
Medieval History	15	5	.....	5	4	17	.....	5
Modern History	30	10	15	15	4	17	2½	7½
United States History	15	20	25	25	32	53	37½	45
English History	15	10	.....	25	32	43	35	50
French History	.....	.....	.....	.....	.....	3	5	10

*The disappearance of natural history should not be regarded as a loss to its field since the subject-matter was taken care of by botany, zoölogy, and biology.

TABLE X—*Continued*

PERCENTAGE OF SCHOOLS OFFERING THE DIFFERENT SUBJECTS FOR THE SEVERAL PERIODS

Subjects	1860–65	1866–70	1871–75	1876–80	1881–85	1886–90	1891–95	1896–1900
General History	15	45	55	50	72	58	62½	65
Universal History	10	.....	5	5	.....	.....	.....	.....
Outlines of History	.....	.....	5	10	.....	.....	2½	.....
Science of Government	15	10	15	15	8	3	.....	.....
Civil Government	.....	40	35	40	60	85	62½	60
United States Civil Government	.....	.....	.....	.....	.....	.....	2½	.....
State Civil Government	.....	.....	.....	.....	.....	.....	2½	.....
Civics	.....	.....	.....	.....	.....	3	17½	25
United States Constitution	40	20	25	20	16	18	.....	5
State Constitution	.....	.....	5	.....	.....	6	.....	.....
United States and State Constitution	.....	.....	.....	.....	.....	.....	2½	.....
Political Economy	20	30	25	15	32	36	27½	40
Historical Reading	.....	.....	.....	.....	.....	3	2½	.....
Social Science	.....	.....	.....	.....	.....	.....	2½	.....
Current Events	.....	.....	.....	.....	.....	.....	2½	.....
Political History	.....	.....	.....	.....	.....	.....	2½	.....
Political Science	.....	5	5	.....	.....	.....	.....	.....
History	10	20	.....	10	20	.....	.....	5
Parliamentary Rules	.....	.....	.....	5	.....	.....	.....	.....
State History	.....	.....	.....	5	.....	.....	.....	.....
History of Civilization	5	.....	.....	.....	4	.....	.....	.....
Chronology	.....	.....	.....	.....	.....	.....	.....	.....
Foreign Languages—								
Latin:	80	85	90	75	92	83	95	97½
One year	.....	5	20	.....	.....	3	2½	.....
Two years	20	15	5	5	12	17	15	7½
Three years	30	20	20	20	40	30	25	15
Four years	5	40	45	45	40	33	63	75
Greek:	35	65	50	40	20	15	17½	25
One year	10	10	20	5	.....	.....	.....	.....
Two years	20	35	20	20	.....	6	7½	20
Three years	10	10	20	15	20	6	5	2½
Four years	.....	.....	.....	.....	.....	.....	.....	2½
German:	35	55	65	60	48	46	52	57½
One year	.....	5	25	5	4	3	10	7½
Two years	20	15	15	10	12	13	27	27½
Three years	.....	15	20	10	8	10	5	.....
Four years	5	15	15	35	24	20	10	22½

TABLE X—*Continued*

PERCENTAGE OF SCHOOLS OFFERING THE DIFFERENT SUBJECTS FOR THE SEVERAL PERIODS

Subjects	1860–65	1866–70	1871–75	1876–80	1881–85	1886–90	1891–95	1896–1900
French:	20	30	60	15	20	10	15	10
One year	10	.....	30	.....	.....	.....	10	.....
Two years	10	15	15	5	16	.....	2½	10
Three years	5	10	15	5	.....	10	.....	.....
Four years	.....	5	5	5	4	.....	2½	.....
Spanish:	5	.....	.....	.....	.....	.....	2½	.....
One year	.....	.....	.....	.....	.....	.....	.....	.....
Two years	.....	.....	.....	.....	.....	.....	.....	.....
Three years	.....	.....	.....	.....	.....	.....	.....	.....
Four years	5	.....	.....	.....	.....	.....	2½	.....
Commercial Subjects—								
Bookkeeping	40	60	50	50	68	80	48	67½
Business Forms	5	.....	.....	5	4	3	5	10
Commercial Law	.....	.....	5	.....	.....	10	12½	22½
Commercial Arithmetic	.....	.....	.....	5	8	6	15	20
Phonography	.....	.....	.....	.....	.....	3	.....	2½
Commercial Geography	.....	.....	.....	.....	.....	.....	2½	7½
Business Practice	.....	.....	.....	.....	.....	.....	2½	2½
Stenography	.....	.....	.....	.....	.....	.....	7½	12½
Typewriting	.....	.....	.....	.....	.....	.....	2½	12½
Banking	.....	.....	.....	.....	.....	.....	.....	2½
Miscellaneous—								
Mental Philosophy	60	75	50	40	24	20	7½	2½
Moral Philosophy	55	45	25	20	12	10	.....	2½
Logic	25	10	10	5	4	.....	.....	.....
Psychology	10	.....	.....	.....	.....	.....	15	22½
Ethics	.....	.....	.....	.....	.....	.....	2½	5
Pedagogy	.....	10	5	.....	4	23	20	15
Art	.....	.....	5	.....	.....	.....	.....	.....
Manual of Art	.....	.....	5	5	.....	.....	.....	.....
Drawing	.....	10	10	5	4	16	7½	15
Manual Training	.....	.....	.....	.....	.....	6	5	5
Classical Antiquities	.....	10	5	5	.....	.....	.....	.....
Evolution of Christianity	10	5	10	.....	.....	.....	.....	.....
Ancient Geography	10	10	10	.....	.....	.....	.....	.....
Biblical Antiquities	.....	.....	5	.....	.....	.....	.....	.....
Domestic Science	10	.....	.....	.....	.....	.....	.....	2½
National Theology	10	.....	.....	.....	.....	.....	.....	.....
Butler's *Analogy*	5	.....	.....	.....	.....	.....	.....	.....

In the first place, from the standpoint of the fields, Table X (and also Tables A–H in more detail) shows that all the schools offered something in mathematics, English, and science in all the periods. The social studies belong to this group after 1870. Prior to that date 10 per cent of the schools offered nothing in this field.

Foreign language was offered in the following percentages of schools for the several periods: 80, 85, 95, 75, 92, 87, 95, and 97½, respectively. Commercial subjects for all the periods show the following percentages: 40, 60, 55, 60, 68, 70, 45, and 65. The miscellaneous subjects are represented by the following in the several periods: 75, 70, 55, 40, 47, 45, and 40.

It will be seen that mathematics, English, and science were the constants, the social studies being in this group after 1870. Foreign language, represented in 80 per cent of the schools in 1860, was offered in 97½ per cent in 1900. The commercial subjects increase from 40 per cent in 1860 to 65 per cent at the close, while the miscellaneous group decreased from 75 per cent to 40 per cent. These subjects fall into two groups. The first includes mental philosophy, moral philosophy, logic, and others mentioned on page 74 which were taught in the earlier years, while psychology, pedagogy, and manual training belong to the second group and were taught in the later years. The comparatively high percentages of the first group hold rather steadily until after 1875 when, with the exception of drawing, they rapidly disappear. The second group, somewhat overlapping the period occupied by the first group, is comparatively unimportant even at the close.

Table X furnishes details concerning constants and variables from the standpoint of subjects offered. As indicated on page 97 the table should not be interpreted as furnishing exact comparative data[1] for the several periods but rather that it shows, first, the relative importance of subjects for the several periods in different degrees, and secondly, the tendencies with respect to the entire period under discussion.

In mathematics, except for the first period, algebra and geometry were the constants. After 1885 there is some overlapping in geometry due to confusion in terminology. Arithmetic is next in importance and was offered in 85 per cent of the schools in 1860 and in 65 per cent at the close. The varying percentages from period to period do not probably indicate that the subject came

[1] The same schools are not used in all the tables.

and went in any such arbitrary fashion in the degree indicated by the table.[1] Tables A–H, however, do show that it was a variable in certain schools being offered at one time and omitted at another.[2] On the whole, the subject declined in importance. Trigonometry stands next in importance, and declines from 60 per cent at the beginning to 22½ per cent at the close. Higher mathematics, as reference to the table will show, was represented in a considerable number of schools in 1860. The decline thereafter was rapid and these subjects had practically disappeared by 1885.

The facts concerning English subjects are not easily determined because of the confusion in terminology. This was caused in several ways. For example, literature, on the one hand, was taught under various titles such as reading, classics, literature, English literature, American literature, and history of English literature. On the other hand, the term "literature" meant history of English literature and sometimes the whole of certain masterpieces. Further uncertainty is added by the introduction of the general term English after 1885.

Grammar,[3] like arithmetic, was a variable and on the whole declined in importance. How much the actual decline was, is not easily determined since it is certain that the subject was taught in some schools under the general title English after 1885. When we take into account, however, that for our purpose here English analysis may be regarded as grammar, it is evident that the decline was considerable.

In the case of composition the table should be interpreted in the light of two facts, viz.: (1) The subject was not so commonly taught in the earlier years as a regular subject as was the case in the later years, the earlier practice being to list it as a footnote along with other subjects such as declamation, music, writing, and the like. (2) The evidence is clear that the subject was taught more or less in connection with grammar, rhetoric, and literature, and in such cases was not always mentioned in the course. Taking into account all the conditions under which the subject was taught, it is clear that its importance increased both from the standpoint of the number of schools offering it and the time devoted to it. It is

[1] The same schools are not used in all the tables.

[2] For example, Chicago, Illinois, and Cleveland, Ohio, offered the subject in 1860-65 but not in 1866-70, while Dubuque, Iowa, offered it during the latter period but not in the former.

[3] As an example of a single school, Madison, Wisconsin, offered the subject in 1860, but it is not included in the curriculum of 1867. It is again included in the list of subjects in 1876, 1883, and 1887. The subject is not offered in 1892 nor thereafter unless included in the general term "English."

usually a first-year subject when listed separately and the decrease of 10 per cent from 1895 to 1900 is exactly balanced by the increase of the use of the term English in designating first-year work.

Rhetoric ranked next to literature in importance and there was not much change relatively in the number of schools offering the subject until 1890. Part of the falling off in the last two periods is probably only apparent since the general term English no doubt included rhetoric. But a study of the table will show that a decrease of approximately 20 per cent from 1890 to 1900 cannot all be accounted for in this way. There was, no doubt, some decline in the subject after the former date.

The facts concerning literature, like those of the other subjects in its field, are not easily determined after 1885 because of the use of the general term English. Confusion is still further introduced because of the lack in some cases of definite information concerning the character of the subject-matter called "reading." Tables A–H show rather conclusively that literature was not a constant until after 1885. Probably not more than 60 per cent of the schools offered the subject in 1860. Under one title or another it increased in importance thereafter and after 1885 it was a constant.

The science field was a constant, some subjects being offered in all the schools. No one subject, however, was strictly a constant, although physics was practically so. It was offered in all the schools included in Tables A–H except for the periods 1871–75, 1876–80, and 1896–1900, the percentage being 95 for each of these.[1] The next nearest approach in this field to being a constant was made by physiology. The average for the several periods was approximately 85 per cent, the maximum being 95 per cent in 1876–80, and the minimum 70 per cent in 1896–1900. Botany ranks next with an average of 78 per cent which is closely followed by physical geography and chemistry, each having an average of 75 per cent. The next highest average, 60 per cent, is held by astronomy although at the close it was offered in less than 25 per cent of the schools. An average of approximately 55 per cent is held by both geology and zoölogy.[2] The former declines rapidly after 1890, being offered in approximately but 25 per cent of the schools at the close. Zoölogy holds rather close to the average throughout except for the period 1876–80 when it reaches its maximum at 75 per cent.

[1] It is probable that subject-matter belonging to the subject was taught in all the schools except for the period 1896-1900, but a positive conclusion is not possible because of confusion in terminology.

[2] Including natural history.

The status of European history is not easily determined from Table X, but Tables A–H show that the subject was offered in some form in all the schools in four of the periods and in 90 per cent of them the other four—first, second, sixth, and seventh.

French history is practically negligible while English history is found in all periods except the third and reached its maximum, 50 per cent, at the close.

United States history does not exceed 25 per cent until after 1880, reaches its maximum, 53 per cent, in 1886–90, and was taught in 45 per cent of the schools at the close. Civics, under its various titles, was offered by a majority of schools in all periods, the minimum being 55 per cent in 1860–65, and is found in approximately 90 per cent of the schools after 1885. Political economy begins with 20 per cent, drops to 15 per cent in 1876–80, and reaches its maximum, 40 per cent, at the close.

Latin[1] was offered in a minimum of 75 per cent of the schools, 1876–80, and in a maximum of 97½ per cent at the close. It will be seen by reference to Table X that with the exception of the first period a plurality, and during three periods, 1871–75, 1891–96, 1896–1900, a majority of the schools offered four years. The general tendency was an increase in the number of schools offering the subject.

Greek was always relatively unimportant and declined rather rapidly after 1875. After 1880 no schools are listed which offer but one year and only one school was found offering four years. The largest number of schools offered two years.

German stands next to Latin in percentage of schools offering the subject. Approximately 50 per cent of the schools taught German, and there is no general movement revealed either as to increased or decreased attention given it. The number of schools offering but one year was relatively small, while there was considerable fluctuation from period to period in percentages of two-, three-, and four-year courses.

French was rather distinctly a large-school subject and this accounts for the high percentage in 1871–75, Table C, Appendix, including a proportionately large number of city schools. The subject was relatively unimportant, and there is on the whole a decrease in schools offering it.

[1] Total percentages for all the foreign languages do not always tally with footings for the several years because detailed data in some cases are lacking.

Table X shows with sufficient clearness the facts concerning commercial subjects. Bookkeeping was the only subject of any particular significance. After 1890 the beginning of the movement to give the commercial subjects an important place in high-school curricula is plainly indicated.

Two facts concerning the miscellaneous subjects are revealed by the table: (1) the wide range of subjects; (2) the relative unimportance of them. As was pointed out on page 75, mental philosophy, moral philosophy, and logic constitute the early group, and psychology, and pedagogy the later group of subjects having any importance. Table X tells the story in detail.

CHAPTER VII

VARIATIONS IN TIME DEVOTED TO FIELDS AND SUBJECTS

The following tables show the variations in time devoted to the several fields and subjects. Tables XI-XVIII show the wide variations in time devoted to fields. Table XIX shows maxima, minima, modes, and averages in time devoted to the fields, and Tables XX–XXVII the same for the subjects.

The tables below indicate the amount of time devoted to each field. It is not possible to include all the schools listed in Tables A–H because some courses of study are not given in sufficient detail.

TABLE XI—1860–65

MATHEMATICS—14 SCHOOLS

Number of Years	Number of Schools
4	3
$3\frac{2}{3}$	1
3	4
$2\frac{2}{3}$	3
$2\frac{1}{3}$	1
$1\frac{2}{3}$	1
1	1

ENGLISH—13 SCHOOLS

Number of Years	Number of Schools
$3\frac{1}{3}$	1
3	2
$2\frac{2}{3}$	1
$2\frac{1}{3}$	1
2	2
$1\frac{2}{3}$	1
$1\frac{1}{2}$	1
$1\frac{1}{3}$	1
1	2
$\frac{1}{3}$	1

SCIENCE—14 SCHOOLS

Number of Schools	Number of Schools
$4\frac{2}{3}$	1
$4\frac{1}{3}$	2
$3\frac{2}{3}$	2
$3\frac{1}{3}$	2
3	3
$2\frac{2}{3}$	1
$2\frac{1}{2}$	1
$2\frac{1}{3}$	1
2	1

SOCIAL STUDIES—13 SCHOOLS

Number of Years	Number of Schools
2	2
$1\frac{1}{2}$	1
$1\frac{1}{3}$	2
1	5
$\frac{2}{3}$	1
$\frac{1}{3}$	2

LATIN—11 SCHOOLS

Number of Years	Number of Schools
4	1
3	6
2⅓	1
2	3

GREEK—8 SCHOOLS

Number of Years	Number of Schools
3	2
2	3
1⅔	2
1⅓	1
1	1

GERMAN—5 SCHOOLS

Number of Years	Number of Schools
4	1
2	4

FRENCH—4 SCHOOLS

Number of Years	Number of Schools
3	1
1	1

COMMERCIAL SUBJECTS—8 SCHOOLS

Number of Years	Number of Schools
1	1
⅔	1
⅓	6

MISCELLANEOUS SUBJECTS—12 SCHOOLS

Number of Years	Number of Schools
2⅔	1
2	1
1⅔	1
1½	1
1	2
⅔	5
⅓	1

TABLE XII—1866–70

MATHEMATICS—15 SCHOOLS

Number of Years	Number of Schools
4⅓	1
4	2
3½	1
3⅓	1
3	4
2⅔	1
2	4
1⅓	1

ENGLISH—15 SCHOOLS

Number of Years	Number of Schools
3⅓	1
2⅓	1
2	1
1⅔	4
1½	1
1⅓	3
1	1
⅔	2
⅓	1

SCIENCE—15 SCHOOLS

Number of Years	Number of Schools
5⅓	1
4⅓	3
3⅔	2
3½	1
3¼	2
3⅙	1
3	3
1⅔	1
1⅓	1

SOCIAL STUDIES—15 SCHOOLS

Number of Years	Number of Schools
2⅙	2
2	2
1⅔	3
1½	1
1⅓	3
1¼	4
1	3
0	1

LATIN—16 SCHOOLS

Number of Years	Number of Schools
4	6
3¾	1
3⅔	1
3	3
2⅔	1
2	3
1	1

GREEK—11 SCHOOLS

Number of Years	Number of Schools
3	2
2	7
1½	1
1	1

GERMAN—10 SCHOOLS

Number of Years	Number of Schools
4	3
3	3
2	3
1	1

FRENCH—6 SCHOOLS

Number of Years	Number of Schools
4	2
3	2
2	3

COMMERCIAL SUBJECTS—12 SCHOOLS

Number of Years	Number of Schools
1	3
⅔	2
½	1
⅓	5
¼	1

MISCELLANEOUS SUBJECTS—12 SCHOOLS

Number of Years	Number of Schools
2¼	1
1⅓	1
1	4
¾	1
⅔	3
½	1
⅓	1

TABLE XIII—1871–75

MATHEMATICS—12 SCHOOLS

Number of Years	Number of Schools
4⅓	1
4	1
3⅔	1
3½	1
3	2
2⅔	1
2½	1
2⅓	3
2	1

ENGLISH—12 SCHOOLS

Number of Years	Number of Schools
3	1
2⅔	1
2	2
1⅔	3
1½	1
1⅓	1
1	3

SCIENCE—12 SCHOOLS

Number of Years	Number of Schools
4⅓	1
4	2
3⅔	1

SOCIAL STUDIES—12 SCHOOLS

Number of Years	Number of Schools
2	2
1⅔	1
1⅓	4

$3\frac{1}{2}$	1
3	2
$2\frac{3}{6}$	1
$2\frac{2}{3}$	1
$2\frac{1}{3}$	1
2	1
$\frac{2}{3}$	1

1	2
$\frac{5}{6}$	1
1	2
$\frac{2}{3}$	2

LATIN—18 SCHOOLS

Number of Years	Number of Schools
4	9
$3\frac{1}{3}$	1
3	3
2	1
1	4

GREEK—12 SCHOOLS

Number of Years	Number of Schools
3	4
2	4
1	4

GERMAN—15 SCHOOLS

Number of Years	Number of Schools
4	3
3	4
2	3
1	5

FRENCH—13 SCHOOLS

Number of Years	Number of Schools
4	1
3	3
2	3
1	5
$\frac{2}{3}$	1

COMMERCIAL SUBJECTS*

MISCELLANEOUS SUBJECTS*

TABLE XIV—1876–80

MATHEMATICS—20 SCHOOLS

Number of Years	Number of Schools
$4\frac{1}{2}$	1
$3\frac{2}{3}$	2
$3\frac{3}{5}$	1
$3\frac{1}{2}$	1
$3\frac{1}{6}$	1
3	3
$2\frac{5}{6}$	1
$2\frac{2}{3}$	2
$2\frac{1}{2}$	3
$2\frac{1}{3}$	2
2	3

ENGLISH—20 SCHOOLS

Number of Years	Number of Schools
3	3
$2\frac{2}{3}$	1
$2\frac{1}{3}$	2
2	4
$1\frac{3}{4}$	1
$1\frac{2}{3}$	2
$1\frac{1}{2}$	1
$1\frac{1}{3}$	1
$1\frac{1}{4}$	1
1	4

SCIENCE—20 SCHOOLS

Number of Years	Number of Schools
5	2
$4\frac{2}{3}$	1

SOCIAL STUDIES—20 SCHOOLS

Number of Years	Number of Schools
$3\frac{1}{3}$	1
3	1

*The courses are so few in this field which makes clear the time devoted to commercial and miscellaneous subjects that no exact data are possible.

$4\frac{1}{3}$	2
4	3
$3\frac{5}{6}$	1
$3\frac{1}{2}$	2
$3\frac{5}{12}$	1
$2\frac{3}{10}$	1
3	1
$2\frac{2}{3}$	3
$2\frac{1}{3}$	1
$1\frac{2}{3}$	1
1	1
$2\frac{1}{2}$	1
$2\frac{1}{3}$	1
2	1
$1\frac{2}{3}$	1
$1\frac{1}{2}$	2
$1\frac{1}{3}$	5
$1\frac{1}{4}$	1
1	3
$\frac{3}{4}$	1
$\frac{2}{3}$	2

LATIN—14 SCHOOLS

Number of Years	Number of Schools
4	9
3	3
$2\frac{2}{3}$	1
$2\frac{1}{3}$	1

GREEK—8 SCHOOLS

Number of Years	Number of Schools
3	3
2	4
$1\frac{1}{3}$	1

COMMERCIAL SUBJECTS—10 SCHOOLS

Number of Years	Number of Schools
2	1
1	2
$\frac{3}{5}$	1
$\frac{1}{3}$	5
$\frac{1}{4}$	1

GERMAN—12 SCHOOLS

Number of Years	Number of Schools
4	7
3	2
2	2
1	1

FRENCH—3 SCHOOLS

Number of Years	Number of Schools
4	1
3	1
2	1

MISCELLANEOUS SUBJECTS—10 SCHOOLS

Number of Years	Number of Schools
$1\frac{1}{2}$	1
$1\frac{1}{3}$	2
1	1
1	1
$\frac{1}{2}$	5

TABLE XV—1881–85

MATHEMATICS—24 SCHOOLS

Number of Years	Number of Schools
$3\frac{2}{3}$	2
$3\frac{2}{5}$	1
$3\frac{1}{2}$	1
$3\frac{1}{3}$	3
3	7
$2\frac{1}{2}$	1
$2\frac{1}{3}$	4
$2\frac{1}{4}$	1

ENGLISH—24 SCHOOLS

Number of Years	Number of Schools
$5\frac{2}{3}$	1
$5\frac{1}{2}$	1
4	2
$3\frac{1}{3}$	2
$3\frac{1}{6}$	1
3	2
$2\frac{1}{2}$	2
$2\frac{1}{3}$	3

2	4

2	4
1⅔	2
1½	1
1⅓	1
1	2

SCIENCE—24 SCHOOLS

Number of Years	Number of Schools
5	2
4⅓	1
4	5
3⅔	2
3½	1
3	3
2⅚	1
2¾	1
2⅔	2
2⅓	2
2	3
1	1

SOCIAL STUDIES—24 SCHOOLS

Number of Years	Number of Schools
3⅓	1
2⅔	1
2½	2
2⅓	3
2	5
1⅔	3
2½	3
1⅓	2
1	3
⅔	1

LATIN—23 SCHOOLS

Number of Years	Number of Schools
4	9
3⅔	1
3⅓	1
3½	2
3	7
2⅓	1
2	2

FRENCH—5 SCHOOLS

Number of Years	Number of Schools
4	1
2	4

GREEK—15 SCHOOLS

Number of Years	Number of Schools
3	5

GERMAN—12 SCHOOLS

Number of Years	Number of Schools
4	5
3⅔	1
3	2
2	3
1	1

COMMERCIAL SUBJECTS—17 SCHOOLS

Number of Years	Number of Schools
1⅓	2
1½	1
1	2
⅔	1
½	2
⅓	9

MISCELLANEOUS SUBJECTS—9 SCHOOLS

Number of Years	Number of Schools
1	3
⅔	2
½	1
⅓	3

TABLE XVI—1886–1900

MATHEMATICS—29 SCHOOLS

Number of Years	Number of Schools
5	1
4	4
$3\frac{2}{3}$	1
$3\frac{1}{2}$	1
$3\frac{1}{3}$	2
$3\frac{1}{4}$	1
$3\frac{1}{6}$	1
3	7
$2\frac{2}{3}$	7
$2\frac{1}{2}$	1
$2\frac{1}{3}$	1
$2\frac{1}{4}$	1
2	1

ENGLISH—28 SCHOOLS

Number of Years	Number of Schools
$6\frac{1}{3}$	1
4	4
$3\frac{2}{3}$	2
$3\frac{1}{2}$	1
$3\frac{1}{3}$	3
3	6
$2\frac{2}{3}$	1
$2\frac{1}{2}$	1
$2\frac{1}{3}$	2
2	4
$1\frac{2}{3}$	1
$1\frac{1}{2}$	2

SCIENCE—29 SCHOOLS

Number of Years	Number of Schools
$6\frac{1}{2}$	1
5	2
$4\frac{5}{6}$	1
$4\frac{1}{2}$	5
$3\frac{2}{3}$	3
$3\frac{1}{2}$	3
$3\frac{1}{3}$	2
3	1
$2\frac{3}{4}$	1
$2\frac{2}{3}$	6
$2\frac{1}{3}$	1
2	3

SOCIAL STUDIES—29 SCHOOLS

Number of Years	Number of Schools
$4\frac{1}{2}$	1
$3\frac{5}{6}$	1
$3\frac{2}{3}$	1
$3\frac{1}{2}$	1
$3\frac{1}{3}$	1
$2\frac{2}{3}$	6
$2\frac{1}{2}$	1
$2\frac{1}{3}$	2
2	4
$1\frac{2}{3}$	4
$1\frac{1}{2}$	3
$1\frac{1}{3}$	2
$1\frac{1}{4}$	1
$\frac{1}{3}$	1

LATIN—25 SCHOOLS

Number of Years	Number of Schools
4	10
$3\frac{1}{2}$	1
3	8
$2\frac{1}{2}$	1
2	4
1	1

GREEK—4 SCHOOLS

Number of Years	Number of Schools
3	2
$2\frac{1}{3}$	1
2	1

GERMAN—14 SCHOOLS

Number of Years	Number of Schools
4	6
3	3
2	4
1	1

FRENCH—3 SCHOOLS

Number of Years	Number of Schools
3	3

COMMERCIAL SUBJECTS—18 SCHOOLS

Number of Years	Number of Schools
$1\frac{2}{3}$	1
$1\frac{1}{2}$	1
$1\frac{1}{3}$	1
1	3
$\frac{2}{3}$	3
$\frac{1}{2}$	4
$\frac{1}{3}$	5

MISCELLANEOUS SUBJECTS—10 SCHOOLS

Number of Years	Number of Schools
$1\frac{2}{3}$	1
1	1
$\frac{2}{3}$	2
$\frac{1}{2}$	1
$\frac{1}{3}$	4
$\frac{1}{4}$	1

TABLE XVII—1891–95

MATHEMATICS—40 SCHOOLS

Number of Years	Number of Schools
$4\frac{1}{2}$	1
4	4
$3\frac{2}{3}$	1
$3\frac{1}{3}$	6
$3\frac{1}{2}$	4
$3\frac{1}{6}$	1
3	11
$2\frac{2}{3}$	3
$2\frac{1}{2}$	3
$2\frac{1}{3}$	5
2	1

ENGLISH—40 SCHOOLS

Number of Years	Number of Schools
6	1
$4\frac{1}{2}$	2
4	5
$3\frac{7}{10}$	1
$3\frac{1}{3}$	2
$3\frac{3}{10}$	1
3	5
$2\frac{2}{3}$	4
$2\frac{3}{5}$	1
$2\frac{1}{2}$	6
2	3
$1\frac{2}{3}$	3
$1\frac{1}{2}$	3
$1\frac{1}{3}$	1
1	1
$\frac{2}{3}$	1

SCIENCE—40 SCHOOLS

Number of Years	Number of Schools
$5\frac{1}{2}$	2
5	1
$4\frac{2}{3}$	1
$4\frac{2}{3}$	3
$4\frac{1}{6}$	1
4	6
$3\frac{5}{6}$	1
$3\frac{2}{3}$	1
$3\frac{1}{2}$	4
$3\frac{1}{3}$	3
$3\frac{1}{6}$	1
3	4

SOCIAL STUDIES—40 SCHOOLS

Number of Years	Number of Schools
$5\frac{1}{3}$	1
4	2
$3\frac{1}{2}$	4
3	4
$2\frac{1}{2}$	3
$2\frac{1}{3}$	2
2	8
$1\frac{4}{5}$	1
$1\frac{2}{3}$	3
$1\frac{1}{2}$	3
$1\frac{1}{3}$	2
1	6

$2\frac{1}{2}$	3
$2\frac{1}{3}$	4
2	1
$1\frac{2}{3}$	1
$1\frac{1}{2}$	3

$\frac{1}{3}$	1

LATIN—38 SCHOOLS

Number of Years	Number of Schools
4	18
$3\frac{2}{3}$	3
$3\frac{1}{3}$	1
3	9
$2\frac{1}{2}$	1
2	5
1	1

FRENCH—6 SCHOOLS

Number of Years	Number of Schools
4	1
2	1
$1\frac{1}{3}$	1
1	3

COMMERCIAL SUBJECTS—20 SCHOOLS

Number of Years	Number of Schools
5	1
$3\frac{1}{3}$	1
3	1
2	2
1	5
$\frac{2}{3}$	2
$\frac{1}{2}$	4
$\frac{1}{3}$	4

GREEK—5 SCHOOLS

Number of Years	Number of Schools
3	2
2	3

GERMAN—22 SCHOOLS

Number of Years	Number of Schools
4	4
3	3
2	11
1	4

SPANISH—1 SCHOOL

Number of Years	Number of Schools
4	1

MISCELLANEOUS SUBJECTS—15 SCHOOLS

Number of Years	Number of Schools
5	1
$2\frac{1}{3}$	1
1	3
$\frac{2}{3}$	3
$\frac{1}{2}$	6
$\frac{1}{3}$	1

TABLE XVIII, 1896–1900

MATHEMATICS—40 SCHOOLS

Number of Years	Number of Schools
$4\frac{1}{2}$	1
4	4
$4\frac{1}{3}$	1
$3\frac{5}{6}$	1
$3\frac{3}{4}$	1

ENGLISH—40 SCHOOLS

Number of Years	Number of Schools
5	1
$4\frac{1}{6}$	1
$4\frac{1}{10}$	1
4	10
$3\frac{5}{6}$	1

3⅔	2
3½	8
3⅓	1
3	3
2⅔	3
2½	1
2⅖	6
2	8

SCIENCE—40 SCHOOLS

Number of Years	Number of Schools
5	1
4½	1
4	6
3⅚	1
3¾	1
3⅔	3
3⅗	1
3½	5
3⅓	2
3	9
2⅔	2
2⅓	1
2	4
1½	1
1	1
½	1

LATIN—39 SCHOOLS

Number of Years	Number of Schools
4⅓	1
4	27
3⅔	1
3⅓	1
3	6
2	3

GERMAN—23 SCHOOLS

Number of Years	Number of Schools
4	9
2	11
1½	1
1	2

3⅔	2
3½	4
3¼	1
3	3
2⅔	2
2½	3
2⅓	1
2	8
1⅔	1
1½	1

SOCIAL STUDIES—40 SCHOOLS

Number of Years	Number of Schools
4	2
3⅔	1
3½	1
3⅓	1
3⅕	1
3	7
2⅔	3
2½	2
2⅓	4
2	7
1⅔	1
1½	7
1⅓	1
1	2

GREEK—10 SCHOOLS

Number of Years	Number of Schools
4	1
3	1
2	8

FRENCH—2 SCHOOLS

Number of Years	Number of Schools
2	4

COMMERCIAL SUBJECTS—
28 SCHOOLS

Number of Years	Number of Schools
7	1
6	1
$2\frac{1}{2}$	
$2\frac{1}{3}$	1
2	2
1	7
$\frac{2}{3}$	2
$\frac{1}{2}$	10
$\frac{1}{3}$	2

MISCELLANEOUS SUBJECTS—
12 SCHOOLS

Number of Years	Number of Schools
$7\frac{2}{3}$	1
$1\frac{1}{2}$	1
1	1
$\frac{2}{3}$	2
$\frac{2}{5}$	1
$\frac{1}{2}$	6

TABLE XIX

SUMMARY SHOWING TIME IN YEARS DEVOTED TO EACH FIELD FOR THE EIGHT PERIODS

Subjects	1860–65	1866–70	1871–75	1876–80	1881–85	1886–90	1891–95	1896–1900
Mathematics—								
Maximum	4	$4\frac{1}{3}$	$4\frac{1}{3}$	$4\frac{1}{2}$	$3\frac{2}{3}$	5	$4\frac{1}{2}$	$4\frac{1}{2}$
Minimum	1	1	2	2	2	2	2	2
Mode	3	2–3	$2\frac{1}{3}$	$2\frac{1}{2}$–3	3	$2\frac{2}{3}$–3	3	2–$3\frac{1}{2}$
Average	$2\frac{4}{5}$	$2\frac{8}{9}$	3	$2\frac{4}{5}$	$2\frac{1}{2}$	$3\frac{1}{10}$	$3\frac{1}{20}$	$3\frac{1}{8}$
English—								
Maximum	$3\frac{1}{3}$	3	3	3	$5\frac{2}{3}$	$6\frac{1}{3}$	6	5
Minimum	$\frac{1}{3}$	$\frac{1}{3}$	1	1	1	$1\frac{1}{2}$	$\frac{2}{3}$	$1\frac{1}{2}$
Mode	1–2–3	$1\frac{2}{3}$	1–$1\frac{2}{3}$	1–2	2	3	$2\frac{1}{2}$	4
Average	$2\frac{1}{4}$	$1\frac{2}{3}$	$1\frac{3}{4}$	$1\frac{3}{4}$	$1\frac{1}{2}$	3	$2\frac{4}{5}$	$3\frac{1}{8}$
Science—								
Maximum	5	$5\frac{1}{3}$	$4\frac{1}{3}$	5	5	$6\frac{1}{2}$	$5\frac{1}{2}$	5
Minimum	2	$1\frac{1}{3}$	$1\frac{1}{3}$	1	1	2	$1\frac{1}{2}$	$\frac{1}{2}$
Mode	3	$4\frac{1}{3}$	3–4	$2\frac{2}{3}$–4	4	$2\frac{3}{4}$	4	3
Average	$3\frac{3}{16}$	$3\frac{1}{3}$	3	$3\frac{1}{2}$	$3\frac{1}{4}$	$3\frac{3}{5}$	$3\frac{3}{8}$	$3\frac{1}{8}$
Social Studies—								
Maximum	2	$2\frac{1}{6}$	2	$3\frac{1}{3}$	$3\frac{1}{3}$	$4\frac{1}{2}$	$5\frac{1}{3}$	4
Minimum	$\frac{1}{3}$	......	$\frac{2}{3}$	$\frac{2}{3}$	$\frac{2}{3}$	$\frac{1}{3}$	$\frac{1}{3}$	1
Mode	1	1–$1\frac{1}{3}$ $1\frac{2}{3}$	$1\frac{1}{3}$	$1\frac{1}{3}$	2	$2\frac{2}{3}$	2	$1\frac{1}{2}$–2–3
Average	$1\frac{5}{12}$	$1\frac{5}{12}$	$1\frac{1}{6}$	$1\frac{1}{2}$	$1\frac{5}{6}$	$2\frac{1}{5}$	$2\frac{1}{5}$	$2\frac{1}{5}$
Latin—								
Maximum	4	4	4	4	4	4	4	$4\frac{1}{3}$
Minimum	2	1	1	$2\frac{1}{3}$	2	1	1	2
Mode	3	4	4	4	4	4	4	4
Average	$3\frac{1}{9}$	$3\frac{1}{10}$	3	$3\frac{4}{7}$	$3\frac{3}{5}$	$3\frac{1}{6}$	$3\frac{2}{3}$	$3\frac{7}{10}$

TABLE XIX—*Continued*

SUMMARY SHOWING TIME IN YEARS DEVOTED TO EACH FIELD FOR THE EIGHT PERIODS

Subjects	1860–65	1866–70	1891–75	1876–80	1881–85	1886–90	1891–95	1896–1900
Greek—								
Maximum	2	3	3	3	3	3	3	4
Minimum	$\frac{2}{3}$	1	1	$1\frac{1}{3}$	3	2	2	2
Mode	2	2	1–2–3	2	3	3	2	2
Average	$1\frac{3}{5}$	2	2	$2\frac{1}{4}$	3	$2\frac{1}{2}$	$2\frac{2}{5}$	$2\frac{3}{10}$
German—								
Maximum	4	4	4	4	4	4	4	4
Minimum	2	1	1	1	1	1	1	1
Mode	2	2–3–4	1	4	4	4	2	2
Average	$2\frac{2}{5}$	$2\frac{2}{5}$	$2\frac{1}{3}$	$3\frac{1}{4}$	3	3	$2\frac{2}{7}$	$2\frac{3}{8}$
French—								
Maximum	3	4	4	4	4	3	4	2
Minimum	1	2	$\frac{2}{3}$	2	2	3	1	2
Mode	1–3	2	1	2–3–4	2	3	1	2
Average	2	$2\frac{2}{3}$	$1\frac{12}{13}$	3	$2\frac{2}{5}$	3	$1\frac{2}{3}$	2
Spanish—								
Maximum	......	......	......	......	......	......	4	......
Minimum	......	......	......	......	......	......	4	......
Mode	......	......	......	......	......	......	4	......
Average	......	......	......	......	......	......	4	......
Foreign Language—								
Maximum	13	10	13	14	15	14	16	$12\frac{1}{3}$
Minimum	2	1	2	3	2	2	3	2
Mode	2–3	5–7	4–6	4–8–11–14	4	3	2	4–6
Average	5	5	7	8	6	6	5	6
*Commercial Subjects**—								
Maximum	1	1	$\frac{2}{3}$	2	$1\frac{1}{3}$	$1\frac{2}{3}$	5	7
Minimum	$\frac{1}{3}$	$\frac{1}{4}$	$\frac{1}{3}$	$\frac{1}{4}$	$\frac{1}{3}$	$\frac{1}{3}$	$\frac{1}{3}$	$\frac{1}{3}$
Mode	$\frac{1}{3}$	$\frac{1}{3}$	$\frac{1}{3}$	$\frac{1}{2}$	$\frac{1}{3}$–1	$\frac{1}{3}$	$\frac{1}{2}$	$\frac{1}{2}$
Average	$\frac{11}{24}$	$\frac{5}{12}$	$\frac{5}{12}$	$\frac{3}{5}$	$\frac{11}{25}$	$\frac{5}{7}$	$1\frac{1}{4}$	$1\frac{5}{7}$
*Miscellaneous Subjects**—								
Maximum	$2\frac{2}{3}$	2	$1\frac{1}{3}$	$1\frac{1}{2}$	1	$1\frac{2}{3}$	5	$7\frac{2}{3}$
Minimum	$\frac{1}{3}$	$\frac{1}{3}$	$\frac{1}{3}$	$\frac{1}{3}$	$\frac{1}{3}$	$\frac{1}{4}$	$\frac{1}{3}$	$\frac{1}{2}$
Mode	$\frac{2}{3}$	1	$\frac{2}{3}$	$\frac{1}{2}$	$\frac{1}{3}$–1	$\frac{1}{3}$	$\frac{1}{2}$	$\frac{1}{2}$
Average	$1\frac{1}{9}$	1	$\frac{2}{3}$	$\frac{4}{5}$	$\frac{4}{7}$	$\frac{3}{5}$	$\frac{4}{5}$	$1\frac{1}{4}$

*For lists of subjects see Appendix, Tables A–H inclusive.

TABLE XX, 1860–65

ANALYSIS OF THE COURSES OF STUDY OF TWENTY SCHOOLS* SHOWING TIME IN YEARS DEVOTED TO EACH SUBJECT†

Subjects	Number of Schools	Maximum	Minimum	Mode	Average
Mathematics—					
Arithmetic	17	1	$\frac{1}{3}$	$\frac{1}{3}$	$\frac{7}{13}$
Algebra	18	$1\frac{2}{3}$	$\frac{1}{2}$	$\frac{2}{3}$–1–$1\frac{1}{3}$	$\frac{8}{9}$
Geometry	19	1	$\frac{1}{3}$	1	$\frac{13}{16}$
Trigonometry	12	$\frac{1}{2}$	$\frac{1}{3}$	$\frac{1}{3}$	$\frac{15}{72}$
Survey and Navigation	8	$\frac{1}{2}$	$\frac{1}{3}$	$\frac{1}{3}$	$\frac{13}{36}$
English—					
Grammar and Analysis	17	$1\frac{1}{3}$	$\frac{1}{3}$	$\frac{1}{3}$	$\frac{4}{9}$
Composition	11	$\frac{2}{3}$	$\frac{1}{3}$	$\frac{1}{3}$	$\frac{3}{7}$
Rhetoric	18	$\frac{2}{3}$	$\frac{1}{3}$	$\frac{1}{3}$	$\frac{4}{9}$
Literature	8	$\frac{2}{3}$	$\frac{1}{3}$	$\frac{1}{3}$	$\frac{11}{21}$
Word Analysis	4	$\frac{2}{3}$	$\frac{1}{3}$	$\frac{1}{3}$	$\frac{4}{9}$
Science—					
Physiology	17	$\frac{2}{3}$	$\frac{1}{3}$	$\frac{1}{3}$	$\frac{7}{15}$
Physical Geography	18	$\frac{2}{3}$	$\frac{1}{3}$	$\frac{1}{3}$	$\frac{3}{7}$
Physics‡	20	1	$\frac{1}{3}$	$\frac{2}{3}$	$\frac{11}{16}$
Chemistry	17	1	$\frac{1}{3}$	$\frac{2}{3}$	$\frac{11}{16}$
Botany	14	$\frac{2}{3}$	$\frac{1}{3}$	$\frac{2}{3}$	$\frac{1}{2}$
Zoölogy§	9	$\frac{2}{3}$	$\frac{1}{3}$	$\frac{1}{3}$	$\frac{1}{2}$
Geology	14	$\frac{2}{3}$	$\frac{1}{3}$	$\frac{1}{3}$	$\frac{4}{9}$
Astronomy	14	$\frac{2}{3}$	$\frac{1}{3}$	$\frac{1}{3}$	$\frac{6}{13}$
Social Studies—					
European History**	13	$1\frac{1}{2}$	$\frac{2}{3}$	$\frac{2}{3}$	$\frac{4}{5}$
United States History	3	$\frac{2}{3}$	$\frac{1}{3}$	$\frac{1}{3}$	$\frac{4}{9}$
Civics††	10	$\frac{1}{3}$	$\frac{1}{3}$	$\frac{1}{3}$	$\frac{1}{3}$
Political Economics	4	$\frac{1}{3}$	$\frac{1}{3}$	$\frac{1}{3}$	$\frac{1}{3}$
Foreign Language‡‡—					
Commercial Subjects—					
Bookkeeping	8	$\frac{1}{3}$	$\frac{1}{3}$	$\frac{1}{3}$	$\frac{1}{3}$
Miscellaneous Subjects—					
Mental Philosophy	12	$\frac{2}{3}$	$\frac{1}{3}$	$\frac{2}{3}$	$\frac{7}{12}$
Moral Philosophy	11	$\frac{2}{3}$	$\frac{1}{3}$	$\frac{1}{3}$	$\frac{1}{3}$
Logic	5	$\frac{1}{3}$	$\frac{1}{3}$	$\frac{1}{3}$	$\frac{1}{3}$

*For the names of towns and cities, subjects offered by each school, and time devoted to each see Appendix, Table A.

†Subjects infrequently offered are not given in this table. For complete list see Appendix, Table A.

‡Natural philosophy was the term in common use.

§Includes natural history and biology.

**Includes ancient, modern, English and general history, and similar titles. For list see Appendix, Table A.

††Includes civil government, United States constitution, State constitution, science of government. See *ibid.*

‡‡See Table XVIII.

TABLE XXI—1866–70

ANALYSIS OF THE COURSES OF STUDY OF TWENTY SCHOOLS* SHOWING TIME IN YEARS DEVOTED TO EACH SUBJECT†

Subjects	Number of Schools	Maximum	Minimum	Mode	Average
Mathematics—					
Arithmetic	12	1	$\frac{1}{3}$	1	$\frac{7}{10}$
Algebra	20	2	$\frac{2}{3}$	1	$1\frac{1}{8}$
Geometry	20	2	$\frac{2}{3}$	1	$\frac{16}{17}$
Trigonometry	14	$\frac{2}{3}$	$\frac{1}{3}$	$\frac{1}{3}$	$\frac{11}{20}$
Survey and Navigation	4	$\frac{1}{2}$	$\frac{1}{3}$	$\frac{1}{3}$	$\frac{3}{8}$
English—					
Grammar and Analysis	14	1	$\frac{1}{3}$	$\frac{1}{3}$	$\frac{2}{3}$
Composition	8	$\frac{1}{2}$	$\frac{1}{3}$	$\frac{1}{3}$	$\frac{7}{18}$
Rhetoric	15	$\frac{1}{2}$	$\frac{1}{3}$	$\frac{1}{3}$	$\frac{4}{11}$
Literature	14	$1\frac{2}{3}$	$\frac{1}{3}$	$\frac{2}{3}$	$\frac{2}{3}$
Science—					
Physiology	15	$\frac{2}{3}$	$\frac{1}{3}$	$\frac{1}{3}$	$\frac{1}{2}$
Physical Geography	13	$\frac{2}{3}$	$\frac{1}{3}$	$\frac{1}{3}$–$\frac{2}{3}$	$\frac{2}{5}$
Physics‡	20	$1\frac{1}{2}$	$\frac{1}{3}$	$\frac{2}{3}$	$\frac{8}{9}$
Chemistry	16	$1\frac{1}{2}$	$\frac{1}{3}$	$\frac{2}{3}$	$\frac{9}{13}$
Botany	15	$\frac{2}{3}$	$\frac{1}{3}$	$\frac{1}{3}$	$\frac{17}{39}$
Zoölogy§	10	1	$\frac{1}{3}$	$\frac{1}{3}$	$\frac{4}{7}$
Geology	12	$\frac{2}{3}$	$\frac{1}{3}$	$\frac{1}{3}$	$\frac{2}{5}$
Astronomy	18	$\frac{2}{3}$	$\frac{1}{3}$	$\frac{1}{3}$	$\frac{7}{15}$
Social Studies—					
European History**	18	$1\frac{1}{6}$	$\frac{2}{3}$	1	$\frac{9}{10}$
United States History	4	$\frac{2}{3}$	$\frac{1}{3}$	$\frac{1}{3}$	$\frac{4}{9}$
Civics††	12	$\frac{2}{3}$	$\frac{1}{4}$	$\frac{1}{3}$	$\frac{1}{2}$
Political Economy	6	$\frac{1}{2}$	$\frac{1}{3}$	$\frac{1}{3}$	$\frac{7}{18}$
Foreign Language‡‡—					
Commercial Subjects—					
Bookkeeping	12	1	$\frac{1}{4}$	$\frac{1}{3}$	$\frac{7}{12}$
Miscellaneous Subjects—					
Mental Philosophy	15	$\frac{2}{3}$	$\frac{1}{3}$	$\frac{1}{3}$	$\frac{6}{13}$
Moral Philosophy	9	$\frac{2}{3}$	$\frac{1}{4}$	$\frac{1}{3}$	$\frac{5}{9}$

*For names of towns and cities, subjects offered by each school, and time devoted to each see Appendix, Table B.

†Subjects infrequently offered are not given in this table. For complete list see Appendix, Table A.

‡Natural philosophy was the term in common use.

§Including natural history and biology.

**Includes ancient, modern, English, and general history, and similar titles.

††Includes civil government, United States Constitution, State Constitution, science of government.

‡‡See Table XVIII.

TABLE XXII—1871–75

Analysis of the Courses of Study of Twenty Schools* Showing Time in Years Devoted to Each Subject†

Subjects	Number of Schools	Maximum	Minimum	Mode	Average
Mathematics—					
Arithmetic	12	1	$\frac{1}{3}$	$\frac{1}{3}$	$\frac{5}{12}$
Algebra	20	$1\frac{2}{3}$	$\frac{2}{3}$	1	$1\frac{1}{8}$
Geometry	20	2	$\frac{1}{3}$	1	1
Trigonometry	15	1	$\frac{1}{3}$	$\frac{1}{3}$	$\frac{5}{11}$
English—					
Grammar and Analysis	13	2	$\frac{1}{3}$	$\frac{1}{3}$–1	$\frac{9}{16}$
Composition	12	2	$\frac{1}{3}$	$\frac{1}{3}$	$\frac{5}{9}$
Rhetoric	17	$\frac{2}{3}$	$\frac{1}{3}$	$\frac{2}{3}$	$\frac{8}{13}$
Literature	20	$1\frac{2}{3}$	$\frac{1}{3}$	$\frac{2}{3}$	$\frac{11}{13}$
Science—					
Physiology	17	$\frac{2}{3}$	$\frac{1}{3}$	$\frac{1}{3}$	$\frac{7}{13}$
Physical Geography	15	$\frac{2}{3}$	$\frac{1}{3}$	$\frac{1}{3}$	$\frac{17}{36}$
Physics‡	19	1	$\frac{1}{3}$	$\frac{2}{3}$	$\frac{7}{12}$
Chemistry	18	1	$\frac{1}{3}$	$\frac{2}{3}$	$\frac{7}{13}$
Botany	17	$\frac{2}{3}$	$\frac{1}{3}$	$\frac{1}{3}$	$\frac{5}{12}$
Zoölogy§	12	$\frac{2}{3}$	$\frac{1}{3}$	$\frac{1}{3}$	$\frac{7}{18}$
Geology	17	$\frac{2}{3}$	$\frac{1}{3}$	$\frac{1}{3}$	$\frac{6}{18}$
Astronomy	16	$\frac{2}{3}$	$\frac{1}{3}$	$\frac{1}{3}$	$\frac{4}{9}$
Social Studies—					
European History**	19	2	$\frac{1}{3}$	$\frac{2}{3}$	$\frac{12}{13}$
United States History	5	1	$\frac{1}{3}$	$\frac{2}{3}$	$\frac{2}{3}$
Civics††	14	1	$\frac{1}{3}$	$\frac{1}{3}$	$\frac{3}{8}$
Political Economy	5	$\frac{2}{3}$	$\frac{1}{3}$	$\frac{1}{3}$	$\frac{17}{30}$
Foreign Language‡‡—					
Commercial Subjects—					
Bookkeeping	10	$\frac{2}{3}$	$\frac{1}{3}$	$\frac{1}{3}$	$\frac{7}{18}$
Miscellaneous Subjects—					
Mental Philosophy	10	$\frac{2}{3}$	$\frac{1}{3}$	$\frac{2}{3}$	$\frac{2}{3}$
Moral Philosophy	6	$\frac{1}{3}$	$\frac{1}{3}$	$\frac{1}{3}$	$\frac{1}{3}$

*For names of towns and cities, subjects offered by each school, and time devoted to each see Appendix, Table C.

†Subjects infrequently offered are not given in this table. For complete list see Appendix, Table A.

‡Natural philosophy was the term in common use.

§Includes natural history and biology.

**Includes ancient, modern, English, and general history, and similar titles. For list see Appendix, Table C.

††Includes Civil Government, United States Constitution, State Constitution, science of government. For list see *ibid.*

‡‡See Table XVIII.

TABLE XXIII—1876–80

Analysis of the Courses of Study of Twenty Schools* Showing Time in Years Devoted to Each Subject†

Subjects	Number of Schools	Maximum	Minimum	Mode	Average
Mathematics—					
Arithmetic	14	$1\frac{1}{3}$	$\frac{2}{3}$	$\frac{1}{2}$	$\frac{6}{7}$
Algebra	20	$2\frac{1}{2}$	$\frac{1}{2}$	1	$1\frac{1}{10}$
Geometry	20	2	$\frac{1}{2}$	1	$1\frac{1}{24}$
Trigonometry	11	$\frac{2}{3}$	$\frac{1}{3}$	$\frac{1}{3}$–$\frac{1}{2}$	$\frac{5}{11}$
English—					
Grammar and Analysis	9	$1\frac{1}{3}$	$\frac{1}{3}$	1	$\frac{3}{4}$
Composition	12	1	$\frac{1}{3}$	$\frac{1}{2}$	$\frac{2}{3}$
Rhetoric	17	1	$\frac{1}{3}$	$\frac{1}{3}$	$\frac{7}{12}$
Literature	16	2	$\frac{1}{3}$	1	$\frac{11}{12}$
Science—					
Physiology	19	1	$\frac{1}{4}$	$\frac{1}{3}$–$\frac{1}{2}$–$\frac{2}{3}$	$\frac{1}{2}$
Physical Geography	13	$\frac{1}{3}$	$\frac{1}{3}$	$\frac{1}{3}$	$\frac{1}{2}$
Physics‡	19	$1\frac{1}{3}$	$\frac{1}{3}$	1	$\frac{25}{29}$
Chemistry	13	1	$\frac{1}{3}$	$\frac{2}{3}$	$\frac{11}{13}$
Botany	17	$\frac{2}{3}$	$\frac{1}{3}$	$\frac{1}{3}$	$\frac{8}{17}$
Zoölogy§	14	$\frac{2}{3}$	$\frac{1}{3}$	$\frac{1}{3}$	$\frac{1}{2}$
Geology	10	$\frac{2}{3}$	$\frac{1}{3}$	$\frac{1}{2}$	$\frac{13}{30}$
Astronomy	13	1	$\frac{1}{3}$	$\frac{1}{3}$	$\frac{17}{39}$
Social Science—					
European History**	20	$1\frac{2}{3}$	$\frac{1}{3}$	1	$1\frac{7}{19}$
United States History	5	1	$\frac{1}{3}$	$\frac{2}{3}$	$\frac{3}{5}$
Civics††	15	1	$\frac{1}{4}$	$\frac{1}{3}$	$\frac{7}{12}$
Political Economy	3	$\frac{1}{2}$	$\frac{1}{3}$	$\frac{1}{3}$	$\frac{7}{18}$
Foreign Language‡‡—					
Commercial Subjects—					
Bookkeeping	10	1	$\frac{1}{4}$	$\frac{1}{3}$	$\frac{11}{20}$
Miscellaneous Subjects—					
Mental Philosophy	8	$\frac{2}{3}$	$\frac{1}{3}$	$\frac{1}{3}$	$\frac{7}{12}$
Moral Philosophy	4	$\frac{2}{3}$	$\frac{1}{3}$	$\frac{1}{3}$	$\frac{13}{24}$

*For names of towns and cities, subjects offered by each school, and time devoted to each. See Appendix, Table D.

†Subjects infrequently offered are not given in this table. For complete list, see *ibid.*

‡Natural philosophy was the term in common use.

§Includes natural history and biology.

**Includes ancient, modern, English, and general history, and similar titles. For list, see Appendix, Table D.

††Includes civil government, United States Constitution, State Constitution, science of government.

‡‡See Table XVIII.

TABLE XXIV—1881–85

ANALYSIS OF THE COURSES OF STUDY OF TWENTY-FIVE SCHOOLS* SHOWING TIME IN YEARS DEVOTED TO EACH SUBJECT†

Subjects	Number of Schools	Maximum	Minimum	Mode	Average
Mathematics—					
Arithmetic	22	2	$\frac{1}{3}$	$\frac{1}{3}$–1	$\frac{3}{5}$
Algebra	25	2	1	1	$1\frac{1}{4}$
Geometry	25	$1\frac{1}{3}$	$\frac{1}{3}$	1	$\frac{4}{5}$
Trigonometry	10	1	$\frac{1}{4}$	$\frac{1}{3}$	$\frac{4}{9}$
English—					
Grammar and Analysis	17	$1\frac{1}{3}$	$\frac{1}{2}$	$\frac{2}{3}$	$\frac{8}{9}$
Composition	8	$1\frac{2}{3}$	$\frac{1}{3}$	$\frac{1}{3}$–$\frac{1}{2}$	$\frac{3}{5}$
Rhetoric	21	1	$\frac{1}{3}$	$\frac{1}{3}$	$\frac{3}{5}$
Literature	23	2	$\frac{2}{3}$	1	1
Science—					
Physiology	23	1	$\frac{1}{3}$	$\frac{1}{2}$	$\frac{1}{2}$
Physical Geography	17	1	$\frac{1}{3}$	$\frac{1}{3}$–$\frac{1}{2}$	$\frac{1}{2}$
Physics‡	25	1	$\frac{1}{3}$	$\frac{2}{3}$	$\frac{3}{4}$
Chemistry	20	1	$\frac{1}{3}$	$\frac{2}{3}$	$\frac{11}{19}$
Botany	18	$\frac{5}{6}$	$\frac{1}{3}$	$\frac{1}{2}$	$\frac{7}{12}$
Zoölogy§	14	$\frac{2}{3}$	$\frac{1}{3}$	$\frac{1}{3}$	$\frac{6}{13}$
Geology	14	$\frac{2}{3}$	$\frac{1}{3}$	$\frac{1}{3}$–$\frac{1}{2}$	$\frac{6}{13}$
Astronomy	12	$\frac{2}{3}$	$\frac{1}{4}$	$\frac{1}{3}$–$\frac{1}{2}$	$\frac{5}{12}$
Social Studies—					
European History**	25	$1\frac{2}{3}$	$\frac{2}{3}$	1	$\frac{11}{12}$
United States History	7	$\frac{2}{3}$	$\frac{1}{3}$	$\frac{1}{2}$	$\frac{1}{2}$
Civics††	21	1	$\frac{1}{3}$	$\frac{1}{3}$	$\frac{1}{2}$
Political Economy	8	$\frac{1}{2}$	$\frac{1}{3}$	$\frac{1}{3}$	$\frac{5}{12}$
Foreign Language‡‡—					
Commercial Subjects—					
Bookkeeping	17	1	$\frac{1}{3}$	$\frac{1}{3}$	$\frac{1}{2}$
Miscellaneous Subjects—					
Mental Philosophy	6	1	$\frac{1}{3}$	$\frac{1}{3}$–1	$\frac{11}{18}$
Moral Philosophy	3	$\frac{1}{3}$	$\frac{1}{3}$	$\frac{1}{3}$	$\frac{1}{3}$

*For names of towns and cities, subjects offered by each school, and time devoted to each see Appendix, Table E.

†Subjects infrequently offered are not given in this table. For complete list see *ibid.*

‡Natural philosophy was the term in common use.

§Includes natural history and biology.

**Includes ancient, modern, English, and general history, and similar titles. For list see Appendix, Table E.

††Includes Civil government, United States Constitution, State Constitution, science of government.

‡‡See Table XVIII.

TABLE XXV—1886–90

ANALYSIS OF THE COURSES OF STUDY OF THIRTY SCHOOLS* SHOWING TIME IN YEARS DEVOTED TO EACH SUBJECT†

Subjects	Number of Schools	Maximum	Minimum	Mode	Average
Mathematics—					
Arithmetic	19	2	$\frac{1}{3}$	$\frac{2}{3}$	$\frac{2}{3}$
Algebra	30	2	1	$1\frac{1}{3}$	$1\frac{3}{10}$
Geometry	30	$1\frac{1}{2}$	$\frac{2}{3}$	1	$1\frac{1}{9}$
Trigonometry	11	$\frac{2}{3}$	$\frac{1}{4}$	$\frac{1}{3}$	$\frac{5}{12}$
English—					
Grammar and Analysis	22	1	$\frac{1}{3}$	$\frac{1}{3}$	$\frac{9}{14}$
Composition	13	1	$\frac{1}{3}$	$\frac{1}{3}$	$\frac{5}{9}$
Rhetoric	25	1	$\frac{1}{3}$	$\frac{2}{3}$	$\frac{15}{22}$
Literature	26	$3\frac{1}{2}$	$\frac{1}{3}$	1	$1\frac{1}{12}$
Science—					
Physiology	26	$1\frac{1}{2}$	$\frac{1}{3}$	$\frac{1}{2}$	$\frac{13}{24}$
Physical Geography	27	1	$\frac{1}{3}$	$\frac{1}{2}$	$\frac{7}{13}$
Physics‡	30	1	$\frac{1}{3}$	1	$\frac{23}{29}$
Chemistry	18	1	$\frac{1}{3}$	$\frac{1}{2}$	$\frac{11}{18}$
Botany	29	$1\frac{1}{2}$	$\frac{1}{4}$	$\frac{1}{2}$	$\frac{1}{2}$
Zoölogy§	18	1	$\frac{1}{3}$	$\frac{1}{2}$	$\frac{8}{17}$
Geology	19	$\frac{2}{3}$	$\frac{1}{4}$	$\frac{1}{3}$	$\frac{5}{12}$
Astronomy	18	$\frac{2}{3}$	$\frac{1}{4}$	$\frac{1}{2}$	$\frac{5}{12}$
Social Studies—					
European History**	25	$2\frac{1}{2}$	$\frac{1}{3}$	1	1
United States History	16	$1\frac{1}{3}$	$\frac{1}{3}$	1	$\frac{3}{4}$
Civics††	28	1	$\frac{1}{4}$	$\frac{1}{3}$	$\frac{1}{2}$
Political Economy	11	$\frac{2}{3}$	$\frac{1}{3}$	$\frac{1}{3}$	$\frac{4}{11}$
Foreign Language‡‡—					
Commercial Subjects—					
Bookkeeping	24	$1\frac{1}{2}$	$\frac{1}{3}$	$\frac{2}{3}$	$\frac{9}{16}$
Miscellaneous Subjects—					
Mental Philosophy	6	$\frac{1}{2}$	$\frac{1}{3}$	$\frac{1}{3}$	$\frac{13}{36}$
Moral Philosophy	3	$\frac{1}{3}$	$\frac{1}{3}$	$\frac{1}{3}$	$\frac{1}{3}$
Pedagogy	7	1	$\frac{1}{4}$	1	$\frac{5}{7}$

*For names of towns and cities, subjects offered by each school, and time devoted to each see Appendix, Table F.

†Subjects infrequently offered are not given in this table. For list see *ibid.*

‡Natural philosophy a term also used.

§Includes natural history.

**Includes ancient, modern, English, and general history, and similar titles. For list see Appendix, Table F.

††Includes civil government, United States Constitution, State Constitution, science of government.

‡‡See Table XVIII.

TABLE XXVI—1891–95

ANALYSIS OF THE COURSES OF STUDY OF FORTY SCHOOLS* SHOWING TIME IN YEARS DEVOTED TO EACH SUBJECT†

Subjects	Number of Schools	Maximum	Minimum	Mode	Average
Mathematics—					
Arithmetic	28	2	$\frac{1}{3}$	$\frac{1}{2}$	$\frac{2}{3}$
Algebra	40	2	1	$1\frac{1}{2}$	$1\frac{7}{10}$
Geometry	40	2	$\frac{2}{3}$	1	$1\frac{1}{7}$
Trigonometry	8	$\frac{2}{3}$	$\frac{1}{3}$	$\frac{1}{3}$–$\frac{1}{2}$	$\frac{11}{24}$
English—					
Grammar	13	1	$\frac{1}{3}$	$\frac{1}{3}$	$\frac{6}{11}$
Composition	20	$1\frac{1}{2}$	$\frac{1}{3}$	$\frac{2}{3}$	$\frac{7}{12}$
Rhetoric	26	1	$\frac{1}{3}$	$\frac{1}{2}$	$\frac{7}{12}$
Literature	35	$3\frac{1}{2}$	$\frac{1}{3}$	1	$1\frac{1}{9}$
Science—					
Physiology	32	1	$\frac{1}{3}$	$\frac{1}{2}$	$\frac{1}{2}$
Physical Geography	29	1	$\frac{1}{3}$	$\frac{1}{2}$	$\frac{1}{2}$
Physics‡	40	1	$\frac{1}{3}$	1	$\frac{5}{6}$
Chemistry	29	1	$\frac{1}{3}$	1	$\frac{5}{6}$
Botany	33	1	$\frac{1}{3}$	$\frac{1}{2}$	$\frac{7}{11}$
Zoölogy§	17	$1\frac{1}{2}$	$\frac{1}{3}$	$\frac{1}{2}$	$\frac{7}{13}$
Geology	19	1	$\frac{1}{3}$	$\frac{1}{2}$	$\frac{1}{2}$
Astronomy	20	$\frac{2}{3}$	$\frac{1}{3}$	$\frac{1}{2}$	$\frac{7}{15}$
Social Studies—					
European History**	38	3	$\frac{1}{3}$	1	$1\frac{1}{3}$
United States History	15	1	$\frac{1}{3}$	$\frac{1}{3}$–$\frac{1}{2}$	$\frac{5}{9}$
Civics††	34	1	$\frac{1}{3}$	$\frac{1}{3}$–$\frac{1}{2}$	$\frac{1}{2}$
Political Economy	11	1	$\frac{1}{3}$	$\frac{1}{3}$	$\frac{1}{2}$
Foreign Language‡‡—					
Commercial Subjects—					
Bookkeeping	19	1	$\frac{1}{3}$	1	$\frac{11}{15}$
Commercial Law	5	1	$\frac{1}{3}$	$\frac{1}{2}$	$\frac{3}{5}$
Miscellaneous Subjects—					
Psychology***	7	1	$\frac{1}{3}$	$\frac{1}{2}$	$\frac{4}{7}$
Pedagogy	8	$\frac{2}{3}$	$\frac{1}{3}$	$\frac{1}{3}$–$\frac{2}{3}$	$\frac{5}{8}$

*For names of towns and cities, subjects offered by each school, and time devoted to each see Appendix, Table G.

†Subjects infrequently offered are not given in this table. For list see *ibid.*

‡Natural philosophy a term also used.

§Includes biology.

**Includes ancient, modern, English and general history, and similar titles. For list, see Appendix, Table G.

††Includes civil government, United States and state constitution.

‡‡See Table XVIII.

***Includes mental philosophy.

TABLE XXVII—1896-1900

ANALYSIS OF THE COURSES OF STUDY OF FORTY SCHOOLS* SHOWING TIME IN YEARS DEVOTED TO EACH SUBJECT†

Subjects	Number of Schools	Maximum	Minimum	Mode	Average
Mathematics—					
Arithmetic	26	1	$\frac{1}{3}$	$\frac{1}{3}$–1	$\frac{9}{13}$
Algebra	40	2	1	$1\frac{1}{2}$	$1\frac{5}{12}$
Geometry	40	$1\frac{2}{3}$	$\frac{2}{3}$	1	$1\frac{3}{20}$
Trigonometry	9	$\frac{1}{2}$	$\frac{1}{3}$	$\frac{1}{3}$	$\frac{4}{9}$
English‡—					
Grammar	14	$1\frac{1}{2}$	$\frac{1}{3}$	$\frac{1}{3}$–1	$\frac{5}{7}$
Composition	17	2	$\frac{1}{3}$	$\frac{1}{3}$–2	1
Rhetoric	25	1	$\frac{1}{3}$	$\frac{1}{2}$	$\frac{7}{11}$
Literature	31	3	$\frac{1}{3}$	1	$1\frac{1}{2}$
Science—					
Physiology	28	1	$\frac{1}{3}$	$\frac{1}{2}$	$\frac{1}{2}$
Physical Geography	30	1	$\frac{1}{3}$	$\frac{1}{2}$	$\frac{7}{12}$
Physics	38	1	$\frac{1}{2}$	1	$\frac{18}{19}$
Chemistry	26	1	$\frac{1}{2}$	1	$\frac{15}{19}$
Botany	33	1	$\frac{1}{3}$	$\frac{1}{2}$	$\frac{1}{2}$
Zoölogy§	22	1	$\frac{1}{3}$	$\frac{1}{2}$	$\frac{6}{11}$
Geology	9	$\frac{2}{3}$	$\frac{1}{3}$	$\frac{1}{2}$	$\frac{1}{2}$
Astronomy	11	$\frac{1}{2}$	$\frac{1}{3}$	$\frac{1}{2}$	[illegible]/11
Social Studies—					
European History**	26	3	$\frac{1}{2}$	1	$1\frac{1}{2}$
United States History	18	$\frac{2}{3}$	$\frac{1}{3}$	$\frac{1}{2}$	$\frac{5}{9}$
Civics††	30	1	$\frac{1}{3}$	$\frac{1}{2}$	$\frac{5}{9}$
Political Economy	16	1	$\frac{1}{3}$	$\frac{1}{3}$	$\frac{1}{2}$
Foreign Language‡‡—					
Commercial Subjects—					
Bookkeeping	29	1	$\frac{1}{3}$	$\frac{1}{2}$	$\frac{3}{5}$
Commercial Law	9	$\frac{1}{2}$	$\frac{1}{3}$	$\frac{1}{3}$	$\frac{8}{21}$
Miscellaneous Subjects—					
Psychology	7	1	$\frac{1}{3}$	$\frac{1}{2}$	$\frac{11}{21}$
Pedagogy	7	1	$\frac{1}{3}$	$\frac{1}{3}$	$\frac{1}{2}$

*For names of towns and cities, subjects offered in each school, and time devoted to each see Appendix, Table H.

†Subjects infrequently offered are not given in this table. For list see *ibid.*

‡Several schools offered English without designating the subjects.

§Includes biology.

**Includes ancient, modern, English and general history.

††Includes civil government.

‡‡See Table XVIII.

1. LACK OF UNIFORMITY IN TIME

Tables XI–XVIII show the great lack of uniformity in time devoted to the various fields. It will be observed, for example, from page 80, that out of fourteen schools offering mathematics there were seven different units of time devoted to this field. In English there were thirteen schools and ten different units, and in science, fourteen schools and nine different units. This lack of uniformity is found to prevail throughout the forty years, although the tendency to standardize some fields is made evident by decrease in number of units and also agreement in a comparatively large number of schools. For example, in 1891–95, out of forty schools offering mathematics [p. 87] there are only twelve units as compared with fourteen schools and seven different units in 1860–65. The tendency to uniformity is also shown by the fact that three units of time include twenty-two of these same schools. The same is true of English. In 1860–65, out of thirteen schools there were ten different units of time, while in 1896–1900, with forty schools there were but fifteen units. As in the case of mathematics, three of these units included twenty schools. Comparing pages 80 and 89 will show the same tendency in both science and the social studies although not in the same degree as in mathematics and English.

These tables, however, very clearly show the lack of standardization of high-school curricula from the standpoint of time devoted to each field even at the close of the century.

Table XIX shows the maximum, minimum, mode, and averages of time devoted to each field for the several periods and Tables XX–XXVII indicate the same for each subject in the different fields.

2. MAXIMUM, MINIMUM, MODE, AND AVERAGE TIME DEVOTED TO SUBJECTS AND FIELDS

MATHEMATICS

The average time devoted to mathematics remained practically constant and was approximately three years. The highest maximum was five and the lowest three and two-thirds. The minimum for 1860–70 was one year and thereafter two years. Three years was the most frequent mode.

Arithmetic.—The average time devoted to this subject never reached one year, the highest being eight-ninths and the lowest five-twelfths. The average time increased two-thirteenths for the entire period. The maximum was as high as two years, one year being the lowest and most frequent. One-third was constant as a minimum. The mode was as high as one year, one-third being the most frequent.

Algebra.—The average except for 1860–65 was above one year. There was a gradual increase and at the close the average time was approximately one and one-half. The lowest maximum was one and two-thirds, the highest two and one-half, and two years most frequent. The lowest minimum was one-half, the highest and most frequent being one. The most frequent mode was one, it being one and one-half at the close.

Geometry.—Average time was approximately one year, increasing from thirteen-sixteenths to one and one-sixth. Lowest maximum was one year, two years being the highest and most frequent. The lowest minimum was one-third, two-thirds being the highest and most frequent. The mode remained one year throughout.

Trigonometry.—The average time ranges from one-third to one-half year. Lowest maximum was one-half, the highest being one year and two-thirds the most frequent. Lowest minimum was one-fourth, one-third being the highest, and most frequent. Practically no change occurred in the amount of time devoted to the subject.

Surveying and navigation was negligible after 1870. It was a short-time subject, the average time devoted to it being between one-third and one-half year.

ENGLISH

The average time devoted to this field ranged from one and one-half to approximately three years at the close. Comparing the first and last period, the average time increased approximately one year. The lowest maximum was three and the highest six and one-third. It is very probable that maxima after 1880 are above the amount actually offered on account of confusion in terminology. The lowest minimum was one-third, the highest one and one-half, one year being the most frequent. There is considerable confusion concerning mode, it being between one and two years before 1880, and between two and four years thereafter.

Grammar.[1]—The average time was below one year, the highest being eight-ninths in 1881–85, and the lowest six-elevenths in 1891–95. The lowest maximum was one, the highest two, and the most frequent one and one-third. The minimum was one-third throughout except for the period 1881–85 when it was one-half. Considerable confusion exists as to the mode, the lowest and most frequent being one-third and the highest one year. Grammar declined in importance both absolutely and also relatively as compared with other subjects in its field.

Composition.[2]—Average time approximately one year at the beginning and one year at the close. The latter was the highest average, the lowest being a trifle above one-third, 1866–70. The lowest maximum was one-half and the highest two years. The minimum was one-third throughout. The lowest and most frequent mode was one-third and the highest two-thirds. On the whole there was an increase in the time devoted to the subject.[3]

Rhetoric.—Average time slightly above one-half, the lowest and highest averages being one-third and two-thirds respectively. The lowest maximum was one-half, the highest and most frequent being one year. The minimum was one-third throughout. The lowest and most frequent mode was one-third, the highest being two-thirds. From the opening to the close there was an increase of time of approximately one-fifth year.[4]

Literature.[5]—The average time devoted to this subject increased from approximately one-half at the beginning to one and one-half at the close. The lowest maximum was two-thirds, the highest three and one-half years, and one and one-half, two, and three and one-half were equal in point of frequency. The lowest and most frequent minimum was one-third and two-thirds was the highest. The lowest mode was two-thirds, the highest and most frequent being one year. The increases in amount of time devoted to English are found chiefly in the increase in literature.

SCIENCE

The average time devoted to science remained practically unchanged comparing 1860 and 1900. There was more or less

[1] The subjects entitled grammar, analysis, sentence analysis, and the like are grouped since it is very apparent that the various titles are used to designate the same general type of subject-matter.

[2] Computations are only approximately correct, since the time devoted to the subject is not clearly indicated, particularly in the earlier years.

[3] The computations in this subject like others in its field are only approximately correct on account of the introduction of the general term "English" about 1880.

[4] *Ibid.*

[5] The term was loosely used and included English literature, American literature, classics, history of literature, reading, etc.

fluctuation from period to period which was probably due to the fact that the same schools do not furnish data for all the tables rather than to any general tendency. The maximum also remains constant except for fluctuations referred to above. The fluctuations are greater in both minimum and mode than in either the average or maximum. The minimum decreases slightly for the whole period while the mode increases two-thirds of a year. The maximum held closely around five years except for one period 1886–90 when it was six and one-half. The average was never below three years or above three and one-half. The highest minimum was two years, the lowest was one year and this was also the most frequent. The highest and most frequent mode was four years and the lowest two and one-third.

Physiology.—The average time devoted to this subject remained approximately one-half year to the close. The maximum increased from two-thirds to one year while the minimum, one-third, remained unchanged. The mode was one-third in 1860 and one-half after 1880. Physical geography was also a short-time subject and its history is almost identical with that of physiology.

Physics.—This was one of the longer-time science subjects and the average increased approximately from three-fourths of a year to one year. The maximum remained one year while the mode increased from two-thirds of a year to one year. The minimum increased from one-third of a year to one-half year.

Chemistry.—The average was the same in 1860 as that of physics and this had increased only by a small fraction in 1900. The subject was identical with physics as to maximum, minimum, and mode.

Botany.—The average time remained one-half year and the mode decreased slightly. The maximum increase from two-thirds of a year to one year and the minimum remains the same. Zoölogy gains slightly in average time and the minimum remains the same. The maximum increases from two-thirds of a year to one year and the mode increased from one-third of a year to one-half.

Geology.—This subject remained unchanged except for negligible fractions. Astronomy shows a slight decrease in time as to average and maximum, the minimum remains the same and the mode increases from one-third to one-half year.

THE SOCIAL STUDIES

The increase in average time devoted to this field amounts to a little less than one year. This was slightly less than the gain in the case of English. The maximum increased two years, the mode from one year to one and one-half and the minimum from one-third of a year to one year. There was little fluctuation in either the average or the maximum, the increase on the whole being steady and uninterrupted. This was not true of the minimum and the mode, although the fluctuations were less pronounced in the latter than in the former.

European history.[1]—The gain in time devoted to the social studies was largely due to increase in time given to European history. The gain in average time was seven-tenths of a year and the maximum increased from one and one-half to three years. The mode increased from two-thirds of a year to one year and the minimum decreased from two-thirds to one-half year. There were some fluctuations, but on the whole the increase in time particularly as to average and maximum was uninterrupted.

United States history.—Except for negligible fractions as to average and mode, no change occurred in amount of time devoted to this subject. Civics shows an increase of two-ninths of a year in average time and one-third in maximum. The minimum remains one-third and the mode changes from one-third to one-half year. Political economy shows no change in minimum or mode each remaining one-third of a year. The average increased from one-third to one-half year and the maximum from one-third to one year.

FOREIGN LANGUAGE

This field presents considerable confusion. One reason for this is that details for foreign language are not given in some of the earlier courses of study. This is particularly true of the modern languages. For example, the mark thus, x, in Table B shows that the schools offered Greek, German, French, or all of these languages, but that no data are given indicating whether one, two, or more years were devoted to each. It is not probable that the maximum was thirteen years during the period 1860–65 and again during 1871–75 and only ten years from 1866–70. It is reasonable to assume that the maximum for foreign language does not suffer such violent fluctuations and it is not probable that the maximum for the period as a whole fluctuated to the extent indicated.

If one takes into account all the data, the conclusion that there was not much change in the amount of time seems justified. The

[1] See footnotes to Tables XX–XXVII.

average time devoted to Latin was approximately three and one-fourth years. The maximum was four years except in the case of one school which devoted four and one-third years to the subject in 1900. One and two years constitute with equal frequency the minimum and four years the most frequent mode.

Greek was practically negligible as a high-school subject particularly after 1880. The table indicates increase in average, maximum, and minimum time devoted to the subject, while the mode remains unchanged except for two periods when it increases from two to three years.

The maximum for German of four years was constant except for the period 1866–70 when it was three years. Two years was the most frequent mode, and the minimum ranged from two-thirds of a year to two years with one year the most frequent. The average ranged from two and one-third to three years and was two and seven-tenths at the close. The average time devoted to French was lowest at one and one-half years, highest at three years, and was two years at the close. The maximum was three years during the first period, two years at the close, and four years was the most frequent. The mode ranged from one to three years, being two years at the close and this was the most frequent. The average was two years at the close. One and two years were equally frequent as the minimum.

COMMERCIAL SUBJECTS

This field received very little attention before 1890, the maximum time being less than two years except for one period (two years, 1876–80) until that date. After that time the maximum increased rapidly and was seven years at the close. This increase was due to the introduction of stenography and typewriting. The average was less than one year until the date mentioned above, the lowest being one-third and the highest was one and three-sevenths years at the close. The most frequent minimum was one-third and the mode ranged from one-third to two-thirds of a year, being one-half at the close.

THE MISCELLANEOUS SUBJECTS

These subjects fall into two groups. The first group consisted of mental philosophy, moral philosophy, logic, Christian evidences, and the like. They were all short-time subjects and declined in importance resulting in less time being devoted to the field. The maximum decreased from two and two-thirds to one year in 1885 and the average also decreased during the same time from one and one-eighth to two-thirds of a year. The manual training group then came in and the maximum was three years in 1885–90 and seven years at the close. The average, however, is still low, approximately one year, due to pedagogy and psychology which were short-time subjects.

3. REQUIRED SUBJECTS AND ELECTIVES

Constants and variables have already been discussed [pp. 75–9], and it was there shown that mathematics, English, and the social studies (after 1870) were offered by all the schools. This does not mean, of course, that the subjects in these fields were required of all the students, since the majority of the schools included in this study, offered opportunity for election.

No subject seems to have been universally required although some were practically so. Algebra and geometry were sometimes not required in commercial courses[1] but this was not the rule particularly in three- and four-year courses.[2] English was not required in some of the earlier classical courses, but the later practice was to require something in this field of all students. In science, the rule was to require physics of all students although exceptions are found.[3] In the field of social studies there seems to have been no one subject universally required of all students.

It will be seen from the above that elective subjects included a wide range, there being no field which did not furnish one or more. As has been pointed out, algebra and geometry, with few exceptions, were required while trigonometry was more frequently an elective. Grammar and composition, if offered, were almost invariably required, while rhetoric and literature were frequently elective. In science, as has been said, physics was usually required. Of the other sciences, botany, physical geography, and physiology were relatively less frequently elective than geology, chemistry, astronomy, and zoölogy. Of the latter group, zoölogy seems to have been more frequently elective than the other three.

Of the social studies, United States history and European history were less frequently elective than civics and political economy. The latter was relatively the most frequently elective.

[1] Cf. p. 39.
[2] Cf. 32.
[3] Cf. 20, 21, 23.

If any foreign language was required, it was almost invariably Latin. When two or more foreign languages were offered it was the common practice to permit election.

Commercial subjects were usually elective and the same was true of pedagogy and psychology.

There seems to have been no generally accepted criteria for determining required subjects and electives. College entrance requirements, of course, determined the subjects required in preparatory courses and these included foreign language and "such other subjects as are requisite to prepare young men for the university."[1] In referring to those who wished to prepare for college the following statement is found in the Chicago report: "Those in preparation for college who desire it can omit the English branches, except the requisite mathematics, and complete the course in three years."[2] English branches as here used meant subjects other than ancient languages. As entrance requirements changed required subjects changed. For example, when little or no English was required for entrance, the subjects in this field were offered in non-preparatory courses in place of the ancient languages. As time went on, more English work was required in all courses irrespective of entrance requirements. The subjects in this field, however, continued to be elective with foreign language to the close. The science subjects were also substitutes for foreign language, the election here being largely on the same basis as was the case in English.

At the beginning of the period covered by Parts I and II, it is clear that the line of cleavage was between foreign language, particularly ancient language, and the so-called "English studies." The courses given on pages 20 and 21 show this distinction. Except for this, however, there was no uniformity in the matter of substitutions. As time went on, and courses were multiplied, the confusion concerning electives increased. This will be seen by a study of electives provided in the courses given on pages 20 to 42. Latin and Greek could be substituted for "other courses" by those preparing for college.[3] Latin was an elective with commercial subjects.[4] History and German were substitutes for Latin,[5] and "English studies"

[1] Cf. p. 20.
[2] Cf. p. 26.
[3] Cf. pp. 21, 22.
[4] Cf. p. 22.
[5] Cf. p. 29.

for German and Greek.[1] Pedagogy was an elective for German and Latin, and Greek for bookkeeping, civics, and science.[2]

Two subjects were required by St. Louis[3] from the following: Latin or German or French; zoölogy or geology, or Greek or Chemistry or mental philosophy or trigonometry. German or French were elective for English history, political science, mental science, and astronomy.[4] In the German-English course, German was a substitute for general history, English history, civil government, and political economy.[5] German and French were also substitutes for English literature and physiology.[6] The following substitutes were allowed for four years of Latin or German: composition, botany, physical geography, civil government, rhetoric, literature, United States history.[7] A comparatively wide range of electives is shown, but no information is given concerning what plan was used in selection.

It is clear as shown on pages 20 to 42 that outside of college preparatory curricula, no uniformity existed concerning content or organization of courses. The same was true of required subjects and electives.

[1] Cf. p. 26.
[2] Cf. p. 29.
[3] Cf. p. 29.
[4] Cf. pp. 26, 29, 30, 33.
[5] Cf. p. 29.
[6] Cf. p. 30.
[7] Cf. p. 31.

CHAPTER VIII

INFLUENCE OF SIZE AND LOCATION OF SCHOOLS

1. LARGE AND SMALL SCHOOLS

The high schools in the cities and larger towns, as would be expected, offered a wider range of subjects than did the schools in the smaller towns, and certain subjects are more frequently found in the curricula of these schools. The modern languages were more frequently taught in the larger schools and this was particularly true of French. Trigonometry, chemistry, and geology were less frequently offered by the small schools. Literature was a large-school subject in the earlier years, and the amount of time devoted to it was usually less in the small schools after it had become a constant in all the schools. Grammar seems to have been offered more frequently in the smaller schools, while the size of the school appears to have had no determining influence in the case of rhetoric. The larger schools provided more electives through a larger number of parallel courses and this, theoretically at least, furnished different types of education for different classes of students.

These different courses, however, resulted from the fact that the large schools were able to offer a wider range of traditional subjects rather than from any attempt to meet in any adequate way the commercial or industrial demands of these urban communities. The president of the Chicago Board of Education in his annual report for 1896 says:

> There is yet one important phase of human activity not touched by our high-school curriculum, a phase which in a large sense dominates and gives direction to all the other elements of public concern. I refer to the commercial interest.[1]

Chicago had already established the English and Manual Training High School and this movement was under way in some other cities. On the whole, however, commercial and industrial courses were not particularly characteristic of city high schools even at the close of the period. A comparison of curricula offered by cities and small towns fails to reveal that either rural conditions or urban conditions affected the character of educational opportunity offered, aside from the fact that cities provided a wider range of traditional subjects. For example, compare Columbus, Ohio and Adel, Iowa,

[1] *Report Board of Education*, 1896, pp. 28-32.

the latter a small county seat town.[1] The curricula differ in no way that would suggest that the former was a large city and the latter a small town school except in amount of work offered. Adel devoted a little more time to mathematics and less time to other fields. Columbus devoted more time to European history, one year more to science, and offered Latin, Greek, French, German, and Spanish, whereas Adel offered only Latin. Both offered commercial subjects, Columbus offering the wider range, and this is the only difference that could be interpreted as reflecting community demands of a definite sort. This interpretation even becomes doubtful when comparison is made of commercial subjects.

2. INFLUENCE OF LOCALITY

Conclusions relating to influence of locality upon curricula are largely negative. As has been pointed out, commercial and industrial demands had but little influence upon the work of the schools up to the close of the nineteenth century. We should not expect, therefore, that locality would determine the character of the curricula from the standpoint of industrial and commercial interests. In so far as bookkeeping was taught, there is no apparent connection between the presence of the subject in a curriculum and the location of the school.[2]

A comparison of individual schools located in various states fails to reveal differences in curricula that are not found by comparing schools located in the same state. In the older settled states, high schools were established earlier and certain traditional subjects sometimes retained their places in the curricula for a considerable time after they cease to appear in the majority of schools. This is not, however, due to the location of the schools, but to the date of establishment.[3]

It is true that some subjects were offered in a higher percentage of schools in one state than in another but these differences were also found among the schools of the same state and have but little significance. Illinois, Michigan, Missouri, and Minnesota have a relatively high percentage of schools offering chemistry while

[1] Cf. Appendix, Table H.

[2] Richmond, Indiana, and Oskaloosa, Iowa, neither of which was a commercial center, offered the subject, while Dayton and Cleveland, Ohio, did not. Columbus, Ohio, offered the subject after 1885, and Springfield, Illinois, after 1870. Madison, Wisconsin, offered it in 1860, 1883, 1887, and 1898, but did not offer it in 1867, 1876, and 1892.

[3] Dayton, Ohio, St. Louis, Missouri, and Madison, Wisconsin, retained mental philosophy until about 1885. These schools were established relatively early.

those of Iowa, Ohio, and Wisconsin rank much lower in this subject.[1] The fact is, however, that if small as well as large schools are taken into account, the majority of schools in no state offered this subject. There are also fluctuations in other sciences but they have no apparent significance in revealing community demands. It is not likely, for example, that the popular interest in astronomy was any greater in Iowa than in Wisconsin and yet 6 per cent of the schools in the former state and only ¼ of 1 per cent in the latter offered the subject in 1896.[2] We find equal percentages of schools offering physical geography in Illinois and Michigan, while the ratio of schools offering geology in the former to those of the latter is 2 to 3.

Algebra and geometry were practically constants. Trigonometry was more frequently offered in the larger schools than in the smaller while the reverse was true of arithmetic. There is no evidence that the English subjects were in any way influenced by locality.[3] Latin was universally required for entrance to classical courses in higher institutions and the percentage of schools offering the subject was no doubt largely determined by the extent to which they attempted to meet these requirements. The highest percentage of schools offering German was in Wisconsin and the next highest, in Michigan.[4] One would expect that states having a large German population would have a higher percentage of schools offering the language, but Minnesota with a large Scandinavian population had a much larger percentage of schools offering German than did Iowa with a relatively large German population.[5]

It is evident that the same generalized educational ideals controlled in all the states included in this study. As has been pointed out, the chief differences in curricula were due to differences in population rather than to the fact that schools were situated in different parts of the area. Sectional differences were minor and had no particular significance.

3. INDIVIDUAL DIFFERENCES IN SCHOOLS

Lack of uniformity in curricula has been pointed out in connection with Table I which shows the wide differences in curricula

[1] Details for all the states given in the *Report United States Commissioner Education*, 1896-97, II, 1893-94.

[2] *Ibid.*

[3] In the earlier years the large schools offered more work in literature, but they were only leaders in a movement participated in by all the schools later.

[4] *Report United States Commissioner Education*, 1896-97, II, 1893-94.

[5] *Ibid.*

organization. Also in Tables XI–XVIII is shown lack of uniformity in time devoted to subjects and fields. The difference between large and small schools has been discussed above. It is very evident in the light of these facts that individual differences were pronounced, but it is clear that any comprehensive treatment of the topic under discussion would require a detailed description of the curricula offered by a large number of schools included in Tables A–H. Few curricula were precisely alike in any period and changes took place in the curricula of all the schools from time to time. These differences consisted in emphasis placed upon the various fields offered by all the schools and the presence or absence of subjects belonging to the miscellaneous group. St. Louis, Missouri, emphasized English, particularly literature, and was one of the few schools which offered instruction in art. Chicago, Illinois, emphasized science, and was one of the schools offering pedagogy. Cleveland, Ohio, was one of the few schools which emphasized English in the earlier years. Madison, Wisconsin, offered commercial subjects and pedagogy. Wilton, Iowa, a small town, offered more work in the social studies in 1876 than was offered in any other schools included in the list of twenty. Springfield, Illinois, offered the maximum in this field in 1891. Oskaloosa, Iowa, offered the maximum in science in the same period and was one of the schools which always offered a large amount of science. A comprehensive treatment of this topic, as has been said, would consist in pointing out the emphasis and neglect of each individual school, all of which is shown in detail in the Appendix, Tables A–H.

4. CHANGES IN CURRICULA OF INDIVIDUAL SCHOOLS

An analysis of the curricula of three schools follows. Parentheses indicate the subjects which were not offered in the other curriculum. Figures show length of time devoted to fields and subjects.

MADISON, WISCONSIN

FOUR-YEAR COURSE IN EACH CASE

1863	1898
Mathematics, 3⅓	Mathematics, 2⅗
Arithmetic, 1	Arithmetic, ⅗
Algebra, 1⅓	Algebra, 1
Geometry, 1	Geometry, 1

English, $2\frac{2}{3}$

Analysis, $\frac{2}{3}$
Word analysis, $\frac{1}{3}$
Rhetoric, 1
Literature, $\frac{2}{3}$

Science, $3\frac{2}{3}$

Physiology, $\frac{2}{3}$
Physical Geography, $\frac{2}{3}$
Natural Philosophy $\frac{2}{3}$
(Chemistry, $\frac{2}{3}$)
(Geology, $\frac{1}{3}$)
(Botany, $\frac{1}{3}$)
(Astronomy, $\frac{1}{3}$)

Social Studies, 1

(Ancient History, $\frac{2}{3}$)
(Political Economy, $\frac{1}{3}$)

Foreign Language, 3

Latin, 3

Commercial Subjects

(Bookkeeping, $\frac{1}{3}$)

Miscellaneous Subjects, $1\frac{2}{3}$

(Mental Philosophy, $\frac{2}{3}$)
(Moral Philosophy, $\frac{1}{3}$)
(Butler's *Analogy*, $\frac{1}{3}$)
(Logic, $\frac{1}{3}$)

English, 2
(Subjects not specified)

First-year English, 3 days per week
Second-year English, 3 days per week
Third-year English, 2 days per week
Fourth-year English, 2 days per week

Science, $3\frac{3}{5}$

Physiology, $\frac{3}{5}$
Physical Geography, 1
Physics, 1
(Biology, 1)

Social Studies, $3\frac{1}{5}$

(United States History, 1)
(Civil Government, 1)
(History, $1\frac{1}{5}$)

Foreign Language, 12

Latin, 4
(German, 4)
(Greek, 4)

Commercial Subjects

None

Miscellaneous Subjects, $\frac{2}{5}$

(Pedagogy, $\frac{1}{5}$)
(Drawing, $\frac{1}{5}$)

CHICAGO, ILLINOIS

FOUR-YEAR COURSE IN EACH CASE

1862

Mathematics, $2\frac{2}{3}$

Algebra, 1
Geometry, 1
Trigonometry, $\frac{2}{3}$

English, $1\frac{1}{6}$

Rhetoric, $\frac{1}{2}$
Literature, $\frac{2}{3}$

Science, 3

Natural Philosophy, $\frac{2}{3}$
Chemistry, $\frac{1}{2}$
Geology, $\frac{1}{2}$
(Botany, $\frac{2}{3}$)
(Physical Geography, $\frac{1}{3}$)
(Physiology, $\frac{1}{3}$)

1892

Mathematics, 3

Algebra, 1
Geometry, $1\frac{1}{2}$
Trigonometry, $\frac{1}{2}$

English $2\frac{3}{5}$

Rhetoric (and Composition $\frac{3}{5}$)
Classics, 1
(History of English Literature, 1)

Science, 4

Physics, 1
Chemistry, 1
Geology, $\frac{1}{3}$
(Biology, 1)
(Astronomy, $\frac{2}{3}$)

Social Studies, 1⅔	**Social Studies, 4**
United States Constitution, ⅓	Civics, ⅓
Universal History, 1	General History, 1
(Political Economy, ⅔)	(Ancient History, 1)
	(Political History, ⅔)
	(History, 1)
Foreign Language, 13	**Foreign Language, 16**
Latin, 4	Latin, 4
German, 4	German, 4
French, 3	French, 4
(Greek, 2)	(Spanish, 4)
Commercial Subjects	**Commercial Subjects, 3**
None	(Bookkeeping, 1)
	(Stenography, 1)
	(Typewriting, 1)
Miscellaneous Subjects	**Miscellaneous Subjects, 5**
(Mental Philosophy, ⅓)	(Psychology, 1)
	(Manual Training, 4)

OSKALOOSA, IOWA

COURSE THREE YEARS IN 1873, FOUR YEARS IN 1897

1873	1897
Mathematics, 3⅓	**Mathematics, 3½**
Arithmetic, 1	Arithmetic, ½
Algebra, 1⅓	Algebra, 1½
Geometry, 1	Geometry, 1½
English 2⅓	**English, 3**
Grammar, 1	Grammar, ½
Rhetoric, ⅔	Rhetoric, ½
(Elocution, ⅔)	Literature, 2
Science, 2⅔	**Science, 3½**
Physical Geography, ⅔	Physical Geography, ½
Natural Philosophy, ½	Physics, 1
Botany, ⅔	Botany, ½
Zoölogy, ⅓	Zoölogy, ½
(Physiology, ½)	(Chemistry, ½)
	(Geology, ½)
Social Studies, ¾	**Social Studies, 3**
Outlines of History, ⅔	Ancient History, ½
	Modern History, ½
	(Civics, ½)
	(United States History, ½)
	(English History, ½)
	(Political Economy, ½)
Foreign Language, 6	**Foreign Language, 5**
Latin, 3	Latin, 4
German, 3	German, 1

Commercial Subjects	Commercial Subjects, 2
None	(Bookkeeping, 1)
	(Commercial Arithmetic, ½)
	(Commercial Law, ½)

No miscellaneous subjects offered in either course.

A comparison of the changes which took place in the curricula of these three schools reveals the same tendencies common to the high schools of the period. Increase of time devoted to English[1] and the social studies, disappearance of the old miscellaneous subjects and the offering of less science subjects with more time devoted to those offered, were all general tendencies. Oskaloosa was an exception to the tendency in science and furnished an example of the survival in some schools of the earlier practice.

These schools also serve as examples to show the lack of uniformity near the close of the period both in subjects offered and in time devoted to fields and subjects. All three schools offered algebra and geometry while two offered arithmetic and one trigonometry. The time devoted to mathematics remained the same in one school, increased in another, and decreased in the third. In science, physiology appears in both curricula of Madison and only in the earlier curricula of the other two schools. Physics was a constant in all the schools, while physical geography was constant in Madison and Oskaloosa and is found only in the earlier curriculum of Chicago. Chemistry and geology were constants in Chicago, are found in the earlier curriculum of Madison and the later one of Oskaloosa. Astronomy was offered in the earlier curriculum of Madison and the later one of Chicago, and in neither of Oskaloosa. Botany persisted in all the schools, while zoölogy is a constant in Oskaloosa and appears in the later curricula of the other two schools.

The increase in time devoted to the social studies in all the schools resulted in important changes in the subjects. One cannot be certain concerning the changes in European history because of the confusion in terminology, but it was offered in each of the curricula of all the schools. None of the schools offered United States history in the earlier curricula, while both Madison and Oskaloosa did in the later ones. Madison and Chicago offered political economy in the earlier curricula and Oskaloosa in the later one. Chicago offered Latin, German, and French in both curricula, Greek

[1] Madison, Wisconsin, as will be seen, devoted less total time to English although it was offered throughout the four years. Decrease in time was due to reduction in number of recitations per week. In the report of that year the principal of the high school recommended that more time be devoted to English and the report of 1900-1901 shows that this was done.

in the earlier, and Spanish in the later. Madison offered Latin and German in both.

None of the commercial subjects were offered in the earlier curricula of Chicago and Oskaloosa, and only bookkeeping by Madison. The latter offered no commercial work in the later curriculum, while Chicago provided bookkeeping, stenography, and typewriting, and Oskaloosa, bookkeeping, commercial arithmetic, and commercial law.

Oskaloosa offered none of the miscellaneous subjects. In the case of Madison, the older subjects were displaced by a meager offering of pedagogy and drawing. Psychology took the place of mental philosophy in the curricula of Chicago.

Madison offered neither commercial nor industrial subjects. Oskaloosa offered the former and Chicago both. The latter city was one of the few leaders in the industrial educational development which has made such rapid progress during the last decade.

PART II

CONDITIONS AND CHANGES IN SUBJECT-MATTER

CHAPTER IX

INTRODUCTORY

In a study of the development of curricula, consideration of the subject-matter used in instruction in the various fields is quite as important as that of the subjects. In fact only by an examination of subject-matter is one able to ascertain the real character of educational opportunity provided by the subjects constituting the curricula under consideration. It is therefore obvious in a comparative study of this kind that subject-matter must receive its due share of attention. Viewed from this standpoint, changes are more radical and important than a study of the subjects alone reveals. It is the purpose of Part II to make analyses of subject-matter taught in the various subjects and to indicate the changes which took place. It should be said in this connection that it is not possible to do more than show the general tendencies which mark the lines of development in the various fields.

Subject-matter will be considered from two standpoints—amount offered and character of material used in instruction. The former has already been considered in Part I in considerable detail and will be treated here only for the purpose of connecting that discussion with the subject-matter of the several subjects.

One of the things revealed by the present study is that fields and subjects differ greatly. In some fields, ancient language for example, very little change either in amount offered or in character of material used has taken place. English furnishes an example of radical changes in literature and little or no change in grammar. In the case of some science subjects, botany for example, important changes have occurred, while in astronomy practically no change is noted.

It is very evident, therefore, that an appearance of unevenness in the treatment of the various subjects is inevitable. Of some subjects, Latin for example, little can be said for the reason that the subject-matter remained practically unchanged. On the other hand, English is an example of a field requiring more detailed treatment in order to make clear the extent and character of the changes which have taken place in the subject-matter used in instruction.

The same general plan of treatment will be followed as in Part I, the various fields and subjects being considered under their appropriate titles.

MATHEMATICS

It has been shown[1] that the amount of time devoted to this field remained practically unchanged throughout the entire period. In view of this, and also as shown by an examination of textbooks, it is probable that no great change occurred in the amount of material offered although t is clear that some diminution took place. Some change, however, is evident in the character of subject-matter. This was brought about in three ways—first, by the decline in importance of trigonometry and the final disappearance of such subjects as analytics, calculus, surveying and navigation, and engineering.[2] It should be said in this connection that the relative importance of trigonometry in 1900 was less than is indicated by Table X since the data were taken chiefly from the curricula of the arger schools. Had this table included data from a proportional number of curricula of the smaller schools, the percentage of the schools offering the subjects would have been correspondingly less.

The first way, then, in which changes took place was by means of elimination. The second way was through an extension of time given to other mathematical subjects, particularly algebra and geometry, resulting in additional material being offered in these subjects. The third, and least important change, was the elimination of material in arithmetic, algebra, and geometry, and the substitution of other content. Clearness in treatment will be best secured by treating each of these subjects separately.

Changes were more pronounced in arithmetic than n either of the other mathematical subjects. A comparison of the textbooks used in the earlier period with those of the later shows that the amount of material decreased and became more simple in character. One of the texts in common use until about 1875 was Ray's *Higher Arithmetic.*[3] This book was an advanced text and contained in addition to the usual arithmetical topics the following: circulating

[1] Cf. Tables XX–XXVII.

[2] Cf. Appendix, Tables A and H; also Table X, chap. vi.

[3] RAY, JOSEPH, *Ray's Higher Arithmetic: The Principles of Arithmetic Analyzed and Practically Applied, For Advanced Students*, 1858.

decimals, aliquot parts, exchanges, accounts current, storage, equation of payments, annuities, series (arithmetical and geometrical), permutations, combinations, systems of notation, duodecimals, mechanical powers, general average, rate bills for schools, allegation.

One of the features of this book was a list of "promiscuous exercises." Two sets of problems were given: fifty examples were to be analyzed presumably for the "mental discipline" derived from the process, and about an equal number was designated "practical examples." The following are typical problems from the first set:

> ⅔ of my money equals ¾ of yours. If we put our money together what part will I own?
>
> I sold an article for ¼ more than it cost me to A who sold it for $6, which was ⅔ less than it cost him. What did it cost me?
>
> At what time between 6 and 7 o'clock are the hour and minute hands 20 minutes apart?

The following are typical of the practical examples:

> How far apart should the knots of a log-line be to indicate every half-minute a speed of 1 mile per hour?
>
> Find the least number which, divided by 2, 3, 4, 5, and 6, leaves a remainder of 1 each time.
>
> Bought eggs on credit, the first time 1 dozen, and each succeeding time 3 more. My last purchase was 7½ dozen. The bill was presented for 120 dozen. How much too large was it?

Scattered throughout the book was a considerable number of problems dealing with business transactions and some emphasis was therefore placed upon what later came to be called commercial arithmetic. On the whole, however, the form of the problems is considered of more importance than the content. In the preface the author says: "In questions of proportion and generally throughout the book, the analytical method of solution has been preferred to mere formal and irrational directions, for no true development of the intellectual powers or satisfactory knowledge of any science can be attained until the spirit of every operation is clearly seen through its form."

Another book of this same general type and still in use as late as 1870, was Greenleaf's *National Arithmetic*.[1] This contains the topics found in Ray's text and also the customary list of pro-

[1] Greenleaf, Benjamin, *The National Arithmetic in the Inductive System: Combining the Analytical and Synthetic Methods Together with the Cancelling System*, 1850.

miscuous examples. He states in the preface that arithmetic has a twofold aim—"a practical knowledge of numbers and the art of calculation and the discipline of the mental powers."

Milne's *Practical Arithmetic*[1] was not so difficult as the texts above mentioned and in reality a grammar-school book. The special topics mentioned in connection with Ray's text are not found in this book. Promiscuous examples, or the familiar puzzle type, are still retained. Robinson's Series were very similar to Milne's in content and arrangement. In one of these texts[2] which seems to have been in common use in the high school and was devoted chiefly to the elementary phase of the subject, allegation is still retained, but the other advanced topics are omitted. The book contains no list of promiscuous examples.

The later editions of the Robinson and Wentworth Series do not differ materially from the earlier editions or from the Milne books. As has been pointed out, the tendency was toward simplification by omitting the more abstract topics and by substituting the more practical problems for the puzzle problems found in the older books. The transition, however, was not sudden and no particular date can be assigned as marking the time when the change took place. Robinson's books were used as early as 1870 and Ray's as late as 1895. The general tendency was to displace the latter type by the former, and this was rather completely accomplished by 1900.

Little need be said concerning algebra. There was practically no change in the character of subject-matter in elementary algebra after the middle of the seventeenth century.[3] The change was in amount of subject-matter used in instruction. Tables XX and XXVII show that the average time devoted to algebra in 1865 was less than one year while in 1900 it was approximately a year and a half. The minimum at the former date was one-half year and at the latter one year. This increase in time means increase in subject-matter as shown by the textbooks, and these constitute the only source of information. College entrance requirements are indefinitely stated and throw but little light upon the question.

[1] MILNE, WILLIAM J., *A Practical Arithmetic on the Inductive Plan, Including Oral and Written Exercises*, 1877.

[2] FISH, DANIEL W. (Editor of Robinson's Series of Arithmetics), *A Complete Arithmetic, Oral and Written*, 1881.

[3] *Cyclopedia of Education*, 1911, I, 92. Textbooks in use 1860-1900 show that the only change of importance in subject-matter had to do with the amount of material used in instruction. Cf. Davies, Loomis, Robinson, Olney, Milne, Wells, and Wentworth texts.

In the earlier years students were admitted only by examination and the requirements are not specific. For example, the University of Illinois in 1868 required a "satisfactory examination in each of the branches ordinarily taught in the common schools of the state."[1] In 1873, algebra is mentioned in the list of subjects in which examinations were required but the extent of preparation is not indicated. Later (1877) the work is specified as "including equations of the second degree and the calculus of radical quantities." This statement of requirements in the subject is repeated in the catalog as late as 1891. This indicates no change in the subject-matter to be offered. The textbooks also show this and further that problems and exercises were more numerous, thereby bringing about a change not in the character of the material used in instruction but merely an increase in the amount of work required.

Geometry, like algebra, has a brief history. "It was from 1850 to 1875 that plane geometry took its definite place in the secondary school."[2] In the earlier type of textbook proofs were given in essay form and there were no exercises provided.[3] This was followed by a text containing exercises and became the typical text in the high school.[4] The next step was the "unit" page; i.e., the material was arranged in steps to aid the eye, one proposition to a page where this was possible.[5] The Wentworth geometry was a pioneer in this respect in this country.[6] These statements represent the only changes of much importance that took place in this subject.

The amount of time devoted to the subject increased somewhat as shown by Tables XX and XXVII. This shows that whereas the average was approximately three-fourths of a year in 1860–65, this had risen to a fraction less than one and one-fifth years in 1896–1900. While the maximum and minimum had increased two-thirds and one-third respectively, the mode had remained the same, one year.

The changes which took place can perhaps be made clear in no better way than by comparing Davies *Legendre*[7] and Wentworth's

[1] *Catalog, University of Illinois*, 1868-69. Entrance requirements.
[2] *A Cyclopedia of Education*, 1911, III, 51.
[3] Smith, D. E., *The Teaching of Geometry*, 1911, p. 72.
[4] *A Cyclopedia of Education*, 1911, III, 32.
[5] Smith, D. E., *The Teaching of Geometry*, 1911, p. 72.
[6] *Ibid.*
[7] The edition of 1862 was used in making comparisons. No exercises and the essay form of demonstration used.

Plane and Solid Geometry.[1] The former is typical of the older type of instruction and the latter of the new. Lists of textbooks do not show that Wentworth was used previous to 1880 and Davies was still in use as late as 1895. In the period 1880–85 the former was used in about one-half and by 1895 in nearly 75 per cent of the schools. Some of the other texts belonging to the older type were Loomis, Olney, and Ray. These were somewhat modified in method of treatment but clearly belong to the older type. Among those adopting essentially Wentworth's method of treatment were the texts of Wells and Welsh.

[1] The edition of 1899 shows the greater contrast in that the original exercises are more extended and the figures tend to greater distinctness in outline. The latter developed into the use of photographs in later books. Wells's *Essentials of Plane and Solid Geometry*, 1898, was very similar to the Wentworth text.

CHAPTER X

ENGLISH

In no other field have the changes been so radical and important as in the field of English. This change is marked in three ways. The first thing that challenges attention in a study of the development of English work in the high school is the increase in the amount of time devoted to the field.[1] It will be observed that the maximum time increased nearly three years, the minimum more than a year, and the mode and average each one year. Next to be noticed is the increasing importance of English as evidenced by the tendency toward greater uniformity among the schools.[2] While the schools are far from being uniform in their practice in 1900, a comparison of the tables cited above shows a marked tendency toward giving Enblish the important place it now occupies. This tendency toward uniformity is also shown in another way. In the earlier years the classical courses frequently required little or no English while requirements as high as three years in this subject were made in the other courses. For example, the classical course of the Ann Arbor high school (1859) required only English analysis.[3] It is also probable that the same course offered by Jacksonville, Illinois (1869), required little English.[4] These schools are fairly representative of the practice during the earlier years.

It is also made clear by a study of college entrance requirements that the earlier college preparatory courses gave very much less attention to English than is the practice at the present time. The increase of attention to the subject is also shown by increase in requirements. For example, in 1867 the University of Illinois required examinations only in orthography, reading, and grammar.[5] As late as 1873 no English requirement is specified except grammar.[6] On the contrary, in 1899–1900[7] this same institution required composition, rhetoric, and literature for entrance and the statement in the catalog specifies that "two years of high-school

[1] Cf. Table XIX.
[2] Cf. Tables XI and XVIII.
[3] Cf. p. 20.
[4] Cf. p. 23.
[5] Cf. *Catalog, University of Illinois*, 1867, p. 24.
[6] *Ibid.*, p. 39.
[7] *Ibid.*, pp. 49-50.

work with five recitations per week will be necessary for the above preparation." Other institutions[1] show the same meager requirements in the earlier years and a gradual increase in requirements to the close of the period.

The third way in which change took place was in the relative emphasis placed upon the different English subjects and in the character of subject-matter. The change in emphasis is shown in Table X and in more detail in the Appendix, Tables A–H inclusive. It is clearly shown in these tables that the relative amount of attention given to grammar and rhetoric decreased while that of literature increased. The status of composition is not so easily determined because it was taught more or less in connection with other English subjects. It is evident, however, that the actual time given to composition increased. The earlier practice was to list it in a footnote of the printed course along with declamation and other general exercises.[2] The later practice of according it a regular place is shown by the fact that it was introduced into the body of the curriculum[3] and in some cases offered as an elective against one of the traditional subjects.[4]

The changes in subject-matter in this field are important and more radical than in most other fields. This is shown by details given in the printed courses of study, by college entrance requirements, and most clearly of all by the textbooks used.

The least change is found in the case of grammar. This was a textbook subject and the texts in use reveal the character of the subject-matter. A comparative study of these reveals that the change which took place was on the whole unimportant. Courses of study show that "Analysis," "English Analysis," and "Sentential Analysis" were terms in common use up to 1875 and they survived even beyond that. These titles fairly represent the character of material and suggest the method of treatment in the older grammars. Welch's text[5] consists of definitions, rules, and abundant material for analysis and parsing. He says in the preface:

> A systematic analysis of the English sentence should hold a prominent rank, merely as a means of mental development.

[1] Cf. *Catalog*, of Indiana University, University of Iowa, Cornell College, and De Pauw University entrance requirements.

[2] Cf. pp. 20, 21, 23, 24, 26, 28, 31.

[3] Cf. pp. 30, 31, 34, 40.

[4] Cf. pp. 30, 40.

[5] WELCH, A. S., *Analysis of the English Sentence, Designed for Advanced Classes in English Grammar*, 1862.

Greene's *Grammar*[1] was very similar both in subject-matter and method of treatment to the text cited above. Clark's *Normal Grammar*[2] was not essentially different from these other books. A system of diagrams was used but this did not change the character of the work. It simply constituted a device probably more or less useful in carrying on the usual type of formal work in analysis and parsing. Except for the use of the diagram in Clark's book no written work is anywhere indicated and the emphases employed in all three books suggest nothing but memorizing definitions and rules and oral exercises in analysis and parsing.

Swinton's book[3] does not differ essentially from the other texts then in use except in the emphasis upon composition. While the author in the preface makes claim that his treatment is not formal, the claim is not justified by the book itself. Mental discipline is stated in the preface as one of the aims in teaching grammar as will be shown by the following:

> The author would state in a single sentence that his aim has been to set forth, in the light of the latest scholarship, the etymology and syntax of the English language and to make this a logical, systematic, and well-ordered prospectus of this great subject with a view to both individual development and wit-sharpening and to the attainment of a fair mastery of the art of speaking and writing our language.

There is bound with this volume a *School Manual of Composition* by the same author. This was also published separately. It is evident that the author places more emphasis than was usual upon written composition as a means of securing drill in grammatical forms. This, however, has to do with method in teaching and not with change in the subject-matter itself.

Reed and Kellogg's text[4] was one of the most widely used books after 1890 as shown by published lists of textbooks. The authors state three aims for the study of a sentence: (1) to give a knowledge of the laws of discourse; (2) to aid in giving ability to translate foreign language; (3) to provide mental discipline. They assert in this connection that the sentence is made the basis of study not from the standpoint of its analysis, but its meaning. Extensive

[1] Greene, Samuel S., *A Grammar of the English Language Adapted to the Use of Schools and Academies*, 1860.

[2] Clark, Stephen W., *The Normal Grammar Analytic and Snythetic: Illustrated by Diagrams*, 1870.

[3] Swinton, William, *A General Etymology and Syntax of the English Language: A Progressive Grammar of the English Language*, 1872.

[4] Reed and Kellogg, *Higher Lessons in English—A Work on English Grammar and Composition: In which the Study of the Science of the Language is made Tributary to the Art of Expression.* 1877, 1885, 1896.

use is made of the diagram as a means of analysis and this seems to have resulted in a continuation of the practice of emphasizing formal analysis and parsing. This conclusion is justified by the contents and method of treatment and is supported by a statement in the preface of the 1896 edition as follows:

> We confess, to some surprise, that so little of what was thought good in matter and method years ago has been seriously affected by criticism.

One reason, no doubt, why criticism did so little to secure reform was that it was confined quite exclusively to statements in the prefaces and found no constructive expressions in the texts themselves, either with regard to contents or method of treatment. A knowledge of grammar as an end in itself and mental discipline, in spite of all statements to the contrary, continued to constitute the chief aims in the teaching of grammar, so far as the texts themselves concerned, to the end of the century. These ideas had become so fixed that composition and later literature were drafted more or less into service to accomplish these aims.

Changes of considerable importance took place in rhetoric. The earlier texts show the relations of this subject to logic, and subject-matter and method of treatment are both largely determined from this point of view. Whateley's *Elements of Rhetorical Composition*[1] is typical of this class of texts. The author claims to have divorced the subject from logic but neither the contents of the book nor the method of treatment justify the claim. The chapter titles are as follows: "Of Propositions," "Of Arguments," "Of Fiction," "Persuasion," "Perspicuity," "Energy," "Elegance," "Elocution." No reference is made to composition, grammatical rules, or forms of speech except in the section devoted to energy. As a matter of fact, it is a treatise on argumentation. Some of the subtopics treated are as follows: presumption pertaining to proof, presumption in favor of existing institutions, presumption of innocence, arguments of cause and effect, how to prepare a sermon, spurious oratory.

Another text[2] of the older type by Alexander Bain shows that the logical viewpoint still prevailed although it is more modern both as to content and method of treatment. More attention is given to rhetorical forms and composition than is found in Whate-

[1] Whateley, Richard, *An Analysis of the Laws of Moral Evidence of Persuasion with Rules for Argumentation, Delivery and Composition.* 1853.

[2] Bain, Alexander, *English Composition and Rhetoric*, 1866.

ley's book. The text is divided into two parts. Part I, "Composition in General," treats of figures of speech, arrangement of words, quality of style, sentences, paragraphing, etc. Part II, "Kinds of Composition," is devoted to narrative, exposition, persuasion, and poetry. This part shows the influence of the logical point of view both in subject-matter and method of treatment.

Haven's *Rhetoric*[1] is another example of the older texts, but suggests very clearly the tendency to emphasize grammatical and rhetorical rather than logical forms. In the preface the author says:

> I would respectfully suggest to teachers that students of rhetoric should always combine practice with study and should always be required to produce either original or selected examples of every form of speech and of every kind of composition and every style described. Once a week the class may present in writing specimens or illustrations of what has been studied during the week. The exercises suggested in Part IV, "Invention" should all be fairly wrought out after the previous parts have been studied. In this way the science and the art are so welded together in the memory as to be of permanent value.

The book is divided into five parts: Part I, "Words." (Emphasis is placed upon the importance of words and direction is given for securing a broader and more useful vocabulary.) Part II, "Figures of Speech"; Part III, "Style"; Part IV, "Invention"; Part V, "Elocution." More than one hundred pages are devoted to figures of speech and about an equal number to composition and style. The following is a good summary of the character of instruction in rhetoric during at least the first half of the period covered by this study:

> Up to about 1880 the work done in rhetoric was of the most formal and artificial sort and was not often accompanied by practical exercises or compositions.[2]

About this time two texts[3] were published which mark a beginning at least of a transition to the second period in the development in the character of subject-matter. This period has been characterized as follows:

> Then came a change in our text books. From about 1885 to 1895, one of the most difficult problems relating to secondary work in English was that of the part played in systematic rhetoric by the correction of "bad" English; i.e., in grammatical and idiomatic expressions. At that time text books most in use

[1] Copyright, 1869.
[2] CARPENTER, G. R., BAKER, F. T. and SCOTT, F. N., *Teaching of English Composition*, 1903, p. 218.
[3] HILL, ADAM S., *Elements of Rhetoric and Composition*, 1878.

concerned themselves largely with exercises of this kind and many colleges made a point of including such texts in their entrance requirements.[1]

The texts above referred to do not, however, represent in any marked way the change of point of view indicated in the quotation, but show the shift of attention from logical to rhetorical forms. A. S. Hill's text has a considerable leaning still to the older type of subject-matter and organization as shown by the emphasis upon "argumentative composition." The text by D. J. Hill emphasizes literary forms to a greater extent and devotes about fifty pages to special forms of composition such as letters, orations, and the like. At the close of the book another fifty pages is given to exercises in style and in the use of punctuation marks and capitals.

Another text by Kellogg[2] which was widely used shows somewhat more clearly the type of work referred to in the quotation characterizing the work from 1885 to 1895. The work is divided into three parts as follows: "Invention," "Qualities of Style," and "Productions." Part I is devoted to the structure of sentences and the material is very similar to that found in Reed and Kellogg's *Higher Lessons in English.* Part II consists in considerable detail in a formal discussion of rhetorical principles. Illustrative material is usually in the form of single sentences indicating the emphasis upon sentence structure and the use of words. Considerable attention is devoted to figures of speech and a knowledge of these is evidently regarded as more important than practice in their proper uses. Part III, devoted to production, occupies about one hundred pages, illustrating the various forms of composition. Of these one hundred pages, however, more than sixty are devoted to poetry and abundant material is used in illustrating its different kinds. Much emphasis is placed upon the classification of poetry under appropriate headings.

The last three books cited represent the type of material used in many of the schools to the close of the century. The relation of rhetoric to composition of a formal sort is emphasized. In fact one of the chief aims apparently of the latter was to provide drill in rhetorical forms. This relationship will be discussed later in more detail.

Textbooks which came into use just at the close of the period indicate the modifications which then took place in character of

[1] HILL, DAVID J., *Principles of Rhetoric and Their Application*, 1878, 1884.

[2] KELLOGG, BRAINARD, *A Text-Book on Rhetoric, Supplementing and Developing All the Senses with Exhaustive Practice in Composition*, 1892. (This text follows closely the plan of the edition of 1880.)

subject-matter and organization. One of these[1] states the point of view thus in the preface:

> That rhetoric in the high school should be regarded simply as a "course" to be pursued and passed and put out of remembrance as quickly as possible is not good either for rhetoric or for composition. In this book, as the name signifies, no such apartness has been recognized. The rhetoric which is found in this book is meant to be the theory of the pupils' practices, nothing more—the explicit statement of principles which are implicit in all successful elementary composition.

The book as a matter of fact deals with the principles and practices of composition and as the authors state, "rhetoric is meant to be the theory of the pupils' practice." Chapter and section titles indicate further this point of view: "External Forms of the Paragraph," "Paragraph Structure," "What to Say," "How to Say It," "In What Order to Say It," "How Much to Say," "What Not to Say." Figures of speech receive only scant attention in six pages of the index, and poetry but thirteen pages. When one compares this text with Kellogg's book, for example, the older viewpoint, with its emphasis upon the formal principles of rhetoric and the use of composition chiefly as a means of drill in learning these, stands out in clear contrast. And after 1885 this viewpoint controlled chiefly in school practice even beyond the close of the century.

Literature is the subject in which the most important changes took place from the standpoints both of amount and character of subject-matter. Table X shows this in terms of percentage and Tables A–H, inclusive, in detail so far as the increase in time devoted to the subject is concerned. It is shown by Table A that at least five of the schools offered no work in literature. A reference to the table also shows that, with one exception, those schools which offered the subject placed the emphasis upon other English subjects. Table H, on the contrary, shows the prominent place given to literature and indicates the increasing importance of the subject.

In a discussion of the character of the subject-matter used in instruction it should be said at the outset that the term "literature" means largely English literature. American literature has received comparatively little attention. For example, in 1865, American literature was not offered in a single one of the schools included in

[1] SCOTT, FRED NEWTON, and DENNY, JOSEPH VELHERS, *Rhetoric, Designed for Use in the Secondary Schools*, 1897.

Table A. This does not quite represent the facts in the case since some of these schools offered reading and the textbooks contained a few selections from American authors. But the emphasis even here was overwhelmingly upon the work of English writers. As time went on more attention was devoted to American literature, but even at the close of the period, Table H shows the decided emphasis still remaining upon English literature. College entrance requirements also show this. For example, the University of Illinois[1] in 1896 required nine classics to be read in high school, six of which were English and three American.

In considering the content of the material used in instruction, three stages in development are evident. It is not possible to say definitely when one of these stages ended and another began since there was considerable overlapping. But from the standpoint of emphasis, at least, there were three rather well-marked stages in the teaching of literature.

The first stage was marked by emphasis upon Select Readings. These consisted of short selections from a relatively large number of authors. Mention of required Select Readings is found in the footnotes of printed courses of study. Reading was regularly taught as shown by the details of the courses.[2] Lists of textbooks contain titles of texts in reading and this shows that the subject was taught as a regular subject. The books themselves show the character of the subject-matter used.[3] Compendiums of literature are also included in lists of textbooks, and they contain material of the same general character as found in the readers.[4]

The work in reading had a twofold purpose—that of training in oral reading and declamation and that of acquainting the student with good literature. The emphasis upon oral reading is shown by the character of the material in the texts, and the almost universal practice of requiring declamation is revealed by the footnotes to the printed courses of study.[5]

Emphasis upon the mechanics of reading is shown by a study of the contents of McGuffy's *Sixth Reader*. About sixty pages are

[1] *Catalog, University of Illinois*, 1896. Entrance requirements.

[2] Cf. Appendix, Tables A, B, and C.

[3] McGuffy's *Fifth and Sixth Readers; The Independent Fifth and Sixth Readers;* Swinton's *Sixth Reader;* Porter's *Exercises in Rhetorical Readings; Standard Fifth Reader* are examples.

[4] Cleveland, *Compendium of English Literature*, 1848, 1874, is an example.

[5] Cf. pp. 20, 22, 23, 24, 25, 26.

devoted to such topics as articulation, inflection, accent, emphasis, reading verse, voice, and gesture. Short selections are furnished in connection with definitions and rules to provide practice in oral reading and speaking. For example, to illustrate the use of the voice in pitch and compass the following examples are given: high pitch—"Gentlemen may cry 'Peace! Peace!' but there is no peace." The following is given as an example of medium pitch:

> Under the spreading chestnut tree
> The village smithy stands.
> The smith a mighty man is he
> With large and sinewy hands
> And the muscles of his brawny arms
> Are strong as iron bands.

Examples are also given of high pitch, slow movement, and so on. Four pages are devoted to instruction in the use of gestures. This book is typical in this respect of the other readers in use. The *Student's Reader*, for example, devotes fifteen pages to general principles of oral reading, with force, pitch, emphasis, inflection, and the l ke, and the *Independent Fifth Reader* devotes attention to similar topics.

The emphasis upon declamatory work, as has been pointed out, is shown by reference to the courses of study. It is also clear that the selections yielded themselves readily to memorizing and oral delivery, if, indeed, many of them were not selected with that specific end in view.

Turning now to the character of the selections from a literary point of view, we find an attempt to furnish a wide range of what was considered to be good literature. In the preface of the *Student's Reader* the author says:

> In this book the attempt has been made to bring together as much and as great a variety of choice literature as a book of this sort can contain. Great care has been taken to secure pieces of positive merit in all respects, and to admit only such. This book is not intended as a treatise on English literature, but is intended to furnish the higher classes in our schools with a class of literature that is at once instructive, interesting, and good taste.

The emphasis upon reading is indicated by the following:

> It is called the *Student's Reader* from the desire to impress the idea that the Reading Lesson ought to be studied.

This book contains 419 pages, of which 325 are given to reading material. An idea of the average length of these selections is indicated by the fact that the 325 pages contain 113 selections, of less than three pages each. The character of the selections can be judged by the titles, some of which are the following: "Expulsion of the Acadians," "The Man Without a Country," "The Universal Prayer," "Washington," "The Bridge of Sighs," "Scene from Henry IV," "Lay of the Last Minstrel," "The Pied Piper of Hamlin," "Faithless Sally Brown," "Contest with a Cannon," "The Tempted Scholar," Cicero's "Impeachment," "Thanatopsis," "Lycidas," "L'Allegro," "Alexander's Feast," "Intimations of Immortality."

McGuffy's *Sixth Reader* devoted 400 pages to 150 selections representing more than 100 authors. *The National Speaker*, while intended primarily to furnish material for declamatory work, contains material of the same general character as contained in the two texts cited above. This book devotes 200 pages to 109 selections. One hundred and eight pages are given to 15 "dialogues, familiar and dramatic." The title of another of these books is *Literary Reader*.[1] This book has about 400 pages containing 179 selections and representing 68 authors. The preface contains the following statement:

> So far as gradation is concerned, this book is intended to fill the place of the *Sixth Reader*. In the original catalogue of the common schools, literature holds practically but a homely place, but public sentiment has fortunately changed touching this matter within a few years; in the hope of further establishing it in its true place in the public schools, this book has been prepared.

The author claims the book to be uncommon in two respects: (1) in the introduction of a liberal representation of American literature; and (2) because of the use of the writings of scientists. Referring to the latter he says:

> This feature of the work seems to make a not undue acknowledgment of the great love of science in these times and it is also a welcome addition to the treasures of literature.

It seems that he is justified in the claim made for the book in both particulars. Other compilers gave little attention to American literature and practically none to scientific writings.

As has been said, no approximate date can be given when the emphasis shifted from the literature itself to its history. From the first, more or less attention was given to the biography of authors, and this for the most part constituted the so-called history of litera-

[1] CATHART, GEORGE R., *Literary Reader: Typical Selections from Some of the Best British and American Authors from Shakespeare to the Present Time*, 1875.

ture. Spaulding's book[1] is an exception to this rule, and while lists of textbooks show that it was used, its use was not general. The introductory chapter covers twelve pages devoted to a brief discussion of the four periods of English history as follows: Roman period to 449, Anglo-Saxon period to 1069, Middle ages to 1509, Modern times to 1852. The plan of the book divides the history of English literature into these four periods and representative authors, of each period were selected. For example, for the period ending 1509, he gives short selections to illustrate the various types of literature. No biographies are given except brief statements in footnotes. The book is devoted chiefly to a discussion of the events of the period and to brief selections of literature which indicate the spirit of the times. The selections chosen are largely those which are directed against some evil practice. The book undertakes to interpret the social and political life of each period of English history.

Another type of texts, the one in more common use, as shown by published lists of textbooks, emphasized the biography of authors. Some of the readers already cited contained short biographies and later books, purporting to be histories of literature, laid such stress upon biography that comparatively little attention was given to writings of the authors. Trimble's *Handbook of English Literature* is an example. In this book more space is devoted to personal biography than to literature.

In referring to the barrenness of the work both in rhetoric and literature, the superintendent of the Chicago schools in his report says:

> The study of rhetoric seems comparatively futile, save in the knowledge acquired of a few terms, and the time devoted to English Literature is often expended on the history of unimportant and forgotten authorities with little appreciation or knowledge of real literature.[2]

An example of the emphasis placed upon the historical aspect of the subject and the persistence of this type of subject-matter is shown in Halleck's *English Literature*.[3] This book contains very meager quotations from the numerous authors in explanation of the types and character of literature produced in the various periods. The biographies of more than one hundred authors are given and a

[1] Spaulding, William, *The History of English Literature with an Outline of the Origin and Growth of English Literature*, 1868.

[2] *Annual Report of Board of Education*, 1883, p. 62.

[3] Halleck, Reuben Post, *History of English Literature*, 1900.

critical analysis made of their writings with, as said before, only meager quotations from the literature. In an appendix is given a "supplementary list of minor authors and their chief works." More than two hundred names are given with dates of birth and death of each and the titles of literary productions.

The third stage is marked by an emphasis upon "classics." This means that emphasis was shifted from the writer to his writings and that wholes were substituted for fragments of literary productions. No date can be fixed for the beginning of this movement, but about 1885 marks the time when this sort of material came into use and by 1890 its use was quite general. The older kinds of material, however, persisted, particularly the historical type, until the close of the century.

College catalogs in their entrance requirements and the printed courses of study of the high schools show clearly the growth in importance of this class of material after the date given above. The University of Illinois[1] did not make any entrance requirement in literature as late as 1892, but gave notice that the following requirements must be met in 1893:

> In 1893 longer essays will be required (except from these offering Greek) upon subjects drawn from the following works: Shakespeare's *Julius Caesar*, Scott's *Marmion*, Webster's *First Bunker Hill Oration*, Goldsmith's *Deserted Village*, Irving's *The Sketch Book*, or one year's work in French or German will be accepted instead of the English Literature described.

The catalog for 1892–93 contains the same list. For 1894 the following list was required: Shakespeare's *Merchant of Venice*, Scott's *Lady of the Lake*, Emerson's *American Scholar*, Longfellow's *Evangeline*, Macaulay's *Second Essay on the Earl of Chatham*. This statement follows the list: "Real equivalents for any of these works will be accepted." It is clear that, up to this time, these masterpieces were used only as a basis for composition work. The catalog[2] for 1895–96 makes specific requirements as follows:

> Each candidate is expected to have read certain assigned masterpieces and will be subjected to such an examination as will determine whether he has done so.

It will be observed that no mention is made of requiring an essay[3] and an examination is substituted therefore. The requirements in English literature are as follows and change from year to year:

[1] Cf. *Catalog, University of Illinois*, 1892. Entrance requirements.

[2] The catalog specifies that candidates will be required to write an essay "correct as to punctuation, etc." but does not indicate the nature of the content.

[3] Cf. *Catalog, University of Illinois*, 1895-96. Entrance requirements.

1896, Shakespeare's *A Midsummer Night's Dream*, Defoe's *History of the Plague in London*, Irving's *Tales of a Traveler*, Scott's *Woodstock*, Macaulay's *Essay on Milton*, Longfellow's *Evangeline*, and George Eliot's *Silas Marner*; 1897, Shakespeare's *As You Like It*, Defoe's *History of the Plague in London*, Irving's *Tales of a Traveller*, Hawthorne's *Twice-Told Tales*, Longfellow's *Evangeline*, and George Eliot's *Silas Marner*; 1898, Milton's *Paradise Lost* (Books I and II), Pope's *Iliad* (Books I and XXII), "The Sir Roger de Coverley Papers" in the *Spectator*, Goldsmith's *The Vicar of Wakefield*, Coleridge's *Ancient Mariner*, Southey's *Life of Nelson*, Carlyle's *Essay on Burns*, Lowell's *Vision of Sir Launfal*, Hawthorne's *House of the Seven Gables*.

It will be seen that the lists for 1896 and 1897 are identical except as follows: *As You Like It* is substituted for *A Midsummer Night's Dream* and *Twice-Told Tales* for *Woodstock* and *Essay on Milton*. The list for 1898 requires nine selections as against six for 1897 and seven for 1896. Other institutions made similar although not identical requirements. DePauw University made the following announcement in the catalog for 1893–94:[1]

> In 1894 and thereafter an additional[2] semester's work will be required in Composition and Rhetoric with written exercises in capitalization, punctuation, paragraph, and sentence structure. The course in literature will include the following masterpieces with the writing of papers and essays on subjects drawn from them as a basis of criticism: Scott's *Marmion*, Longfellow's *The Courtship of Miles Standish*, Irving's *The Sketch Book*, Dickens' *David Copperfield*, Defoe's *History of the Plague in London*, Goldsmith's *Vicar of Wakefield*, George Eliot's *Silas Marnor*, and Webster's *Bunker Hill Oration*, or equivalent.[3]

The University of Indiana[4] made requirements similar to those of Illinois.

To what extent the entrance requirements in English were influenced by what was actually being taught in the high schools is not easily determined. It is entirely clear that some high schools were offering work in literature consisting of material very similar to the entrance requirements above cited several years before the higher institutions adopted the requirements. It is not improbable, therefore, that the agreement on the part of the higher institutions in the general plan was determined somewhat

[1] Requirement in composition is as follows: The candidate will be required to write two biographies of about one hundred and fifty words each as a test of his ability to use the English language.
[2] Cf. *Catalog, DePauw University*, 1893-94. Entrance requirements.
[3] Three semesters' work in English required for entrance in the previous catalog.
[4] Cf. *Catalog, University of Indiana*, 1895-96. Entrance requirements.

by what the high schools were already doing. On the other hand, the lack of uniformity in the details of entrance requirements shows that the work was not standardized by the high schools and that the higher institutions had not yet worked out uniform requirements.

When we turn to the high schools for information concerning the work in literature, we find that the practice of substituting classics more generally for short selections antedates the requirements of higher institutions in this regard. The courses of study[1] of Milwaukee, Wisconsin, as early as 1877 included English Classics. These are, however, not specified and no information is given concerning their number or character. An outline of the work in English in the Laporte, Indiana, high school (1883), contains the ollowing:

> Extracts from Irving, Hawthorne, Longfellow, Whittier, Holmes, Lowell, Thoreau, Emerson, Bryant, Poe, Scott, Wordsworth, Tennyson, Dickens, Thackeray, Ruskin, Macaulay, and Carlyle. Preparation of short biographical sketches of these and other recent writers. Classification of authors and works. Collections of weighty thoughts and beautiful sayings. . . . . Critical reading of one of Shakespeare's plays and of some extracts from Bacon, Milton, Addison, Samuel Johnson, Hume or Gibbon, and Herbert Spencer. A general survey of English literature in short lectures.[2]

It will be observed that with the exception of one play from Shakespeare the work consists of extracts and the emphasis upon biography still holds.

The printed courses of study, however, for the period 1886–90 show conclusively the tendency to substitute classics for extracts. The following statement is found in the school report of Lawrence, Kansas, under the heading English Classics:

> The following course of supplementary reading is outlined for the pupils of the high school, with a desire to acquaint them with standard productions and to implant in their minds a love for choice literature. Junior class: *Lady of the Lake*, *Legend of Sleepy Hollow*, *Miles Standish*, Virgil's *Aeneid* (2 books), *Macbeth;* Middle class: *Snowbound*, *Rasselas*, *Julius Caesar*, *Evangeline*, Bacon's *Essays;* Senior class: *Vision of Sir Launfal*, *Merchant of Venice*, *Paradise Lost* (2 books).[3]

Kankakee, Illinois, high school provided the following list in 1890:

> First year: *Legend of Sleepy Hollow*, *Thanatopsis*, *Deserted Village*, Gray's *Elegy*, *Lady of the Lake*, Campbell's *Pleasures of Hope*, *Merchant of Venice;*

[1] *Annual Report of the School Board*, 1877, p. lxxvii.

[2] Calendar of the Laporte Public Schools for 1883-84, pp. 18-19.

[3] *Annual Report of Board of Education*, 1887, p. 53.

Second year: *Bunker Hill Oration, The Sketch Book, Ancient Mariner, Tales from Shakespeare,* Macaulay's *Warren Hastings,* Dickens' *Christmas Carol, Julius Caesar;* Third year: "Sir Roger de Coverley," *Lycidas, As You Like It, Paradise Lost* (Book I), Tennyson's *Two Voices, Round About Papers, Henry VIII;* Fourth year: *In Memoriam, The Tempest, Modern Painters, Macbeth,* Chaucer's *The Life Squire's Tale, Hamlet.*[1]

Other schools[2] during this period offered similar lists. Some of these are extensive, others very meager. The Grand Rapids list contains thirty-three titles while that of Richmond, Indiana, presents but two, and these are not specified—being simply designated as "two of Shakespeare's plays." The ten years following 1890 show a rapid development in this kind of work. From this time on, the older type of literature declined in importance and a list of classics became a part of the English work. There was lack of uniformity both in the number and character of the classics read but this kind of material had come into general use. College entrance requirements no doubt exerted an influence in the direction of securing some degree of uniformity, but even these lacked uniformity practically until the close of the century.

The following will show the relative importance of some of the masterpieces from the standpoint of frequency of occurrence in the lists of the various schools.[3] The ranking in the order named of the ten highest is as follows:

1. *Merchant of Venice*
2. *Julius Caesar*
3. *Bunker Hill Oration*
4. *The Sketch Book*
4. *Evangeline*
4. *Vision of Sir Launfal*
5. *Snowbound*
6. *Macbeth*
7. *Lady of the Lake*
8. *Hamlet*
9. *Deserted Village*
10. Gray's *Elegy*
10. *Thanatopsis*
10. *As You Like It*

They appear in the reading lists of more than 25 per cent of the schools and the one ranking first being found in nearly 70 per cent of the lists.

It will be seen that Shakespeare's writings constitute five out of the fourteen holding the first, second, sixth, eighth, and tenth ranks, and of the fourteen listed, eight are English and six American.

A second list is given below. These titles were included in the reading lists of not more than 25 per cent of the schools and the

[1] *Annual Report of the Public Schools,* 1890, p. 38.

[2] Geneseo, Illinois, Belvidere, Illinois, Evansville, Indiana, Fairbury, Nebraska, Grand Rapids, Michigan, Richmond, Indiana, as shown by printed courses of study.

[3] The data are furnished by the printed courses of study for the periods 1886-90, 1891-95, and 1896-1900. Cf. Appendix, Tables F, G, and H.

range is as low as 10 per cent in some cases. The arrangement is in the order of frequency.

1. *Miles Standish*
2. *Il Penseroso*
2. *Paradise Lost*
3. *L'Allegro*
3. *Lycidas*
4. *Ivanhoe*
4. "Sir Roger de Coverley Papers" from the *Spectator*
4. *David Copperfield*
4. *Silas Marner*
5. *In Memoriam*
5. *Enoch Arden*
5. *Behavior*
5. *Marmion*
5. *Tales of the Whi e Hills*
5. *Lays of Ancient Rome*
5. *A Midsummer Night's Dream*
5. *Vicar of Wakefield*
5. *Iliad*
6. *Henry VIII*
6. *Among the Hills*
6. *Cotter's Saturday Night*
6. *Chambered Nautilus*
6. *Comus*
6. Bryant's *Favorite Poems*
6. *The Princess*
6. *Saul*
6. *King Lear*

A third list contains those titles that are found in less than 10 per cent of the reading lists. Many of these are not found except in the list of a single school. The purpose of this list is to show the lack of uniformity and the wide range of material used. No attempt is made to arrange the titles in order of frequency.

Prisoner of Chillon
Rasselas
Last of the Mohicans
Warren Hastings
Christmas Carol
The Tempest
Culture
Books and Libraries
Autocrat of the Breakfast-Table
Gettysburg Speech
Sesame and Lilies
Macaulay's *Addison*
Childe Harold
The Faerie Queene
Odyssey (2 books)
Flight of the Tartars
Carlyle's *Essay on Burns*
Aeneid
Plutarch's *Lives*
Hiawatha
Mosses from an Old Manse
Adam Bede
Selections from the *Spectator*
Pickwick Papers
Idyls of the King
Shakespeare's English Historical Plays
The Rape of the Lock
Middlemarch
The Task
Essays of Elia
The Excursion
Venice Preserved
English Traits
Ancient Mariner
Scenes from Clerical Life
Essay on Man
Vanity Fair
Knight's Tale
Alexander's Feast
The Spanish Student
Ladder of St. Augustine
The Alhambra
House of Seven Gables
Representative Men
Essays on Character
Circles
Gifts

Views Afoot
Bigelow Papers
The Cathedral
A Few Thoughts for Young Men Entering Life
A Few Thoughts on the Powers and Duties of a Woman
Lotus Eaters
Rip Van Winkle
To a Water Fowl
Poor Richard's Almanac
Letters of Samuel Mather
Letters to Reverend Lathrop
Boston Letters to Benjamin Webb
The Plowman
The Iron Gate
The Great Stone Face
My Visit to Niagara
The Ship Builders
The Worship of Nature
The Pilgrim Fathers
Essays on Lincoln
Boston Hymn
The Cricket on the Hearth
The Traveler
To a Mouse
To a Mountain
For A' That
Burke's Speeches
Faust
Samson Agonistes
The Divine Comedy
Johnson's *Lives of the Poets*
Uncle Tom's Cabin
Ben Hur
Bitter Sweet
Selections from Katrine
Timothy Titcomb's Letters
Bacon's *Essays*
Tales from Shakespeare
Two Voices
Round About Papers
Modern Painters
The Squire's Tale
Romola
Essay on Lord Bacon
Tom Brown
The Newcomes
Wild Apples
Abraham Lincoln (Lowell)
Character of Washington
The Hunt of the Deer
Succession of Forest Fires
Selected Essays (Emerson)
Adonais
Reply to Hayne
The Whit Murder Trial
Eulogy on Garfield
Legends of New England
The School Boy
Frederic the Great
Compensation
Books
Songs of the Cavalier
Duke of Wellington
Henry VI
Richard II
Works of Patrick Henry
Tale of Two Cities
Fifteen Decisive Battles
Oliver Twist
Tales of a Traveler
Woodstock
Essay on Milton
History of the London Plague
Twice Told Tales
Speech on Conciliation
Life of Samuel Johnson
Sohrab and Rustum
The Closing Scene
The Fire Worshippers
Life and Death of Jason
The Pleasures of Hope
Elaine
Lady of Lyons
Dream of Fair Women
Adams and Jefferson
Othello
Henry VI
Conduct of Life
Chaucer's *Prologue*
Alcestes
Intimations of Immortality
Les Misérables
Buddha
Pompei

Hypatia
The Voyage
Westminster Abbey
Holmes' *Favorite Poems*
My Hunt after the Captain
Lowell's *Favorite Poems*
Burns' *Select Poems*
Fable for Critics
Palamon and Arcite
Macaulay's *Milton*
Reply to Hayne
Pope's *Essay on Macaulay*
Sella
Selections from Ruskin
Selected Poems of Wordsworth
The Coming of Arthur
Guinivere
The Passing of Arthur
Essay on Johnson
Heroes and Hero Worship
Emerson's *Social Aims*
Selections from Browning
Legend of Sleepy Hollow
Death of the Flowers
True Stories of England
The Atomic Theory
Conservation of Energy
The Blind Preacher
Oratory and Oratory
Old Mortality
Battle of Blenheim
Marcella
Social and Present Day Problems
Sketch of Creation
Homes Without Hands
Prince of India
Essay on Character
Geraint and Enid
History of Our Own Times
Forms of Water
Clincote and Time
The Atmosphere
Robert of Sicily
The Arrow and the Song
The Over Soul
Plain Folks
Prince of the House of David

Approximately two hundred titles are contained in the above list. They represent a wide range of themes and for the most part they indicate the fragmentary character of the material typical of the periods preceding 1885. Schools differed greatly in respect to this kind of subject-matter. Some offered a wide range of it and others none at all as shown by the published courses of study. It is evident, however, that it occupied an important place in English work and its prevalence continued to the close of the century.

Two practices prevailed in the use of classics. One was that of securing a wide range of reading, and the other placed the emphasis upon a critical study of a few masterpieces. Higher institutions after about 1895 began to publish two lists of requirements, one for "minute and critical study," and another for "general reading and composition work." In 1895 Indiana University published two such lists as a part of the entrance requirements in English. The language used raises a doubt concerning whether the work was actually required for entrance or merely suggested as desirable. However, it may have been that the lists were as follows: "For minute and critical study"—*Merchant of Venice*, *L'Allegro*, *Il Penseroso*, *Comus*, *Lycidas*, and Maculay's *Essay on Milton*; "for general reading and composition work"—*Twelfth Night*, *Sketch Book*, Scott's *Abbot*, *Bunker Hill Oration*, *Evangeline*, and Macaulay's *Essay on Milton*.[1]

The University of Illinois made similar requirements or suggestions in 1896. The list "for critical study" was the same as that of Indiana except for Macaulay's *Essay on Addison*. The list for "general reading and composition work" contained only *Evangeline* and Macaulay's *Essay on Milton*. The others were as follows: *Midsummer Night's Dream*, *The History of the Plague in London*, *Tales of a Traveler*, *Woodstock*, and *Silas Marner*.[2]

Some of the high schools provide two lists, making in a general way the same distinction as indicated above. In 1900, Emporia, Kansas,[3] published two such lists—one designated to be studied in class, the other at home. Lawrence, Kansas (1891), designates one classic to be read critically in class and three to be read outside of school, "the latter to be tested by essays on same."[4] In 1893 the part of the report devoted to English contains the following statement:

> To familiarize the pupils with the treasures of English literature and to develop thought power, they are given for outside work a list of books on various lines of thought, which are required to be read carefully. Reports are frequently made and questions answered concerning meaning, etc., of authors.[5]

The foregoing represents the character of the work done in a considerable number of the high schools. It is evident, however, that a wide range of reading was neither sought nor secured in many of the schools. In the first place, the lists were meager and comparatively little time was devoted to literature. For example the Belvidere, Illinois, list for 1880 contains but six titles as follows: *Sketch Book*, *Lady of the Lake*, *Merchant of Venice*, *Thanatopsis*, *Bunker Hill Oration*, and *Vision of Sir Launfal*.[6] The point of view is also clearly indicated thus:

> These works are to be studied critically. Unusual expressions, figures of speech, interesting words are all to receive careful attention.

Evansville, Indiana, furnishes another example of emphasis upon the critical type of work. The list is somewhat more extended

[1] Cf. *Catalog, University of Indiana*, 1894-95. Entrance requirements.
[2] Cf. *Catalog, University of Illinois*, 1895-96. Entrance requirements.
[3] Cf. *Annual Report of Board of Education*, 1900, pp. 97-98.
[4] *Annual Report Board of Education*, 1890-91, p. 301.
[5] *Annual Report Board of Education*, 1893, p. 131.
[6] Cf. *Course of Study and Regulations of the Public Schools*, 1889-90, p. 80.

than that of Belvidere, but the selections are all of the literary type in the narrow sense. The statement following the list indicates the point of view:

> To be critically read in class with attention given to the formation of words, construction of sentences, expressions of thought, characteristics of style, and figures of rhetoric used by the author.[1]

In summary it may be said that the emphasis upon classics dates from about 1885. The list of fourteen titles shows the ones which were in most common use, and the second list indicates approximately thirty titles of those used in from 10 to 25 per cent of the schools. The third list shows the lack of uniformity because none of these were taught in 10 per cent of the schools and many of them only in a single school. The increasing emphasis upon the larger wholes of literature is evident. Nevertheless, the practice of using numerous shorter selections discussed on pages 137-140 continued to the close of the century. Two aims were attempted in teaching literature, indicated by the emphasis upon "critical study" and "general reading and composition work." It is clear, however, that the first aim mentioned received the most attention and that even the composition work was dominated by this aim, resulting in an emphasis upon grammatical, rhetorical, and literary forms rather than upon content.

The discussion of composition has been deferred until last because of its dependence upon, and vital relation to, the other English subjects. Before entering upon the consideration of this, the increasing attention given to the subject will be noted.

The subject was given a place in the curriculum of the Boston High School at the beginning of 1821 and was taught more or less in high schools throughout the period under consideration. Not until near the close of the century, however, did it receive the attention at all approximating that which it now receives. Previous to about 1890 it was not generally listed in the course of study, but included in a footnote along with declamation, select reading, music, and other general exercises.[2] There were occasional exceptions[3] to this but the general practice was as stated. The amount of time given to the subject cannot be determined from the general statement found in the footnotes that composition continues throughout the course.[4] The fact, however, that it was listed with

[1] *Course of Study*, 1888.
[2] Cf. pp. 20, 21, 22, 23, 25, 26, 28, 31, 33.
[3] Cf. p. 24. [4] Cf. pp. 21, 22, 28, 31, 33.

other general exercises indicates clearly that it did not receive the attention given to other subjects. Then in some cases the infrequent character of the work is plainly indicated by such statements as the following: "Declamation and composition semi-monthly";[1] "Exercises in declamation and composition weekly throughout the Course";[2] "Beginning with the third year original addresses and essays will be required once in three weeks to the end of the Course."[3] In the later years of the period increase of time is implied from the fact that the subject is given a place in the body of the curriculum.[4] It is also shown by the further fact that one and two days per week were assigned to the work in some schools.[5] Further evidence of increased attention being given to the subject is found in the outlines in English work published in the school reports and in the college entrance requirements.

The composition work, not only in the early schools, but also at a later date, was no doubt of an informal sort in connection with general exercise. Literary societies were maintained and the literary part of the programs was made up of declamations and compositions or essays. "Rhetorical exercises occur every Friday during the fall and winter terms."[6] "Four rhetorical exercises each term to be required of each pupil."[7] "Literary exercises monthly," was a requirement in the Oskaloosa, Iowa, high school in 1876.[8] The Alliance, Nebraska, high school made the following requirement in 1890: "Each member of the third-year class will be required to write at least three essays on subjects chosen by the leader." Madison, Wisconsin, required the "delivery of competitive essays or orations at morning exercises or on graduation day."[9] The Canal Fulton, Ohio *Annual School Report*, 1892, contains the following statement: "During the three years in the high school, literary exercises consisting of recitations, essays, and debates are required." Fredonia, Kansas (1896), required "composition on various subjects during high-school work."

It is evident that composition work as indicated above was of an informal sort and that topics were derived from the reading and

[1] Cf. p. 20.
[2] Cf. p. 21.
[3] Cf. p. 22.
[4] Cf. pp. 27, 28, 29, 34.
[5] Cf. pp. 34, 40.
[6] *Annual Catalog of the Public Schools*, Appleton, Wisconsin, 1886-87, p. 19.
[7] *Annual Report of Public Schools*, Napoleon, Ohio, 1888, p. 29.
[8] *Rules and Regulations*, p. 13.
[9] *Rules, Regulations*, and *Course of Study*, 1896, p. 33.

experience of the pupils. The work was carried on in connection with literary society work, opening exercises, Friday afternoon programs, and commencement exercises. A comparatively large place was given to select reading and declamations, and training in oral expression no doubt received more attention than work in written composition.

Some attention was necessarily paid to the technique of the work in the earlier years, but the formal side of composition was a later development. This earlier practice was to regard composition only in its relation to grammar, and the emphasis upon this phase of the work continued to the close of the century.[1] The formal character of the work in grammar has already been pointed out and in the earlier years composition was evidently regarded chiefly as a means of securing drill in the work in grammar. Textbooks show this both in the titles and in the exercises designated as composition. One of the later books[2] devoted forty pages to composition work, and while some attention is given to practical forms of composition, the chief emphasis even in the latest edition (1896) is upon grammatical forms. College entrance requirements in English as late as 1893 show clearly the survival of this earlier practice.

The next phase in the development of formal work in composition is marked by a shift of attention from grammar to rhetoric. It has already been shown that the older texts which presented the logical aspect of the subject were superseded about 1880 by other texts emphasizing figures of speech, literary forms, and the like. This change in character of subject-matter in rhetoric was accompanied by use of composition exercises as a means of drill in rhetorical forms. In the preface of one of these books[3] is the following statement:

> The cry that comes up from teachers on all sides is that they need something more in the text books, something that after the principles of the sciences have been followed and clearly unfolded shall come on immediately to mark out work for the pupil to do in illustration of what he has learned and shall exact the doing of it, not in the recitation room, but in preparation for it, as appertaining to his lesson.

The third stage in the development of composition work is marked by the emphasis upon its relation to literature. The

[1] Carpenter, G. R., Baker, E. T., and Scott, F. N., *Teaching of English Composition*, 1903, p. 230.

[2] Reed, Alonzo, and Kellogg, Brainard, *Higher Lessons in English*, 1877, 1885, 1896.

[3] Kellogg, Brainard, *A Text-Book in Rhetoric with Exhaustive Practice in Composition*, 1880. This book and the later edition of 1892 were widely used as shown by lists of textbooks published in school reports.

classics served two purposes—furnished themes and provided models of style. The amount of work increased and the pupils were given some practice in writing themes of some length instead of writing single sentences solely for the purpose of illustrating the application of grammatical and rhetorical rules. It is apparent, nevertheless, that the older forms of composition continued to predominate to the close of the century.

One of the evidences of this is the emphasis already pointed out in connection with the discussion of literature, upon "critical and minute" study of classics. Since this point of view prevailed in the study of literature, it would naturally control in composition work. There is also some direct evidence available. The Fort Scott, Kansas, report contains the following statement:

> Each term's work in English requires nine essays upon subjects specified by the instructors bearing upon the work in classics.[1]

It is clear that this had reference to the classics "to be studied critically in class" and not those for general reading since a knowledge of the latter was tested by examinations "at stated times."[2] An explanation is also given of the character of the work to be done in class which also indicates the character of the composition work. The explanation is as follows:

> The phrase to be studied critically in class means careful syntactical and etymological analysis in addition to style, thought, and literary value. The language of poetical structures must be paraphrased, the author's meaning fully brought out, the mechanical forms explained, and choice extracts memorized.[3]

Other courses of study indicate the same character of work in composition. Entrance requirements also show the formal character of the work and the survival of the old emphasis upon grammatical forms. DePauw University made the following requirement in 1893:

> In 1894 and thereafter an additional semester's work will be required in Composition and Rhetoric with written exercises in capitalization, punctuation, paragraph, and sentence structure.[4]

The University of Illinois in 1895 states the following requirement under the caption "Composition and Rhetoric":

> Correct spelling, capitalization, paragraphing, idioms, definitions, and proper use of rhetorical figures.[5]

This statement is repeated for 1899–1900.

[1] *Annual Report*, Ft. Scott City Schools, 1892, p. 63.
[2] *Ibid.*, p. 64.
[3] *Ibid.*
[4] Cf. *Catalog, DePauw University*, 1893. Entrance requirements.
[5] Cf. *Catalog, University of Illinois*, 1895. Entrance requirements.

In spite of increase of attention given to composition and the changes in the character of the work already indicated, it is apparent that the emphasis upon grammatical and rhetorical forms continued. The growth in importance of literature, and particularly the introduction of classics, stimulated the work in composition. The prevalence, however, of the severely critical point of view of teaching literature resulted in narrowing composition work to a mere drill in the use of grammatical, rhetorical, and literary forms. The larger aims and purposes of composition, through correlation with other school subjects and extra-school interests and activities, and the technique of working this out, belong to a later period in its development. This is foreshadowed somewhat by the textbooks published at the very close of the century.

Scott and Denney's book[1] is one of these. The authors state in the preface the following purposes of the book:

> First, it is desirable that a clearer union than has prevailed hitherto be brought about between secondary composition and secondary rhetoric.

The rhetoric referred to has already been explained on pp. 126–128:

> Second, it is desirable in secondary composition that greater use be made of the paragraph than has hitherto been done in the majority of schools. . . . .[1] A third idea underlying the work is the idea of growth. A composition is regarded not as a dead form, to be analyzed into its component parts, but a living product of an active, creative mind. . . . . In working out these ideas, care has been taken to provide illustrative material of a kind that should be thought-provoking, interesting, and valuable in itself, but not too far above the standard of literary practice, material which the pupil can appreciate readily and can turn to account at once in his own written work. . . . . Care has also been taken in the way the text is stated, as well as in the way the exercises are presented, to suggest that the study is pursued for the purpose of acquiring constructive rather than critical power and the authors venture to advise that until chapter iv is reached, minute criticism be avoided; let criticisms be made solely with reference to the matter treated in the current lesson, and to bad English that may be used by the pupil.

The book exphasizes the composition as a whole and abounds in suggestive material and in constructive directions for writing. It differs radically from the older critical type of work which emphasized grammatical and rhetorical forms. As has been said this type of work belongs rather to the years following the close of the period.

[1] Scott, F. N., and Denney, J. V., *Composition-Rhetoric*, 1897.

CHAPTER XI

THE SCIENCES

This field presents a rather confused situation as regards the subject-matter of the various subjects. They differ widely as to amounts and character of change and there is much overlapping due to different points of view presented by textbooks and the continued use of old textbooks in some schools when new books of a different type had been introduced in other schools. In spite of this confusion, however, changes in subject-matter in most of the science subjects is rather marked and these different types of material fall into periods more or less clearly defined.

It has been shown in Table XIX that the average time devoted to this field remained practically the same comparing the period 1860–65 with that of 1896–1900. It will also be observed that at the beginning the average exceeded the mode by approximately one-fourth year while at the close they were three and one-eighth years respectively. This indicates that greater uniformity prevailed in the later years, although there were, no doubt, many small schools that gave comparatively little attention to the science subjects. Table XIX, furthermore, shows that some of the subjects decline in importance and this means, of course, that more attention was given to other subjects in this field.

Taking the schools as a whole then, and the field as a whole, the first way in which science instruction changed was in this shift of attention from some of the subjects to others. Table X should not be interpreted literally in this regard, but it is clear, nevertheless, that a much smaller percentage of schools was offering geology and astronomy in 1900 than in 1865, and that more attention was being given to the biological sciences, and also, through increase of time, to physics.

The most important changes in subject-matter were due to the various aims or points of view which determined the selection of material and its organization, and the emphases employed in teaching. As has been said, there was considerable confusion in this regard and it is only by a careful study of the aims set forth in school reports and in the prefaces of texts and, most of all, an analysis of the subject-matter itself, that one is able to arrive at anything like a correct interpretation of the character of instruction given. Three aims or points of view are clearly revealed.

1. The religious aim, which survived from earlier schools, is still evident in 1860. This was apparently not very important but references are made to it in the prefaces of textbooks, and this practice survived almost to the close of the century. The aim is also revealed by the subject-matter in an occasional text.[1]

2. An aim far more influential than the religious one was the knowledge aim. This really represented two points of view. The first of these emphasized the value of knowledge as such—truth for truth's sake—and to the end that the learner might be regarded as an intelligent person.[2] As one author[3] phrased it in reference to the text, in the preface:

> It includes only that which every well-informed person ought to know of the subject.

The other point of view emphasized the importance of science from the standpoint of its practical utility as distinguished from a knowledge which merely contributed to one's general intelligence. The distinction was not always clear in the statement of aims, and some of the authors who claimed the twofold aim failed to emphasize the so-called practical aspect in the subject-matter itself.[4] Steele's texts,[5] throughout, emphasized more or less the latter viewpoint.

3. The third viewpoint, the controlling one, particularly during the latter part of the period, was that of mental discipline. Whatever else the author claimed as the aim of teaching science, he only infrequently failed to state that discipline was one of the aims, if, indeed, not the chief one. Each of these viewpoints will be discussed in detail in connection with the treatment of the various science subjects.

1. THE BIOLOGICAL SCIENCES

Natural history, as shown by Table X, occupied a relatively important place in the curriculum during the period 1860–65. This is followed by a decline and final disappearance of the subject from the high school. The subject-matter, however, continued as

[1] Hitchcock, Edward, and Hitchcock, Edward, Jr., *Elementary Physiology*, 1860, pp. 420-32.

[2] Hooker, Washington, *Natural History for the Use of Schools and Families*, 1860.

[3] Hooker, Washington, *Chemistry*, 1863.

[4] *Ibid.*

[5] A Series of Science Texts by J. Dorman Steele.

biology and more particularly as zoölogy. The author of one of the texts[1] in use states in the preface the aims in teaching the subject:

> First this study has a practical bearing upon many of the most valuable and extensive occupations of man—agriculture, horticulture, etc.

He further says:

> The practical benefit to be derived from the study of Natural History or, indeed, any of the natural sciences, is the discipline which it gives the mental powers. It develops the perceptive and reasoning powers together thus forming that habit of intelligent observation which marks the possessor, as a matter of course, as a person of extensive information, and is an essential element of success in almost any pursuit in which he may engage.

In spite of the emphasis which he placed in the preface upon the practical value of a knowledge of the subject in its relation to agriculture and horticulture, the book itself gives scant attention to this phase of the subject. The first chapter is devoted to a summarized discussion of the classification of animals. Then a more detailed discussion is given of quadrupeds, rodents, ruminants, etc.; birds of prey, scratchers, wading and swimming birds; reptiles, fishes, and insects of all sorts and descriptions. In fact, a large section of the book is devoted to insects. The text as a whole is descriptive of the various types of animal life, the descriptions dealing chiefly with the physical characteristics of animals although some attention is paid to their habits of life. The emphasis upon the knowledge aspect of the subject without much reference to its "practical bearing upon the occupations of man" is shown clearly not only by the contents but by the lists of questions provided at the close of each chapter.

Another book[2] of this same period was similar in many respects to Hooker's text. It is, however, simpler in content and method of treatment and places somewhat less emphasis upon anatomical structure and classification. The following statement in the preface is a fair characterization of the book:

> Upon the whole, the general design of this publication is to convey to the minds of youth, and of such as may have paid little attention to the study of nature, a species of knowledge which is not difficult to acquire. The knowledge will be a perpetual and inexhaustible source of many pleasures; it will afford innocent and virtuous amusement, and will occupy agreeably the leisure or vacant hours of life.

[1] Hooker, Washington, *Natural History for the Use of Schools and Families*, 1860, p. 211.
[2] Ware, John, *Physiology of Natural History* 1860.

This book like the other one introduces the subject by means of a summarized classification of animals from the standpoint of anatomical structure but does not continue the emphasis. Attention soon shifts to supposed or real characteristics of the different types of animal life. The author discusses modes of communication, education of the senses, reproduction, coverings of animals, their migrations, and habitations. In their relations to man he discusses their education and domestication and gives interesting and naïve accounts of what he calls the artifices of animals. These accounts are mostly of the "we are told" sort, and while interesting are probably not true. His chapter on the mental constitution of animals, their instincts, and intelligence, is on the same plane as the "we are told" sort of stories. The concluding chapter is devoted to the religious value of scientific knowledge. As has been said, this subject, as such, declined and was finally dropped from the curriculum and changes in subject-matter will be discussed in connection with zoölogy.

The subject-matter of zoölogy roughly divided itself into four periods. In the earlier years the material was of the same general character as that already described in the discussion connected with natural history. The tendency, however, was toward the more formal aspect of the subject and the old type of material finally disappears. In the second stage, comparative anatomy was made the basis of the work and anatomical structure and the classification of animals received the emphasis of attention. This point of view was evident even in the earlier books. One[1] of these shows very clearly this emphasis. It abounded in technical terms and gave extensive and minute classifications. Anatomical structure received a large share of attention to the exclusion practically of habits of life and general characteristics of animals. Packard's text[2] is an example of the emphasis upon anatomical structure. Quotations from the prefaces of the various editions will indicate the point of view and method of treatment. In the preface of the first edition the author says:

> Before taking up the book each member of the class should be required to examine a fish . . . .; the pupil should draw it with all the fins expanded; then, with the aid of directions on pages 154–57, by means of a small scalpel, forceps, and scissors, the student should dissect the fish, drawing the heart, stomach, etc.,

[1] Chambers, *Elements of Zoölogy or Natural History of Animals.* Edited by D. M. Reese, M.D., 1866.

[2] Packard, A. S., *Zoölogy,* 1883. Revised in 1885, 1886, 1892.

and a transverse section; a preparation of the brain can be easily made with the aid of a competent teacher. Having thus obtained some notion of the structure of a common vertebrate animal as a basis of comparison, the class can begin to study the book; meanwhile, once or twice a week, if not oftener, taking a laboratory lesson, drawing, and dissecting a star-fish, clam, or fresh water mussel; a lobster or crayfish; a horseshoe crab, locust or grasshopper; and finally a fish, frog, and cat. A small collection of corals, shells, and a few dried or alcoholic insects and skeletons of a fish, frog, reptile, bird, and cat should also be examined and referred to constantly in using this or any other textbook. In this way and with an occasional field excursion after living animals, the study of zoölogy can be made of the highest interest and value, calling out both the observing and reflective faculties.

The preface to the edition of 1885 shows the importance attached to those things which could be of interest only to the specialist.

The most important discovery made since this book was published is that the two lowest mammals, i.e., the duckbill and the Echidna, both lay eggs; . . . . nervous system of the Echinodernis has been found to consist of a delicate sheet lying under the integument.

The edition of the next year calls attention to the following:

The Tunicates are placed in the sub-kingdoms as the Vertebrates; the Merostomata and Trilobites are regarded together, forming a class of Anthropoda called Podostomata; the sub-kingdom Anthropoda is subdivided into six classes; the Molacopoda, Myriopoda, Arachnida and Insecta being regarded as classes, instead of sub-classes as in the former edition. The orders of insects have been increased from eight to sixteen.

The various editions of the text itself show the same technical classificatory treatment as indicated by the prefaces. Anatomical structure is described in detail and the method suggested in the preface of the edition of 1883 indicates the importance placed upon dissection.

The third stage is in reality a broadening of the work of the preceding stage. Anatomical structure still remained the basis of the work but the morphological point of view was emphasized. This type of work placed much stress upon the lower forms of animal life and upon laboratory work. The amoeba, sponge, Hydra, earthworm, mussel, frog, and the like received emphasis to an almost entire neglect of the higher forms commonly found in the older books. Some of the texts emphasized this phase of the subject to such an extent that the courses provided were more truly in animal and plant morphology than biology in the broader sense. Boyer's *Elementary Biology*[1] is an example of this type of

[1] BOYER, F. R., *A Laboratory Manual in Biology: An Inductive Study in Animal and Plant Morphology*, 1894.

book. The disciplinary point of view prevailed as shown by the following quotation from the preface:

> The aim is to develop rather than to inform; hence the laboratory method is more important than the information involved. Accuracy in observation is a prerequisite to accuracy and clearness in description or statement, as well as to logical inference or conclusion.

When one compares the material in this type of text with that of the earlier years of the period the contrast is very striking. There was certainly nothing in these later books which would "afford innocent and virtuous amusement and occupy agreeably the leisure or vacant hours of life."

The fourth stage really lies beyond the scope of this chapter. It was marked by an attempt to combine the earlier natural history type of material with the more formal anatomical and morphological types immediately preceding it. Field work is combined with laboratory work and the emphasis was upon the functional aspect of animal life. Davenport's *Introduction to Zoölogy* (1900) was influential in bringing about the changes which mark the period.

Botany as shown by Table X has occupied an important place in science instruction. It was a short-time subject and except for the change from the three-term to the semester plan the time devoted to it remained practically constant. Attention has already been called to the lack of correlation between this subject and zoölogy after the older type of material called natural history ceased to be taught. Toward the close of the century biology begins to receive attention, but on the whole, botany remained detached from other science subjects to the close of the century.

The teaching of botany may with some degree of accuracy be divided into four periods. The subject was regarded as a premedical study and was offered by higher institutions for medical students. This type of instruction, however, belongs to a time preceding 1860 and the aim has probably had little, if, indeed, any influence in determining subject-matter or method of treatment since that date. The secondary texts were nothing more than abridgments of the more advanced texts and contained merely a less amount of the same kind of material. During these early years the religious aim was among those stated in the prefaces, and in the mind of the author of the book[1] most in use after 1860 this aim seems to have exerted some influence. It is probable that

[1] Gray, Asa, *How Plants Grow*, 1858.

teachers were more or less influenced by it in their interpretations and applications, but there is not much direct evidence bearing upon the question.

The second period is characterized by an emphasis almost to the entire seclusion of everything else upon anatomical structure. The chief aim to be realized in teaching the subject, if one draws his conclusions from the subject-matter and its organization, was to train students in the technique of analyzing and classifying flowers and plants. Much attention was given to a minute description of plants from the standpoint of structure and to a classification of these with reference to kind, genera, and species.

Botany furnishes an exception in the field of science in that two books, as shown by lists of texts published in school reports, were used more than all others combined. Gray's text, already cited above, was used almost exclusively until 1895 and even in the period 1896–1900 it was used in more schools than any other single text and in nearly half of the schools listed in Table H. This book, therefore, constitutes the chief source of information concerning the character of instruction to 1895 and from that date to 1900 for nearly one-half of the schools.[1] The other book[2] belongs to the third period and will be discussed later. It stands next to Gray's text, and these two were used in about 75 per cent of the schools during the period 1896–1900.

Since Gray's text was so largely used it will be taken as a basis for explanation of the character of the subject-matter and method of treatment which characterized the second period. This book was published first in 1858 and continued to be published practically without revision. The book is divided into two parts. Part I contains four chapters having the following titles: chapter I, "How Plants Grow and What Their Parts or Organs Are," fifty pages; chapter II, "How Plants Are Propagated or Multiplied in Numbers," twenty-nine pages; chapter III, "Why Plants Grow, What They Are Made for and What They Do," eight pages; chapter IV, "How Plants Are Classified, Named, and Studied," fourteen pages. Part II consists of "Popular Flora, A Classification and Description of the Common Plants of the Country, Both Wild and Cultivated under Their Natural Orders," one

[1] There were other texts by Gray but this book was the one in use in most of the schools. The other texts by this author do not differ in character of subject-matter.

[2] Bergen, J. Y., *Elements of Botany*, 1896.

hundred and eleven pages. Chapter IV really belongs to Part II since it consists of minute instructions in the art of classifying, naming, and studying plants.

The viewpoint of the author can be stated by quoting from the preface:

Consider the lilies of the field, how they grow: they toil not, neither do they spin: and yet I say unto you, that even Solomon in all his glory was not arrayed like one of these.—Matthew vi, 28, 29. Our Lord's direct object in his lesson of the lilies was to convince the people of God's care for them. Now this clothing of the earth with plants and flowers—at once so beautiful and so useful, so essential to all animal life—is one of the very ways in which He takes care of his creatures. And when Christ himself directs us to consider with attention the plants around us—to notice how they grow, how varied, how numerous, and how elegant they are, and with what exquisite skill they are fashioned and adorned—we shall surely find it profitable and pleasant to learn the lessons which they teach.

"Now this considering of plants inquiringly and intelligently is the study of botany. It is an easy study when pursued in the right way and with diligent attention. There is no difficulty in understanding how plants grow, are nourished by the ground, the rain, and the air, nor in learning what their parts are, how they are adapted to each other, and the way the plants live. And any young person who will take some pains about it may learn to distinguish all our common plants, and to find out their names.

"Interesting as this study is to all, it must be particularly so to young people. It appeals to their natural curiosity—to their lively desire to know about things; it calls out and directs, i.e., educates, their powers of observation, and is adapted to sharpen and exercise, in a very pleasant way, the faculty of discrimination. To learn *how to observe* and *how to distinguish things* correctly is the greater part of education, and is that in which people otherwise well educated are apt to be deficient. Natural objects, everywhere present and endless in variety, afford the best field for practice; and the study when young, first of botany, and afterwards of the other natural sciences, as they are called, is the best training that can be in these respects. This study ought to begin even before the study of language, for to distinguish *things* scientifically, i.e., carefully and accurately, is simpler than to distinguish *ideas*. In natural history the learner is gradually led from the observation of things, up to the study of ideas or the relation of things."

"The first and most important thing for a student is to know well the general plan of a plant and the way it grows, the parts of plants, the uses of the several parts, their general forms, and the names which are used to distinguish them. This is all very interesting and very useful in itself, and it is indispensable for studying plants with any satisfaction or advantage to find out their names, their properties, and the family they belong to, i.e., to ascertain the kinds of plants."

An occasional reference is made to the religious aspect of the subject in the textbook itself as the following will show:

> In learning as we have done, How Plants Grow and Why They Grow, have we not learned more of the lesson of the text placed at the beginning of this book, and of the verses that follow? "Wherefore if God so clothed the grass of the field, shall He not much more clothe you? . . . . Therefore, take no thought, saying What shall we eat? or, What shall we drink? or Wherewithal shall we be clothed? For your Heavenly Father knoweth that ye have need of all these things." And we now perceive that causing plants to grow is the very way in which He bountifully supplies these needs, and feeds, clothes, warms, and shelters the myriads of beings He has made, and especially *Man* whom he made to have dominion over them all.[1]

> In order that the vegetable creation might be adapted to every soil, situation and climate, and to the different wants of the greatest variety of animals as well as to the many peculiar needs of mankind, God created plants in a vast number of kinds. And in order that these should be perpetuated and kept distinct He ordained that each should yield and seed fruit "after its kind." So each sort of plant multiplies and perpetuates itself from generation to generation.[2]

It will be observed from the statements concerning the divisions of the book that about one-half is devoted to the "Popular Flora" and instructions concerning how to classify, name, and study plants. The emphasis of the text is almost entirely upon a study of the anatomical structure of plants and flowers in order to classify them with reference to class, order, or family, genus, and specie. This is carried out in great detail as shown by the treatment of leaves. More than fifty figures are used to illustrate the minute descriptions of the various kinds. More than forty figures are employed to illustrate the descriptions of the forms and kinds of flowers. These descriptions abound in technical terms and a strictly logical order of treatment prevails. There is nowhere any suggestion of the application of the knowledge gained except in gaining more of the same kind. At the close of each section an "analysis of the section" is given. The following is a sample of the analysis:

> Leaves: Their parts—blade footstalk, stipules; simple and compound; structure and veining of leaves—woody or fibrous part, cellular tissue or green

[1] GRAY, ASA, *How Plants Grow*, 1858, chap. iii, p. 92.
[2] *Ibid.*, chap. iv, p. 93.

pulp, epidermis or skin; ribs; veins and veinlets; nerves, so-called; netted veined and reticulated.[1]

This is carried out still farther in the shapes of leaves. Seeds, flowers, stems, and roots are all treated in the same detailed manner.

The author no doubt intended that the student should have opportunity to study plants and flowers first hand as shown by the following statement in the preface:

Let the learners, or the class under their teacher, in the first place go carefully once through the First Part, or at least through the first two chapters, verifying the examples and illustrations given, as far as possible with their own eyes, and searching for other examples in the plants and flowers around them.

He indicates the emphasis upon the subject-matter of the text in the following:

Then they may begin to study plants by the Flora, or Second Part of the book, according to directions given in the last section of Chapter IV.

Probably very little laboratory work was done. There is not much evidence found either way in the printed courses of study but what there is of it is nearly all negative. Some statements are found deploring the lack of laboratory facilities and the purely textbook character of the work, while only very rarely is anything said on the positive side. In these cases the statements are no more detailed than to say that pupils are expected to prepare herbariums consisting of forty or fifty specimens.

The third period is characterized by the emphasis upon the morphology of plants. Bergen's text referred to on page 153 is typical of the books published after 1890, emphasizing the morphological aspect of the subject. The author mentions other phases of botany in the preface such as geographical distribution, vegetable physiology, and vegetable ecology. He says, however:

There is not usually time to take up botanical geography or to do much more than mention the important subject of economic botany, the study of the uses of plants to man. It ought, however, to be possible for the student to learn in his high-school course a good deal about the simpler parts of morphology and of vegetable physiology.[2]

The text itself shows the same emphasis upon morphology as indicated in the preface. The explanation of the term morphology in the preface is a fair characterization of the text.

Morphology, or the science of form, structure, and so on, deals with the plant without much regard to its character as a living thing. Under this head are

[1] GRAY, ASA, *How Plants Grow*, 1858.

[2] BERGEN, J. Y., *Elements of Botany*, 1896.

studied the forms of plants and the various shapes or disguises which the same sort of organ may take in different kinds of plants, their gross structure, their classification, and the successive stages in the history of the germs from which all but a few of the simplest plants are formed.

Thirty-three experiments are called for and much other laboratory work contemplated. There are two hundred and eight figures used to illustrate the descriptive material of the text. The nature of the work is explained in brief as follows:

> One does not become a botanist—not even much of an amateur in the subject—by reading books about botany. It is necessary to study plants themselves, to take them to pieces and make out the connection of their parts, to examine with the microscope small sections of the exterior surface and thin slices of all of the variously built materials or tissues of which the plant consists.

The method of treatment here suggested is further emphasized in Appendix A by a detailed description of how to use a compound microscope. Appendix B supplies an extended list of apparatus and Appendix C indicates the material for study in connection with each chapter. Appendix E is devoted to a detailed discussion of the purpose and use of the notebook. Two books are recommended—one for drawing and one for written notes. The importance of systematized work is stressed and the reason for this is stated as follows:

> It will go far toward training the pupil into a scientific habit of mind if he is required in his notes and his recitations to distinguish clearly the sources of his knowledge.[1]

The point of view of the author, the methods of teaching and learning insisted upon, and the text itself all lead to the conviction that the work was very formal and even highly technical. Knowledge of plant life except in the most narrow sense, certainly was not the controlling aim in instruction. On the contrary, it seems to have been that of mental discipline stated in terms of "training into a scientific habit of mind." The century closed with this type of instruction prevailing in many schools and within a very short time it became practically universal in secondary education. The fourth period will be discussed in Part III.

Physiology, like grammar and arithmetic, was taught in the grades as well as the high school. It has therefore never been regarded as distinctively a secondary subject as have the other biological sciences and clear lines of demarcation between elemen-

[1] Bergen, J. Y., *Elements of Botany*, 1896. Appendix E.

tary, high-school, and college texts are not always drawn. In consequence of this, the work is not standardized and varied from very elementary in character to that of college grade, depending upon the particular kind of textbooks in use. For example, one school would use Martin's *Human Body*,[1] a college text, while another would use *The Eclectic Physiology*,[2] an elementary text. On the whole, however, the latter class of books as shown by published lists of texts, were in most common use.

In a general way physiology has passed through stages similar to those of the other biological sciences. For example the religious aim was more or less common in the earlier years. The knowledge aim functioned considerably throughout the whole period, i.e., knowledge as an end in itself. The other aim which controlled more or less was the so-called practical or hygienic aim. This, however, came rather late, not much emphasis being placed upon it until near the close of the century. The subject-matter which received the most attention throughout the whole period was of the anatomical sort.

The authors of one of the earlier books[3] state the following in the preface:

> This work is offered to the public in the hope that it has some desirable features as a textbook not found in any of the able elementary works on anatomy and physiology now extant. One is the introduction of more microscopic work in anatomy than is usual. Another is the large addition of comparative anatomy which has now become a science of great importance. The third is the religious application of this science.

The author states that he has attempted to give a condensed yet clear exposition of the leading principles and facts. What particular value these would have for anyone save a physician or a teacher of anatomy is not readily seen. In this book one hundred pages are devoted to a study of bones; fifty pages to the muscles; fifty pages to the nutritive system, and still another fifty pages to the circulation of the blood. The other usual topics follow with less space devoted to each. The emphasis throughout the book is upon anatomy of a rather technical sort. Considerable attention is given, as has been promised, to "comparative anatomy and physiology," and finally about fifteen pages are devoted to what

[1] MARTIN, H. NEWELL, *The Human Body: An Account of Its Structure and Activities and the Conditions of Its Healthy Working*, 1880 and 1890.

[2] BROWN, ELI F., *The Eclectic Physiology for Use in Schools*, 1884.

[3] HITCHCOCK, EDWARD, and HITCHCOCK, EDWARD JR., *Elementary Physiology*, 1866.

he calls "religious inferences from anatomy and physiology." His discussion falls under these general topics as follows: I. Proofs of the existence of God. II. Proofs of divine benevolence. III. Anatomy and physiology furnish presumptive evidence that the world is in a fallen condition. IV. Anatomy and physiology furnish proof of divine unity. V. Anatomy and physiology disprove the atheistic hypothesis that the development of animal organs is the result of mere law. He attacks what he calls the development hypothesis as follows:

> This hypothesis supposes that the organs were not contrived and constructed by an intelligent mind for the uses to which they are applied but that the influence of the living mass of almost amorphus matter led to such efforts as ultimately to form an organ.[1]

VI. Anatomy and physiology show the unreasonableness of objecting to mystery in religion.

> The cases of mystery in anatomy and physiology are more striking than in religion.[2]

The emphasis upon hygiene, theoretically at least, began about 1875 with the publication of Hutchison's text. The author was a physician and the book clearly shows the influence of the professional point of view. Anatomical structure comes in for considerable attention but more emphasis is given to physiology than was the case in Hitchcock's book. Its technical character is illustrated by considerable attention being given to the use of the microscope and to dissection. As a matter of fact, about all of the so-called practical subject-matter in the book is placed in an appendix and deals with poisons and their antidotes.

Another book[3] in quite general use, published ten years later, contains the same general character of subject-matter and the method of treatment is very similar to the book described above. This book is in fact a text on anatomy, very little attention being given to hygiene. The emphasis is upon descriptions of the various parts of the human body and the physiological processes that go on. For example, in the chapter on the digestive organs and digestion, most of the discussion is devoted to an explanation of the digestive process with but little reference to the health side of the matter. A great deal of emphasis is placed throughout the book upon dis-

[1] Elementary Physiology, Hitchcock, Edw. and Hitchcock, Edw. Jr., 1866, p. 431.
[2] *Ibid.*
[3] CUTTER, JOHN S., *Comprehensive Physiology, Anatomy and Hygiene*, 1885.

section and the use of the microscope. About twenty pages at the close of the book are devoted to the care of the sick and emergency cases. This is intended to be of a practical sort, but the language and the instructions are such that it is very doubtful whether anyone except a physician or a trained nurse would be able to get very much out of it.

The books began soon after 1880 to include a treatment of the effects of stimulants and narcotics and to place relatively more emphasis upon hygiene. The *Eclectic*, for example, devotes nine pages to "Elementary Sanitary Science." This chapter includes such topics as, what to eat and drink, clothing and cleanliness, pure air, and care of the sick. Four pages are given to "Emergency and Accident" and fourteen pages to "Alcohol—Its Effects upon the Body and Mind." Short paragraphs throughout the book are devoted to hygiene of the skin, of the eyes, of the ears, and the like.

2. THE PHYSICAL SCIENCES

This constitutes the most important branch of the sciences from the standpoint of the percentage of schools offering science as shown by Table X. Physics was the one constant among the sciences and chemistry was offered in more than three-fifths of the schools[1] at the close, and the average was above this for the entire forty-year period. Theoretically, at least, the points of view controlling in the biological sciences obtained here, except the religious, and that seems to have had no influence in determining the selection of subject-matter or emphasis in instruction.

Physics, natural philosophy being the older term, was the one science taken over from the earlier schools whose place was firmly established in the curriculum of all the high schools and whose increasing importance is shown by any considerable increase in time devoted to the subject.

The teaching of physics was controlled by two aims and the character of instruction was determined by the emphasis upon one or the other of these. Roughly speaking, the knowledge aim controlled during the first twenty years and the disciplinary one thereafter. The earlier period was really characterized by an attempt, theoretically at least, to realize both aims, while in the later period, both theoretically and practically, the disciplinary controlled almost entirely.

[1] Chemistry, as stated in Part I, was confined to the larger schools in a greater degree than physics, and this percentage would not represent the exact status if the same schools were represented proportionally in the tables.

As pointed out in connection with the discussion of the aims in teaching the science subjects, pages 147–8, the knowledge aim was really a twofold one. Knowledge was valuable for its own sake and also because of its use in the practical affairs of life. The earlier books all emphasized in their prefaces the importance of knowledge from both these standpoints. Only an occasional book, however, made good in the text the promise made in the preface. In commenting upon textbooks in physics, Professor Woodhull says:

> In 1850, in the preface of his Natural Philosophy, Wells wrote: "The principles of physical science are so intimately connected with the arts and occupations of everyday life, with our very existence and continuance as sentient beings, that public opinion at the present time imperatively demands that the course of instruction in this subject shall be as full, thorough, and complete as opportunity and time will permit." . . . . Of the fifty or more high-school texts written in the last fifty years there is scarcely one which has not repeated the sentiment in its preface. When, however, we come to look into the body of the text we are invariably disappointed. Those who have written within the last fifteen years have noticeably been circumscribed in this matter.[1]

Examination of textbooks reveals that the above is a fair characterization, not only of later books, but also of some of the earlier ones. On the whole, however, the period preceding 1880 was characterized by a type of instruction which emphasized the more practical phase of the subject. After that date attention was shifted to laboratory work involving the performing of experiments by pupils, and instruction became not only formal but also rather barren of useful knowledge of any sort. Commenting upon this contrast, Professor Woodhull says:

> Wells, under the head "Strength of Material" gives an interesting and illuminating account covering eight pages, dealing with hollow bones of animals, hollow stalks of grain, columns of buildings, and other interesting things. Within the last fifteen years, however, the exigences of college preparation have substituted for all this a laboratory exercise in which each pupil attempts to find out the number of grains required to break a piece of small wire. We certainly need common sense instruction about strength material.

All of the earlier books, however, do not emphasize the "philosophy of common things." Comstock's text[2] is an example. It is almost wholly descriptive and without any practical applications of the facts learned. There are no mathematical problems and the

[1] WOODHULL, J. F., *The Teaching of Physical Science*, 1910, p. 5.

[2] COMSTOCK, J. L., *A System of Natural Philosophy*, 1840. There were later editions not differing essentially from the edition of 1840.

book abounds in cuts and drawings to illustrate the principles studied. It is evident that no experiments are performed by the pupils but it calls for or at least suggests considerable demonstration work to be given by the teacher. The knowledge aim controls and is of a sort that "every well-informed person ought to know," but with no suggestion of practical application.

Parker's Philosophy[1] is similar to Comstock's except that it contains a number of mathematical problems. It abounds in definitions, and the general plan of organization is that of question and answer. There is no suggestion anywhere in the book of emphasis upon a knowledge of "common things" as was the case in Wells's text and a later one by Steele. No experimentation is required of students and probably no demonstration work expected of the teacher. This book shows that it belongs to the older order by including about sixty-five pages of subject-matter belonging to astronomy.

Cooley's text[2] was one of the books published before 1880 that emphasized the disciplinary aim. In the preface the author says:

> The great aim of this little book is to present the most elementary facts of "Natural Philosophy" in such a way as to cause the student to thoroughly and consistently observe phenomena and to draw inferences from what he observes. The study is not only easy and interesting; it is also in the highest degree beneficial to the young partly because of the value of the facts which it imparts but even more on account of the mental power it develops. The object of primary education should be to discipline the senses to habits of quick and accurate observation and the mind to the habit of forming correct judgments from the facts which the senses reveal. Natural Philosophy furnishes abundant material of the most excellent kind by means of which this may be accomplished.

The author states that the subject is to be introduced by means of easy experiments with phenomena of common occurrence and the pupil called upon to notice what these suggest. This is to be followed by a precise and accurate statement of the principle involved. Many of the paragraph titles are in the form of questions. The experiments are of the most simple sort and seem to be rather remotely related to the experience of the average high-school student. It is evident, however, that demonstration by the teacher and no experiments by the student is the real intent of the author. On the whole the book is concrete and contains a wide range of information.

[1] *Parker's Philosophy*. Revised by George W. Plympton, 1871.

[2] Cooley, Roy C., *Natural Philosophy for Common and High Schools*, 1872.

Another book[1] of the same period emphasizing the general knowledge aim and also experimentation as a method is one by Rolfe and Gillett. It consists of two parts also published as separate volumes. Part I is entitled "Elements of Natural Philosophy" but it might better be "Mechanics" since it treats quite exclusively that phase of the subject. The title to Part II is "Light, Sound, and Heat" and is justified by the contents. The book as a whole is evidently intended to give general information without any suggestions relating to its application. Concerning experiments, the authors say in the preface:

> As the principles of physical science are all established by fact and observation, the method has been adopted in this course of first establishing the fact by experiment when this is possible, and then drawing out the principle. From their experience as teachers, the authors strongly recommend that each lesson be explained and illustrated with the class before being given out to be studied.

The emphasis, however, upon the descriptive work of the text is shown by the list of questions at the close which suggest no problems or experiments but call merely for a knowledge of the contents of the book.

A book[2] in wide use after 1870 and in fact still in use in a considerable number of schools in 1900 emphasized the more familiar and practical aspects of the subject. The author wrote in the preface of one of the earlier editions (1873) as follows:

> From the multitude of principles only those have been selected which are essential to the information of every well-read person. . . . . The aim is to lead young people to become lovers and interpreters of nature. . . . . Choose simple experiments within the reach of every pupil at home.

This is one of the books in which the text fulfils in large measure the promise contained in the preface. There was considerable emphasis upon "common things" and the experiments were simple, dealing with material in which the pupil would likely be interested and with which he would be more or less familiar. The whole method of treatment, however, is clearly of the descriptive type. The intention of the author in this regard is shown by the following under "Suggestions to Teachers":

> Scholars are expected to obtain information from this book without the aid of questions as they almost always do in their general reading. When the subject of the paragraph is announced, the pupil should be prepared to state all he knows about it.

[1] Rolfe and Gillett, *A Book of Natural Philosophy*, 1868.
[2] Steele, J. Dorman, *Fourteen Weeks in Natural Philosophy*, 1868.

At the close of the book four pages are devoted to descriptions of simple apparatus and a list of easy experiments. The reference to the importance of experiments found in the prefaces of the books between 1870 and 1880, and even earlier, begin to find expression in the texts themselves after 1880. The fact that laboratory work is receiving some attention, and also the prevalence still of textbook methods, is shown by the following quoted from *Circular of Information, Bureau of Education, 1880*:

In high schools and academies the teaching of chemistry and physics varies between widely separated limits. In the great majority of cases mere textbook work is done, only a few experiments being performed by the teacher. In some instances the scholars have laboratory practice in both subjects, the work in chemistry extending through a full year and including the outlines of analysis. Between these extremes all conceivable variations are to be found. . . . . That laboratory practice is feasible for young people, all teachers familiar with that kind of instruction will testify. But as there are some who still doubt the practicability of laboratory methods, a little evidence may be presented here.[1]

Following this is a brief summary of the results of an investigation dealing with the prevalence and character of laboratory work. No distinction is made, however, between the work in physics and that in chemistry. Fifty schools report that laboratory work is "permitted." About double that number require it. The following are some of the extracts from these reports: "Thirty hours required—work elementary;" "twenty-four hours required—four hours per week for six weeks;" "only simple experiments are required;" "laboratory once a week;" "each pupil does a little laboratory work;" "the pupils have limited practice in a small laboratory."

Textbooks even before this time began to show the emphasis upon laboratory work which had begun in chemistry at an earlier date. After 1885, the older type of instruction had ceased except as it survived through the use of such texts as Steele's. The books published after this date show conclusively that the era of supremacy of the "Science of common things" had passed and that the new era of formal instruction had taken its place. Gage's text[2] was a typical one. The following from the preface indicates the author's point of view:

An experience of about six years in requiring individual laboratory work from my pupils has constantly tended to strengthen my conviction that in this way alone can a pupil become a master of the subjects taught. . . . . With a text-

[1] *Circular of Information, No. 4, Bureau of Education*, 1880.
[2] GAGE, A. P., *Introduction to Physical Science*, 1887.

book prepared on the induction plan, and with classroom instruction harmonizing with it, the pupil will scarcely fail to catch the spirit and method of the instigator, while much of his limited time may profitably be expended in applying the principles acquired in making physical measurements.[1]

A brief statement of my method of conducting laboratory exercises may be of service to some until their own experience has taught them better ways.[1] As a rule the principles and laws are discussed in the classroom in preparation for subsequent work in the laboratory. The pupil then enters the laboratory without a textbook, receives his notebook from the teacher, goes at once to an unoccupied (numbered) desk containing apparatus, reads on a mural blackboard the questions to be answered, the directions for the work to be done with the apparatus, measurements to be made, etc. . . . . These notebooks are deposited in a receptacle near the door as he leaves the laboratory. Nothing is ever written in them except at the times of experimenting. These books are examined by the teacher; they contain the only written tests to which the pupil is subjected, except the annual test given under the direction of the Board of Supervisors.

The book contains three hundred and fifty-five pages and two hundred and forty-four experiments are provided. Numerous exercises are given consisting of questions and problems and at the close is a list of review questions. These are in keeping with the subject-matter and method of treatment and indicate the formal character of the work. They show the emphasis upon such matters as the "number of grains required to break a piece of small wire."

Carhart and Chute's texts[2] are similar to Gage's book in all essential respects. A great deal of emphasis is placed upon the mathematical phase of the subject and the questions and problems indicate the same general character of material and plan of treatments. Other texts of this period show the absence of the older type of subject-matter, and of the practical point of view, in the application of principles to matters of common interest in the fields of vocational activity.

Professor Woodhull[3] quotes from several authors of textbooks to indicate the points of view prevailing in the physical sciences near the close of the century and especially to show the emphasis upon laboratory work. Some of these, however, show a beginning of the reaction against the formal and barren character of the work.

Chemistry has suffered from the irrepressible wave of laboratory madness which has swept over the whole educational world. . . . . Nothing too severe can be said against the mechanical and demoralizing system of notebooks with

[1] Dr. Gage was instructor in physics in the English High School, Boston.

[2] Carhart, H. C., and Chute, H. N., *Elements of Physics*, 1896; *Physics for High School Students*, 1901 and 1907.

[3] Woodhull, J. F., *The Teaching of Physical Science*, 1910, pp. 9-11.

"operations, observations" and "inference" headings. They are wholesale breeders of dishonest and superficial work. [Torrey.] A few years ago it seemed necessary to urge upon teachers the adoption of the laboratory methods to illustrate the textbook; in not a few instances it would now seem almost necessary to urge the use of textbook to render intelligible the chaotic work of the laboratory. [Carhart and Chute.] Physics in too many of our schools ranks as a most difficult subject. . . . . An elementary presentation of physics should begin by resuming what might be called the experience of the average lad of sixteen years. . . . . The demand, therefore, is not so much for new facts, or for sheer facts of any kind, as for an orderly arrangement and an ability to use these facts. [Crew.]

Chemistry followed much the same line in its development as physics except that laboratory work came in earlier and the narrow, technical type of work also developed earlier. Gage remarks of his physics text (1882) that "chemistry has been taught by the laboratory method for twenty years" and urges the introduction of laboratory method in physics.

Two of the earlier texts agree in that they are descriptive and call for comparatively little experimentation. In some other respects they differ. Comstock's text[1] follows very closely the method of treatment found in his physics text.[2] It is evidently intended to give a rather comprehensive knowledge of chemistry by means of description. Numerous cuts and drawings are provided. There is an absence of experiments called for although not in the same degree as in the case of his physics. It abounds in definitions and explanations of chemical phenomena.

Hooker's Chemistry[3] (1863) contains the following in the preface:

> A large proportion of the experiments can be treated with very simple apparatus.

The experiments are very simple and not numerous. The text is primarily descriptive and makes good the claim of the author that it is largely a chemistry of "common things." The practical concrete nature of the book is shown by the topics treated as follows: vegetation—the seed, its growth, source of carbon in plants, organic food of plants, water in plants, etc.; soil—soil in manures, humus, how soil was originally made, different kinds of soils, rotation of crops, manures, volatile substances, bone dust, lime, gypsum, vegetable refuse; products of vegetables—vegetable acids, tonic acid, coloring matter, oils and fats, glycerine, soaps,

[1] Comstock, J. L., *Elements of Chemistry; Designed for the Use of Schools and Academies*, 1861.

[2] Cf. p. 161.

[3] Title-page destroyed.

liniment, emulsion, varnish, oils, petroleum, camphor; fermentation—fermentation in bread, how ether is obtained, vinegar, sour bread.

At the close of the book is a list of questions covering the text and occupying about twenty-five pages. While they do not call for applications of knowledge gained and are simply tests upon the contents of the book, they clearly emphasize the chemistry of common things.

Steele's book[1] was very similar in method of treatment to his work on physics.[2] In the preface of the former he says:

> Unusual importance is given to that practical part of chemical knowledge which concerns everyday life.

He maintains that throughout the study of chemistry a clearer relation should be established between the "schoolroom and the kitchen, farm, and shop."

The emphasis upon laboratory practice which began about 1880 in physics had its beginning in chemistry at an earlier date and its influence upon subject-matter extends over a longer period. The effect of this was to direct attention away from the value of content, from the things which "every well-informed person ought to know" and from its relation to "kitchen, farm, and shop" to the technique of laboratory work.

This shift of emphasis is foreshadowed by some of the texts already cited and is shown clearly by the books published after 1880. Greene's text[3] published in 1884 is rather typical of the books of that date. The author was a high-school teacher and the book no doubt fairly represents what was actually being taught in chemi stry. There is no suggestion in the book of relating the work of the classroom to vocational activities of any sort. The treatment if formal and numerous experiments are called for which indicate the emphasis upon laboratory work.

Another book,[4] and one widely used, belongs to the same type of texts as the one cited above. The author says in the preface:

> It should be remembered that the object of the course laid down in this book is not to make chemists but to help develop sound minds and at the same time to awaken an interest in the subject of natural phenomena of great importance to mankind. This book represents the ideal in the teaching of chemistry in that it contains a relatively large number of experiments.

[1] STEELE, J. DORMAN, *Fourteen Weeks in Chemistry*, 1869.

[2] Cf. p. 243.

[3] GREENE, WILLIAM H., *Lessons in Chemistry*, 1884.

[4] REMSEN, IRA, *Elements of Chemistry: A Text for Beginners*, 1887.

In the two hundred and forty-two pages constituting the text proper, one hundred and thirty-two experiments are called for. Neither the descriptive material nor the experiments, however, contain any hint of the chemistry of "common things" such as was found in the earlier books. At the close about fifteen pages are devoted to questions and problems intended to supplement the experiments contained in the main body of the text. A comparison of this book with that of Hooker or Steele shows clearly the two periods into which chemistry instruction falls. Other texts[1] after 1885 show the same emphasis and general method as Remsen's book.

In speaking of the character of the work of physical science during the last years of the nineteenth and the first years of the twentieth century, Professor Woodhull says:

> Certainly whatever we may profess in the preface of our textbooks, we are actually doing less in our schools today than we did fifty years ago to make science minister to the needs of our common life. The fact that it requires a certain number of grams to break a piece of No. 24 brass wire is of no concern to any of us—not even to the bridge-builder. It would seem that laboratory teachers, like kindergarten folks, have been at much pains to invent "busy work."[2]

3. THE EARTH SCIENCES

Geology declined in importanc as shown by Table X and this decline continued as shown by courses of study after 1900. It was taught from the standpoint of giving a general knowledge of geological facts in the earlier years and little or no change in point of view in this particular takes place throughout the period. The evolutionary theory received much less consideration in the older books than in the later ones but this does not materially change the older emphasis upon knowledge for its own sake without reference to economic considerations and values. The prevalence of the aim in teaching geology manifest in the second edition of Dana's book[3] is shown in a revised edition (1897).[4] The older book consists of four parts. Part I deals very briefly with physiographic geology—size, form, and surface structure of the earth. Part II is devoted to kinds, structure, and stratification of rocks, and a "view of the animal and vegetable kingdoms." The latter is simply the classification of plants and animals the same as found

[1] ELIST and STORER'S, WILLIAMS'S and SHEPARD'S texts are examples.

[2] WOODHULL, J. F., *The Teaching of Physical Science*, 1910, p. 6.

[3] DANA, JAMES D., *A Text-Book on Geology Designed for Schools and Academies*, 1874. This does not differ essentially from the edition of 1863.

[4] DANA, JAMES D., *Revised Text-Book on Geology*, 1897. Edited by William North Rice.

in the texts in botany and zoölogy of that time. Part III is devoted to historical geology with the usual divisions of time—Archaean, Palezoic, etc. Part IV consists of a discussion of dynamical geology—the causes or origins of events in geological history such as power of gravitation, atmosphere, heat, water, and the like.

The editor of the revised edition published in 1897 says in the preface:

> It was proposed in the plan of revision that the distinctive characteristics of the book should be preserved as far as possible. It was to be brought down to the present time as regards its facts, but it was still to express the well-known opinions of its author.

He then states that a more radical revision than was at first contemplated was found necessary and continues as follows:

> The zoölogical and botanical classifications used in the former edition were judged to be obsolete. The endeavor has been made to substitute for them, as nearly as practical, the classifications which are followed in the majority of recent manuals on zoölogy and botany. It was decided that the theory of evolution required fuller recognition than it had received in the previous edition of this work or the last edition of his Manual. . . . . In the present edition the bearing of various events in geological history upon the theory of evolution is pointed out in the appropriate places; and in the closing chapter which has been entirely rewritten the general bearing of paleontology upon evolution is discussed.

The book contains more material than the former edition, the facts are brought up to date, and the evolutionary theory emphasized. These represent practically the only changes noted in the revised edition.

Lists of texts found in the printed courses of study show that Dana's books were used more than any other text during all the periods and more than all others in most of the periods.

A text[1] occasionally mentioned in the published list of texts differs from the Dana texts chiefly in a discussion of the "bearings of geology upon religion," [17 pages] and in a brief account of "economical geology" [12 pages]. The most of this discussion is devoted to mining, one page being given to "agricultural geology."

Other texts such as Norton's (1871) and Geikie's (1890) show the same general character of material and method of treatment as found in Dana's books. Geikie's text places rather unusual emphasis upon the classification of plants and animals but presents no other distinguishing characteristics.

[1] HITCHCOCK, EDWARD, and HITCHCOCK, CHARLES H., *Elementary Geology. Second Edition*, 1867. "This differs from the edition of 1860 chiefly by the insertion of such new numbers, summaries and special details in technical statement as are required by the late rapid accumulation of interesting facts." (Preface)

Physical geography was one of the more important science subjects as shown by Table X. The number of schools offering it remained practically constant and there was no change in time devoted to it except as incidentally resulted from the change from a three-term to a two-term school year.

The character of the subject-matter remained practically unchanged until near the close of the century and can be classified roughly under two heads. The older type of material was of the general information sort and the textbooks were on the order of compendiums of knowledge selected from several of the science subjects. The new standpoint in teaching the subject becomes evident in the very last years of the century and this resulted in a restriction of the subject rather closely to the earth sciences. The standpoint as expressed in the preface of one of the later books[1] was as follows:

> They (the earth's physical features) must not be presented apart from the manner in which they affect man's ways of living; attention must frequently be drawn to the association of human conditions with the environment by which they have been determined, in order to form the habit of looking at the features of the earth as prime factors in guiding the development of mankind.

These two points of view then, the one supplying general information without any guiding aim or principle, and the other presenting these facts with reference to how "they effect man's ways of living" are the indexes to the character of the subject-matter.

An example of the older type of text is Mitchell's *Physical Geography*.[2] In the preface he says:

> In the following the writer has endeavored to unfold concisely, yet in their completeness, the principles and facts of Physical Geography, and has sought by the mode of presenting them and by freshness of illustration to uphold the intrinsic interest in this department of science.

No mention is made of the relations which the subject may have to life upon the earth or to any particular use to which the information may be put. The following, quoting again from the preface, shows also the religious viewpoint:

> The physical phenomena of the world reveal in their harmonious action a unity of plan and purpose, and display in an infinite variety of ways, the Power, Wisdom, and Goodness of the Almighty Designer.

The text itself is a compendium, descriptive of the various physical features of the earth such as rivers, oceans, plains, moun-

[1] Davis, William Morris, and Snyder, William Henry, *Physical Geography*, 1898.
[2] Brickleby, John, *Elements of Physical Geography*, 1867.

tains, valleys, and the like, physical phenomena such as earthquakes and volcanoes. Part V is devoted to meteorology and Part VI to geographical zoölogy, geographical botany, and ethnology. The religious point of view is not much in evidence but an occasional reference is made to it in the topic title "Proofs of Design." It is noticeable that while the author in his chapter on ethnology discusses classification as to races, differences in anatomical structure and other physical features, that there is an absence of any attempt to relate these topics to the subject-matter of the text preceding this chapter.

Guyot's text,[1] published a little later, is very similar to the one referred to above. No reference, however, is made to the religious phase of the subject either in the preface or the text proper. The same character of subject-matter is emphasized with some difference from the standpoint of classification. The following statement in the preface is a fair classification of the text itself:

> In every part of the work a strict geographical point of view has been preserved. From the kindred sciences—geology, natural philosophy, meteorology—only such facts and principles have been borrowed as were necessary to illustrate geographical phenomena. In the exposition of the life system, the associations of plants, animals, and races of men in geographical groups, characterizing the great natural divisions of the globe, have been defined, and not the botanical, zoölogical, or ethological classification.

Houston's book[2] does not differ from Guyot's in any essential particular. The author claims in the preface to have omitted certain unnecessary details and to have added certain subjects "usually omitted in works on Physical Geography" but no striking illustrations are found in the book either of omissions or additions. "Electrical and optical phenomena" receive some attention and "cultivated plants" is stressed a little more than in the other texts cited above, but this text does not differ essentially from them.

Appleton's Physical Geography[3] was published in 1887. This book is a compendium written by several authors. Ten are named on the title-page and the contributions of others acknowledged in the preface. This would indicate that it was a book prepared by specialists in the various subjects and fields. The reason given for the "new and original plan" is stated in the preface as follows:

> As Physical Geography is a singularly comprehensive science, requiring application from a great variety of cognate sciences, it is presumable that no one

[1] Guyot, Arnold, *Physical Geography*, 1873.
[2] Houston, Edwin J., *The Elements of Physical Geography*, 1875.
[3] *Appleton's Physical Geography; Prepared on a New and Original Plan*, 1887.

author possesses the depth or variety of knowledge essential to the preparation of a successful textbook on the subject, especially in view of the important advances recently made in many diverse fields of inquiry through the researches of specialists.

Special features of the book are referred to as follows:

The most recent views in regard to vulcanology and earthquakes are presented with illustration to the present year. The theory of ocean currents is clearly unfolded in the light of the latest discoveries. . . . . The general motions of the atmosphere are made plain by the application of Terrel's Law; while the perplexities environing the consideration of cyclonic storms are more thoroughly disentangled than in other American school books. The chapters devoted to geology, botany, zoölogy, and ethnology will be found as fascinating as they are instructive.[1]

The book claims scientific accuracy and thoroughness of treatment of the various subjects. No point of view is presented except that of knowledge for its own sake and no applications attempted.

The text by Davis and Snyder, already referred to, presents a new point of view in the teaching of physical geography. Quoting further from the preface:

Extraneous subjects, however interesting or important in themselves, such as the non-geographical elements of astronomy, the principles of physics, and the divisions of geological time, are carefully excluded.

An analysis of the book under such headings as agriculture, forests animals, plants, and the like, shows that considerable attention is devoted to these subjects and the point of view controls as stated in the preface. The older books discussed in detail the actual distribution of animals and plants. This text shows how physical conditions affect such distributions. The student is given the point of view at the outset by means of an introduction the chapter title being "The Relation of Man to the Earth." The following are other chapter titles indicating the character of the text, "The Relation of Man to the Climate;" "The Geographical Control of Population;" "The Lifelike Behavior of Rivers."

The emphasis throughout the book is upon physical conditions and phenomena in their relation to the earth as the home of man. A comparison of this book with Guyot's or Appleton's reveals clearly the change in point of view and character of subject-matter. Since this book did not come into use until the very last years of

[1] *Appleton's Physical Geography Prepared on a New and Original Plan*, 1887.

the century, the other books cited are the ones that determined almost exclusively the character of instruction in physical geography. From the standpoint of work actually done in the schools, texts, of which Davis' and Snyder's book is an example, belong to the first years of the present century.

CHAPTER XII

THE SOCIAL STUDIES

Under this general head are included history, civics, and political economy. Table XIX shows that there was an increase of a little more than a year in the time devoted to this field from 1860 to 1900. This increase was practically all given to history. The time devoted to civics and economics remained practically unchanged, the only change in these subjects being due to the fact that an occasional school devoted a whole year to one or the other and that the change from a three-term to a two-term plan had a tendency to increase the time from one-third year to one-half year. It will be seen also by reference to Table XIX that the maximum time doubled and that the minimum increased from one-third to one year.

1. HISTORY

European history, both from the standpoint of the number of schools offering it and also in the amount of time devoted to it, received a larger share of attention than did United States history. The character of the subject-matter in the former did not undergo very important changes. Different types of subject-matter are discoverable. Continental history was taught under various titles, such as ancient, medieval, modern, general, universal, and outlines of history. These titles, however, are not accurate descriptions of the character of material emphasized. As a matter of fact, ancient history received an undue proportion of attention regardless of the title of the textbook, and an examination of texts leads one to believe that the titles of books was the determining factor in giving titles to the courses. The texts also furnish practically the only reliable source of information concerning the character of subject-matter.

As pointed out above, ancient history received an undue amount of attention throughout the entire period. There was an occasional exception to this in a textbook, but on the whole the above statement holds true. Whatever particular emphasis the author may have employed, the matter dealt largely with political history, with a good deal of stress upon those periods in which the countries were engaged in war. Comparatively little attention was given to the economic or social life of the people, and education was almost entirely ignored.

One of the earlier books[1] used is characteristic of the texts of that date. A chronological table and index occupies thirty-two pages in the front part of the book, and on examining this, one is impressed by the emphasis placed upon wars and events directly connected with them. The text itself shows this same emphasis. About one-half of this book is devoted to what the author calls "Ancient and Middle History," and the balance to the "Modern Period." At the bottom of each page is given a list of questions on the text. These questions reveal clearly the emphasis upon political and military history in all the periods treated.

Another text[2] which was still in use after 1860, as shown by the printed lists of textbooks, shows the same emphasis as Willard's upon the political and military history. This book devotes three hundred and seventy-four pages to the history of the Asiatic countries and the remainder to Greece and Rome.

As stated above, history material does not seem to have been standardized, as shown by the textbooks. Some of these show that the authors were conscious of the fact that material other than accounts of political and military events should be included and incorporated in their books. One of these was the text[3] by William Swinton. Of the 487 pages, 305 are devoted to the "History of the World Preceding the Fifteenth Century," 67 pages of this being given to the Asiatic peoples and the balance to European. The emphasis in this book is clearly upon political and military affairs, but toward the close he devotes some attention to what he calls "The Progress of Civilization," occupying about 10 pages. This consists chiefly of the names of philosophers and scientists of the eighteenth century. Then at the very close of the book he gives five pages to great names of the nineteenth century. His chronological method of treatment is shown by the analytic synopses for reviews, which are provided at the close of the sections devoted to each of the periods. This book was widely used, as shown by the lists of textbooks published in school reports.

[1] WILLARD, EMMA, *Universal History: Divided into Three Periods, Ancient, Middle and Modern*, 1865.

[2] GOODRICH, S. G., *Complete History from the Creation to the Fall of Rome*, 1848.

[3] SWINTON, WILLIAM, *Outlines of the World's History, Ancient, Medieval and Modern with Special Relation to the History of Civilization and Progress of Mankind*, 1874.

Another book[1] of this same general type treats quite exclusively political and military events. This text, as well as the others above cited, seems to lack any point of view other than the presentation of a great array of events chronologically arranged.

Barnes's General History[2] is rather an exception to the books of that date and marks a beginning of a movement in history-teaching receiving considerable attention at the present time. There is an agreement with other texts from the standpoint of its emphasis upon ancient history, devoting more than one-half of the book to this period. It differs in that considerable attention is devoted to what the author calls "Civilization, Manners and Customs." Under the former the following are discussed: society, the army, education, literature, libraries and writing materials, monuments and art; under the latter: religion, games and festivals, marriage, burial and dress. A total of 112 pages are devoted to "civilization," and 60 pages to "manners and customs." Of the 172 pages devoted to this kind of material, 132 pages are taken up with an account of the civilization, manners, and customs of the ancient peoples, only 40 pages being devoted to the medieval and modern periods. The book, however, does not contain less material of the political and military sort. It was a larger book than was in common use at that time and this humanized material was simply added.

A protest against this sort of material is voiced in the preface of Anderson's *General History.*[3] This was not a protest against the text above cited since the two books came out almost simultaneously, but it is very likely that the former text was issued to meet a popular demand. The Anderson text was also issued in two volumes, one devoted to ancient history and the other to medieval and modern periods. In the preface to the *General History* he says:

> There has been for some time a growing tendency in the public mind to study rather those things that directly concern the life of the people as such, than the facts of National or Political History. Certainly this department of knowledge has a most fascinating interest: but it must be borne in mind that the greater movements of mankind are connected rather with the nation, than their social history: and hence it is a false system that makes the former subordinate to the

[1] QUACKENBOS, JOHN D., *Illustrated School History of the World from the Earliest Ages to the Present Time: Accompanied with Numerous Maps and Engravings*, 1876.

[2] *Barnes's History. A Brief History of the Medieval and Modern Peoples with Some Accounts of Their Movements, Institutions, Arts, Manners and Customs.*

[3] ANDERSON, JOHN J., *Manual of General History with Particular Attention to Ancient and Modern Civilization: With Numerous Engravings and Maps for Use in Colleges, High Schools, Academies, etc.*, 1882.

latter. . . . . The old masters of education, though more severe than those of the present time in their imposition of tasks, are less anxious to consult the uncultured palates of their pupils. Probably on that account they imparted more solid and enduring accomplishments. The present work while giving a brief sketch to the history of every nation both Ancient and Modern, aims also to afford in a pleasing and instructive style all the information needed by the young students. In regard to social peculiarities of the people and their progress in each department of civilization, care has been exercised to keep this branch inside of its just limits.

The book devotes some attention to what he calls "civilization" particularly of the ancient period. Practically no attention is devoted to this topic in modern times. The text as a whole makes good the contention of the author cited above in the preface. It is essentially a political and military history.

A book[1] published in 1885 is very different in method of treatment than the other high-school texts of that time. It is in fact a source book quoting very extensively from historical sources. The author says in the preface:

This book is not a history, but a collection of historical materials: it contains just the sort of things historians must deal with when they want to describe or judge any period of history, and just the kind of things, moreover, which we Americans must constantly attend to. In Greek History it gives bare chronology of deeds, pictures of buildings and statues, extracts from speeches, laws and poems. From these materials you must form your own judgment of the Greeks, discover their style of thinking, acting, living, feeling; you must in short imagine you yourself there, too, writing a Greek History, or that you are a Greek citizen called upon to judge the life about you. This helps you in this advantage, inserted in the midst of material such questions and problems which the Historian or citizen must always be asking himself, or rather must always be putting to the laws, events, poetry and ruins which he studies, whether they belong to peoples and times far away or near at hand. In this way you can learn to judge and interpret what you see before you in your own country and help to make of America that which she may become.

This book represents no point of view apparently which would be of value to a high-school teacher or a high-school student. In fact it is primarily a collection of historical matter and contains "just the sort of things which historians deal with."

Quotations from sources are abundant. For example, under the general title "Studies on the Athenian Leadership" several pages are devoted to stories and extracts illustrative of the period. Some of these quotations are of some length as "Character of Pericles" [Plutarch], "Funeral Speech of Pericles over the First Dead

[1] SHELDON, MARY D., *Studies in General History*, 1885.

in the Peloponnesian War" [Thucydides], and "The Defense and Death of Socrates" [Plato]. A large number of "Short Quotations from the Tragedians" are given. At the close of these is found a summary of the "Political and Military and Naval Events." This method of treatment is characteristic of the entire book. The author gives some interpretations and conclusions, but it is not a textbook in the usual sense. It was in all probability an attempt to encourage the source method, sometimes called laboratory method, in history, which was being advocated in certain quarters at that time. It is, however, the only book of its kind that is listed among the textbooks used in the high school as shown by the printed lists found in the courses of study, and its method of treatment was not adopted by other writers of textbooks.

Myers's texts in European history came into use about 1885, and during the period 1891–95 were used in more high schools than any other single text as shown by lists of textbooks published in the school reports. After 1895 they were used more than all other texts combined. The *General History*,[1] after its publication, largely displaced the earlier works by the same author as indicated by the published lists referred to above. The printed courses of study also show the prevalence of the term "General History" as revealed by Tables VII and VIII. So far as the Myers' texts are concerned, however, the subject-matter is not materially changed by a change of title. In the preface of the *General History* the author says:

> This volume is based upon my *Ancient History* and *Medieval* and *Modern History*. In some instances I have changed the perspective and the proportions of the narrative, but in the main, the book is constructed upon the same lines as those drawn for the earlier work.

The influence of the point of view controlling in Willard's, Swinton's, and Anderson's texts is evident in this book as shown by the emphasis upon political and military history. On the other hand, the material against which the author of the latter protests is given some attention. It is noticeable, too, that this does not appear to have been done as an afterthought or merely in response to a popular demand. The subject-matter dealing with the social life, art, commerce, religion, language, etc., of the various peoples is woven into the story in such a way as to make it an integral part of it.

[1] MYERS, P. V. N., *A General History for High Schools and Colleges*, 1889.

The proportion of space devoted to this sort of material is not large, although during the Greek period it received considerable attention. One hundred and thirty-four pages are devoted to the history of Greece and of these, forty-five pages are given to architecture, sculpture, painting, literature, philosophy, science, and social life. Under the last topic such things as education, banquets, occupation, and slavery are discussed. Little detail, however, is given, as indicated by the number of general topics considered. The chapter devoted to Greek philosophy and science consists chiefly of biographies of noted men. Much less space relatively is given, however, to those phases of life among the Romans, and still less in succeeding periods. A short account is given of the Revival of Learning and a brief notice is made of the literature of the Elizabethan Era. The book belongs to the same class as the Barnes and Anderson texts, and like them, the amount of subject-matter devoted to political and military history is not decreased as compared with texts in use previous to 1880. The movement toward more emphasis upon the social, industrial, and commercial aspects of history gained but little momentum, and the development of this phase of history-teaching belongs to the period lying beyond the close of the nineteenth century.

The subject-matter of United States history and the changes occurring therein need but brief attention. This subject, like arithmetic, grammar, and physiology, was taught in the upper grades and rural schools as well as in the high schools. It was in fact primarily a grade subject, and textbooks of this type, as shown by the published lists of texts, were used almost exclusively in the high schools.

Table XX shows that it was a short-time subject and that the time devoted to it remained practically unchanged. Tables II–IX, inclusive, indicate that it increased somewhat in importance from the standpoint of the number of schools offering it. It remained, however, relatively unimportant, European history receiving far more consideration.

One of the characteristics possessed in common by the textbooks in United States history is the relatively larger amount of attention devoted to wars. The earlier books show this and texts published after 1860 reveal the influence of the Civil War in this particular. Willard's[1] text devotes about one-fourth the entire space to an

[1] WILLARD, EMMA, *Abridged History of the United States*, 1853. New and enlarged edition. First edition published in 1849.

account of the Revolutionary War and more than twenty pages to the War of 1812. About forty pages are devoted to the Mexican War and the Indian and Colonial Wars receive a large share of attention. Political history occupies the remainder of the book almost to the entire exclusion of everything else, particularly after the beginning of the national period.

Wilson's book[1] was very similar in contents and method of treatment. It was a larger book than Willard's, the additional pages being devoted to an account of the Civil War. These books are mentioned more frequently than any others in the published lists prior to 1870.

The book most used after this date to 1890 was Barnes's *Brief History of the United States.*[2] The revised edition (1880) contained three hundred and two pages and of these about one hundred and twenty were devoted to the Revolutionary, Mexican, and Civil Wars. In addition to this, detailed accounts are given of Indian fighting and Indian Wars. As in the texts above cited, political history is stressed to the neglect of social and industrial affairs. This book is, however, a departure in one particular—the inclusion in footnotes of a good deal of material tending to throw light upon and add interest to the subject-matter of the text proper. In enumerating the "general methods of teaching this study" the author states:

> To furnish copious notes containing collateral facts, minor events, sketches of the lives of presidents and noted men, and especially those anecdotes of heroism and devotion that so brighten the record of our national growth.[3]

There is also introduced into the body of the text a little subject-matter bearing upon the daily life of the people bearing the title, "Condition of the Colonies." This occupies seven pages and such topics as the laws regulating the affairs of private life, manners and customs, and education are discussed. This material is all in fine print similar to the footnotes and deals only with colonial life.

The Barnes text and Montgomery's "Leading Facts of History Series"[4] were used more than all other books[5] combined after 1870.

[1] WILSON, MARCIUS, *History of the United States from the Earliest Discoveries to the Close of the Great Rebellion in 1865. Containing also the Constitution of the United States with Explanatory Notes and Questions*, 1866.

[2] It was published first in 1871 and revised in 1879 and 1880.

[3] *Ibid.*, Preface.

[4] MONTGOMERY, D. H., *The Student's American History*, 1897.

[5] *The Leading Facts of American History*, a Grammar School text, was published a few years previous to the student's edition. Other texts in use did not differ essentially from Barnes's and Montgomery's. Some of them are: EGGLESTON, EDWARD, *A History of the United States and Its People*, 1888; SCOTT, DAVID B., *A School History of the United States* (Harper's School History), 1870; SCUDDER, HORACE E., *A New History of the United States*, 1897; THALHEIMER, M. E., *An Eclectic History of the United States*, 1881.

The students' edition is the only text named in the published lists intended primarily for high-school use. It differs from the smaller book[1] only in the following particulars:

> It is much fuller in its treatment of political and constitutional history, and of the chief events bearing upon the development of the nation. It quotes the statements of public men, original documents, and authorities, in order that the history of our country may speak for itself on the points of greatest interest to the student and the teacher.[2]

This book contains none of the "anecdotes of heroism and devotion" found in the Barnes text and only an occasional reference to industrial or social life.

The books referred to above show clearly that the political and constitutional point of view controlled in history-teaching to the very close of the century. The slight attention given after 1870 to social and industrial life does not indicate any essential change in aim, or materially change the character of the subject-matter.

2. CIVICS

The term civics is a recent one. Politics, political philosophy, constitution, science of government, and civil government were the more common terms employed throughout the most of the period. It has already been shown that the subject increased somewhat in importance from the standpoint of the number of schools offering it and that the average amount of time devoted to it remained practically the same. The only change affecting the latter being the shift from a three-term to a two-semester plan. This, of course, eliminated the practice of devoting one-third of a year to a subject and substituted one-half year. This, however, was only incidental and does not represent an increase of importance attached to the subject.

Instruction in civics falls into two fairly well-defined periods. The first of these is characterized by an emphasis upon the formal, theoretical aspect of the subject. The work during the first period consisted largely of interpretations of constitutions, federal and state, and the texts used were scarcely more than analyses. Practically nothing was done to give pupils a knowledge of government in its practical workings, or to teach the duties of citizens except in an abstract, formal way. Titles of some of the early books are

[1] MONTGOMERY, D. H., *The Students American History*, 1879.
[2] *Ibid.*

fair indexes of the contents and method of treatment. The title of one of these books,[1] *The Science of Government*, is an illustration. The author in the preface quotes Professor F. D. Huntington in an address before the Massachusetts legislature as follows:

It is absurd that pupils should go through their whole term of preparation for life committing the rules of grammar and rules of arithmetic, to the total neglect of the principles of legislation under which they are to live or to the facts of the country to which they belong, and of the constitution of their liberties.

He adds he would have every young person

carefully and conscientiously taught those distinctive ideas which constitute the substance of our Constitution, and which determine the policy of our politics . . . . and to this end there ought forthwith to be introduced in our schools a simple and comprehensive manual, whereby the needed tuition should be planted at that early period.

The book is in fact an analysis and interpretation of the federal constitution. Enough historical material is introduced to furnish somewhat of a background. One chapter is devoted to the institutions of the several states. This chapter, however, contains little more than information concerning the date of adoption of these constitutions, then some comment upon the distribution of powers among the several departments of government, and the scattered, unconnected facts concerning the length of residence required to be a voter, meager details of judicial systems, and the like. Another chapter is devoted to international law, and the final chapter to a brief discussion of different kinds of law defined, as constitutional, international, municipal, statute, and common law.

Townsend's *Analysis of Civil Government*[2] came into use at about the same time as the book cited above. The following statement is found in the preface.

The Analytic Method of this work furnishes its first claim of superiority over others as a textbook on Civil Government. The Constitution of the United States is our fundamental law. To understand this law is to understand the whole theory: and to analyze this is to analyze the entire American System. The proper aim therefore of this work is to present *analytically* the subject of Civil Government as administered in this country. . . . . In the tabular arrangement in the sections and clauses of the Constitution nothing is omitted or added, and as far as possible the precise language of that document is retained.

The introduction is written to the book by Rev. James E. Lapham, in which he says in part:

He has drawn the materials from his work from original sources and from commentaries and from classic excellence. We see traces of interminable rum-

[1] ALDEN, JOSEPH, *The Science of Government in Connection with American Institutions*, 1866.
[2] TOWNSEND, COLVIN, *Analysis of Civil Government*, 1868.

magings of The Madison Papers, the Federalist, Elliott's Debates, Story and Rawle on the Constitution, Kent's and Blackstone's Commentaries, as well as the most patient learnings from official statistical and chronological tables.

This is one of the books at least in which promises made in the preface are rigorously kept. The contents of the book itself constitute an analysis of the constitution, and the method of treatment further emphasizes that point of view. The division into heads and subheads and arrangement of material on the page all add in bringing before the student in very clear outline the analytical method of treatment. In the comments that are made it is evident that the statement made in the introduction concerning the materials from commentaries and from classic excellences, are true. The author, as the title-page indicates, was a lawyer, and the lawyer's point of view is evident throughout the book. A glossary is provided at the close, containing a long list of definitions of legal terms. As a matter of fact this book was not a pioneer in the field as an examination of Alden's text above referred to will show. It simply placed further emphasis upon the analytical method of treating the constitution of the United States. Another book of this same general type was Andrews's *Manual of the Constitution.*[1] The author indicates in the preface the same point of view as the other books just described contained, as the following will show:

> The proper instruction of students in the important subject of Civil Government, a clearer exposition of the great principles of the Constitution, is met with a summary of the legislative Provisions in which they have been embodied.

As has been said, this book belongs to the same class as those referred to above, but differs in two particulars. In the first place, the method is not so severely analytical, the treatment being in descriptive form, and, as he indicates in the preface, an explanation is given to the "legislative provisions," in which the principles of the constitution have been embodied. In the second place, the book contains some historical information which has the constitution as a background. For example, in the discussion of the executive department, he gives a list of the names of the presidents up to date. This also was followed by lists of the names of the secretaries of the various executive departments. He devotes a short chapter to state governments, but this information is very much condensed and fragmentary. In the appendix he gives in

[1] ANDREWS, ISRAEL WARREN, *Manual of the Constitution of the United States*, 1874.

full the Articles of Confederation, the Declaration of Independence, the Ordinance of 1787, and the Federal Constitution.

The type of instruction represented by these books above cited certainly continued to about 1885 or a little after. There is, however, some sign of change of point of view in the textbooks published a little before 1880. This formal type of instruction however prevailed throughout the most of the period through the use of the older type of books in many schools.

The second period is marked by an emphasis upon state and local government, and while the legal point of view is the prevailing one, the emphasis upon constitutions and the analytical method of treatment no longer completely dominates. One of the books which represents a short step in advance in this particular was Martin's *Civil Government*.[1] This text was in no sense a radical departure since the organization and method of treatment reveals the predominance of the old ideal in teaching civil government. There was, however, a tendency manifested to give more attention to a discussion of the functions of government and less to mere constitutional and legal principles, and also to give a place, although a very subordinate one, to state and local governments.

Two books[2] came into use after 1885 that represent the new point of view—viz., emphasis upon the function of government and more attention to the smaller units of government. McCleary's text reverses the accustomed order of treatment in that it begins with a discussion, covering about sixty pages, of local forms and functions of government. The author takes up the town, village, city, and county. Another feature of this book is the introduction of a brief discussion of commercial law. This subject occupies twenty pages. These two features distinguish this book very clearly from the texts published before 1885. The balance of the book, however, is devoted largely to the constitutional type of material and really belongs to the old order of textbooks. In the preface the author says:

> The Constitution of the United States, not a mere abstract of it but a careful study of the text, is properly given much space but is not allowed a monopoly of it.

It is perhaps not allowed a monoply but certainly receives a large share of attention.

[1] MARTIN, GEORGE H., *A Text-Book on Civil Government*, 1875.

[2] MCCLEARY, J. F., *Studies in Civics*, 1888 and DOLE, CHARLES F., *The American Citizen*, 1891.

In Dole's book a new note is sounded in the preface as follows:

> There seems to be a growing demand for the more adequate teaching of morals in the schools, especially with reference to the making of good citizens. But it is difficult to teach morals directly or apart from the concrete subjects about which moral questions grow. Neither can sound morals be taught at all without a touch of enthusiasm.
>
> We have, however, in the great and interesting subjects of the conduct of governments, business and society precisely the kind of material to furnish us indirectly with innumerable examples. The consideration of the public good, the welfare of the nation, or the interests of mankind, lies in the very region where patriotic emotion and moral enthusiasm are most naturally kindled.

He says further:

> Every intelligent boy or girl, indeed, may be presumed to wish to know the facts about the government of our country and our social institutions. The object of this book, however, is not merely to state these facts, but also to illustrate the moral principles that underlie the life of civilized man. . . . . It will be obvious to the intelligent teacher that the kind of study which this book is designed to serve must not be made mere task work. The main hope of its usefulness is by awakening the interest of students and stimulating them to think and talk about the various subjects considered.

The book is a radical departure from the books that preceded it and represents a very different point of view and emphasis, as shown by the quotations from the preface, and the text itself fulfils the promise of the preface. It is divided into five parts, and each part presents the rights and duties of citizenship from a particular angle. Part I deals in general with the "Beginning of Citizenship." The chapters deal with the family, the school, the playground, clubs and debating societies, the principles that bind men together, the different duties that men owe each other and the like. Part II deals with "The Citizen and the Government; or the Rights and Duties of Citizens." Topics discussed in the several chapters are the purpose and forms of government, local government, cities and their government, the machinery of government, the judicial branch of the government, the treasury and the taxes, the school system, voting, and so on. Part III deals with "Economic Duties; or the Rights and Duties of Business and Money." Under this general head some of the topics discussed are as follows: wealth, its nature, conditions of, to whom it belongs, honest money, labor and competition, the grievances of the poor. Part IV takes up "Social Rights and Duties; or the Duties of Men as they Live Together in Society." Under this are discussed the rights and duties of neighbors, the treatment of crime (not from a legal but a social point of view), how to help the poor, and the problem of temperance. Part V is devoted to "International Duties; or the Rights and Duties of Nations." This general topic is divided into sub-international law and how it grows, the rights of nations, the duties of nations, and war, arbitration, and patriotism.

The book is written in simple language. The style is attractive, and in both content and method of treatment is suited to the interests and abilities of high-school students.

A book[1] published just at the opening of the present century, while not belonging strictly to the period covered by our study, shows the influence of the point of view so clearly revealed in the book just discussed. This text reveals something of the old legislative viewpoint; it represents nothing of the constitutional mode of treatment, and deals largely with the concrete relationships of the people as these relate to keeping order, making laws, providing schools, maintaining roads, transportation and distribution of mail, collection and spending taxes and the like.

In view of the textbooks used quite exclusively up to 1890 and the persistence of some of these until 1900, it is clear that the civics teaching was entirely dominated by the legislative point of view until the former date, and that the influence of this was felt to the very close of the century. A new order of things, however, had been initiated to be worked out more completely in the early years of the present century.

3. ECONOMICS

Economics, or political economy, has not held as important a place in the high-school curriculum as civics. This is clearly shown by Tables II–IX and also by Table X. The increase of importance from the standpoint of the number of schools offering it was considerable as shown by Table X. The time devoted to it remained practically constant, the only change of any consequence being due to a slight increase brought about by a change from the three-term to the two-term plan of organization.

The teaching of the subjects falls into two periods not very well defined in point of time. The first is marked by an emphasis upon principles or the philosophical aspect of the subject. Wayland's text,[2] although published nearly twenty years before the beginning of the period covered by this study, was still in use as late as 1875.

[1] Clark, S. T., *The Government—What It Is and What It Does*, 1902.
[2] Wayland, Francis, *The Elements of Political Economy*, 1841.

In fact, it was the only text mentioned previous to 1870 in the lists of texts examined. In the preface of the edition cited the author says:

> When the author's attention was first directed to the Science of Political Economy, he was struck with the simplicity of its principles, the extent of its generalizations and the readiness with which its facts seemed capable of being brought into natural and methodical arrangement.

The text bears abundant evidence that the above quotations represent the controlling point of view. It is a discussion of principles which are of the abstract sort, the generalizations are based upon abstractions, and the treatment is methodical although the method was evidently borrowed from the field of philosophy of that time. He says in the preface:

> The principles of Political Economy are so closely analogous to those of Moral Philosophy that almost every question in the one may be argued on the grounds belonging in the other. He has not, however, thought it proper in general to intermingle them, but has argued economical questions on merely economical grounds.

In spite of the promise made in the last sentence, the method of treatment smacks of the philosophical point of view. Political philosophy certainly, if not moral philosophy, entered into not only the method of treatment, but also the contents. The book contains "in substance the Lectures on Political Economy which have been delivered for some years past to the Senior class in Brown University." This will indicate the method, treatment, and also the degree of difficulty which high-school students would encounter in an attempt to master it.

Another text[1] which was evidently not written specifically for high-school students was Champlin's *Political Economy.* In the preface the author states:

> It is prepared for "schools" as well as "colleges" because the author believes that a science so practical and essential to all classes of society should be more generally studied in our schools. There is nothing in the science above the comprehension and mastery of the average scholars in our academies and high schools. . . . . At the same time, it is hoped that they will not be found inadequate to the wants of college classes.

The book is more modern than Wayland's in that it contains practically none of the material belonging more strictly to political science, and there is given to the subject a more distinctive eco-

[1] CHAMPLIN, J. F., *Lessons in Political Economy, Designed as a Basis for Instruction in that Science in Schools and Colleges*, 1868.

nomic emphasis throughout the text. It, however, is very similar to the older book in discussing almost wholly abstract principles and in its formal descriptive style. The lack of concreteness is marked, and this was no doubt intended as indicated by the following quotation from the preface:

> It is believed that they (the lessons) contain all the fundamental principles of the science, and all indeed that are required in a general course of education. Subordinate principles and details can be added by the teacher; but if the principles here presented are mastered, the student will have a competent knowledge of the science for all ordinary purposes.

The influence of Wayland's point of view and of the text itself is revealed by a book published in 1878.[1] On the front cover of the book are the words, *Wayland Series Political Economy, Wayland—Chapin* and in the preface the following reference is made to the author of the older book:

> His effort was attended with remarkable success and no other textbook on the subject has gained such general acceptance and been so extensively and continuously read.

After referring to the fact that "many practical problems of political economy have come to be studied in a new light" Chapin says:

> While these things have caused little change in the real elements of the science as presented by our author they demand that as a text-book of instruction adapted to our times, his work should be very considerably modified.[2]

This review in part consists of new material such as gold and silver and the double standard, politics, and the enlargement of the discussion of credit in its various forms, and railway corporations. The subjects of free trade and protection receive extended consideration, and banks and currency are treated in detail. In method of treatment, however, and to a considerable extent in content, the books are much alike.

Walker's text[3] marks somewhat of a transition in that it devotes about a hundred pages to "Some Applications of Economic Principles," while the subtopics under this general head are similar to those treated in the older books. The application of the principles is practical and concrete. The failure to distinguish between the need of college and high-school students is not recognized, as is shown by the following statements in the preface:

> This work has been abridged from the third edition of my *Manual of Political Economy* published in 1883. The object in view has been to present a text-book

[1] WAYLAND, FRANCIS, *The Elements of Political Economy. Recast by Aaron L. Chapin*, 1878.
[2] *Ibid.*
[3] WALKER, FRANCIS A., *Political Economy (Briefer Course)*, 1884.

adapted to use in colleges and academies where but one term is devoted to the study of Political Economy.

Later *The Elements of Political Economy*[1] by the same author was issued. This book was little more than an abridgment of his *Political Economy* and was widely used in the high schools. These books really marked the transition from the old to the new point of view, and other texts such as Bullock's[2] made the transition complete.

The following quotation from the preface of the Bullock text represents the point of view:

> This work is designed for an introductory text-book of Economic Science. The first three chapters aim to familiarize the student with an orderly treatment with some leading facts of the Economic history of the United States before the study of Economic theory is commenced. Throughout the book economic principles are discussed with special reference to American conditions and their workings are illustrated by frequent allusions to American experience.

The historical background, dealing with the facts of Economic History and the illustration of principles by "frequent allusions to American experience," marks the complete transition from the formal and theoretical to the concrete and scientific method of treatment. The emphasis which the author places upon money and credit, and also his concrete method of treatment, indicate clearly the interest manifested in free silver issue of that time. His treatment of monopolies, socialism, the economic function of government, and the like, further illustrate the practical point of view and the changes which had then taken place in the subject-matter of political economy.

[1] Walker, Francis A., *The Elements of Political Economy*, 1884.
[2] Bullock, Charles Jesse, *Introduction to the Study of Economics*, 1897.

CHAPTER XIII

FOREIGN LANGUAGE AND MISCELLANEOUS SUBJECTS

1. FOREIGN LANGUAGE

No changes of importance occurred in the teaching of foreign languages so far as subject-matter is concerned. The amount of material offered evidently remained about the same except as affected by increase of time devoted to it. Even this increase in time did not mean a proportional increase in amount of material. For example, in the case of Latin the earlier three-year courses appear to have covered approximately the same ground as the later four-year courses. This is shown by comparing the data in Table A with that of succeeding tables. The earlier practice of requiring but three subjects to be carried by the student instead of the requirement of four subjects in the later years would account for doing the same amount of work in any subject in a shorter time.

It is also evident that there were no important changes in the character of the subject-matter taught in any of the foreign languages. The grammatical method of teaching prevailed practically without exception as shown by the textbooks used. The technique of teaching particularly in the ancient languages had been worked out in the older types of schools and both method and subject-matter were taken over by the high schools. The modern languages seem to have been inherited in the same way. At any rate, the same method in teaching and the same character of subject-matter was emphasized. It has already been pointed out in Chapter II the extent to which the grammatical method prevailed in the teaching of English. Its effect upon the teaching of modern language was even more marked.

Greek is almost negligible so far as the number of schools offering it are concerned at the close of the period. The amount of subject-matter offered in the few schools that still taught it remained the same as in 1860 and there is no evidence of even the slightest change in the character of material. The *Grammar and Reader*,[1] the *Anabasis*, and the *Iliad* made up the course. No other subject-matter is mentioned in the printed courses of study.

[1] Usually Goodwin's text.

The history of Latin is very similar to that of Greek. The First-Book, Caesar, Cicero, and Virgil constituted the work except for minor modifications.[1] In the early years an occasional school offered Sallust, Nepos, and Horace, but this practice was not general and soon ceased entirely. The fixed order was a first-year book, followed by Caesar, and this usually by Cicero and Virgil in the order named. Occasionally Virgil would precede Cicero as shown by the courses of study. So far as the work in Latin, after the first year is concerned, the courses of study show conclusively that no change in the character of subject-matter took place.

It remains then to consider only the work of the first year and the textbooks furnish a reliable source of information. The books from first to last consist chiefly of grammar and exercises for use in drill. One of the noticeable things about these exercises is the large amount of material selected from Caesar's *Commentaries on the Gallic War*. The reason for this no doubt was that it furnished excellent material for grammatical drill and also afforded specific preparation for the work of the second year. One of the older reading books[2] shows this same emphasis upon Caesar. Another book[3] published about ten years later devotes twenty-two pages of the seventy-one pages (exclusive of notes, vocabularies, etc.) to the Helvetian War. In addition to this, extracts from the commentaries are abundant.

Leighton's *Latin Lessons*[4] contains no less material chosen from Caesar than the books cited, but additional reading matter is provided consisting of biographical sketches and stories. The following statement is made in the preface:

> The Reading Lessons which follow are largely made up from modern Latin—a few *Fables* from Aesop and extracts from *Viri Romae*—owing to the almost absolute lack in classic authors of matter at once simple in style and suitable for elementary practice. These are followed by Woodford's *Epitome of the First Book of the Gallic War*, which gives the main thread of the narrative in Caesar's own words, omitting the parenthetical clauses.

These two classes of material, after 1860, with the emphasis upon selections from Caesar, constitute the reading lessons of first-year texts.

[1] See Appendix, Tables A–H. If the columns contain figures or are numbered thus *x* it indicates that the subject named in the margin was taught. The mark thus *o* indicates no specification.

[2] *The New Liber Primus*, 1858.

[3] ALLEN, WM. F., and ALLEN, J. H., *Latin Lessons Adapted to the Latin Grammar. Fourth Edition*, 1869.

[4] LEIGHTON, R. F., *Latin Lessons Adapted to Allen and Greenough's Latin Grammar*, 1872.

Two first-year books in common use were *First Lessons in Latin*[1] and the *Beginner's Latin Book*.[2] The former shows the emphasis in the title upon preparation for work in Caesar and the text itself furnished evidence of the same fact. Collar and Daniell's text is apparently intended to serve the purpose of both grammar and reader and the material in reading is relatively less extensive. It does not, however, differ essentially in character from that found in the Jones text.

One thing that indicates very clearly the fact that the character of the work in first-year Latin remained practically unchanged was the wide use of Harkness' text. This book appears in every list made up from the printed courses of study from 1860 to 1900. The first-year books already mentioned did not differ in any essential particular from the Harkness *Grammar* and *Reader* except in some reduction in the details of Latin grammar.

The modern languages apparently have a history very similar to that of Latin from the standpoint of character of subject-matter and method of treatment. Since it was usual to offer but two years and in some schools but a single year as shown by Tables A–H, the work consisted chiefly of grammar and exercises for grammatical drill. The grammar translation method rather than the so-called natural or the direct method has prevailed. Professor Handschin has the following to say as late as 1912:

> Our readers, texts, and for the most part, our grammars are not adapted to the direct method of teaching.[3]

In speaking of the teaching of German, he says:

> Consider a typical two year high school course as we find it today. It consists of (beside the grammar and reader) . . . . let us say of *Immensee*. . . . . Next follows *L'Arrabbiata*, a gem of literature, but an eratic story of Italian life that has nothing German about it but the language. Then follows a long prose tale or at best a short modern comedy, and *Wilhelm Tell* and the course is finished.

Since the course consisted of grammar and reading, *Immensee* and *Wilhelm Tell* were no doubt common throughout the period covered by this study as shown by the printed lists of texts contained in the school reports. The German readers such as Sheldon's, and grammars (Worman's and Heidner's are examples) show the emphasis upon grammatical drill and that the reading matter is selected primarily for its value in this particular.

[1] Jones, Elisha, *First Lessons in Latin*, 1877.
[2] Collar, William C., and Daniell, M. G., *The Beginner's Latin Book*, 1886.
[3] Handschin, C. H., *The Teaching of Modern Languages in the United States*, 1912.

2. THE MISCELLANEOUS SUBJECTS

These occupied only a secondary place in the curriculum and information is meager concerning the details of subject-matter and method of treatment.

As has been pointed out in connection with the discussion of the commercial subjects in Part I, they were comparatively negligible until the last decade of the period. Bookkeeping was taught from the first and thus constituted the chief, and in most schools the only, commercial subject taught. A few schools list business forms, but the information available concerning the nature of this work indicates that it was only a part of bookkeeping. In the school report[1] of Newark, Ohio, the principal says:

> For some time there has been a demand in this city that the high school should give to its members a more thorough knowledge of business forms. To meet this demand as an elective study alternate with Political Economy, a course with recitations is provided three times a week throughout the year in the D High School.

The commercial arithmetic differed but little from the other texts used. The commercial texts were little more than the usual grammar-school books with a slight emphasis upon the class of problems involving commercial transactions.

There is no evidence revealed by a study of the school reports that what was later called business English received any attention. The so-called commercial courses were for the most part made up of subjects only remotely connected with training for business of any sort. Stenography and typewriting were taught in a few schools after 1890. The whole field of commercial education so far as the high schools were concerned, remained practically undeveloped until after the beginning of the present century.

Of the industrial subjects only manual training is listed in the high-school curricula and this only in a small percentage of schools at the very close of the period. It is probable that no textbooks were used since none are mentioned in the published lists of high-school texts. The courses of study indicate the lines of work and from these one can gain a general idea of the character of the work.

[1] *Bi-annual Report of the Superintendent of the Newark, Ohio, Public Schools*, 1881 and 1882, p. 27.

Appleton, Wisconsin, offered work in manual training in 1887. The following statement is found in a footnote to the printed course of study:

A department of Manual Training has been added. This includes bench work, wood carving and mechanical drawing. This course is optional.[1]

The character of the work and also the point of view in teaching manual training in the Chicago schools in 1886 is shown by the following statement of the superintendent:

Much attention and discussion has been given to this question during the year and it was determined to make an experimental beginning this present year. A convenient room has been furnished with benches and tools for pupils of the first grade in the high schools. Some seventy pupils are at present engaged in mechanical drawing and bench work in the afternoon. The interest manifested and the progress made has thus far exceeded our highest expectations. The greatest benefit of this work, in my opinion, is the habit of industry and the dignifying of labor. The study of things rather than of words and the application of philosophical principles of daily labor is by no means to be overlooked.[2]

He states further that bench work should not begin much earlier than the high school and doubts whether work in iron should be introduced. His objection is that it would be expensive and would probably not receive popular approval.

The rapid development of the work, however, is shown by a statement of the superintendent in the Report of 1888 as follows:

For the first year the pupils have carpenter work with free hand and mechanical drawing; for the second year they have wood turning, pattern making, mechanical drawing, modeling, molding, and casting of soft metals.[3]

In discussing the work further he says:

We have drawing, freehand and mechanical, nice geometrical constructions, the graphic solution of problems, geographical and historical illustrations; with much work in botany and chemistry requiring accurate observation and nice manipulation.[4]

The following concerning the work in Cleveland, Ohio, shows the way in which it was introduced and also its character:

Manual Training in Cleveland was started in February, 1885. A small carpenter shop was opened in a barn near the Central High School for the benefit of the boys in that school. The same year a stock company of Cleveland business men was incorporated to build a manual training school for the interests of the

[1] *Annual Catalog of the Public Schools*, 1886-87, p. 19.
[2] *Annual Report Board of Education*, 1886, pp. 56-57.
[3] *Annual Report Board of Education*, 1888, p. 80.
[4] *Ibid.*, p. 86.

Cleveland High School boys. The school was opened in January, 1886. In 1887 a law was passed by the Ohio State Legislature providing a tax levy for the support of Manual Training in Cleveland. This money was turned over to the Manual Training High School Company by the Board of Education in return for the free tuition of high school pupils. In 1890 the Board of Education established the West Side Manual Training School wholly supported by the Board. The work consisted of mechanical drawing, carpentry, wood turning, pattern making, forging and machine shop practice, the course usually given in manual training of that period.[1]

Mr. Milo Stewart, principal of the Manual Training High School, Indianapolis, Indiana, says in a personal letter:

> The subject was offered first in 1895. The program of work from 1895 to 1900 was as follows: Stenography, bookkeeping, penmanship, wood working, mechanical drawing and iron and steel forging.

"Mechanical drawing and bench work" is the only description given of the work in manual training in the Omaha, Nebraska, High School in 1889.[2]

Further development of the work in the Chicago English High and Manual Training School is shown by the course of study for 1895.[3] The course includes mechanical and freehand drawing, joinery and wood-turning, cabinet and bench work, pattern work, foundry and blacksmith work, machine shopwork—chipping, filing, and fitting—and use of lathe planer and milling machine, lectures on wood, iron, and machinery, and its work constituted a part of the regular work of the course.

The work provided in the course offered by the Appleton, Wisconsin, High School[4] in 1900 is grouped under two heads—drawing and shopwork. Under the former are listed notes on experimental geometry, geometrical solution of problems with draughting instruments, block and freehand lettering, shade-lining, tracing, blue printing and mounting prints, freehand drawing, dimension sketches, notes on pattern making, molding and casting, pattern and machine drawing, elementary mechanism, notes on forging, welding and tool making, orthographic projection, and machine design.

The shopwork is described as follows: instruction in construction, care, and use of bench tools and joinery; instruction and

[1] Information furnished by a letter to the author by Mr. Roberts who had charge of the manual training work in Cleveland for a number of years.

[2] *Report Board of Education*, 1889.

[3] *Annual Report Board of Education*, 1895, pp. 319-20.

[4] *Catalog of Public Schools*, Appleton, Wisconsin, 1900, pp. 54-61.

practice in putting bench tools in order, wood carving; lathe work in wood (hand tools); pattern making, molding and casting (in brass, zinc, and plaster of Paris); forging (in iron and steel), welding, case hardening and hardening and tempering steel; bench work in metals, machine work in metals and machine finishing, polishing, and grinding.

In a footnote to the work of the first year is found the following statement:

> The shop work includes a finished article—such as a stand, table, grille—which shall be as far as possible, the product of the pupil's work.[1]

The work of the two schools last cited was much more extensive than was offered in most of the schools even as late as 1910 as shown by the printed courses of study. Usually little or no work was done in iron and the work in wood was less extensive than either of the above courses indicate. The emphasis in these early years of the work was placed upon learning to use hand tools and in making a "finished article such as a stand, table" and the like.

[1] *Catalog, Appleton, Wisconsin, Public Schools*, 1900.

PART III

RECENT DEVELOPMENTS

CHAPTER XIV

ORGANIZATION OF CURRICULA AND RANGE OF SUBJECTS

The close of the nineteenth century witnessed certain definite tendencies in secondary education. No radical readjustments had yet taken place but tendencies were developed during the last decade of the century which have resulted in a great movement changing the scope and character of secondary education in marked degree. As pointed out, however, in Part I, the old order of things held until the close of the century in spite of the tendencies referred to above during the last decade. The first decade of the present century shows an increase in these tendencies, but the readjustments have really taken place for the most part since 1910. Since that date radical changes have already occurred or are well under way.

One of the very marked changes is in the scope of secondary education. The junior high school adds two years to the high-school curriculum from below, making six years instead of four. The junior college adds two years beyond the twelfth grade. In case a high school includes both of these, the curriculum includes eight years of work. The latter type of school is not classified definitely as a secondary institution, but a number of schools are so recognized and others are in prospect of establishment. Chicago[1] now maintains a junior college in connection with the Crane Technical High School and one has been established in Grand Rapids,[2] Michigan. The State Department of South Dakota reports two in that state "all connected with high schools." Statistics are rather meager concerning this institution but it is evident that the movement has considerable momentum and may result in a general extension upward of the scope of secondary education.

Every indication at the present time is that the movement to establish junior high schools will result in a fixed policy of including at least six years in the scope of high-school education. The move-

[1] Cf. *Course of Study*, 1917.

[2] Cf. *School Survey*. Grand Rapids, Michigan, 1910, pp. 267 ff.

ment is now widespread in the North Central states as shown by data collected and tabulated by Professor C. O. Davis for the North Central Association of Colleges and Secondary Schools.[1] His report shows that there were 1,140 schools accredited by the association in 1918 and this number includes two hundred and ninety-three which maintain junior high schools. It is true that this type of school is far from being standardized, either from the standpoint of organization or curriculum. In fact, the name "junior high school" is applied to but one hundred and sixty-eight of these schools. Other names being employed are: "department school," forty-six; "six-year high school," twelve; other names, sixty-seven. There is lack of uniformity also regarding the grades included as this same report shows: eighty-nine include grades seven, eight, and nine; twenty-two, grades six, seven, and eight; eight, grades eight and nine; one hundred and thirty-three, grades seven and eight; eleven, only the eighth grade; and eleven designated as including other grades. Eighteen having the six-six plan do not make distinction between junior and senior high school organization, but it is clear that all grades beyond the seventh are included. If the recommendation of the Commission on Units and Curricula of the North Central Association made to the Association in 1917 and adopted the present year is accepted as a standard, uniformity will prevail in the number of years included. The recommendation reads as follows:

The Junior High School shall normally include the seventh, eighth, and ninth years of public school work.[2]

Lack of standardization is also shown by an examination of the curricula of these schools. In some cases elementary subjects predominate to such an extent that there is little difference between the work of the first two years and the traditional seventh- and eighth-grade work. In others the work is predominately of secondary grade so far as the subjects are concerned. This difference is also shown by different schools from the standpoint of curricula organization. Some schools offer a single curriculum with few or no electives during the first two years while others recognize the needs of pupil groups and provide parallel curricula. The recommendation of the North Central Association also touches upon this point.[3]

[1] Leaflet published 1918.
[2] *Proceedings of North Central Association Colleges and Secondary Schools*, 1917, p. 56.
[3] *Ibid.*, pp. 56-57.

The following are typical junior high school curricula:

DULUTH JUNIOR HIGH SCHOOLS

ACADEMIC COURSES | PREVOCATIONAL COURSES

SEVENTH GRADE

Required Subjects (Academic)	Periods per Week	Required Subjects (Prevocational)	Periods per Week
English	5	English	7
Arithmetic	4	Arithmetic	4
History & Geography	5	History & Geography	5
Physical Training	2	Physical Training	2
Music and Penmanship	2	Music and Penmanship	2
Drawing	2	Drawing	2
Shopwork or Home Training	2		
	22		22

Choose One	Periods	Boys	Periods	Weeks	Girls	Periods	Weeks
English	5	Wood work	10	9	Housekeeping	10	....
Latin	5	Metal work	10	9	Garment Making	10	....
French	5	Printing	10	9	Physiology and Home Nursing	5	....
		Physiology & Hygiene	5	9	Textiles	5	

EIGHTH GRADE

Required Subjects (Academic)	Periods per Week	Required Subjects (Prevocational)	Periods per Week	
English	5	English	7	Through the year
Mathematics	4	Applied Mathematics	4	
American History and Civics	5	American History and Civics	5	
Physical Training	5	Music and Penmanship	2	
Music and Penmanship	2	Drawing	2	
Drawing	2	Physical Training	2	
Shopwork or Home Training	2		—	
Additional			22	
French, Latin, or English	5			
	30			

Boys	Periods	Weeks	Girls	Periods	Weeks
B 8th Typewriting	5	18	Household management or	8	18
or Science	5	18	Garment-making	8	18
A 8th Electricity	10	18	A 8th Typewriting or	5	18
			Science	5	18

NINTH GRADE

Required Subjects	Periods per Week	Required Subjects	Periods per Week
English	5	Prep. English or Business English	5
Algebra	5	Econ. Hist. and Occupations	5
Physical Training	2	Physical Training	2
Drawing or Music	2	Drawing or Music	2
European Hist	5		
	19		14

Boys	Periods	Weeks	Girls	Periods	Weeks
B 9th Mech. Dr. Advanced	10	18	Large Quantity Cookery and	10	12
A 9th Advanced Wood work and Concrete or Machine Shop	10	18	B 9th Art Needle Work	10	8
			A 9th Elementary Dressmaking	10	16

Choose One	Periods		Choose One	Periods	
Latin or French	5	Through the year	Latin or French	5	Through the year
European Hist	5		Algebra	5	
Stenography	5		European Hist	5	
Typewriting	5 or 10		Commercial Arith	5	
Bookkeeping	10		Stenography	5	
Science	7		Typewriting	5 or 10	
			Bookkeeping	10	
			Science	7	

On the advice of the Principal students may specialize on some Industrial subject.

The seventh grade prevocational students will take two shop subjects each semester in the order in which they are offered. They are required of all prevocational students.

Notes for the Ninth Grade.—

1. Those who expect to take only two years of the Commercial Course in the Senior High School should choose Commercial Arithmetic and either Stenography and Typewriting or History and Bookkeeping.

2. Those who have taken the Prevocational Course in the Seventh and Eighth Grades and who expect to take the General Academic Course in the Senior High School should choose either Science or Language.

3. For those who do not expect to continue longer than the Ninth Grade in school, a special arrangement may be made by which they will be required to take English, Physical Training, and Drawing or Music, and in addition they may choose, with the approval of the Principal three subjects or group of subjects.

4. Girls who intend to pursue the Home Training Course in the High School should elect Science in the Ninth Grade.

GARFIELD JUNIOR HIGH SCHOOL—RICHMOND, INDIANA

Seventh-Grade Work

REQUIRED SUBJECTS TWENTY-FIVE PERIODS PER WEEK	Periods per Week	ELECTIVE SUBJECTS FIVE PERIODS PER WEEK	Periods per Week
English	5	Latin	5
Arithmetic	5	German	5
History	5	English Composition	5

Physical Education	3	Industrial or	
Industrial or		Household Arts	5
Household Arts	3	Agriculture	5
Music	2	Commercial Work	5
Drawing	2	Orchestra	2 (extra)

Eighth-Grade Work

REQUIRED SUBJECTS TWENTY PERIODS PER WEEK	Periods per Week	ELECTIVE SUBJECTS TEN PERIODS PER WEEK	Periods per Week
English	5	Latin	5
Arithmetic	5	German	5
Geography (8B),		English Composition	5
Civics (8A)	5	Industrial or	
Physical Education	3	Household Arts	5 or 10
Chorus or Drawing	2	Agriculture	5 or 10
		Commercial Work	5 or 10
		Drawing and Design	5
		Music	5
		Orchestra	2 (extra)

Ninth-Grade Work

REQUIRED SUBJECTS FIFTEEN PERIODS PER WEEK	Periods per Week	ELECTIVE SUBJECTS FIFTEEN PERIODS PER WEEK	Periods per Week
English	5	Latin	5
General Science	5	German	5
Physical Education	3	Industrial or	
Chorus or Drawing	2	Household Arts	5 or 10
		Agriculture	5 or 10
		Drawing and Design	5 or 10
		Music	5
		Mathematics	
		Algebra, Commercial or	
		Industrial Arithmetic	5
		Civics	5
		History	5
		Orchestra	2 (extra)

AURORA PUBLIC SCHOOLS

Tentative Course, Junior High School

FIRST SEMESTER

Required		Optional	
English	5	English Grammar	5
Literature		Latin	5
Composition		German	5
Spelling	1	Algebra	5
Civics	2½	Commercial Arithmetic	5

General Science	2½	Cooking	1
		Sewing	1
		Manual Training	2
		Music	1
		Drawing	1
		Penmanship	2

SECOND SEMESTER

Required		Optional	
English	5	English Grammar	5
Literature		Latin	5
Composition		German	5
Spelling	1	Algebra	5
Civics	2½	Commercial Arithmetic and Bookkeeping	5
General Science	2½	Cooking	1
		Sewing	1
		Manual Training	2
		Music	1
		Drawing	1
		Penmanship	2

Forty-six semester units required to complete the year's work.

The numeral set opposite the various subjects indicates the unit credits allowed for each, and measures as nearly as possible the comparative time and effort required to satisfy requirements in each.

These curricula clearly show the secondary character of the work. One provides parallel curricula and the other two each a single curriculum with electives. The first two include the seventh, eighth, and ninth grades while the last provides only one year's work. Each of the first two schools maintains a senior high school of three years with parallel curricula corresponding to the junior high school. In the case of Aurora, the term "senior high school" is not used. Six parallel curricula are offered following the "tentative course" of one year. Four of the six curricula are four years in length; the other two, five years.

1. CURRICULA ORGANIZATION

No uniformity exists in the plan of organization of curricula. Certain tendencies toward uniformity have been manifest for about twenty years and these are in process of being worked out. Two things should be taken into account in any fruitful discussion of this topic: first, the plan of organization, and secondly, the educational aims involved. Taking up first the question of educational aims, it is evident both from the titles of curricula and also their content that aims are becoming more definite and that they are being expressed more and more in terms of the needs of various pupil groups. Some of the old titles still remain, but on the whole, titles have become more meaningful, and differentiation of curricula with reference to the needs of student groups is on the increase. This tendency is increasing so far as curricula titles are concerned, at least, as shown by a comparison of (1) and (2) in Table XXVII.

Three plans of organization prevail—a single course with electives, parallel courses, and the major-minor system. The latter, however, is rare, but it is probable that its use will become more general.[1]

The following table shows the number of courses offered, their designations, and the number of each.

TABLE XXVIII

1.—SIXTY SCHOOLS, 1906–11

Number of Schools	Number of Courses
23	1
7	2
4	3
14	4
9	5
3	6

Designation of Courses	Number of Schools
Academic	1
Art	1
Art and Manual Training	1
Business	2
Classical	5
Classical Preparatory	1
College Preparatory	8
Commercial	29
Commercial Industrial	1
Domestic Science	1
Elective	2
Engineering	1
Engineering Preparatory	1
English	8
English and Latin	1
English Scientific	2
English Commercial	1
Five-year General	1

[1] *Report North Central Association of Colleges and Secondary Schools*, 1917, pp. 58-59.

Five-year Latin	1
Foreign Language	1
General	8
General Science	1
German	3
German-English	2
Historical	1
History	3
Industrial	2
Language	3
Language and Science	1
Latin	11
Latin-English	1
Latin-German	3
Latin-Scientific	2
Literary	1
Manual Arts	1
Manual Training	4
Modern Classical	1
Modern Language	1
Normal Training	3
Physical Science	1
Regular	2
Science	5
Scientific	9
Scientific English	1
Scientific Preparatory	1
Teachers'	2

2.—SIXTY SCHOOLS, 1915–18

Number of Schools	Number of Courses
15	1
5	2
5	3
8	4
7	5
4	6
6	7
3	8
2	9
1	10
1	11
1	12
1	13
1	19

Designation of Courses	Number of Schools
Academic	2
Accounting	2
Agricultural	5
Architectural	1
Art	2
Business	4
Business-English	1
Civil Service	1
Classical	5
Classical Preparatory	20
College Preparatory and Domestic Science	1
College Preparatory for Engineering, Agricultural, and Technical Courses	1
College Preparatory in Pharmacy	1
Combined Commercial and Manual Training—Boys	1
Combined Commercial and Manual Training—Girls	1
Commercial	31
Commercial Course for Boys	1
Commercial Course for Girls	1
Contractor	1
Course in Millinery	1
Course in Needle Arts	1
Dentistry	1
Domestic Science	2
Domestic Science and Arts	1
Engineering	4
English	10
English-Scientific	2
Fine Arts	1
Five-year Latin	1
Five-year General	1
Household Studies	1
General	16
General College Course	1
General College Preparatory	1
German	4
History	4
Home	1
Home Arts	1
Home Economics	5
Household Arts	2
Household Economics	2
Household Science	2
Industrial	1
Industrial Arts	1
Industrial Course for Boys	1

Industrial Course for Girls	1
Industrial and Engineering	1
Industrial and Vocational	1
Language	2
Latin	9
Latin-French	1
Latin-German	2
Latin-Scientific	1
Local	1
Law	1
Manual Arts	4
Manual Training	11
Mathematics	1
Mechanic Arts	1
Medicine	1
Modern Classical	1
Modern Language	3
Normal College Preparatory	1
Normal Training	5
Office Preparatory	1
Pharmacist	1
Preparatory	1
Rural Economics	1
Science	10
Scientific	8
Scientific College Preparatory	2
Special Preparatory	1
Stenography	3
Teachers'	10
Telegraphy	1
Technical	1
Vocational	1

*The above titles indicate four-year courses with the exceptions noted.

The following are titles of two-year courses:

Designation of Courses	Number of Schools
Accounting	1
Agriculture	1
Bookkeeping	1
Domestic Science and Arts	1
Electricity	1
Industrial	1
Machine Shop	1
Printing	1
Stenography	1
Shorthand	1
Commercial (one year)	1

Turning to the titles listed on pages 205–06, such as the following are significant showing the specific character of educational opportunity provided: Agriculture, Commercial Courses for Boys, Commercial Courses for Girls, Courses in Millinery, Course in Needle Arts, Normal Training, Teachers', Bookkeeping, Accounting, Electricity, Printing, Machine Shop, and Stenography. The preparatory curricula have also felt the influence of professional and industrial influences. Such titles as the following show this: College Preparatory for Engineering, College Preparatory in Pharmacy, Pharmacist, Law, and Dentistry. How recent these specific terms are is shown by a comparison of titles in (1) and (2) of Table XXVIII, and the contrast between present practice and that of the closing years of the nineteenth century is shown by comparing the titles in Table XXVIII with those in (8) Table I.

It is true, of course, that specific titles do not always mean a high degree of specialization, but many of these industrial and commercial curricula do provide a rather highly specialized type of education.

Survival of the earlier practice of using titles derived from the various fields and subjects is shown by such terms as Latin, English, History, Latin-Scientific, etc. Also, indefinite titles such as General, Elective, Academic, and the like, still prevail. A comparison, however, of Tables I and XXVIII shows the recent decline of this practice, and a comparison of (8) in Table I with that of (2) in Table XXVIII indicates the change which has taken place in this particular during the last twenty years.

The plan of organization—one curriculum with electives or several parallel curricula—may or may not be significant, depending upon (1) the range of subjects offered, and (2) the plan of administering the elective system. For example, one school may provide a single curriculum with electives so administered that the same educational opportunity is provided as is furnished by another school which offers two or more parallel curricula. In evaluating these plans it is therefore necessary to know something of the details of administering them. Some printed courses of study furnish this information and others do not. From the evidence available, however, it is evident that an attempt is being made by the schools which publish a single curriculum to provide through a system of electives for differentiation to meet the needs of the various pupil groups. As has been pointed out, this attempt to provide special types of education to meet the various commercial and industrial demands is clearly revealed both by curricula organization and the range of subjects offered. The following are typical high-school curricula for the periods 1906–11 and 1915–18.

CHEBOYGAN, MICHIGAN, 1909–10

FIRST YEAR—NINTH GRADE

First Semester	Second Semester
Required	*Required*
English	English
Algebra	Algebra
General Electives	*General Electives*
Latin	Latin
Zoölogy	Botany
Ancient History	Ancient History
Manual Training	Manual Training
Domestic Science	Domestic Science
Commercial Electives	*Commercial Electives*
Penmanship and Spelling	Commercial Arithmetic
	Penmanship and Spelling

SECOND YEAR—TENTH GRADE

Required	*Required*
English	English
Algebra	Plane Geometry
General Electives	*General Electives*
Latin (Caesar)	Latin (Caesar)
Medieval and Modern History	Medieval and Modern History
Physiography	Physiography
Manual Training	Manual Training
Domestic Science	Domestic Science
Commercial Electives	*Commercial Electives*
Bookkeeping	Bookkeeping

THIRD YEAR—ELEVENTH GRADE

Required	*Required*
English	English
Plane Geometry	Solid Geometry*
Physics	Physics
General Electives	*General Electives*
Latin (Cicero)	Latin (Cicero)
German	German
Commercial Electives	*Commercial Electives*
Commercial Geography	Stenography and Typewriting

FOURTH YEAR—TWELFTH GRADE

Required	*Required*
American History and Civics	American History
	Civics
English	English

*Not required of students who take the full commercial course.

General Electives	General Electives
Latin (Virgil)	Latin (Virgil)
German	German
Chemistry	Chemistry
English Grammar Review	Algebra Review
	Advanced Physiology
Commercial Electives	**Commercial Electives**
Commercial Law	Bookkeeping
Stenography	Stenography
Typewriting	Typewriting

CHEBOYGAN, MICHIGAN, 1916

LATIN COURSE

First Year	Second Year	Third Year	Fourth Year
English	English	English	Latin
Algebra	Algebra and Geometry	Geometry	German
Latin	Latin	Latin	Physics
Ancient History	Modern History	German	American History

LATIN-GERMAN COURSE

English	English	English	English
Algebra	Algebra and Geometry	Geometry	German
Latin	Latin	Chemistry	Physics
Ancient History	Modern History	German	American History

ENGLISH COURSE

English	English	English	English
Algebra	Algebra and Geometry	Geometry	Physics
Biology, Zoölogy, and Botany	Physiography	Chemistry	German or Latin
Arithmetic and Commercial Correspondence	Modern History	German or Latin	American History
Correspondence			

COMMERCIAL COURSE

English	English	English	English
Algebra	Algebra and Geometry	Geometry or Chemistry	Physics
Biology, Zoölogy, and Botany	Physiography	Stenography and Typewriting	Stenography and Typewriting
Arithmetic and Commercial Correspondence	Bookkeeping	Commercial Geography and Law	American History
Correspondence			

DELAVAN, WISCONSIN, 1910–11

English Course

FIRST YEAR

First Semester	Second Semester
Algebra	Algebra
English	English
Physical Geography	Physical Geography, Botany
Physiology	Geography

SECOND YEAR

First Semester	Second Semester
Ancient History	Ancient History
English	English
Botany	Bookkeeping
Arithmetic	Civics

THIRD YEAR

First Semester	Second Semester
Geometry	Geometry
Medieval History	Modern History
English	American Literature
Political Economy	English Grammar

FOURTH YEAR

First Semester	Second Semester
Physics	Physics
American History	American History
English Literature	English Literature
Theory and Art	Algebra or Reviews

Modern Classical Course

FIRST YEAR

First Semester	Second Semester
Algebra	Algebra
English	English
Physical Geography	Physical Geography, Botany
Latin	Latin

SECOND YEAR

First Semester	Second Semester
Ancient History	Ancient History
English	English
Botany	Latin
Latin	Bookkeeping or Civics

THIRD YEAR

First Semester	Second Semester
Medieval History	Modern History
Geometry	Geometry
Latin	Latin
German	German

FOURTH YEAR

First Semester	Second Semester
Physics	Physics
American History	American History
Latin	Latin
German	German

German Course

FIRST YEAR

First Semester	Second Semester
Algebra	Algebra
English	English

Physical Geography	Physical Geography
Physiology	Botany
	Geography
SECOND YEAR	
Ancient History	Ancient History
English	English
Botany	Bookkeeping
Arithmetic	Civics
THIRD YEAR	
Medieval History	Modern History
Geometry	Geometry
German	German
Political Economy	English Grammar
FOURTH YEAR	
Physics	Physics
American History	American History
German	German
English Literature	English Literature

YANKTON, SOUTH DAKOTA, 1911

Latin Course	Scientific Course
FIRST YEAR	
Required	Required
English	English
Algebra	Algebra
Latin	Ancient History
Penmanship	Penmanship
Elective	Elective
Ancient History	Physical Geography
Music	Commercial Geography
Drawing	Music
	Drawing
SECOND YEAR	
Required	Required
English	English
Latin	German
Geometry	Geometry
Elective	Elective
Modern History	Modern History
German I	Botany
Music	Agriculture
Drawing	Music
	Drawing
THIRD YEAR	
Required	Required
English	English
Solid Geometry, Algebra	Solid Geometry, Algebra
Latin	German
	Chemistry

Elective	Elective
English History	Music
French History	Drawing
German II	
Music	
Drawing	

FOURTH YEAR

Required	Required
English	English
Physics	Physics
Latin	
Elective	**Elective**
German III	German III
American History, Arithmetic	American History, Arithmetic
Economy, Commercial Law	Economy, Commercial Law
	Physiology, Biology

YANKTON, SOUTH DAKOTA, 1917

Normal Course

FIRST YEAR

Required	Elective
English	German or Latin
Algebra	Domestic Science or Manual Training
Latin	Art
Penmanship	Physical Geography and General Science
Physical Culture	
Music	

SECOND YEAR

English	German or Latin
Latin	Modern History
Algebra and Plane Geometry	Domestic Science or Manual Training
Biology and Physiology	Music
Physical Training	Art

THIRD YEAR

English	Chemistry
Plane Geometry and Solid Geometry	Public Speaking and Debating
Physical Culture	Music
American History and Civics	Art
German or Latin	Agriculture

FOURTH YEAR

English	German or Latin
Psychology and Pedagogy	Public Speaking and Debating
Arithmetic	Music
	Art
	Agriculture
	Physics

Scientific Course

FIRST YEAR

Required	Elective
English	Ancient History
Algebra	Latin
Physical Culture	Music
	Art
	General Science
	Manual Training or Domestic Science
	Physical Geography and General Science

SECOND YEAR

Required	Elective
English	Modern History
Algebra and Plane Geometry	Latin
Physical Culture	Music
	Art
	Manual Training or Domestic Science
	Biology and Physiology

THIRD YEAR

Required	Elective
English	Latin
German	Public Speaking and Debating
Chemistry	Music
Physical Culture	Art
	American History and Civics
	Plane Geometry and Algebra

FOURTH YEAR

Required	Elective
English	Latin
Physics	Public Speaking and Debating
German	Political Economy and Arithmetic
Physical Culture	Music
	Art

Industrial and Engineering Course

FIRST YEAR

Required	Elective
English	Latin
Mechanical Drawing and Bench Work	Ancient History
Algebra	Physical Geography and General Science
Physical Culture	Music
	Art

SECOND YEAR

Required	Elective
English	Latin
Algebra and Plane Geometry	Modern History
Mechanical Drawing	Music
Bench Work	Art
Physical Culture	Physiology
	Biology

THIRD YEAR

English	Latin
Plane Geometry and Solid Geometry	Public Speaking and Debating
German	Chemistry
Architectural and Mechanical Drawing and Forge and Machine Work	Music
Physical Culture	Art
	German
	Spanish

FOURTH YEAR

English	Latin
Physics	Public Speaking and Debating
Architectural and Mechanical Drawing, Forge and Machine Work	Political Economy and Arithmetic
German	Music
Physical Culture	Art
	German
	Spanish

Home Economics Course

FIRST YEAR

Required	Elective
English	Ancient History
Home Economics	Physical Geography and General Science
Algebra	Music
Latin	Art
Physical Culture	

SECOND YEAR

English	Modern History
Home Economics	Algebra and Plane Geometry
Latin	Music
Physical Culture	Art
Biology and Physiology	

THIRD YEAR

English	Latin
Home Economics	German
Physical Culture	Chemistry
American History and Civics	Public Speaking and Debating
Chemistry	Music
	Art

FOURTH YEAR

English	German or Latin
Home Economics	Public Speaking and Debating
Physical Culture	Political Economy and Arithmetic
Physics	Music
	Art

Classical Course

First Year

Required	Elective
English	Ancient History
Algebra	Music
Latin	Art
Physical Culture	Manual Training or Domestic Science
	Physical and General Science

Second Year

Required	Elective
English	Modern History
Latin	Music
Algebra and Plane Geometry	Art
Physical Culture	Biology and Physiology
	Manual Training or Domestic Science

Third Year

Required	Elective
English	German
Plane Geometry and Solid Geometry	Music
Latin	Art
American History and Civics	Public Speaking and Debating
Physical Culture	Chemistry

Fourth Year

Required	Elective
English	German
Physics	Public Speaking and Debating
Latin	Music
Physical Culture	Art
	Political Economy and Arithmetic

Commercial Course

First Year

Required

- Algebra
- Commercial Geography and Commercial Arithmetic
- Typewriting
- Physical Training
- Penmanship
- Latin

Second Year

Required

- English
- Algebra and Plane Geometry
- Typewriting
- Bookkeeping
- Penmanship
- Biology and Physiology
- Physical Training

Third Year

Required

- English
- Bookkeeping and Shorthand Principles
- American History and Civics
- Physical Training
- Spanish

Fourth Year

Required

- Shorthand
- Political Economy and Commercial Law
- Typewriting
- Physical Training
- Spanish

AGRICULTURAL COURSE

FIRST YEAR

Required

English
Algebra
Manual Training or
Domestic Science
Latin

Physical Training

Elective

Ancient History
Physiology and General Science

SECOND YEAR

Required

English
Manual Training or
Domestic Science
Latin
Physical Training

Elective

Biology
Algebra and Plane Geometry

THIRD YEAR

Required

English
Agriculture
Chemistry

Physical Training

Elective

American History and Civics
Public Speaking and Debating
Manual Training or
Domestic Science

FOURTH YEAR

Required

English
Agriculture
Physical Training

Elective

Political Economy and
Commercial Law
Public Speaking and Debating
Manual Training or
Domestic Science

NOTE.—Students wishing to take electives other than those given may possibly do so upon consultation with principal. Such selections, however, should be confined to subjects corresponding to the respective classification of the student.

It will be seen that Cheboygan offered a single course in 1909 with two groups of electives designated "general" and "commercial." In 1916 four parallel courses were offered. Delavan offered three courses in 1910 and in 1916 a single course with electives. Yankton offered two courses in 1911 each with electives. In 1918 seven courses were provided with no electives. As has been pointed out, the plan of organization may or may not be significant, depending upon how the choice of electives is administered. The tendency, however, is clearly toward parallel curricula organized on the basis of meeting the needs of the various pupil groups. Those who enter higher institutions are provided for in this particular as well as those who enter immediately upon the active duties of life.

The following table shows the number of schools offering the various fields and subjects, 1906–11.

TABLE XXIX

FORTY SCHOOLS, 1906–11

Mathematics, 40

Arithmetic, 18
Algebra, 40
Plane Geometry, 40
Solid Geometry, 36
Trigonometry, 20
College Algebra, 3

English, 40*

Science, 40

Astronomy, 5
Biology, 7
Botany, 34
Zoölogy, 22
Physics, 40
Chemistry, 37
Physical Geography, 33
Physiology, 26
Geology, 4
General Science, 1

Social Studies, 40

Ancient History, 37
Medieval and Modern History, 34
English History, 24
American History, 37
Civics, 33
Economics, 18
General History, 1

Foreign Language, 40

Latin, 40
French, 15
German, 38
Greek, 10
Spanish, 3

Commercial Subjects, 35

Commercial Arithmetic, 22
Commercial English, 9
Commercial Geography, 23
Commercial Law, 22
Commercial and Industrial History, 3
Typewriting, 25
Stenography, 27
Bookkeeping, 31

Practical and Fine Arts, 28

Agriculture, 4
Domestic Science, 16
Domestic Art, 5
Domestic Economy, 1
Mechanical Drawing, 1
Manual Training, 24
Art, 1

Education, 10

Pedagogy, 8
Psychology, 5
Ethics, 1

The following table shows the number of schools offering the various fields and subjects, 1915–18.

TABLE XXX

FORTY SCHOOLS, 1915–18

Mathematics, 40

Arithmetic, 13
Algebra, 40
Plane Geometry, 40
Solid Geometry, 39
Trigonometry, 20
College Algebra, 3

English, 40*

Science, 40

Astronomy, 1
Biology, 18
Botany, 27
Chemistry, 37
Geology, 3
General Science, 19
Zoölogy, 16
Physics, 40
Physical Geography, 21
Physiology, 21

Social Studies, 40

Ancient History, 38
Medieval and Modern History, 34
English History, 21
American History, 37

*Subjects not specified.

Civics, 34
Economics, 25
State History, 2
Citizenship, 1
Contemporary Life, 1

Foreign Language, 40

Latin, 40
French, 14
German, 37
Greek, 6
Spanish, 15
Swedish, 1

Commercial Subjects, 40

Commercial Arithmetic, 26
Commercial English, 16
Commercial Geography, 27
Commercial Law, 31
Commercial and Industrial History, 10
Typewriting, 38
Stenography, 38
Bookkeeping, 37
Accounting, 5
Business Methods, 9
Banking, 3
Salesmanship, 5
Office Practice, 4
Advertising, 3

Practical and Fine Arts, 39

Agriculture, 22
Domestic Science, 30
Domestic Art, 7
Domestic Economy, 6
Manual Training, 31
Mechanical Drawing, 5
Pattern Making, 4
Machine Shop, 6
Metal Work, 2
Pottery, 1
Household Chemistry, 5
Camp Cooking, 1
Forging, 6
Machine Fitting, 1
Printing, 3
First Aid, 1
Electricity and Applied Mechanics, 1
Building Construction, 1
Carpentry, 1
Home Management, 3
Design, 1
Telegraphy, 1
Home-Nursing, 1
Millinery, 2
Art and Needlework, 2
Laundry and Sanitation, 1
Household Physics, 1

Education, 13

Pedagogy, 13
Psychology, 7
Biblical Literature, 1

2. RANGE OF SUBJECTS

The range of subjects in the traditional fields remains practically unchanged since 1900. Increase of uniformity of terminology, particularly in English, science, and the social studies, gives an appearance of less wide range, but such is not the case in fact, except in a limited way. In the case of English, for example, less attention no doubt is being given to the formal aspects of grammar and rhetoric and more emphasis is being placed upon composition and the content of literature. Astronomy has practically disappeared and geology is negligible. The loss through the decline of these subjects is more than compensated for by extension of subject-matter in other science subjects. The standardization of terminology in the case of the social studies has greatly reduced the number of the names of subjects without, however, involving any actual loss.

The commercial subjects and the fine and practical arts, on the other hand, show great increase in range of subjects. The most of this extension has taken place since 1910, as shown by a study of Tables IX, XXIX, and XXX. The latter table, particularly, shows lack of uniformity in the use of terms, but making full allowance for this, it is still evident that considerable extension has taken place. Such terms, for example, as salesmanship, accounting, advertising, and the like show that the work in commercial subjects is being extended beyond merely clerical lines.[1]

The fields in which greatest extension has taken place are those of the commercial and the fine and practical arts.[2] We find here also evident lack of standardization of terms, but again making full allowance for this, it is very clear that the work in this field is being greatly extended. Such terms as millinery, printing, nursing, design, telegraphy, and the like conclusively show this. There is no doubt much similarity in lines of work designated by the use of different names. For example, domestic science, domestic art, and domestic economy do not always signify different lines of work. The first two are frequently used synonymously and all three are sometimes so used. It is clear, however, that three general lines of work are now recognized. The first has to do with food, its values, its preparation, and the serving of it. The second emphasizes the artistic side of home life including decoration, selection and arrangement of furniture, and the like. In this line is also included needlework of all sorts, millinery, and a study of textiles. The third group of subjects emphasizes management in the home. This subject is not clearly defined but the point of view is clearly that of training in directing all the forces in the home and conserving all its interests. As has been said, there is much overlapping and terms are used very loosely. It is evident, however, that the process of differentiation and classification is going on rapidly and unit courses and curricula are being definitely worked out which will result in a fairly definite organization of these lines of work.

The general terms "manual training" and "mechanical drawing" include a relatively wide range of subjects. These two lines of work have been recognized from the first and the distinction is still maintained. The former has been much extended as shown by the use of such terms as carpentry, building construction, machine

[1] Cf. Tables XXIX and XXX.

[2] *Ibid.*

shop, electricity, and applied mechanics. The greatest extension of this work is found in technical schools such as the Harrison, Lane, and Crane Technical high schools of Chicago.[1] Similar schools are maintained by other large cities, but since these schools are relatively few and are not typical, data from their curricula are not included in the tables.

The following table shows the constants and variables in terms of percentages for the various fields and subjects.

TABLE XXXI

	1906–11	1915–18
Mathematics	100	100
English	100	100
Science	100	100
Social Studies	100	100
Foreign Language	100	100
Commercial Subjects	90	100
Fine and Practical Arts	70	97½
Education	25	32½

	1906–11	1915–18
Mathematics—		
Arithmetic	45	32½
Algebra	100	100
Plane Geometry	100	100
Solid Geometry	90	97½
Trigonometry	50	50
College Algebra	7½	7½
English—		
Composition*	100	100
Literature	100	100
Science—		
Astronomy	12½	2½
Biology	17½	45
Botany	85	67½
Zoölogy	55	40
Physics	100	100
Chemistry	92½	92½
Physical Geography	82½	52½
Physiology	65	52½
Geology	10	7½
General Science	2½	47½
Social Studies—		
Ancient History	92½	95
Medieval and Modern History	85	85
English History	60	52½
American History	92½	92½
Civics	82½	87½
Economics	45	62½
Foreign Language—		
Latin	100	100
French	32½	35
German	95	92½
Greek	25	15
Spanish	7½	37½
Commercial Subjects—		
Commercial Arithmetic	55	65
Commercial English	22½	40
Commercial Geography	57½	67½
Commercial Law	57½	77½
Commercial and Industrial History	7½	22½
Typewriting	62½	95
Stenography	67½	92½
Bookkeeping	77½	92½
Accounting		17½
Banking		7½
Office Practice		10
Salesmanship		12½
Advertising		7½

*Grammar and rhetoric are no doubt taught more or less, but the tendency to teach these in connection with composition and literature has been steadily increasing since 1900. For this reason they are not listed separately.

[1] Cf. *Printed Course of Study for Chicago High Schools*, 1917.

Fine and Practical Arts†		
Agriculture	10	55
Domestic Science	40	75
Domestic Economy	2½	15
Domestic Art	12½	17½
Manual Training	60	77½
Mechanical Drawing	2½	12½
Pattern Making	0	10
Household Chemistry		12½
Household Management		7½
Machine Shop		15
Forging		15
Printing		7½
Education—		
Pedagogy	20	32½
Psychology	12½	17½

3. CONSTANTS AND VARIABLES

It will be seen by reference to Table XXXI that all the fields are constants in the period 1915–18 except that one school offers nothing in the fine and practical arts. In the period 1906–11, approximately 90 per cent offer commercial work and 70 per cent provide courses in the fine and practical arts. Comparing Tables IX and XXXI a considerable increase is shown in the number of schools offering commercial work. The same comparison shows that the increase of the work in the fine and practical arts has practically all taken place since 1900.

The only field not a constant is what is now generally called education. In certain of the states this work is emphasized far more than in other states.[1] This field is growing in importance and a decided increase is shown since 1900.

The only constants in the field of mathematics are algebra and geometry. Solid geometry is nearly so. Trigonometry was offered in 50 per cent of the schools in both periods and has increased since 1900, as shown by reference to Table X. Arithmetic has declined since 1900 and is still on the decline as shown by comparing the two periods in Tables XXXI.

The reorganization of the work in English which has been going on for some time has resulted in a breaking down of the old divisions. This has resulted in a decline of formal grammar and rhetoric and an increase in attention to composition and literature. It is probably true that all teach grammar and rhetoric although these terms are frequently not included in explanations of the work in English.

Physics is the only science subject offered by all the schools. Chemistry stands next having to its credit 92½ per cent of the schools

†For subjects offered in only one or two schools see Tables XXIX and XXX.

[1] Cf. *Report United States Commission of Education*, 1916, II, 452-55.

in each period. A decided increase is shown since 1900. Botany stands next to chemistry and is followed by physical geography. Both of these subjects show a decided decline, comparing periods 1906–11 and 1915–18. Physiology follows physical geography, having to its credit 65 per cent of the schools in 1906–11 and declines to 52½ per cent in the last period. Zoölogy loses 15 per cent and is offered in 40 per cent of the schools in 1915–18. Astronomy and geology are negligible in the last period. Biology more than doubles and general science represented by only one school on 1906–11, is offered by 47½ per cent of the schools in the last period. The decrease in the importance of botany, zoölogy, physical geography, and physiology is no doubt fully accounted for by the increase in the number of schools offering biology and general science.

No subject in the field of the social studies is strictly a constant although ancient history and American history are nearly so, each being offered in more than 90 per cent of the schools. Medieval and modern history stands next with 85 per cent of the schools for both periods. Civics follows with 82½ per cent and 87½ per cent for the two periods. All these subjects show decided increase since 1900, as shown by reference to Table X. The increase in the case of European history is, however, not as much as it appears to be due to the disappearance of the term "general history." The material formerly so designated is now classified as ancient history and medieval and modern history. Not much change, as a matter of fact, has taken place in the number of schools offering European history. English history is offered in a little more than one-half of the schools and shows some decline. Economics offered in 45 per cent of the schools in 1906–11 increases to 62½ per cent in the last period.

Latin is the constant in the field of foreign language followed closely by German. It is a matter of common knowledge that the latter has declined rapidly in the last few months and present indications are that it will become almost negligible. Whether or not this decline almost to the point of extinction is permanent, cannot be determined at present. French, offered in approximately one-third of the schools in both periods, will be introduced into many schools next year. As in the case of German it is too early to tell what the final outcome will be. Spanish was offered in 7½ per cent of the schools in 1906–11 and in 37½ per cent in the last period.

The most significant fact revealed by Table XXXI concerning commercial subjects and the fine and practical arts is the tremendous increase since 1900 in the number of schools offering these subjects. The table also shows the rapid increase since 1910. This is shown both by increase in percentages and also by the new subjects added.

None of the commercial subjects are constants, although stenography, typewriting, and bookkeeping are nearly so in the last period. Commercial law, geography, and arithmetic stand next in the order named with 77½ per cent, 67½ per cent, and 65 per cent respectively.

Table XXXI does not present the true status concerning the fine and practical arts, due to lack of uniformity in the use of terminology. For example, take the terms "domestic economy," "domestic science," and "domestic art." They are not used in the same sense by all the schools. A reference to Table XXXI shows that 97½ per cent offer some work in this general field in 1915–18. The same is true in the case of the vocational subjects for boys. Approximately 97½ per cent of the schools also offer work in the subjects included in the general subject manual training. As shown by Table XXX all but one school offered something in this general field in the last period.

Pedagogy and psychology are not as yet very important, but an increase is shown from 1900 to 1910 and further increase since the latter date.

4. REQUIRED SUBJECTS AND ELECTIVES

English is the only field in which subjects are universally required. All the schools at present require at least two years work, approximately 90 per cent require at least three years, and about 50 per cent require four years. This practice of requiring English of all students dates back previous to 1900, and the amount required has constantly increased up to the present time.

Approximately 80 per cent of the schools require algebra and about 60 per cent require plane geometry. Of this number about 50 per cent require two years, one year of algebra and one year of plane geometry, and the remainder require an additional semester of algebra. The number of schools requiring any mathematics beyond this is negligible. Previous to 1900 practically all high schools required both algebra and plane geometry. The decline in this practice has taken place chiefly since 1910.

About 50 per cent of the schools require some work in science, usually one or two years. Of this number 20 per cent do not specify what science is required, giving students opportunity to choose. Physics is required in 25 per cent of the schools and physiology in about 10 per cent. A few schools require some other science subject, but the number is negligible. On the whole, the practice of requiring science is decreasing, the only exception being in general science. This subject has been introduced only recently and the increasing tendency to require the subject is evident.

Something in the field of the social studies is required in 60 per cent of the schools. American history leads with 40 per cent and ancient history and civics are each required by 15 per cent of the schools. The practice of requiring American history has developed since 1900 and the same is true of civics. The requirement in the case of ancient history is no doubt a survival of the practice of requiring general history. The number of schools requiring American history and civics is increasing, and this may be expected to continue. The growth of sentiment in favor of requiring American history is shown by a resolution adopted by the North Central Association of Secondary Schools and Colleges, March 22, 1918. The resolution reads as follows:

> It is urgently recommended that a course in American history be required for graduation by all secondary schools; that the course be so placed in the curriculum, in so far as such arrangement is possible, that all who enter the schools may receive the benefit of instruction; that the subject matter be selected with special reference to the inculcation of proper social and economic ideals; and that methods of teaching be chosen and supervised with special reference to the accomplishment of this aim.

This does not represent at all what schools do actually require, but since the resolution was unanimously adopted, it is significant in indicating the sentiment of teachers and administrators in secondary schools and higher institutions. The number of schools requiring subjects other than those named above are so few that they may be disregarded.

Some foreign language, usually not specified, is required in about 10 per cent of the schools. When the language is specified, it is invariably Latin.

No school in the list considered requires commercial subjects. It is rather interesting to note, however, that 10 per cent of the schools require something in the field of fine and practical arts.

While it is not the practice to specify, it is clear that requirements for boys and girls are different.

The relative importance at present of subjects, from the standpoint of the number of pupils pursuing them, is not easily determined in most cases, since several determining factors enter into the situation. First, the relative number of schools requiring the various subjects has to be taken into account. This has been discussed in the preceding pages, and if it were the only factor, one could determine the minimum percentages, at least, of pupils pursuing the various subjects. For example, it could be said that at least 25 per cent study physics while the minimum for those studying physiology is only 10 per cent. The second factor here enters in, viz., the year or years in the course in which the subject is offered. This is discussed in the section immediately following. Taking the two subjects mentioned, physiology is usually a first-year subject while physics is usually offered in the last year. In any given schools requiring both of these subjects, it is clear that many more pupils, perhaps double the number, would study the former as compared with the number pursuing the latter. Computing the number on the basis of 10 per cent of the schools requiring physiology and 25 per cent physics, it is probable that the minimum number is about the same in each case. Another question entering into the situation is whether a subject is required of all pupils or only in certain specified curricula. For example, a school might maintain five curricula and require a specified subject in four of the five, while another school having an equal enrolment and an equal number of curricula would require it in only one. If curricula titles were more definitely descriptive of content, inferences, at least, could be drawn with some degree of accuracy. There are some titles, of course, which clearly indicate that one or more subjects are pursued by all who elect the curricula. For example, such titles as agriculture, domestic science, manual training, and commercial, indicate groups of subjects, at least, which are pursued by large numbers of pupils. Another title, college preparatory, indicates another group of subjects which are pursued by the large number of pupils preparing for higher institutions. For example, foreign language, while required by only 10 per cent of the schools, stands relatively high in the number of pupils pursuing it.

Taking into account all the factors it is possible to arrive at certain conclusions with varying degrees of accuracy. It is clear for example, that English leads all other subjects. It is offered four years, two years is required in all schools, three years in 90 per cent and four years in 50 per cent of them. Algebra probably stands next because it is a first-year subject and is required in a high percentage of schools. History of some sort probably stands relatively high since the average time devoted to this field is four years and something is required in 60 per cent of the schools. When one undertakes, however, to determine the relative importance of the different units in history, definite conclusions are quite impossible. American history is required in nearly one-half of the schools and ancient history in less than one-sixth. But the latter is usually offered in the first year and the former in the last year, and it is therefore probable that these subjects are about equal in importance.

From the standpoint of the percentage of schools making requirements, science stands next to the social studies. The maximum requirement, 25 per cent, in the case of physics does not mean that this subject leads for the reason already pointed out, and it is probable that the number of pupils in each of the subjects, physical geography, physiology, physics, and botany, is about equal.[1] Foreign language is required in only about 10 per cent of the schools, but it is no doubt elected by a large number of pupils. This is especially true in the case of Latin.[2] It is offered four years in practically all the schools and is nearly always required in college preparatory courses.

In summary it may be said that the order of importance of fields and subjects is as follows: English, with emphasis upon composition and literature; algebra, history, science, probably quite equally distributed as suggested above; foreign language (with Latin leading) and increasing emphasis on commercial and practical arts subjects.

5. SIZE AND LOCATION OF SCHOOLS

It is evident that general uniformity in content of curricula prevails in the North Central states. As pointed out in Part I, neither the size of a school nor its location seems to have much influence except that schools in the larger centers of population offer a wider range of subjects. The rapid development of com-

[1] This estimate is corroborated by the *Report of the United States Commission of Education*, 1916, II, 500-4.

[2] *Ibid.*

mercial and industrial education is widespread and extends to the smaller schools as well as to the larger ones. The latter, however, offer a wider range of subjects and also those more highly specialized and more strictly vocational in character. Commercial and industrial education is by no means confined to localities where one would expect occupational interests and activities to demand these specific types of education. Agriculture, for example, is taught in urban as well as in rural communities. Commercial subjects are offered in the latter as well as in the former, although the range is not so wide nor are the subjects usually so highly specialized.

The fact seems clear that specific community interests and demands initiated the movement for these types of education. Then two influences have been at work to cause the spread of the movement—widespread interest in commerce and industry, and the always prevailing tendency to imitate in matters social and institutional. The essential unity in the thought and purpose of the people of these states is clearly revealed by the fact of general uniformity in the character of the curricula of the secondary schools. It is no doubt true that less uniformity would in many cases be desirable. Smaller schools are sometimes overambitious to imitate larger schools, and attempts to imitate result in undertaking to do things which are not done well. But the facts are as stated. The American high school early in its history undertook to perform two functions, that of preparing for college, and that of preparing for life, and both these functions are still attempted by all high schools having a minimum curriculum of four years. As the commercial and industrial demands have increased and become more specific, the schools have responded by attempting to meet the demands through the introduction of commercial and industrial subjects. Rural as well as urban communities vary in these demands, and small schools as well as large ones have attempted to meet them.

CHAPTER XV

CHANGES IN SUBJECT-MATTER

Changes in subject-matter since 1900 have been marked in some fields and subjects while in others little or no change has taken place. One cause of change, if not indeed the chief cause, has been the emphasis placed upon industrial and commercial education. The increased attention given to these types of education as shown by the multiplication of subjects in these fields and by the increase in time devoted to the subjects is also shown by the influence upon the subject-matter of some of the traditional subjects. This influence, for example, is shown by such terms as business English, commercial arithmetic, vocational mathematics, industrial history, household chemistry, shop and farm physics, agricultural botany and the like.

In this respect, the changes since 1900 are radically different from those which took place before that date. For example, the shift in botany from the anatomy of plants to morphology was clearly due to professional influence. On the contrary, the present emphasis upon agricultural and horticultural aspects of the subjects, in so far as this emphasis exists, is manifestly due to industrial influences. The same thing is true concerning the other sciences. The changes previous to 1900 were apparently in no way determined by industrial demands but were due to the shift of interest and point of view of the teachers of sciences. In the field of foreign language the growth of interest in Spanish is no doubt due to commercial influences. Attempts are also being made to have Latin contribute to the demands for a more practical education. Whether these latter subjects are capable of making any considerable contribution to vocational training is another question. The fact is that the advocates of these subjects are attempting to have them make such contribution. Further evidence of the influence of industrial and commercial demands will be noted later.

MATHEMATICS

The influence of commercial demands upon arithmetic is clearly revealed by the attention devoted to commercial arithmetic. A reference to Table J will show the percentage of schools offering this subject at the present time, and comparison of this table with Table I will show the rapid gain made by this subject since 1910. The recent textbooks also show the emphasis placed upon the commercial phase of the subject. An examination of these reveals that the old type of subject-matter discussed in Part II has been largely supplanted, so far as high-school work is concerned, by material determined theoretically at least by industrial and commercial demands.

Algebra and geometry have also felt the influence of these demands as shown by the claims of these subjects set up in the prefaces of the later texts. An examination of the texts themselves, however, fails to reveal any radical change in the character of the subject-matter of either of these subjects. The so-called practical values which they possess have received more attention than formerly and that these values have been stressed is an undoubted result of the vocational movement in education. But after all, this has not resulted in any marked change in character of the material in either subject.

Except for the change noted in connection with arithmetic, the only real significant change in the field of mathematics is found in the reorganization of material. Texts in "unified" or "mixed" mathematics are being substituted for separate texts in the various mathematical subjects. For example, a three-book series[1] for junior high schools by Wentworth, Smith, and Brown includes arithmetic, algebra, geometry and trigonometry. Book I is devoted to arithmetic and geometry, Book II to algebra and arithmetic, and Book III to algebra, geometry, and trigonometry. A total of less than three-fifths of the space in Books I and II is devoted to arithmetic and a little more than one-fifth to each of the other subjects. The subject-matter of arithmetic emphasizes to some extent the industrial and commercial aspects of the subject. The quantity of algebra is reduced and the work is simplified. Otherwise the material is no different than found in the traditional text. The work in geometry is greatly reduced in amount and is also simplified. It is in fact reduced to the geometry of form and position in Book I and is designed chiefly as propaedeutic to more advanced work. About one-half of Book III is devoted to geom-

[1] WENTWORTH, G. H., SMITH, D. E., and BROWN, J. C., *Junior High School Mathematics. Book I, II and III.* 1916, 1918.

etry, a little less than one-third to algebra, and the remainder to trigonometry.

The Breslich texts[1] is another example of this type of organization. The author claims that the "practical is emphasized," but one fails to note any significant change in the type of material selected. The purpose of the series is well set forth in the editor's preface.

> During this process of reform, mathematics has changed less perhaps than any other subject. The text books in algebra have modified but little their list of topics or other mode of exposition. Most of the later books introduce graphs and have graded their problems better and have omitted some of the intricacies which were included a generation ago. These improvements are welcome but insufficient and if algebra has been conservative, what shall one say of Euclidian geometry. . . . . To those who examine this book from the point of view of the critical mathematician, it ought to be said that it is a pedagogical rather than a logical organization of general and fundamental mathematical notions. Rigor in the pure mathematical sense is not attempted in definitions, axioms, or principles. Insight has everywhere been the controlling consideration. Experimentation, intuition, and induction are fully employed.

Another book of this same general type is Evans and Marsh's *First Year Mathematics*.[2] The material is chiefly algebra with a considerable number of arithmetical and geometrical exercises. There is less material than in the other texts cited above and there is no new subject-matter introduced. The book is chiefly intended to serve as an introduction to a further study of mathematics. From this standpoint the material is well selected and the organization has taken into account the propaedeutic value of the various topics and exercises.

These books represent the new movement in high-school mathematics. Two things characterize the movement. The first is a breaking down of the hard and fast divisions of subject-matter into arithmetic, algebra, geometry, and trigonometry. This results in new units of instruction which consist of material selected from two or more of the mathematical subjects. The second characteristic naturally follows, viz., a reorganization of material. As indicated above in the preface quoted "it is a pedagogical rather than a logical organization of general and fundamental mathematical notions."

[1] Breslich, Ernst R., *First-Year Mathematics*, 1915 (1906, 1909); *Second-Year Mathematics*, 1916 (1910); *Third-Year Mathematics*, 1917.

[2] Evans, G. W., and Marsh, J. A., *First Year Mathematics*, 1916.

An examination of a number of texts in both algebra and geometry published since 1900 does not reveal any significant changes either in material selected or in organization. Certain devices have been used in some of the newer books which have perhaps aided more or less in better teaching. For example, in Reitz, Crathorne, and Taylor's Algebra text emphasis is placed upon the propaedeutic value of the subject-matter as it relates to higher mathematics and science. Principles and rules are printed in black-faced type or italics and numerous historical notes are given. Ford and Amerman's *Geometry* is another example of the use of devices to aid the teacher. In accordance with the recommendation of the Committee of Fifteen, theorems of supposedly greatest value, are printed in bold-faced type, those of somewhat less importance in italics, and the remainder in ordinary type. Historical notes are also provided.

Except for the change noted in the organization of material and the increasing importance of commercial arithmetic, little change has taken place in the field of mathematics.

ENGLISH

Some of the newer texts in English show that important changes have taken place since 1900 both in the character of material used and also in its organization. It is interesting first of all to note that unified English as well as unified mathematics represents the new type of organization. Brubaker's and Snyder's *High-School English*[1] is an example. The following is found in the preface of Book I:

> The purpose of this book is to unify the teaching of English in the high school. English as a school study is more than grammar, more than composition, more than literature. It is a judicious combination of these three component parts.

In the preface of Book II, the following statement is made:

> High school English is here considered a unit. During the secondary school period the pupil should become familiar with the structure of the English language by the study of the uncontroverted rules of usages embodied in grammar; he should acquire the habitual use of forceful and appropriate language in speaking and writing by the practice of oral and written self-expression; he should form a discriminating taste for good literature by much reading, together with profitable discussion regarding the form and content of the literature read. This volume seeks to be a guide in such work.

[1] Brubaker, A. R., and Snyder, Dorothy, *High School English. Books I and II*, 1910.

As indicated in the prefaces the authors have ignored the traditional divisions, grammar, composition, rhetoric, and literature, and have attempted to present English as a unit. In this they seem to have succeeded. They have left off labels and selected the material and organized it with reference to training in composition, both oral and written, and have used literature as one of the means to this end and also for the purpose of forming "a discriminating taste for good literature by much reading." The material dealing with grammar is put in an appendix covering about fifty pages.

Another text of this same general type is Webster's *English for Secondary Schools*.[1] It is made clear by a statement in the preface that the author has not sought to unify the work so much as he has to make composition the center around which to organize the work.

> In presenting *English for Secondary Schools* it will serve a purpose to state the principles that have guided in making the book. It is some years since the study of literature gave way to the more practical study of composition in which the mass of rules concerning diction has been superseded by a few principles designed simply to secure clearness of expression. Furthermore, it is now evident that no mere statement of these principles, however clear and accurate it may be, is as illuminating to the young learner as a clear exposition of how successful writers have done their work. Few teachers would now have the hardihood to separate the study of composition from the study of literature and all teachers know that the best instructors in English composition are those writers who have served their apprenticeship and have been accepted in the world of literature as masters of their craft.

This no doubt indicates the use of literature as a source of material in composition but its chief use is clearly for acquiring the technique of expression. Commenting further concerning the source of material and the motivation of the work he says:

> There must be a definite, concrete problem upon which the student is to focus his energy and ingenuity. Among these concrete problems, none are so sure to call forth eager active minds as those which have immediate and local interest. So that, while the exercises given here are good as models and suggestions, those most certain to bring out expression are the ones that every instructor finds ready at hand in the life of the community where he labors.

Frank's *Elements of High-School English*[2] is another instance of the use of a title similar to the ones already cited. Like Webster's

[1] Webster, W. F., *English for Secondary Schools*, 1912.

[2] Frank, Maude M., *Elements of High School English*, 1915.

text this one is essentially a composition book. Emphasis is placed upon oral as well as written composition, and provision is made for "dramatic effort in the classroom." This book devotes considerable attention to spelling and an undue amount of space is devoted to grammar. No attempt is made to use literature either as a source of material or as a model for technique in composition.

These texts will serve as illustrations of the movement under way to break up the traditional organization of subject-matter in the field of English. It is no doubt due in part to the practice now becoming prevalent of regarding all instruction in English from two standpoints, viz., composition and literature. This is clearly shown by the report of the Commission on Units and Curricula of the North Central Association.[1] This report reads as follows:

> The acquisition of ideas and the development of skill, habits, ideals and attitudes which the English studies are designed for have reference to the two aspects of life—work and leisure, production and play—may be found the basis for a vital and economical organization of the English course. The study of books of an informational or persuasive character should support the study of oral and written composition for utilitarian purposes; likewise the practice of literary or creative composition, of reading aloud, and of dramatizing should aid the appreciative reading of novels, dramas, essays and poems. The terms "composition" and "literature" are used to designate these two types of activities in this report and they should represent separate units with equal credits in the high school.

This recognition of "separate units' is not always found in the texts but the two terms "composition" and "literature" are used to include all of the subject-matter presented.

Another way in which this breaking up of traditional divisions is manifested is in the courses in commercial and business English. These courses are primarily composition courses and in this respect are unlike the texts referred to above. But in this class of texts, grammar and rhetoric are not considered as separate subjects or even as separate units. Material is chosen from these subjects and this together with the content material is organized as a unit. An example of this class of texts is Buhlig's *Business English.*[2]

Literature has from the beginning been regarded as a separate unit. In the case of composition this has become true only recently. The evolution of this subject from being regarded as an irregular general exercise to its present status has been explained in Part II.

[1] *Report of Commission on Units and Curricula, North Central Association of Secondary Schools and Colleges*, 1918, p. 10.

[2] Buhlig, Rose, *Business English*, 1914.

Its first direct connection with other English subjects as there pointed out was with grammar, next with rhetoric, and finally with literature. Titles of textbooks such as *Elements of Composition and Grammar*, *Composition and Rhetoric*, and *Composition-Literature* show this development. Composition has now come to occupy an equal place with literature, and in the most of these texts, such titles as *First Year English* and the like, chief attention is directed to composition. The courses in English given in more or less detail in the published courses of study also show this same emphasis.

The books bearing the older titles indicate this emphasis upon composition. Scott and Denney's *New Composition and Rhetoric*[1] is an example. This is essentially a composition text and a considerable amount of literature is included as a source of material. Concerning this matter of topics and composition material the authors have the following to say in the preface:

> Composition topics are drawn not only from literature and student life but from the vocations toward which the various classes of students are naturally tending. The teacher is thus enabled to take advantage of a powerful means of interest and incitement in making assignments and to consult the known tastes and inclinations of the individual students.

The same emphasis upon these sources for topics and material is indicated in the report of the Commission on Units and Curricula.[2]

> There should be a constant effort to relate the work in composition with the pupils' experience and interest, both in and out of school. This will include drawing upon among other things, his school work and other school activities, social and athletic, as well as his extra school work, amusements, home, and other interests.

The history of literature has continued to hold an important place in the curriculum. No marked change has taken place since 1900 in the character of subject-matter. A recent tendency, however, is evident to place more emphasis upon literature itself and relatively less upon biography of authors. The text by Moody and Lovett[3] is an example of the older sort which contained comparatively little literature. A text quite similar to the above, so far as content is concerned, is that by Pancoast and Shelley.[4] Newcomer's book[5] places more emphasis upon the literature itself,

[1] Scott, F. N., and Denney, J. V., *New Composition and Rhetoric*, 1911.
[2] Cf. p. 10.
[3] Moody, W. V., and Lovett, R. M., *A History of English Literature*, 1902.
[4] Pancoast, Henry S., and Shelly, Percy Van Dyke, *First Book in English Literature*, 1910.
[5] Newcomer, Alfonso Gerald, *English Literature*, 1905.

selections being used liberally for purposes of illustration. A revision of Halleck's earlier work (1900) shows the same tendency.[1] The text[2] by Rankin and Aiken shows more clearly the later emphasis as the following statement in the preface indicates:

> The chief value in the discussion of literature is gained when the student has learned to read the literature under discussion.

The author carries out this viewpoint by including in the text numerous selections from literature.

As would be expected, numerous classics have largely furnished the reading matter in courses in English. Recently, as shown by published courses of study, current literature is coming to be used much more than formerly. The whole tendency of the recent movement in teaching English is away from the formal. Old divisions of subject-matter are being ignored, the interests of students are being more fully taken into account, and social demands of various sorts are beginning to function in the selection of material. Theoretically the correlation of English with other school subjects is receiving emphasis but not much, apparently, in practice has been accomplished.

SCIENCE

The extremely formal types of subject-matter in the various sciences referred to in Part II resulted in widespread dissatisfaction with science-teaching. Evidence of this is found in the decline of interest particularly in the physical sciences as shown by substantial relative decrease in the number of pupils pursuing these subjects. General dissatisfaction is also revealed by the discussions of science-teaching in educational meetings and in some of the publications dealing with the pedagogy of science subjects. As a result of this, an attempt has been made to eliminate one of the chief causes of highly specialized courses in each of the sciences by organizing courses in general science. This movement had its beginning about 1905 and has made considerable progress since that time. Table XXIX shows that only one school offered such a course while Table XXX contains nineteen schools offering the subject.

It is very obvious that the movement so far as it has affected educational practice is of very recent origin and at the present time more than half of the schools provide no such course. It should be

[1] HALLECK, REUBEN POST, *New English Literature*, 1913.
[2] RANKIN, THOMAS E., and AIKEN, WILFRED A., *English Literature*, 1917.

noted also that even in the schools which offer a course in general science, the traditional units as botany, physics, and the like are still provided. The texts in this subject thus far published are manifestly not intended to supplant the texts in the different science subjects, but are intended rather to serve as an introduction to them. In this respect, the general science texts differ from the texts in English and mathematics referred to in previous sections of this chapter. Several texts have been published since 1910 which purport to ignore the traditional divisions and which claim to present subject-matter chosen with reference to definite educative values. At first glance, these books remind one of the older type of organization called natural history. It requires but a superficial examination, however, to reveal the difference. In spite of the fact that they are books dealing with general science, each is written more or less from the point of view of the particular science in which the author was trained. All are not open to this charge in the same degree, but the fact does hold true of all of them. In view of this, as would be expected, the various texts differ widely as to character of subject-matter and plan of organization. The books also differ as to the purpose of such a course. Not all the books reveal either in the preface or context the point of view as to purpose while in others the purpose is stated or clearly manifest.

Snyder's text[1] is essentially a physical geography. The author says in the preface:

> First year science deals with the earth and the sun in their relation to man. This treatment has three advantages; it gives the book unity; it gives it practical interest, and it offers all the earth science needed to meet such requirements as those of the College Entrance Examination Board.

The reason for including material from all the sciences is stated as follows:

> All the subjects of elementary school science—physics, chemistry, meteorology, botany, zoölogy, astronomy, physiography, forestry, and agriculture—are treated so that the pupil can find out for himself what ones he wishes to study later in the course.

Another text[2] definitely rejects this purpose. In the preface the following statement is made:

> This book is written in the belief that science instruction in the first year high school should not aim primarily to survey the entire field of nature and

[1] SNYDER, WILLIAM H., *First Year Science*, 1914.

[2] BARBER, F. D., FULLER, M. L., PROSSER, J. L., and ADAMS, H. W., *First Course in General Science*, 1916. This book is a revision and enlargement of the *Elements of Physical Science* by the senior author in 1906.

present scattered bits and choice morsels from every special science in order that the pupil may decide which he will omit. Nor should first year general science be regarded primarily as an introduction to a foundation for the special sciences he may study later. . . . . It must be justified by its own intrinsic value as a training for life's work.

The book is predominantly physical science which may be accounted for by the fact that it is a revision of an earlier text by the senior author who is a teacher of physics. Sharp divisions from the standpoint of the several sciences is avoided, the material is well blended, and the organization is good.

Hessler's text[1] is manifestly intended as introductory to the physical sciences. He says in the preface:

While physics and chemistry as such ought not to be put into the early years of the high school, yet instruction in the simpler principles of these sciences can be given in a first-year General Science course. The most important part of this course will be introductory notions of physical and chemical phenomena but the course should include more than this.

Other science material, chiefly botany and physiology, is included but is of secondary importance.

Another book having a different purpose than Snyder's text is Clark's *An Introduction to Science.*[2] The purpose of the book and also the general character of the contents is revealed in the preface.

The purpose of this book is to start young high school pupils on scientific projects which will influence their present lives and which under different guises will equally influence for good their future lives. Among the scientific projects presented to the pupils are those of the selection of economic means of dietary standards; the selection of suitable paints, oils and varnishes for actual daily use; the examination of different fuels and their adaptation to furnace and kitchen range; the investigation of home and school lighting and its influence on eyesight; the utilization of simple labor saving devices to relieve physical exertion; the employment of chemical agents to transform useless waste products, such as grease and sewage into useful products such as soaps and fertilizers; and the application of hygienic facts and theories to school, home and community sanitation.

The projects show as does also an examination of the text itself that physical science is stressed with special emphasis upon chemistry of an applied sort.

One further example[3] of this class of texts will be mentioned. This book is evidently similar in its purpose to the one by Clark,

[1] Hessler, John C., *The First Year of Science*, 1914.
[2] Clark, Bertha M., *An Introduction to Science*, 1915.
[3] Caldwell, O. W., and Eikenberry, W. L., *Elements of General Science*, 1914.

viz., "to present a body of science material that will appeal to the everyday experiences of young people and that will function in their daily living." The emphasis is perhaps more evenly distributed over the various sciences than in the other books named, thus indicating less than the usual bias of specialists. No attempt is made to present a section of this science and of that one as such, and pedagogical rather than logical considerations control in the organization of material. The book is divided into five parts, each part being designated as follows: Part I, "The Air," Part II, "Water and Its Uses," Part III, "Work and Energy," Part IV, "The Earth's Crust," Part V, "Life Upon the Earth." Numerous applications are made to the practical needs of life and the everyday experiences of the students are taken into account.

As has been said the chief thing of interest connected with this so-called general science material is the departure from the older type of organization of science material and the forming of a unit made up of material selected from several of the sciences. This, however, has not been the only result. An attempt is made to choose material having what is assumed to be a more practical value. This means that less emphasis is placed upon scientific training and more upon the content value of the subject-matter. The quotation given from the preface of Clark's text is an illustration of this. That some authors have succeeded in greater degree than others is obvious, and it is entirely probable that the degree of difference in this respect is not a matter of accident but of purpose.

When we turn to the more recent texts in the separate sciences, we find that the authors of these have been more or less influenced by the same considerations that have resulted in the modified character of the subject-matter in the general science text, viz., the purpose to make science instruction less formal and more vital. It is true that some of the recent books do not give evidence of any significant change in the character of the subject-matter, but many of them do, and enough of them to make it clear that profound changes are taking place in science instruction.

The titles of some of these books indicate the change that has come about. Examples of such titles are as follows: *Practical Chemistry for High School Students*,[1] *Practical Applied Chemistry*,[2]

[1] Cook, Charles G., *Practical Chemistry for High School Students*, 1913.

[2] Allyn, Lewis B., *Elementary Applied Chemistry*, 1912.

Elements of Household Chemistry,[1] *Practical Physics for Secondary Schools*,[2] *Physics for the Household*,[3] *Practical Zoölogy*,[4] *Practical Botany*,[5] and the like.

Cook says in his preface:

> This book is intended for students in the second year of the high school. It is its purpose to bring the pupil into closer contact with the things of everyday life, to give him an insight into the nature of chemical processes with which all of us come more or less into contact, to furnish him with some chemical knowledge of the type necessary for his health and comfort, and thus adjust him to his environment. In doing this no attempt is made to treat the subject in a theoretical way. In fact, but little of the theory of chemistry is mentioned. . . .

The mathematical side of chemistry finds no place in a text of this sort, but a chapter on "Chemical Arithmetic" is included in the appendix. Not all texts fulfil the promises of the prefaces, but the author of this book holds rather closely to his purpose.

One of the early books of the new type of physics is the text[6] by Mann and Twiss. This is a revision of an earlier edition published in 1905. The plan is that of the project or problem. The authors state a rewriting of the book was necessary in order to apply the principles to subject-matter more likely to be of interest to the pupils. "Part one contains material that should be of interest to everybody." The problems selected are rather closely related to to the experiences and interests of high-school students and call for the practical application of the principles. The organization of the material shows that pedagogical considerations have controlled. Another book[7] of this class is the one by Black and Davis. The authors say in the preface:

> In the preparation of this book, we have tried to select only those topics which were of vital interest whether or not they intend to continue their study of Physics in the college course. Particularly we have decided that the value of the *information* side of such a course lies in its application to the machinery of everyday living. Everybody needs to know something about the making of electric motors, optical instruments, automobiles, and all those labor-saving devices, vacuum cleaners, fireless cookers, pressure cookers, and electric irons, which will be found in many American homes. We have, therefore, drawn as much of our illustrative material as possible from the common devices in modern

[1] SNELL, JOHN F., *Elements of Household Chemistry*, 1914.
[2] BLACK, HENRY, and DAVIS, HARRY D., *Practical Physics for Secondary Schools*, 1913.
[3] LYNDE, CARLTON J., *Physics of the Household*, 1914.
[4] HIGNER, ROBERT W., *Practical Zoölogy*, 1915.
[5] BERGEN, J. Y., and CALDWELL, O. W., *Practical Botany*, 1913.
[6] MANN, CHARLES R., and TWISS, GEORGE R., *Physics*, 1910. Revised edition.
[7] BLACK, HENRY, and DAVIS, HARRY D., *Practical Physics for Secondary Schools*, 1913.

life. We see no reason why this should detract from the educational value of the study of physics, for one can learn to think straight by thinking about an electric generator as well as by thinking about a Geissler tube.

The criticism of the formal type of text implied in the last sentence is quite in harmony with Woodhull's characterization of physics-teaching found in Part II. The new point of view in teaching the physical sciences is evidently not shared by the makers of some of the books still widely used. Carhart and Chute[1] in referring to the dissatisfaction with science-teaching have the following to say in their preface:

> Attempts have been made to meet this vague dissatisfaction by presenting many familiar illustrations of the practical application of physics but with an unsatisfactory treatment of the fundamental principles upon which these applications are based. As a result pupils reach the end of their study with few definite ideas and little knowledge of physics. This condition was plainly so much worse than the former one that teachers who had been drawn into the experiment have generally perferred to return to the regular type of book.

How accurately this describes the situation in 1912, it would be difficult to say. That it is not descriptive of conditions now, so far as returning to the regular type of book is concerned, is evident from the number and the character of the newer types of books in use in the schools.

In the biological sciences the same general tendency is apparent as in the case of the physical sciences. One of the first texts in botany of the newer type was one by Bergen and Caldwell.[2] This book is marked by an emphasis upon the practical, i.e., the agricultural and horticultural phases of the subjects. Larger units are chosen than in a morphological type of book and are chosen from the standpoint of these practical utilities. Plant nutrition, relation of nutrition to soil, of parasitic plants to other plants and to man, plant breeding, and forestry are examples of topics considered. In treating lower plant forms, fungi receive special attention because of the practical bearing upon the economic phase of botany. Quoting from the preface:

> The elements of plant life and structure are presented synthetically rather than by use of special divisions of botanical study which are more helpful to advanced students than beginners.

The book was avowedly written to meet the practical demands of everyday life and the organization is indicated by the quotation

[1] Carhart, Henry A., and Chute, H. N., *Principles of Physics*, 1912.
[2] Bergen, J. Y., and Caldwell, O. W., *Practical Botany*, 1913.

above. The fact of promise of similar change in the character of text in zoölogy was indicated in Part II by brief reference to Davenport's *Introduction to Zoölogy* published in 1900. The change, however, came about slowly and no radical departure from the old order of things is noted until after 1910. A good example of a text in zoölogy which attempts much the same thing in its field as Bergen and Caldwell's book does in botany is one by Higner.[1] In the preface the author says:

> The word "practical" in the title chosen, shows that an effort has been made to present those facts and theories about animals which will have the most practical bearing upon the daily life of the student. It refers not only to the economic side of the subject, but also to the elements that are of greater intellectual value. . . . . The constant reference to the relations of animals to environment and the selection of common animals, especially those of economic importance, for illustrative purposes, tend to stimulate the natural interest of boys and girls in animal life.

The following are examples of the topics discussed in the text: "Insects of the Household," "The House Fly and Disease," "Mosquitoes and Disease," "The Relation of Birds and Man," "The Relation of Mammals to Man."

Physiology does not seem to have shared with other biological science the influence of this new movement in science-teaching. The textbooks used in the high school at least do not show the same marked tendency to get away from the old anatomical kind of material. The texts used in the grades, on the contrary, do show this influence. The coming in of general science has no doubt been responsible for the decline of physiology as a high-school subject. These books contain more or less material which might properly belong in texts on hygiene as also do the botanies and zoölogies. Even chemistry makes its contribution to health instruction in much greater degree than formerly. All of these things taken together might readily account for the failure of physiology as a separate subject from sharing in the general movement.

In the earth sciences, there seems to have been no significant change since 1900. Geology has declined in importance almost to the vanishing point and physical geography has also declined although not in the same degree. It will be remembered that both of these subjects underwent important changes in the last years of

[1] Higner, Robert W., *Practical Zoölogy*, 1915.

the nineteenth century somewhat similar to the changes which have been taking place in the other sciences more recently. The character of these changes is explained in Part II and further discussion is unnecessary.

THE SOCIAL STUDIES

Changes in this field in the character of subject-matter have been very important. The emphasis upon commercial and industrial education finds expression here to a considerable extent. History has witnessed rather remarkable modification in the character of material found in textbooks. In the first place, this change is made clear by a new type of text—commercial and industrial histories. The second evidence of change is found in the character of material contained in the type of textbooks which formerly gave little attention to anything except political and military history. Some of these books now stress the industrial and commercial life of the people, and all recent books give more or less attention to social history. Texts in European history show conclusively this trend toward a discussion of events other than political and military. This change has taken place chiefly in the text published since 1910 although some exceptions are found in earlier books. An example of the new type of text is found in Webster's *History of Commerce.*[1] This text places a good deal of emphasis upon the history of commerce but also devotes a good deal of attention to political history which seems to bear little relation to the purpose of the book as indicated in the title. Two later books[2] show clearly the importance attached to events pertaining to the development of commerce and industry. The point of view determining the organization of material is indicated by Smith in the preface as follows:

> In the part dealing with the United States, I have described the industries rather than regions and states. The wheat industry, for example, forms certain environmental conditions that exist in many states and countries. Therefore, I have not hesitated to refer by way of comparison to the great wheat-producing regions in other countries.

This significant statement is found in the preface of Herrick's text:

> Not many years ago Edward A. Freeman's famous dictum "history is past politics and politics are present history," found general acceptance, but this sentiment is no longer generally approved. Clearly there is at present a desire

[1] WEBSTER, W. C., *General History of Commerce*, 1903.

[2] SMITH, J. R., *Commerce and Industry*, 1916, and HERRICK, C. A., *History of Commerce and Industry*, 1917.

to select those interests of the past which most clearly bear on the present. For a considerable time, the tendency has been obvious for both writers and teachers to emphasize economic and social history rather than the history of war or the evolution of governmental systems.

One might expect, of course, this point of view in the books referred to above, but it is not confined to texts of this sort. West, in the revised edition of his *Ancient World*[1] has this to say in his preface:

> It is doubtful if a textbook of this sort should give room to any incident which the student cannot articulate with the life of to-day—or *which is not essential to understanding the evolution of important conditions* which *can* be so articulated.

The content of the text itself shows that this point of view has prevailed in the selection of material. The following topics are examples: "Contributions of Civilization," "Industry and Art," "Literature and Learning," "Society and Culture," "Religion and Morals," "Culture and Morals," and the like.

The modern history text by Knowlton and Howe[2] shows clearly the departure from the traditional type of historical material. In the preface the authors say:

> An understanding of contemporary Europe is largely dependent upon an application of two lines of development which have their origin back in the early years of the eighteenth century. The one gave rise to modern methods of carrying on commerce and industry; the other gave us a new conception of the relation of government and governed. In other words to form a proper estimate of existing conditions in Europe we must follow step by step the revolutionary changes in commerce and industry and the tremendous advance of democracy which have in a special manner characterized the history of the past century and a quarter.

These two points of view evidently control the selection of subject-matter.

Further evidence of this important change in the character of history material is furnished by other texts.[3] Ashley is the author of a series of texts published recently which show the change that has taken place. Other texts show the same tendency in less degree.[4] These revised texts, however, show the continued influence of the earlier viewpoint in the emphasis placed upon the traditional types of material.

[1] West, William M., *The Ancient World from the Earliest Time to 800 A.D., Revised Edition.*

[2] Knowlton, D. C., and Howe, S. B., *Essentials in Modern European History*, 1917.

[3] Ashley, Roscoe Lewis, *Ancient Civilization*, 1915; *Medieval Civilization*, 1915; *Modern Civilization*, 1918.

[4] Webster, Hutton, *Ancient History*, 1913; Myers, P. V. N., *Ancient History*, 1916, second revised edition; Morey, Wm. C., *Ancient Peoples: A Revision of Morey's Outlines of Ancient History*, 1915.

The influence of the same point of view is also evident in the case of United States history. Thompson[1] in the preface of his text says:

> In preparing the following pages for students who are about to enter seriously on the study of United States history, I have been guided in the selection of material and in the presentation of the material by a desire to place more emphasis on the industrial and social activities of the American people than is usually placed by writers of textbooks which we may for convenience call political histories.

About fifty pages are devoted to growth and improvement in agriculture, country life, commerce, transportation, and communication. Considerable attention is also devoted to the merchant marine and to the development of industry since the Civil War. Mussey's[2] text shows the same general emphasis.

The importance of the industrial phase of history is recognized to some extent by McLaughlin in the 1913 edition of his *History of the American Nation.*[3] He says in the preface:

> Every passing year seems to add significance to the important general phases of industrial growth during the last fifty years, while the relations of government to industry and to tasks of social betterment are more and more the subject for discussion. This does not mean that history should be written from the point of view of industrial growth alone; on the contrary, perhaps never before was there such need for understanding political history . . . . because political activity, the state, the government and law are now clearly involved in every problem of industrial control, in every plan for social regeneration.

The text itself emphasizes political history but devotes considerable space to social questions [pp. 128–98] and to agriculture and industrial development in general [pp. 340–85]. Some attention is devoted to commercial and industrial topics. Channing's text[4] shows the same tendency in less degree. Other books[5] are similar to this one in the relatively small amount of space devoted to history other than political and military.

A comparison of the history texts published since 1910 with those published prior to that date clearly reveals the larger amount of space devoted to social and industrial history. The older books are still used more or less and some of the newer books and recent

[1] Thompson, James M., *History of the United States: Political, Industrial, Social,* 1915.

[2] Mussey, David S., *American History,* 1911.

[3] McLaughlin, Andrew C., *History of the American Nation,* 1913, revised edition. See also *Readings in the History of the American Nation* by the same author, 1914.

[4] Channing, Edward, *A Student's History of the United States,* 1913.

[5] Montgomery, D. H., *The Student's American History,* 1913. Revised edition. James, James A., and Sanford, Albert H., *American History,* 1909.

revisions of others, as already pointed out, still stress the old type of material. Some of the books which stress the new viewpoint most are of very recent publication. It is therefore evident that the actual change in the teaching of history is not as radical as the latter text would indicate. It is clear, however, that conditions are changing rapidly and that changes of considerable significance have already taken place.

Civics as well as history has been undergoing important changes in recent years. Dole's *American Citizen*, published in the last decade of the nineteenth century, was the pioneer book in the field of what is usually called functional civics as distinguished from the traditional text which emphasized governmental forms and machinery. This book has already been discussed in Part II. Since its publication, authors have been inclined to deplore in prefaces the lack of emphasis upon the functional aspects of civics and then to neglect to make subject-matter conform to the demands of the functional viewpoint.

Changes of any great importance in the character of subject-matter are very recent. One of the textbooks which has had wide use in secondary schools is *Government in State and Nation* by James and Sanford[1] published in 1901. This book places the emphasis upon governmental forms and machinery and is fairly representative of the type of texts used almost universally until after 1910. In fact, Ashley's text[2] published that year contains the same emphasis. Another text[3] by Ashley published seven years later is a very different type of book and is representative of the new viewpoint in the teaching of civics. The following are some of the topics which show that emphasis is being placed upon the functional aspects of the subject: "Individual Needs and Civic Relations," "Individual Needs and Public Needs," "Childhood Rights of Life and Health," "Beginning of Civic Training in the Home," "Training Citizens in the School," "Degree of Self-Government in Different Schools," "The Citizen in Business."

Another text which gives some recognition to the newer type of material is a book by Guitteau.[4] Some of the topics treated are as follows: "Important Aids to the Public Health," "Public Parks and Playgrounds," "Public Charities," "Why Government Aids

[1] James, J. A., and Sanford, A. H., *Government in State and Nation*, 1910.
[2] Ashley, Roscoe L., *American Government for Use in Secondary Schools*, 1910.
[3] Ashley, Roscoe L., *The New Civics*, 1917.
[4] Guitteau, William B., *Preparation for Citizenship*, 1914.

Agriculture," "Work of the National Government in Improvement of Highways."

A characterization of the two types of texts, the old and the new, is found in the preface of Beard's book[1] published in 1914.

> An examination of the collection in the Library of Congress which mentions all of the most recent books in civics fall into two parts, those which are formal and legal and those which are sociological in character.

An examination of published lists of texts shows that most of the texts in use belong to the class called "formal and legal." The newer texts, however, now coming into use indicate that radical changes are taking place in the character of civic instruction.

These new texts in history and civics do not furnish all the evidence of changes going on in the social studies. The most striking evidence, perhaps, is found in a type of text that represents not only marked changes in the character of subject-matter but a new plan of organization as well. Two of these[2] will be used as illustration of the new movement. Towne says in his preface:

> The work is intended primarily for beginners in the field of social studies—for those who may desire a better understanding of social questions. . . . . This, then, has been the aim: to bring before students of social problems these facts regarding present day conditions; to indicate certain weaknesses in our own social order; to show what has been done and is being done toward the elimination of these weaknesses; and to impress upon these students through the presentation of such facts, the possibilities of wise, sane, constructive social action.

The following are some of the chapter titles and indicate the general character of subject matter: "Influence of Natural Conditions on Economic and Social Development," "Child Labor," "Women and Industry," "Unemployment," "The Blind and the Deaf," "Crime and Punishment," "The Liquor Problem," "Conservation of Natural Resources," "Conservation of Plant and Animal Life," "Conservation of Human Life."

The other book is similar in its purpose but differs considerably in character of subject-matter and even more in method of treatment. The authors have the following to say in the preface:

> This book has grown out of an attempt to socialize one phase of secondary education and to bring it into harmony with present day demands. It is designed to meet the needs of an elementary course in the study of society—especially of American society. A conscious attempt has been made to emphasize the social

[1] Beard, Charles A., and Beard, Mary R., *American Citizenship*, 1914.

[2] Towne, Ezra T., *A Study of Present Day Social Conditions*, 1916, and Burch, Henry R., and Patterson, S. H., *American Social Problems*, 1918.

aspect of American life, rather than the political or economic. Although three phases naturally overlap and are in many cases inseparably interwoven, the main stress has always been placed on the social point of view. . . . . The method of treatment has been evolutionary and historical because growth and development is the very essence of social institutions. It is also hoped that this method of approach and the material presented will help meet the demand for what has been termed "socialized history."

Some of the chapter titles are as follows: "The Life of the Past" (evolution), "The Past and the Present" (tradition and social survivals), "The Influence of Environment," "History of the Family," "The Problem of Immigration," "The American Race Problem," "Social Effects of Industry," "The Problem of Crime," "The Problem of Prohibition," "Evolution of the Schools," "Moral Progress."

It is evident that radical changes in the character of subject-matter and its organization are well under way. The revision of texts in history, dealing with the general field, the use in many schools of industrial and commercial histories and the new type of civics bear abundant evidence of the change going on. Added to this is the evidence of the movement to reorganize the material something after the plan already referred to in connection with mathematics, English, and science. In the field of social studies as well as in these other fields, old divisions are being ignored and a new era in secondary education is being ushered in. Whether this movement in its present form is permanent is perhaps too early to say, but that we shall ever return to the old, hard and fast plan of organization is extremely doubtful.

The subject-matter of the foreign languages has apparently been affected very little by the influences which have caused important changes in other subjects. Modern language, except for the increased attention being given to Spanish, does not appear to have been appreciably influenced. Latin, so far as the second, third, and fourth years are concerned, remains unchanged. Caesar, Cicero, and Virgil continue to constitute the work of these years. There is some evidence[1] of an attempt to revise the work of the first year but as long as Caesar continues to constitute wholly or chiefly the work of the second year, the subject-matter of the first year will have to be propaedeutic to this work.[2]

[1] Scott, Harry F., *First Latin Book for Junior High Schools*, 1918.

[2] Pearson, Henry C., *Essentials of Latin*, 1905. Revised 1911, 1912, 1915. Also Smith, M. L., *Latin Lessons*, 1913.

The subject-matter of the vocational subjects has already been discussed in part in connection with the discussion of other fields. The influence of the vocational movement upon mathematics, English, science, and the social studies was there pointed out. The character of the subject-matter of the more strictly vocational subjects is rather clearly revealed by the titles of the various subjects. The most of these have come into the curriculum so recently that no comparative study in development can be made at this time.

CHAPTER XVI

SUMMARY

The forty years included in the study covered by Parts I and II have been grouped into periods of five years each for convenience in determining conditions and in noting any changes that should take place from time to time. In this summary it will not be necessary to treat each of these periods separately since no changes of importance occurred in some of them. For this reason, except in cases where the recognition of these arbitrary groupings aid in interpretations, they will be ignored.

The year 1860 fairly approximates the beginning of the widespread movement in the North Central states to establish public secondary schools. Comparison of earlier and later courses show that the schools included therein attempted to fulfil the purpose of the Boston school, that of fitting for life. It is clear that four of them did not undertake to prepare for higher institutions because of the absence of foreign languages. Four-fifths of the schools undertook to perform both functions, and this type of high school became the prevailing type. Along these two lines high-school curricula developed.

The line was not clearly drawn for a considerable time between the work of high schools and that of higher institutions. This is shown by the wide range of subjects offered particularly in mathematics, foreign language, and the miscellaneous subjects. It was probably the conscious purpose of some of these early high schools to enter the field of higher education, following in this respect the schools of Boston, Lowell, Philadelphia, and Baltimore.

One of the changes taking place in organization of curricula is manifested by a change in terminology, the word "Department" being superseded by the word "Course." "Classical department" and "English department" gave way to "Classical Course" and "English Course" and these in turn ceased to be used exclusively to designate courses intended to prepare for higher institutions and those to prepare for life. This tendency is noticeable at the very beginning of our study and courses and titles multiply as time goes on. The extent to which this practice was carried on means that the schools were no longer attempting to provide two types of education but several types. Theoretically, the purpose was to furnish education that would meet the needs of the various classes of pupils enrolled in the schools. This practice grew in favor after 1880 and was a forerunner of the more specific differentiation in curricula receiving so much attention at the present time.

Another change which took place was the disappearance or decline in importance of a number of subjects taught in the earlier schools. Mental philosophy, moral philosophy, logic, evidences of Christianity, biblical antiquities, classical antiquities, and ancient geography had all disappeared by 1890 except the first two named, and they were found in only one school thereafter. The higher mathematics, except trigonometry, ceased to be offered after 1885, and that subject declined in importance after 1880. In science, astronomy and geology, ranking with botany in 1860, declined after 1875 and were offered in approximately only one-fourth of the schools at the close. It will be seen that, roughly speaking, 1880 marks the disappearance or decline of those subjects which occupied an important place in the earlier curricula.

Subjects from a new field did not take the place of these discontinued and declining subjects. Less time was not devoted to either mathemathics or science, but more time was given to the subjects remaining. Also more time was given to both English and the social studies. The year 1880 marks the beginning of increase of time devoted to these fields. The gain in each was approximately one year.

The increasing tendency to greater uniformity in curricula from the standpoint of time devoted to both subjects and fields was another change which took place. This was neither sudden nor marked. No single date or period can be designated as marking the transition. A comparison of Tables A and H and also Tables XI and XVIII makes it clear that greater uniformity prevailed at the close.

Lack of uniformity in terminology is very pronounced, particularly in the earlier periods. This is especially true in English and the social studies and continued, although in less degree, to the close. In mathematics, all terms disappear about 1880 except those now used to designate high-school mathematics. The general term "English," used to designate all the subjects in that field, came into use about 1880 and was employed in about 25 per cent of the schools at the close. United States Constitution, science of government, and civil government tended to give way to the term "civics." General history became the term in more general use to take the place of several terms used in the earlier periods. In science, the term "natural history" ceased to be used to any considerable extent after 1875 and biology came in about 1880. Specific terms such as meteorology, mineralogy, electricity, and mechanics had practically disappeared by 1880. The term "natural philosophy" gradually gave way to that of "physics" and the latter was used by a majority of the schools at the close.

The beginning of both commercial and industrial education is found in the closing years of the century. One commercial subject, bookkeeping, was offered from the first, but it was practically the only one in its field until 1890. An occasional school offered commercial law and commercial arithmetic, but it is evident that no serious attention was given to commercial education previous to that date in spite of the fact that a few schools offered so-called commercial courses. That date, however, marks the beginning of the movement that resulted in commercial courses in fact and later in commercial high schools. The industrial courses make their first appearance about 1885, and this also was the beginning of another important movement in secondary education. The development of both of these movements, however, belongs to the present century.

The two purposes of the high school, that of preparing for college and fitting for life, continue evident in the courses of study. The courses intended to prepare for higher institutions undergo rather marked changes.[1] Greek ceases to be a constant and other subjects are added, including English, science, and the social studies. These changes were no doubt due in part to changes in entrance requirements and in part to an attempt to broaden the type of education and thus fulfil, in some degree, both aims of the high school.

As has been pointed out,[2] the other type of courses do not seem to have been controlled either by well-defined educational ideals or specific social aims. Judging from the titles of courses,[3] it seems to have been assumed that the various fields furnished real bases for differences in educational and social values, but no criteria except

[1] Cf. courses of study, pp. 20-42.

[2] Cf. pp. 50 ff.

[3] Cf. Table I.

of the most generalized sort are discoverable. When these courses are examined in detail, it is found that the descriptive titles are not safe guides in determining emphases in subjects or the character of organization. Except for the few normal, commercial, and manual training courses, differentiation in courses was not accompanied by equal differentiation in character of education provided.

The majority of schools furnishing data provided four-year courses. Some of the early ones were not given in sufficient detail to determine the length, and these cannot be included in the summaries. Tables A to H, Appendix, show the number of courses of four, three, two, and one year respectively. These make clear that four-year courses were in the majority throughout the forty years, and after 1885 the ratio is about three to one in favor of the four-year course. The study made in 1894 by Superintendent W. F. Cramer of more than one hundred courses offered in Iowa high schools shows about the same proportion of four-year courses.[1]

It should be said, however, that in the present study as well as in that made by Mr. Cramer, many of the smaller schools are not included simply because data are not obtainable. This class of schools is not so apt to publish courses and the present study has revealed that in many schools these documents are not preserved even if published. It needs to be said, therefore, that it is not probable that three-fourths of the high schools either in Iowa or in the North Central states offered four-year courses. The conclusion is nevertheless justified that four years was regarded, except in the early years of our study, as the standard high-school course.

In the discussion of the order in which subjects appear in curricula, it was shown that considerable confusion prevailed. Arithmetic was taught either alone or simultaneously with algebra in the first year. Frequent exceptions to this, however, are found. Algebra always preceded geometry.[2] Grammar was usually a first-year subject, sometimes being offered as a review subject in the last year. Rhetoric was a middle-course subject—second or third year—and literature was confined largely to the third and fourth years.

In science, physiology and physical geography are found almost exclusively in the first two years, and physics, chemistry, geology, and astronomy in the last two. Botany and zoölogy are more often

[1] Pamphlet published by Northeastern Iowa Teachers Association, 1894.
[2] In some cases a third semester of algebra was offered following plane geometry.

found in the first two years, but the tendency toward distributing them over the entire course is more pronounced than in the other sciences. This is particularly true of zoölogy. Lack of correlation of science subjects, except physics and chemistry, is evident.

United States history was usually a first-year subject and political economy a last year. European history was on the whole a middle-course subject and civics tended toward distribution over the entire course. Toward the close the latter subject is found more frequently than formerly in the first year, and European history shifts somewhat to this year. There is evident lack of sequence of courses in this field. A narrow range of commercial subjects appears in the earlier years of the curricula and the miscellaneous subjects in the later ones.

The range of subjects offered is shown in Tables II–IX. In mathematics and the miscellaneous subjects, the range was wide in the earlier years. After 1880, the latter subjects practically disappear as do also the higher mathematical subjects, except trigonometry which declines in importance. Lack of uniformity in terminology in English and the social studies accounts for the apparent wide range of subjects in these fields. The fact is that the range was comparatively narrow prior to 1880.

In science a wide range was offered throughout the entire period with a tendency to reduce the number of subjects toward the close without diminution of time devoted to the field.

Foreign language included Latin, Greek, German, French, and Spanish, the latter being practically negligible. Latin leads both in number of schools offering the subject and in time devoted to it. German stands next to Latin in importance.

The range of commercial subjects was very narrow, an occasional school near the close devoting considerable time to this field. The wide range of miscellaneous subjects offered in 1860 largely disappears after 1880, and near the close industrial subjects begin to appear in a few schools.

Table X indicates that mathematics, English, and science were constants and the social studies belong to this group after 1870. Strictly speaking no subject was a constant although algebra, geometry, physics, and literature, after 1885, were practically so. Of the variables Latin, physiology, botany, physical geography, and rhetoric represent the highest percentages of frequency. The degree of variability indicated in Table X is accounted for in two ways: first, all the schools do not appear in all the tables,[1] and secondly, subjects that were offered by a school at one time would be omitted at another.[2]

The pronounced lack of uniformity in curricula from the standpoint of time devoted to fields and subjects is shown in Tables XI–XVIII, XIX, and XX–XXVII. Lack of standardization is very evident in all the fields and in many of the subjects. In a group of schools offering English there were ten different units of time devoted to the field, and in science, fourteen schools represented nine different units of time. Extreme differences between individual schools is shown in the maxima and minima of the tables. The increasing tendency toward uniformity is shown by comparing Tables XI and XVIII.

The chief difference between curricula of large and small schools was that the former offered a wider range of subjects in the fields offered by practically all the schools. Trigonometry and other higher mathematical subjects, in the earlier years, belonged chiefly to the curricula of the larger schools. These schools also offered English, particularly literature, in the earlier years, and the modern languages were less frequently offered by the smaller schools. This was especially true of French. In science, chemistry and geology were the subjects more frequently provided by the larger schools. The larger schools were not distinguished by offering commercial and industrial subjects until near the close of the century.

Aside from the difference between city and large town schools, and small town schools, there is no evidence that locality had any appreciable influence upon curricula. It is true that some subjects received more emphasis in one state than in another, but differences in this regard were quite as great between schools of the same state as between schools located in different states.

Individual differences in schools from the standpoint of subjects offered regardless of location were very pronounced as shown in the Appendix, Tables A–H. A greater degree of similarity prevailed among small schools than large ones. This is explained by the fact that they offered a narrower range of subjects and provided less electives. The constants common to both large and small schools would result in similarity of curricula while the variables

[1] Cf. Appendix, Table A–H.

[2] Examples as to arithmetic and grammar given in footnotes, p. 76.

offered in larger number by the larger schools caused greater variation among the schools.

Regarded from the standpoint of time devoted to fields and subjects, the individual differences are also very pronounced. Tables XI–XVIII, XIX, and XX–XXVIII show this in detail. Comparisons of curricula, pp. 20–42, make this clear in regard to particular schools.

In some fields changes in the character of subject-matter is practically negligible. Mathematics and foreign language are examples. English, particularly literature, some of the sciences, and the social studies furnish examples in varying degrees of importance.

The subject-matter of grammar did not differ essentially in 1900 from what it was in 1860. Literature on the contrary passed through three rather distinct stages in its development. The first was characterized by a wide range of short selections. The second was marked by stress placed upon the history of literature and more particularly by the amount of attention devoted to biographies of authors. The more general use of classics which marks the third stage began about 1885. The classics were grouped into two classes—one for critical study and the other for general reading.

The subject-matter of rhetoric in the earlier years was characterized by emphasis on the logical aspect of the subject. Later the attempt to make the subject function in connection with the correct use of English is evident. Much attention is devoted to the correction of "bad" English, i.e., to "grammatical and idiomatic expressions." About 1895 one witnesses a further shift in the same direction, viz., increased emphasis upon the relation of the subject to composition.

Composition received apparently little attention in the early years of the period under discussion. This has been pointed out in Part I. The character of the subject-matter was determined largely in the various stages of its development by its relation to the other English subjects. The first stage is marked by the stress placed upon grammatical forms. Composition exercises were used to secure drill in the use of these forms. Drill on rhetorical forms constituted the emphasis in the second stage. The third stage is characterized by the use of literature as a source of material.

The biological subjects, particularly botany, witnessed important changes in subject-matter. The religious point of view is somewhat in evidence early in the period. In the case of botany, the premedical standpoint is also noticeable. Both this subject and zoölogy later received the anatomical emphasis to the exclusion practically of other material. Near the close of the period the morphological aspects of the subjects predominated. The subject-matter of physiology was almost wholly anatomy, the shift of attention to hygienic material becoming somewhat noticeable near the close of the century.

Physics and chemistry followed practically the same lines of development. The "science of common things" was displaced by formal types of subject-matter. The development of laboratory work seems to have been influential in bringing about this change. The earth sciences as well as the biological were influenced by the evolutionary theory, and changes in the character of subject-matter are readily apparent. The economic phases of the subjects began to receive some attention in the very last years of the period. Astronomy steadily declined in importance after 1880 and no change of importance occurred in subject-matter.

European history was largely ancient history in the early years and this period continued to receive the emphasis of attention to the close. The older texts were devoted quite exclusively to political and military history. After 1875 a tendency is noticeable to include some material dealing with social life. The emphasis, however, upon the political and military aspects of the subjects continued to prevail. The stress on United States history was the same as that on European history with respect to political and military events. The earlier texts show this conclusively. Later the Barnes and Montgomery texts devote some attention to the affairs of social life.

Civics passed through three fairly well-defined periods. The early texts were little more than manuals of constitutions. This material continued to be used in the second period, but more or less statutory material was introduced and governmental machinery was considered in considerable detail. The third period is marked by a tendency to stress the functions of government. The old points of view, however, continued to dominate in the teaching of the subject to the close of the century. The teaching of political economy falls roughly into two periods. In the first the subject-matter dealt with principles or the philosophical aspects of the subject. The relation of the subject to moral philosophy is stressed.

The second period is characterized by a shift of emphasis to the practical application of principles. These principles also change in that they are more or less completely derived from existing economic conditions.

The vocational subjects were just beginning to receive serious attention at the close of the century and the development of subject-matter was not important.

Important changes have taken place in high-school education since 1900 and more particularly since 1910. The scope of the work has been greatly increased especially since the latter date. This has been accomplished in two ways: (1) by an increase in the number of commercial and industrial subjects and in the time devoted to these subjects; (2) by a reorganization which results in two years being added to the period devoted to secondary education in those schools in which a junior high school is maintained, and four years in case of the junior college. The former does not mean in many cases an actual increase of two years of secondary work since elementary subjects are still included in the curricula. The movement does represent, however, a well-developed tendency to limit the work of the elementary school to six years and to extend the work of the secondary school downward two years.

The organization of curricula has also witnessed marked changes. The two purposes of the high school—fitting for college and fitting for life—are still maintained, but the latter functions much more definitely than it did previous to 1900. Differentiation in college-preparatory curricula has also developed considerably. The so-called "Regular" or "General" courses, and titles derived from the traditional fields such as "English," "science," "Latin" and the like, have decreased in number. In place of these titles we find such as the following: "Agricultural," "Commercial Course for Boys," "Commercial Course for Girls," "Domestic Science," "Fine Arts," and "Stenography." This attempt to differentiate curricula to meet specific vocational needs began prior to 1900 but the development of the practice has taken place largely since 1910.

The range of subjects has greatly increased since 1900 and more especially since 1910, as shown by a comparison of Tables IX, XXIX, and XXX. This increase has taken place chiefly in the general field of vocational subjects.

The matter of constants and variables is treated in Table XXXI and is discussed in the pages immediately following. Not much change has occurred in practice as related to the traditional subjects except as brought about by reorganizations of subject-matter. For example the introduction of "general" science has resulted apparently in a decline in importance of some of the science subjects. The rapid increase in the teaching of vocational subjects is clearly shown.

The practice of requiring all pupils to take the same subjects has rapidly declined. English is the only field required of all students during the period 1915–18. Mathematics stands next with approximately 80 per cent of the schools requiring algebra and 60 per cent geometry. The social studies stand third with 60 per cent, American history leading with 40 per cent. About 50 per cent require science, physics being specified in 25 per cent of the schools. Few schools require foreign language and none specify commercial subjects as a requirement. Approximately 10 per cent require something in the field of the fine and practical arts.

The changes that have been pointed out are important, but the most significant readjustments relate to the character of subject-matter and its organization. Subject-matter has been differentiated in the commercial field and in the fine and practical arts. New types of material have been introduced into the traditional subjects. This latter change has been radical particularly in the sciences and the social studies, and the influence has been felt, though less marked, in English. The subject-matter of mathematics has not apparently undergone any important change and the same is true of foreign language.

The tendency to get away from the traditional organization of subject-matter is evident. Unified mathematics and general science are examples of this, the development of the latter subject being particularly significant. English furnishes another example. This is shown not only by the titles of textbooks and the point of view of authors revealed in prefaces, but also by the emphases employed and the organization of the subject-matter itself. The tendency to disregard the traditional types of organization and to unify subject-matter is also seen in the social studies. Courses in social problems are being introduced and textbooks having this type of organization are coming into use.

The last decade, roughly speaking, has witnessed the development of these tendencies both as to the character of subject-matter and its organization. The preceding decade, and, to much less extent, the last years of the nineteenth century present evidence of important impending changes. The actual readjustments, however, particularly in subject-matter and its organization have taken place chiefly since 1910. There seems to be abundant evidence that this movement to extend the scope of secondary education and to make it more vital is destined to continue until permanent readjustments shall have been made.

APPENDIX

The following tables show the names of the towns and cities, the length in years of the courses, and the date of each. The figures indicate the time in years devoted to the several subjects and fields.

TABLE A—1860–1865

Town or City	Years in course	Date	Mathematics: Arithmetic	Algebra	Geometry	Trigonometry	Analytics	Surveying and Navigation	Engineering	Total	English: Grammar	Analysis	Word Analysis	Reading	Composition	Rhetoric	English Literature	Literature	Classics	Elements of Criticism	Elocution	Total
Adrian, Michigan	3	1857	....	....	1/3	....	....	1/3	1/3	1	....	x	....	x	x	1/3	....	....	....	1/3	....	2/3
Ann Arbor, Michigan	3	1857	1/2	1/2	1	....	....	....	....	2	1/2	....	....	....	1/2	1/2	....	....	....	1/2	....	2
Battle Creek, Michigan	3	1859	1/3	2/3	2/3	1/3	....	1/3	....	2 1/3	2/3	....	....	....	1/3	1/3	2/3	....	....	....	....	2
Burlington, Iowa	4	1864	2/3	2/3	1	1/3	....	1/3	....	3	2/3	....	....	....	....	2/3	....	....	....	....	1/3	1 2/3
Charlotte, Michigan	?	1859	x	....	....	....	....	....	....	?	x	x	x	....	....	x	....	....	....	....	....	?
Cleveland, Ohio	4	1852	2/3	1 1/3	2/3	1/3	....	....	....	3	1	....	....	....	2/3	2/3	1/3	....	....	1/3	....	3
Chicago, Illinois	4	1862	....	1	1	2/3	....	....	....	2 2/3	....	....	....	....	....	1/2	2/3	....	....	....	....	1 1/6
Cincinnati, Ohio	4	1857	1/2	1 1/2	1	1/2	....	1/2	....	4	....	....	....	....	2/5	1/2	....	....	1/2	....	....	1 2/5
Detroit, Michigan	3	1859	....	2/3	2/3	2/3	1/3	....	....	2 1/3	....	1 1/3	2/3	2/3	1/3	1/3	....	....	....	....	....	3 1/3
Dubuque, Iowa	3	1858	1/3	1 1/3	1 2/3	....	....	1/3	....	2 2/3	1/3	2/3	1/3	....	2/3	1/3	....	....	....	....	....	2 1/3
Galesburg, Illinois	2	1865	1/3	2/3	2/3	....	....	....	....	1 2/3	....	....	....	....	....	1/3	....	....	....	....	....	1/3
Grand Rapids, Michigan	?	1857	1/3	1 1/3	2/3	1/3	....	....	....	2 2/3	....	2/3	....	....	....	2/3	....	....	....	....	....	1 1/3
Kalamazoo, Michigan	4	1864	1/3	1 2/3	2/3	1/3	....	....	....	3	1/3	1/3	....	....	1/3	1/3	2/3	....	....	....	....	2
Lacon, Illinois	3	1859	1	1	1	....	....	....	....	3	1	2/3	....	....	....	....	....	....	....	....	....	1 2/3
Madison, Wisconsin	4	1863	1	1 2/3	1	....	....	....	....	3 2/3	....	2/3	1/3	....	....	1	2/3	....	....	....	....	2 2/3
Monroe, Michigan	?	1857	x	x	x	x	....	x	....	?	x	....	....	....	....	x	....	x	....	....	....	?
Mt. Pleasant, Iowa	4	1863	1	1	1	1/3	....	1/3	1/3	4	1	....	....	1	1/3	1/3	....	....	....	....	1/3	3
Racine, Wisconsin	3	1858	2/3	2/3	1	1/3	1/3	....	....	3	....	2/3	....	1/3	....	1/3	1/3	....	....	....	....	1 2/3
Rock Island, Illinois	?	1857	x	x	x	....	....	x	....	?	x	x	....	x	x	....	....	....	....	....	....	?
Ypsilanti, Michigan	?	1857	x	x	x	....	....	....	....	?	x	x	....	x	x	x	....	....	....	x	....	?

x indicates time not specified.

TABLE A—1860–1865, *Continued*

Town or City	Science: Physiology	Physical Geography	Natural Philosophy	Physics	Chemistry	Geology	Botany	Natural History	Zoölogy	Astronomy	Geography	Total	Social Studies: Ancient History	Medieval History	Modern History	United States History	English History	General History	Universal History	Science of Government	United States Constitution	Political Economy	History	History of Civilization	Total
Adrian, Michigan	....	x	2/3	....	x	1/3	x	....	1/3	2/3	....	2	....	....	....	....	....	2/3	....	....	....	....	....	1/3	1
Ann Arbor, Michigan	1/2	1/2	1	....	1/2	1/2	1/2	1/2	....	....	....	4	....	....	....	....	....	....	....	....	....	....	1	....	1
Battle Creek, Michigan	1/3	2/3	1/3	....	2/3	1/3	2/3	....	1/3	1/3	....	3 2/3	....	....	....	....	....	....	....	1/3	....	1/3	2/3	....	1 1/3
Burlington, Iowa	2/3	1/3	2/3	....	2/3	1	2/3	1/3	1/3	....	....	4 2/3	....	....	....	....	....	....	2/3	....	1/3	....	....	....	1
Charlotte, Michigan	....	x	x	....	....	....	x	....	....	....	....	?	....	....	....	....	....	....	....	....	....	....	....	....	....
Cleveland, Ohio	2/3	1/3	2/3	....	1	1/3	2/3	1/3	1/3	1/3	1/3	5	1/3	....	1/3	1/3	....	....	....	....	1/3	....	....	....	1 1/3
Chicago, Illinois	1/3	1/3	2/3	....	1/2	1/2	2/3	....	....	....	....	3	....	....	....	....	....	....	1	....	1/3	1/3	....	....	1 2/3
Cincinnati, Ohio	....	....	1	....	1	....	....	....	....	1/3	....	2 1/3	1/2	1/2	1/2	....	....	....	....	....	x	....	....	....	1 1/2
Detroit, Michigan	1/3	1/3	1	....	1/3	....	2/3	....	....	2/3	....	3 1/3	2/3	1/3	....	....	1/3	....	....	....	....	....	....	....	1 1/3
Dubuque, Iowa	2/3	2/3	1	....	1	2/3	1/3	....	....	....	....	4 1/3	....	....	....	....	1/3	1	....	....	1/3	....	....	....	1 2/3
Galesburg, Illinois	1/3	1/3	2/3	....	....	....	1/3	1/3	....	2/3	....	2 2/3	....	....	....	....	....	....	....	....	1/3	....	....	....	1/3
Grand Rapids, Michigan	1/3	1/3	1/3	....	2/3	2/3	2/3	2/3	2/3	2/3	....	5	1/3	....	1/3	....	....	....	....	1/3	....	....	....	....	1
Kalamazoo, Michigan	2/3	1/3	1/2	....	2/3	1/2	....	....	....	1/3	....	3	....	....	1/3	....	1/3	....	....	1/3	....	....	....	....	1
Lacon, Illinois	1/3	2/3	2/3	....	2/3	....	1/3	....	....	2/3	....	3 1/3	....	....	....	2/3	....	....	....	....	....	1/3	....	....	1
Madison, Wisconsin	2/3	2/3	2/3	....	2/3	1/3	1/3	....	....	1/3	....	3 2/3	2/3	....	....	....	....	....	....	....	....	1/3	....	....	1
Monroe, Michigan	x	x	x	....	x	x	x	....	....	x	....	x	x	....	....	....	....	x	....	....	....	....	....	....	?
Mt. Pleasant, Iowa	1/3	1/3	1/3	1/3	1/3	1/3	....	....	....	1/3	....	2 1/3	....	....	....	....	....	....	....	....	1/3	....	....	....	1/3
Racine, Wisconsin	1/3	1/3	1/3	....	....	1/3	1/3	....	....	1/3	1/3	2 1/3	1/3	1/3	1/3	1/3	....	....	....	....	1/3	1/3	....	....	2
Rock Island, Illinois	x	x	x	....	x	....	x	....	....	....	....	?	....	....	....	....	....	....	....	....	....	....	....	....	....
Ypsilanti, Michigan	x	....	x	....	x	x	....	....	....	....	....	?	x	....	x	....	....	....	....	....	....	....	....	....	?

x indicates time not specified.

TABLE A—1860–1865, *Continued*

Town or City	Latin: First year Latin	Latin: Caesar	Latin: Cicero	Latin: Virgil	Latin: Sallust	Latin: Horace	Latin: Total	All Foreign Languages: German	All Foreign Languages: French	All Foreign Languages: Greek	All Foreign Languages: Total	Commercial: Bookkeeping	Commercial: Total	Miscellaneous: Mental Philosophy	Miscellaneous: Moral Philosophy	Miscellaneous: Logic	Miscellaneous: Psychology	Miscellaneous: Evidence of Christianity	Miscellaneous: Domestic Science	Miscellaneous: Ancient Geography	Miscellaneous: Natural Theology	Miscellaneous: Butler's Analogy	Miscellaneous: Total
Adrian, Michigan	x	...	x	x	...	...	?	...	...	...	?	...	...	½	...	...	...	...	...	...	...	...	½
Ann Arbor, Michigan	1	x	x	x	...	...	?	...	2	x	6	...	...	...	⅔	...	...	...	...	...	...	...	⅔
Battle Creek, Michigan	1⅓	⅔	⅔	⅔	...	...	3⅓	2	...	...	5⅓	⅓	⅓	⅓	⅓	...	...	...	...	...	...	...	⅔
Burlington, Iowa	1	x	x	x	...	...	?	2⅓	...	...	6	⅓	⅓	⅔	⅓	...	...	...	...	⅓	...	...	1⅓
Charlotte, Michigan	...	...	...	...	...	...	...	x	...	...	x	x	?	...	...	...	...	...	...	...	...	...	...
Cleveland, Ohio	1	⅔	⅔	⅔	⅓	...	3⅓	2	...	...	5⅓	...	...	⅔	...	...	...	...	⅓	...	...	...	1
Chicago, Illinois	1	0	0	0	...	...	?	4	3	2	13	...	...	⅓	...	...	...	...	...	...	...	...	⅓
Cincinnati, Ohio	1	0	0	...	...	...	?	2	2	2	11	...	...	...	...	...	...	...	...	...	...	...	...
Detroit, Michigan	1	0	0	0	...	...	?	...	...	2	6	...	...	...	⅓	⅓	...	...	...	...	...	...	⅔
Dubuque, Iowa	1	⅔	⅓	1	...	...	3	2	1	1⅓	7⅓	⅓	⅓	⅔	...	...	...	...	...	...	...	...	⅔
Galesburg, Illinois	1	0	...	...	...	...	?	...	...	...	2	...	...	⅔	⅓	⅓	⅓	...	⅔	⅓	...	...	2⅔
Grand Rapids, Michigan	1⅓	...	...	...	⅔	...	2	...	...	...	2	...	...	...	...	...	...	...	...	...	...	...	...
Kalamazoo, Michigan	1	⅔	1	⅔	...	⅔	4	...	...	...	4	⅓	⅓	⅔	⅔	...	...	...	...	...	...	...	1⅓
Lacon, Illinois	⅓	0	0	...	...	...	?	...	...	⅔	3	⅓	⅓	...	...	...	...	...	...	...	...	...	...
Madison, Wisconsin	1	0	0	...	...	...	?	...	...	...	3	⅓	⅓	⅔	⅓	⅓	...	...	...	...	...	⅓	1⅔
Monroe, Michigan														x	x	...	x	...	...	...	...	...	?
Mt. Pleasant, Iowa	⅔	⅓	⅓	⅔	...	...	2	...	...	...	2	...	...	⅓	⅓	⅓	...	⅓	...	...	⅓	...	1⅔
Racine, Wisconsin	...	...	...	...	...	...	...	...	...	...	...	⅓	⅓	⅓	⅓	...	...	...	...	...	⅓	...	1
Rock Island, Illinois	...	...	...	...	...	...	...	...	...	...	...	...	...	...	x	...	...	...	...	...	...	...	?
Ypsilanti, Michigan	...	...	...	...	...	...	...	...	...	x	?	...	...	...	...	x	...	x	...	...	...	...	?

x indicates time not specified; o indicates subject was offered but the character of subject matter not given. For example, in the case of second year o merely indicates that Latin was offered but Caesar is not specified.

TABLE B—1866–1870

Town or City	Years in course	Date	Mathematics: Arithmetic	Algebra	Geometry	Trigonometry	Calculus	Analytics	Surveying	Engineering	Total	English: Grammar	Analysis	Reading	Composition	Rhetoric	English Literature	American Literature	Etymology	History of English Literature	English Language	Elocution	Total
Beloit, Wisconsin	4	1869	x	x	x	....	....	....	....	....	?	x	....	x	....	x	x	....	....	....	....	....	?
Clinton, Iowa	3	1869	....	1	1	....	....	....	....	....	2	....	1/3	1/3	....	2/3	1/3	....	....	....	....	....	1 2/3
Cleveland, Ohio	4	1870	1/3	1	1	2/3	....	....	....	....	3	....	....	....	....	....	....	....	....	1/3	....	....	1/3
Chicago, Illinois	4	1867	1/3	1	1	1/3	....	....	1/3	....	3	1/3	....	....	....	1/3	2/3	....	....	....	....	....	1 1/3
Cincinnati, Ohio	4	1867	....	1 1/2	1	1/2	....	....	1/2	....	3 1/2	....	....	....	1/2	....	2/3	....	....	....	2	....	3
Dubuque, Iowa	3	1867	....	1 1/2	2	1/2	....	....	....	....	4	....	....	....	....	1	....	....	....	....	....	....	1
Detroit, Michigan	?	1878	....	x	x	x	....	....	....	....	?	....	....	x	x	x	....	....	....	....	....	....	?
Danville, Illinois	4	1870	1	2/3	1	1/3	....	....	....	....	3	1/3	2/3	....	x	2/3	2/3	....	....	....	....	....	2 1/3
Decatur, Illinois	4	1870	....	1	2/3	1/3	....	....	....	....	2	1	....	x	....	2/3	2/3	....	1/3	....	....	....	2 2/3
Iowa City, Iowa	1	1869	....	....	2/3	1/3	....	....	....	....	1	2/3	1/3	....	....	....	....	....	....	....	....	....	1
Jacksonville, Ill.	3	1869	2/3	1	1	....	....	....	....	....	2 2/3	2/3	1/3	....	....	2/3	....	....	....	....	....	....	1 2/3
Leavenworth, Kansas	4	1867	2/3	1	2/3	2/3	....	....	1/3	....	3 1/3	....	1/3	x	x	1/3	2/3	....	....	....	....	....	?
Marengo, Iowa	4	1869	1	2	2/3	2/3	....	....	....	....	4 1/3	....	2/3	....	1/3	1/3	1/3	....	....	....	....	....	1 2/3
Madison, Wisconsin	2	1867	2/3	1 1/3	1	....	....	....	....	....	3	....	....	1	....	1/3	....	....	....	....	....	....	1 1/3
Normal, Illinois	3	1870	1/3	1 1/3	2/3	....	....	....	....	....	2 1/3	....	1/3	....	1/3	2/3	2/3	....	....	....	....	....	2
Oshkosh, Wisconsin	4	1878	1	1 1/3	2/3	1/3	....	....	....	....	3 1/3	1	....	....	....	1/3	2/3	....	....	....	....	....	2
St. Louis, Missouri	4	1867	....	1	1	1/2	1/2	1/2	1/4	1/4	4	....	1/2	....	....	....	....	1	....	....	....	....	1 1/2
Springfield, Illinois	3	1867	....	1	1	....	....	....	....	....	2	....	....	....	....	....	2/3	1	....	....	....	....	1 2/3
Waterloo, Iowa	3	1870	1	1	2/3	1/3	....	....	....	....	3	....	....	....	....	....	2/3	....	....	....	....	....	2/3
Watertown, Wisconsin	2	1869	x	x	x	x	....	....	....	....	?	x	....	....	x	x	x	....	....	....	....	x	?

x indicates time not specified.

TABLE B—1866–1870, *Continued*

Town or City	Science: Physiology	Physical Geography	Natural Philosophy	Physics	Chemistry	Astronomy	Geology	Botany	Zoology	Natural History	Mineralogy	Meteorology	Geography	Mechanics	Total
Beloit, Wisconsin	x	x	x	...	x	x	x	x	...	x	...	...	...	...	?
Clinton, Iowa	...	...	2/3	...	2/3	1/3	...	...	...	...	...	...	...	...	1 2/3
Cleveland, Ohio	...	1/3	1	...	1	1/3	1/3	1/3	2/3	1/3	...	...	...	...	4 1/3
Chicago, Illinois	1/2	1/2	1	...	1/2	1/3	1/2	2/3	...	...	...	...	1/3	...	4 1/3
Cincinnati, Ohio	1/2	...	1	...	1	1/2	1/4	...	...	...	...	...	...	...	3 1/4
Dubuque, Iowa	1/2	...	1 1/2	...	1 1/2	...	...	...	...	...	...	...	...	...	3 1/2
Detroit, Michigan	x	x	x	...	x	x	x	x	...	...	...	...	x	...	?
Danville, Illinois	...	2/3	2/3	...	1/3	1/3	1/3	1/3	...	1/3	...	...	...	...	3
Decatur, Illinois	...	2/3	2/3	1/3	2/3	1/3	1/3	1/3	1/3	...	...	...	...	...	3 2/3
Iowa City, Iowa	1/3	...	1/3	...	...	...	...	1/3	...	...	...	...	...	...	1
Jacksonville, Ill.	2/3	1/3	2/3	...	2/3	2/3	2/3	2/3	1/3	1/3	...	...	1/3	...	5 1/3
Leavenworth, Kansas	2/3	2/3	2/3	...	1	1/3	1/3	1/3	...	...	...	1/3	...	...	4 1/3
Marengo, Iowa	1/3	1/3	2/3	...	...	2/3	...	2/3	...	2/3	...	...	...	1/3	2 2/3
Madison, Wisconsin	1/3	1/3	2/3	...	...	1/3	1/3	1/3	...	...	...	...	...	...	2 1/3
Normal, Illinois	1/3	2/3	2/3	...	1/3	1/3	...	1/3	...	1/3	...	...	...	...	3
Oshkosh, Wisconsin	1/3	..	2/3	..	2/3	2/3	1/3	1/3	...	...	...	...	...	...	3
St. Louis, Missouri	1/2	1/2	1/2	...	1/2	1/2	...	1/2	1/2	...	...	...	...	...	3 1/2
Springfield, Illinois	...	...	2/3	...	2/3	1/3	1/2	2/3	...	...	...	...	1/3	...	3 1/6
Waterloo, Iowa	2/3	...	1/3	...	...	1/3	...	...	...	...	...	...	...	...	1 1/3
Watertown, Wisconsin	x	x	x	...	x	x	...	...	...	...	x	x	x	...	?

Town or City	Social Studies: Ancient History	Modern History	History	English History	General History	United States History	Science of Government	Civil Government	United States Constitution	Political Economy	Political Science	Total
Beloit, Wisconsin	...	...	...	...	x	...	...	x	...	...	x	?
Clinton, Iowa	2/3	...	...	...	...	...	...	1/3	...	...	...	1
Cleveland, Ohio	1/3	...	...	1/3	1/3	...	1/3	...	...	1/3	...	1 2/3
Chicago, Illinois	...	...	...	...	1	...	...	1/3	1/3	1/2	...	2 1/6
Cincinnati, Ohio	...	...	...	...	1/2	2/3	...	...	...	...	...	1 1/3
Dubuque, Iowa	...	...	...	...	...	...	...	...	...	...	...	...
Detroit, Michigan	x	...	...	...	...	...	...	...	...	...	...	?
Danville, Illinois	...	...	...	...	1	...	...	1/3	...	1/3	...	1 2/3
Decatur, Illinois	...	...	1/3	...	...	2/3	...	1/3	...	...	...	1 1/3
Iowa City, Iowa	...	...	...	...	...	...	...	...	...	...	...	...
Jacksonville, Ill.	1	...	...	...	...	...	1/3	...	...	1/3	...	1 2/3
Leavenworth, Kansas	...	...	...	...	2/3	...	...	...	...	1/3	...	1
Marengo, Iowa	1/3	2/3	2/3	...	...	...	...	...	1/3	...	...	2
Madison, Wisconsin	1/3	...	1/3	...	1/3	...	...	1/3	...	...	...	1 1/3
Normal, Illinois	1/3	...	...	1/3	...	...	...	1/3	...	...	...	1
Oshkosh, Wisconsin	...	...	...	...	1	...	...	...	...	...	...	1
St. Louis, Missouri	1/2	1/2	...	...	...	...	...	...	1/4	...	...	1 1/4
Springfield, Illinois	...	...	...	...	...	1	...	...	...	1/2	...	1 1/2
Waterloo, Iowa	...	...	...	...	...	1	...	...	...	...	...	1
Watertown, Wisconsin	...	...	x	...	x	...	...	x	...	...	...	?

x indicates time not specified.

TABLE B—1866–1870, *Continued*

Town or City	Latin: First year Latin	Latin: Caesar	Latin: Cicero	Latin: Virgil	Latin: Sallust	Latin: Juvenal	Total	All Foreign Languages: German	All Foreign Languages: French	All Foreign Languages: Greek	Total	Commercial: Bookkeeping	Commercial: Total	Miscellaneous: Mental Philosophy	Miscellaneous: Moral Philosophy	Miscellaneous: Logic	Miscellaneous: Drawing	Miscellaneous: Classical Antiquities	Miscellaneous: Evidences of Christianity	Miscellaneous: Ancient Geography	Miscellaneous: Pedagogy	Total
Beloit, Wisconsin	1	0	0	0	....	....	4	x	x	x	?	....	....	x	....	....	....	....	....	....	....	?
Clinton, Iowa	⅔	⅔	⅔	⅔	....	....	2⅔	x	....	x	?	1	1	....	....	....	....	....	....	....	....	....
Cleveland, Ohio	1	1	⅔	1	⅓	....	4	....	....	1	1	....	....	⅓	....	....	....	⅓	....	....	....	⅔
Chicago, Illinois	1⅓	⅔	1	1	....	....	4	x	x	x	?	⅔	⅔	½	....	....	....	....	....	....	....	½
Cincinnati, Ohio	1	1	1	....	....	....	3	1	1	2½	7½	¼	¼	½	¼	....	....	....	....	....	1	1¾
Dubuque, Iowa	1	½	½	½	....	½	3	1	1	1½	6½	....	....	....	....	....	....	....	....	....	....	....
Detroit, Michigan	1	....	0	0	0	....	4	....	....	....	4	....	....	x	....	....	....	....	....	....	....	?
Danville, Illinois	1	0	0	0	....	....	4	....	....	3	7	⅓	⅓	⅔	....	....	....	....	....	....	....	⅔
Decatur, Illinois	1	x	x	x	....	....	?	....	....	3	?	⅓	⅓	⅓	⅓	....	....	....	....	....	....	⅔
Iowa City, Iowa	....	....	....	....	....	....	....	....	....	....	....	....	....	....	....	....	....	....	....	....	....	....
Jacksonville, Ill.	⅔	⅔	⅔	⅔	....	....	3	....	....	2⅔	5⅔	⅔	⅔	⅔	⅓	....	....	....	....	....	1⅔	2⅔
Leavenworth, Kansas	1	....	....	....	....	....	1	....	....	....	1	⅓	⅓	⅓	⅔	⅓	....	....	....	....	....	1⅓
Marengo, Iowa	1	....	....	....	....	....	1	1	....	....	2	1	1	....	....	....	....	....	....	....	....	....
Madison, Wisconsin	1	0	....	....	....	....	2	x	x	x	?	....	....	⅔	⅓	....	....	....	....	....	....	1
Normal, Illinois	....	....	....	....	....	....	....	....	....	....	....	⅓	⅓	⅓	....	....	....	....	....	....	....	⅓
Oshkosh, Wisconsin	1⅓	⅔	1	1	....	....	4	3	....	3	10	....	....	⅓	⅔	....	....	....	....	....	....	1⅓
St. Louis, Missouri	1	¾	1	x	¼	....	3	x	x	x	?	½	½	½	½	....	½	....	....	⅓	....	2
Springfield, Illinois	1	⅔	⅓	1	....	....	3	1	....	2⅓	6⅓	....	....	⅓	⅓	....	....	....	....	½	....	1⅓
Waterloo, Iowa	1	1	0	....	....	....	3	1	....	....	4	1	1	⅓	⅓	⅓	....	⅓	⅓	....	....	1
Watertown, Wisconsin	....	....	....	....	....	....	....	....	....	....	....	x	?	....	....	....	x	....	....	....	....	?

x indicates time not specified; o indicates subject was offered but the character of subject matter not given. For example, in the case of second year o merely indicates that Latin was offered but Caesar is not specified.

TABLE C—1871–1875

Town or City	Years in course	Date	Mathematics: Arithmetic	Algebra	Geometry	Trigonometry	Calculus	Analytics	Surveying	Total	English: Grammar	Analysis	Composition	Rhetoric	History of English Literature	English Literature	American Literature	Etymology	Elocution	English Languages	Total
Adrian, Michigan	?	1875	....	x	x	....	....	....	....	?	⅓	x	....	x	....	x	....	....	....	....	?
Ann Arbor, Michigan	?	1874	....	x	x	....	....	....	....	?	....	....	....	x	....	x	....	....	....	....	?
Bedford, Indiana	4	1875	⅓	1⅔	⅔	⅔	....	....	⅓	3⅔	....	....	....	⅔	....	⅔	....	....	⅓	....	1⅔
Chicago, Illinois	4	1872	....	1	1	⅓	....	....	....	2⅓	....	....	....	....	....	1	....	....	....	....	1
Columbus, Ohio	?	1873	x	x	x	x	....	....	....	?	x	....	x	x	....	x	....	....	....	....	?
Dayton, Ohio	4	1875	....	1	1	½	....	....	....	2½	....	....	....	½	....	1	....	....	....	....	1½
De Witt, Iowa	3	1873	x	x	x	x	....	....	....	?	x	x	....	x	....	x	x	x	....	....	?
Joliet, Illinois	3	1873	....	1⅓	1	....	....	....	....	2⅓	....	....	x	⅔	....	⅔	....	....	....	....	1⅓
Kankakee, Illinois	4	1875	⅓	1	1	⅓	....	....	⅓	3	1½	½	....	⅓	....	⅔	....	....	....	....	3
Keokuk, Iowa	4	1873	⅓	1⅔	1	⅓	....	....	....	3⅓	1	....	⅔	⅔	....	1⅔	....	....	....	....	4
Lansing, Michigan	4	1871	1	1	⅔	⅓	....	....	....	3	....	⅓	....	⅔	....	1	....	....	....	....	2
Laporte, Indiana	4	1875	⅓	1⅙	⅔	⅓	....	....	....	2½	⅔	....	⅓	⅓	....	⅔	....	....	....	....	2
Milwaukee, Wisconsin	4	1874	⅓	1	1	⅓	....	....	⅓	3	⅓	....	⅓	⅓	....	1	....	⅓	....	....	2⅓
Macomb, Illinois	3	1875	1	1	2	⅓	....	....	....	4⅓	1	....	....	⅔	....	....	....	....	....	....	1⅔
Muscatine, Iowa	3	1871	⅓	1	1⅓	1	....	....	....	3⅔	....	....	....	⅔	....	⅓	....	....	....	....	1
Oberlin, Ohio	3	1873	⅓	1	⅓	⅔	....	....	....	2⅓	....	⅓	....	....	....	⅓	....	....	....	⅓	1
Oskaloosa, Iowa	3	1873	1	1⅓	1	....	....	....	....	3⅓	1	....	....	⅔	....	....	⅔	....	....	⅓	2⅔
Richmond, Indiana	4	1875	....	⅔	1⅔	1	⅓	....	....	3⅔	....	....	2	⅓	....	⅔	....	....	....	....	3
Springfield, Illinois	3	1872	....	1	1	....	....	....	....	2	....	x	x	⅔	....	1	....	....	....	....	?
St. Louis, Mo.	4	1871	....	x	x	x	x	x	....	?	....	x	....	....	x	....	....	....	....	....	?

x indicates time not specified.

TABLE C—1871–1875, *Continued*

Town or City	Science: Physiology	Physical Geography	Natural Philosophy	Physics	Chemistry	Geology	Botany	Zoölogy	Natural History	Mineralogy	Geography	Mechanics	Astronomy	Natural Science	Electricity	Light and Heat	Total
Adrian, Mich.	x	x	x	....	x	x	x	x	....	....	....	....	x	....	....	....	?
Ann Arbor, Mich.	x	x	x	x	x	x	....	x	....	....	....	....	x	....	....	....	?
Bedford, Ind.	1/3	1/3	1/3	....	1/3	1/3	1/3	....	....	....	....	....	1/3	....	....	....	2 1/3
Chicago, Ill.	1/3	2/3	....	1	1/3	1/3	1/2	....	1/2	....	....	x	2/3	....	....	....	4 1/3
Columbus, Ohio	x	....	....	x	x	x	x	....	....	....	....	....	x	....	....	....	?
Dayton, Ohio	1/2	....	1/2	....	1/2	1/2	1/2	....	....	....	....	1/2	1/2	....	....	....	3 1/2
De Witt, Iowa	....	....	x	x	x	x	x	x	....	....	....	....	x	....	....	....	?
Joliet, Ill.	2/3	2/3	....	....	2/3	1/3	2/3	1/3	....	....	....	....	1/3	....	....	....	3 2/3
Kankakee, Ill.	2/3	....	2/3	....	1/3	1/3	1/3	1/3	....	....	....	....	1/3	....	....	....	3
Keokuk, Iowa	1/3	2/3	2/3	....	2/3	2/3	1/3	....	....	1/3	....	....	1/3	....	....	....	4
Lansing, Mich.	1/3	1/3	2/3	....	2/3	1/3	1/3	....	....	....	....	....	1/3	....	....	....	3
Laporte, Ind.	1/3	1/3	1/2	....	1/2	1/3	1/3	1/3	....	....	....	....	1/3	....	....	....	3
Milwaukee, Wis.	1/3	1/3	....	2/3	1/3	1/3	....	1/3	....	....	....	....	1/3	....	....	....	2 2/3
Macomb, Ill.	1/3	2/3	1/3	....	2/3	1/3	2/3	....	1/3	....	1/3	....	1/3	....	....	....	4
Muscatine, Iowa	1/3	1/3	....	....	2/3	2/3	1/3	....	....	....	....	1/3	2/3	....	1/3	1/3	4
Oberlin, Ohio	....	1/3	....	....	....	....	1/3	....	....	....	....	....	....	....	....	....	2/3
Oskaloosa, Iowa	1/2	2/3	1/2	....	....	....	2/3	1/3	....	....	....	....	....	....	....	....	2 2/3
Richmond, Ind.	2/3	1/3	2/3	....	1/3	2/3	1/3	....	2/3	....	....	....	....	....	....	....	3 2/3
Springfield, Ill.	....	....	1/3	....	2/3	1/2	2/3	....	1/3	....	....	....	1/3	....	....	....	2 5/6
St. Louis, Mo.	x	x	x	....	x	....	....	....	....	....	....	....	....	x	....	....	?

Town or City	Social Studies: Ancient History	Modern History	Medieval History	United States History	General History	Universal History	History	Science of Government	Civil Government	United States Constitution	State Constitution	Political Economy	Political Science	Outlines of History	Total
Adrian, Mich.	....	....	....	....	x	....	....	....	....	....	....	....	....	....	?
Ann Arbor, Mich.	....	....	....	x	x	....	....	....	....	x	....	....	....	....	?
Bedford, Ind.	....	....	....	1	1/3	....	....	....	1/3	1/3	....	....	....	....	2
Chicago, Ill.	....	....	....	....	1	....	....	....	1/3	....	....	2/3	....	....	2
Columbus, Ohio	....	....	....	....	x	....	....	....	....	....	....	....	....	....	?
Dayton, Ohio	....	....	....	....	1/2	....	....	....	....	1/2	....	....	....	....	1
De Witt, Iowa	....	....	....	....	....	....	x	....	x	....	....	....	....	....	?
Joliet, Ill.	....	....	....	1/3	2/3	....	....	1/3	....	....	....	....	....	....	1 1/3
Kankakee, Ill.	....	....	....	....	2/3	....	....	....	1/3	....	....	1/3	....	....	1 1/3
Keokuk, Iowa	2/3	1	1/3	....	....	....	....	....	....	....	1/3	....	2/3	....	2 2/3
Lansing, Mich.	1/3	....	....	....	1	....	....	....	1/3	....	....	....	....	....	1 2/3
Laporte, Ind.	....	1/3	....	....	2/3	....	2/3	1/3	....	....	....	....	....	....	1 1/3
Milwaukee, Wis.	....	....	....	....	....	....	....	....	1/3	....	....	....	1/3	....	1 1/3
Macomb, Ill.	....	....	....	2/3	....	2/3	....	....	1/3	....	....	....	....	....	1 2/3
Muscatine, Iowa	1/3	1/3	....	....	....	....	....	....	....	....	....	....	....	....	2/3
Oberlin, Ohio	2/3	....	....	....	....	....	....	1/3	....	....	....	....	....	....	1
Oskaloosa, Iowa	....	....	....	....	....	....	....	....	....	....	....	....	....	2/3	2/3
Richmond, Ind.	....	....	....	....	1	....	....	....	....	1/3	....	1	....	....	2 1/3
Springfield, Ill.	....	....	....	....	....	....	1/3	....	....	....	....	1/2	....	....	5/6
St. Louis, Mo.	....	....	....	....	....	....	x	....	....	x	....	....	....	....	?

x indicates time not specified.

TABLE C—1871–1875, *Continued*

Town or City	All Foreign Languages: First year Latin	Caesar	Cicero	Virgil	Sallust	Latin	German	French	Spanish	Greek	Total	Comm'l Subjects: Bookkeeping	Commercial Law	Total	Miscellaneous: Mental Philosophy	Moral Philosophy	Logic	Evidences of Christianity	Mythology	Pedagogy	Ancient Geography	Biblical Antiquities	Art	Total
Adrian, Mich.	1	....	....	....	....	1	x	....	x	....	?	....	....	?	....	....	....	....	....	....	....	....	....	....
Ann Arbor, Mich.	1	....	....	....	....	1	x	x	....	1	?	....	x	?	x	....	....	....	....	....	x	....	....	?
Bedford, Indiana	2/3	1/3	1/3	2/3	....	3	....	....	....	....	3	....	....	....	....	....	....	....	....	....	....	....	....	....
Chicago, Illinois	1	0	0	0	....	4	2	2	....	3	11	2/3	....	2/3	1	....	....	....	....	....	....	....	....	1
Columbus, Ohio	1	....	....	....	....	?	....	....	....	1	?	....	....	....	x	x	....	....	....	....	....	....	....	?
Dayton, Ohio	1	1	1/2	1	....	3½	2	4	....	2	11½	....	....	....	1/3	....	....	....	....	....	....	....	....	1/3
De Witt, Iowa	1	x	x	x	....	?	....	....	....	....	?	x	....	?	x	x	....	....	....	....	....	....	....	?
Joliet, Illinois	1	....	1	1	....	3	....	....	....	2	5	....	....	....	....	....	1/3	....	....	....	....	....	....	1/3
Kankakee, Illinois	1	0	0	....	....	3	3	3	....	....	9	1/3	....	1/3	1/3	....	....	....	....	....	....	....	....	1/3
Keokuk, Iowa	1 1/3	2/3	2/3	1	1/3	4	4	....	....	....	8	....	....	....	2/3	1/3	....	....	....	....	....	....	....	1
Lansing, Mich.	1	1	1	1	....	4	3	1	....	....	8	1/3	....	1/3	2/3	....	....	....	....	....	2/3	....	....	1 1/3
Laporte, Indiana	1	0	0	0	....	4	3	3	....	2	12	1/3	....	1/3	....	....	....	....	....	....	....	....	....	....
Milwaukee, Wisconsin	1	0	0	0	....	4	4	2	....	2	12	1/3	....	1/3	....	....	....	....	....	x	....	....	....	?
Macomb, Illinois	....	....	....	....	....	....	....	....	....	....	....	....	....	....	....	....	....	....	....	....	....	....	....	....
Muscatine, Iowa	....	....	....	....	....	....	2	....	....	....	2	....	....	....	....	....	....	....	....	....	....	....	....	....
Oberlin, Ohio	1	1/3	2/3	2/3	....	2 2/3	2/3	2/3	....	2	6	....	....	....	....	....	....	....	1/3	....	....	1/3	....	2/3
Oskaloosa, Iowa	1	0	0	....	....	3	3	....	....	....	6	....	....	....	....	....	....	....	....	....	....	....	....	....
Richmond, Indiana	1	2/3	2/3	2/3	....	3	....	....	....	....	3	1/3	....	1/3	1	1/3	....	....	....	....	....	....	....	1 1/3
Springfield, Illinois	1	2/3	1/3	1	1/3	3 1/3	3	....	3	3	12 1/3	1/3	....	1/3	....	1/3	....	1/3	....	....	....	....	....	2/3
St. Louis, Mo.	1	0	0	0	....	4	4	2	....	3	13	x	....	?	x	x	....	....	....	....	....	....	x	?

x indicates time not specified; o indicates subject was offered but the character of subject matter not given. For example, in the case of second year o merely indicates that Latin was offered but Caesar is not specified.

TABLE D—1876–1880

Town or City	Years in course	Date	Mathematics: Arithmetic	Algebra	University Algebra	Geometry	Trigonometry	Analytics	Mensuration	Surveying	Plane Geometry	Solid Geometry	Total	English: Grammar	Analysis	Word Analysis	Reading	Composition	Rhetoric	History of English Literature	English Literature	American Literature	Elements of Criticism	English Language	Elocution	Total
Appleton, Wisconsin	4	1876	1⅓	1	....	....	....	....	....	....	⅔	⅔	3⅔	1	⅓	....	....	....	⅓	....	....	....	....	....	....	1⅔
Burlington, Iowa	4	1879	1	2	....	1	½	....	....	....	....	....	4½	....	....	....	....	1	....	....	½	½	....	....	....	2
Cincinnati, Ohio	4	1879	....	½	....	1	½	....	....	½	....	....	2½	....	....	....	....	....	....	....	1¼	....	....	....	....	1¼
Cleveland, Ohio	4	1876	....	1	....	1	⅓	....	....	....	....	....	2⅓	....	....	....	....	½	½	⅓	....	....	....	....	....	1⅓
Columbus, Ohio	4	1878	....	1	....	1	⅓	....	....	....	....	....	2⅓	⅓	....	....	....	....	1	....	⅔	....	....	1	....	3
Dayton, Ohio	4	1878	⅓	1	....	1	½	....	....	....	....	....	2⅚	....	....	....	....	x	½	....	1	....	....	....	....	?
Dubuque, Iowa	4	1878	½	1	....	1	½	....	....	....	....	....	3	....	....	....	....	½	½	....	....	....	....	....	....	1
Galena, Illinois	4	1879	⅔	1	....	⅔	⅓	....	....	....	....	....	2⅔	⅔	....	....	⅓	....	⅓	....	⅓	....	⅓	....	....	2
Grand Rapids, Mich.	4	1880	1	1	....	1	....	....	....	....	....	....	3	1	....	....	x	....	⅔	....	1	....	....	....	....	2⅔
Jacksonville, Illinois	4	1878	....	1	....	1	....	....	....	....	....	....	2	....	....	....	....	....	⅔	....	⅓	....	....	....	....	1
Laporte, Indiana	4	1879	⅓	1	....	1	....	....	....	....	....	....	2⅓	....	....	....	....	....	⅓	....	⅔	....	....	....	....	1
Madison, Wisconsin	3	1876	⅔	1	....	1	....	....	....	....	....	....	2⅔	⅔	⅓	....	....	⅓	⅓	....	....	....	....	....	....	1⅔
Mattoon, Illinois	3	1877	⅓	1	....	1	⅓	....	....	....	....	....	2⅔	⅓	⅔	⅓	....	x	⅓	....	⅓	....	....	....	....	2
Oberlin, Ohio	3	1877	⅔	1	½	1½	....	....	....	....	....	....	3⅔	....	....	....	....	⅓	....	....	....	....	....	⅔	....	1
Omaha, Nebraska	4	1877	....	x	....	x	....	....	....	....	....	....	?	....	....	....	....	x	x	....	x	....	....	....	x	?
Oskaloosa, Iowa	4	1878	½	2⅓	....	½	....	....	....	....	....	....	3½	....	....	....	....	½	½	....	....	1	....	....	....	2
Richmond, Indiana	4	1877	½	1	....	....	⅓	....	⅓	⅓	⅔	....	3⅙	....	⅓	....	....	1	⅓	....	....	⅔	....	....	....	2⅓
Springfield, Illinois	4	1880	....	1⅓	....	1	⅔	....	....	....	....	....	3	....	....	....	....	1	1	....	1	....	....	....	....	3
St. Louis, Missouri	3	1876	1	1	....	⅔	½	½	....	....	....	....	3⅔	....	....	....	....	....	....	1	¾	....	....	....	....	1¾
Milton, Iowa	3	1880	½	1	....	....	....	....	....	....	1	....	2½	....	⅔	....	....	....	1	....	⅔	....	....	....	....	2⅓

x indicates time not specified.

TABLE D 1876–1880, *Continued*

Town or City	Science: Physiology	Physical Geography	Natural Philosophy	Physics	Chemistry	Geology	Botany	Zoölogy	Natural History	Astronomy	Meteorology	Geography	Natural Science	Total	Social Studies: Ancient History	Medieval History	Modern History	U. S. History	English History	General History	Universal History	Outlines of History	Total
Appleton, Wisconsin	2/3	2/3	1/3	....	....	....	2/3	....	....	....	....	....	....	2 1/3	....	....	....	2/3	....	1/3	....	....	....
Burlington, Iowa	1	....	1	....	1	1/2	1/2	1/2	....	1/2	....	....	....	5	1	....	1/2	....	....	....	....	....	....
Cincinnati, Ohio	1/4	....	1	....	1	1/2	1/3	....	1/3	....	....	....	....	3 5/12	....	....	....	....	....	....	....	....	1/2
Cleveland, Ohio	....	1/3	1	....	1	1/3	1/3	1/3	1/2	1/3	....	....	....	4	1/3	....	....	....	1/3	1/3	....	....	....
Columbus, Ohio	1/3	....	....	2/3	2/3	....	....	....	....	....	....	....	....	1 2/3	2/3	....	....	....	....	....	....	....	....
Dayton, Ohio	1/2	....	1/2	....	1/2	1/2	1/2	....	....	1/2	....	....	....	3	....	....	....	....	....	1/2	....	....	....
Dubuque, Iowa	1/2	....	1	....	1	....	1/2	....	....	....	....	....	....	3	....	....	....	....	....	1	....	....	....
Galena, Illinois	2/3	1/3	2/3	2/3	....	....	1/3	1/3	....	1/3	....	2/3	....	4	1/3	....	....	2/3	2/3	....	....	....	....
Grand Rapids, Mich.	1/3	2/3	....	....	....	....	2/3	2/3	....	2/3	....	....	....	2 2/3	1/3	1/3	1/3	....	2/3	....	....	....	1
Jacksonville, Illinois	1/2	1/2	....	1	2/3	1/3	1/3	2/3	....	1/3	....	....	....	4 1/3	....	....	....	....	....	1/3	....	....	....
Laporte, Indiana	1/3	1/3	2/3	....	1/3	....	1/3	1/3	....	1/3	....	....	....	2 2/3	....	....	1/3	1/3	....	2/3	....	....	....
Madison, Wisconsin	1/2	1/2	2/3	....	....	....	1/2	....	1/2	....	....	....	....	2 2/3	....	....	....	....	1/3	1	....	....	....
Mattoon, Illinois	2/3	....	2/3	2/3	2/3	1/3	2/3	1/3	....	1/3	....	2/3	....	5	....	....	....	2/3	....	2/3	....	....	....
Oberlin, Ohio	1/3	1/3	1/3	....	....	....	....	....	....	....	....	....	....	1	....	....	....	....	....	....	....	2/3	....
Omaha, Nebraska	x	x	....	x	x	x	x	x	....	....	x	....	....	?	x	....	....	....	x	x	....	....	....
Oskaloosa, Iowa	1/2	1/2	1	....	....	1/2	1/2	1/2	....	....	....	....	....	3 1/2	....	....	....	....	....	....	....	....	1
Richmond, Indiana	2/3	1/3	2/3	....	1/3	2/3	1/3	....	2/3	1/3	....	....	....	4	....	....	....	1/3	....	....	2/3	....	....
Springfield, Illinois	1	2/3	1	....	2/3	1/3	2/3	....	2/3	1/3	....	....	....	5 1/3	....	....	....	....	....	1	....	....	....
St. Louis, Missouri	2/3	....	1	....	2/3	....	....	....	....	1/2	....	....	1	3 3/10	....	....	....	....	....	....	1	....	....
Milton, Iowa	2/3	1	1/3	....	....	....	1/2	....	1/3	1	....	....	....	3 5/6	....	....	....	....	....	....	....	....	....

x indicates time not specified.

TABLE D—1876–1880, *Continued*

Town or City	Social Studies: Science of Government	Civil Government	United States Constitution	Political Economy	Parliamentary Rules	History of Michigan	Total
Appleton, Wisconsin		1/3					1 1/3
Burlington, Iowa							1 1/2
Cincinnati, Ohio			1/4				3/4
Cleveland, Ohio	1/3			1/3			1 2/3
Columbus, Ohio							2/3
Dayton, Ohio			1/2				1
Dubuque, Iowa				1/2			1 1/2
Galena, Illinois		1/3					2 1/3
Grand Rapids, Mich.	1/3					1	4
Jacksonville, Illinois	1/3						2/3
Laporte, Indiana		2/3					2
Madison, Wisconsin		1/3					1 2/3
Mattoon, Illinois							1 1/3
Oberlin, Ohio	1/3						1
Omaha, Nebraska		x					?
Oskaloosa, Iowa		1/2					1 1/2
Richmond, Indiana		1/3					1 1/3
Springfield, Illinois			1/3	1/3			1 2/3
St. Louis, Missouri			1/4		1/3		1 1/4
Milton, Iowa		1					2 1/3

Town or City	Latin: First year Latin	Caesar	Cicero	Virgil	Sallust	Livy	Horace	Total	Foreign Languages: German	French	Greek	Total
Appleton, Wisconsin	1	1	2/3					2 2/3	2			4 2/3
Burlington, Iowa	1	1	1	1	1/3			4	4			8
Cincinnati, Ohio												
Cleveland, Ohio	1	1	2/3	1				3 2/3	4	2	3	12 2/3
Columbus, Ohio	1	x	x	x				4	4		2	10
Dayton, Ohio	1	1	1/2	1	1/2			4	4	4	2	14
Dubuque, Iowa	1	1	1	1				4	2		2	8
Galena, Illinois	1	1	2/3	1	1/3			4	1			5
Grand Rapids, Mich.												
Jacksonville, Illinois	1	0	0	0				4	4	2	3	13
Laporte, Indiana	1	0	0	0				4	4			8
Madison, Wisconsin	1	0	0					3				3
Mattoon, Illinois												
Oberlin, Ohio	1	2/3	2/3					2 1/3			1 1/3	3 2/3
Omaha, Nebraska	0	0	0	0				4				4
Oskaloosa, Iowa												
Richmond, Indiana	1	x		x				3	3			?
Springfield, Illinois	1	0		1		1/3	2/3	4	4		3	11
St. Louis, Missouri	1	0	0					3	3	3	2	11
Milton, Iowa												

Town or City	Commercial Subjects: Bookkeeping	Business Forms	Commercial Arithmetic	Total	Miscellaneous: Mental Philosophy	Moral Philosophy	Logic	Classical Antiquities	Manual Arts	Drawing	Total
Appleton, Wisconsin						1/3					1/3
Burlington, Iowa					1/2	1/2	1/2	x			1 1/2
Cincinnati, Ohio	1/4			1/4	1/2						1/2
Cleveland, Ohio					1/3						1/3
Columbus, Ohio											
Dayton, Ohio					1/3						1/3
Dubuque, Iowa	1			1							
Galena, Illinois	1/3			1/3	1/3						1/3
Grand Rapids, Mich.	1	1		2							
Jacksonville, Illinois					2/3	2/3					1 1/3
Laporte, Indiana											
Madison, Wisconsin											
Mattoon, Illinois											
Oberlin, Ohio	1/3			1/3							
Omaha, Nebraska	x		x	?	x	x					?
Oskaloosa, Iowa	1			1							
Richmond, Indiana	1/3			1/3	1/3						1/3
Springfield, Illinois	1/3			1/3							
St. Louis, Missouri	3/5			3/5					x	x	?
Milton, Iowa											

x indicates time not specified; o indicates subject was offered but the character of subject matter not given. For example, in the case of second year o merely indicates that Latin was offered but Caesar is not specified.

TABLE E—1881–1885

Town or City	Years in course	Date	Mathematics: Arithmetic	Algebra	Geometry	Trigonometry	Surveying	Total	English: Grammar	Analysis	Word Analysis	Reading	Composition	Rhetoric	History of English Literature	English Literature	American Literature	History of American Literature	Literature	Elocution	Etymology	Elocution	Total
Ashland, Nebraska	3	1881	1	1 1/3	2/3	....	....	3	1/3	1/3	....	1/3	1/3	1	....	1	....	1/3	....	1	....	1	5 2/3
Auburn, Indiana	4	1882	1 1/3	1 1/3	2/3	....	....	3 1/3	1 1/3	....	....	1	....	....	....	....	....	....	....	....	....	....	2 1/3
California, Missouri	4	1883	x	x	x	x	x	?	x	x	....	x	x	....	....	....	....	....	x	....	....	....	?
Cedar Rapids, Iowa	4	1882	1/2	1 1/2	1	....	....	3	1/2	....	....	....	1	....	....	....	....	....	0	....	....	....	2 1/2
Chicago, Illinois	4	1883	....	1	2/3	1/3	....	2	....	....	....	....	....	1/3	....	2/3	....	....	....	1/3	....	....	1 1/3
Danville, Illinois	4	1881	2/3	1 1/3	2/3	1/3	....	3	....	1	....	....	....	2/3	....	1	....	....	....	....	....	....	1 2/3
Dayton, Ohio	4	1883	....	1	1	1/4	....	2 1/4	....	....	....	....	....	1/2	....	1	....	....	....	....	....	....	1 1/2
Emporia, Kansas	3	1885	1/4	1	1	....	....	2 1/2	....	....	....	....	1/2	1/2	....	1/2	1/2	....	....	....	....	....	2
Fargo, North Dakota	4	1885	1/3	1 1/3	2/3	....	....	2 1/3	1/3	....	....	1	....	2/3	....	2/3	....	....	....	2/3	....	....	3 1/3
Fort Scott, Kansas	3	1883	1/2	1 1/2	1	....	....	3	....	....	....	....	....	....	....	1/2	1/2	....	....	....	....	1	2
Forrest, Illinois	4	1885	....	1	1/3	....	....	3 1/3	2	....	....		....	2/3	....	....	....	....	2/3	....	....	....	5 1/3
Kansas City, Missouri	4	1883	1/2	1 1/2	1	1/2	1/2	4	....	....	....	....	....	1	....	1	....	....	....	....	....	....	2
Lincoln, Nebraska	2	1882	1/3	1	2/3	....	....	2	....	....	....	....	1/3	1/3	....	1/3	1/3	....	....	1/3	....	....	1 2/3
Lawrence, Kansas	3	1884	1	1 1/2	1	....	....	3 1/2	1	....	....	....	....	1	1/2	1/2	....	1	....	....	....	1/2	4 1/2
Laporte, Indiana	4	1883	1/3	1	1	....	....	2 1/3	....	....	....	....	....	1/3	....	2/3	....	....	....	....	....	....	1
Monticello, Illinois	4	1881	1	1	1 1/3	....	....	3 1/3	....	2/3	....	1/3	....	2/3	....	2/3	....	....	....	....	....	....	2 1/3
Madison, Wisconsin	4	1883	1	1	1	....	....	3	....	1	....	....	....	1/3	....	....	....	....	0	....	....	....	1/3
Moline, Illinois	4	1881	1/3	1	1	....	....	2 1/3	....	1/2	....	....	1 2/3	....	....	1	....	....	....	....	....	....	3
Milwaukee, Wisconsin	4	1884	1/3	1	2/3	1/3	....	2 1/3	2/3	....	....	....	....	1/3	....	2/3	....	....	....	1	2/3	....	3 1/3
Newark, Ohio	4	1882	1/3	1 1/3	1	1/3	....	3	....	....	....	....	....	1/3	....	2/3	....	....	....	....	....	....	1
Oskaloosa, Iowa	4	1884	2/3	2	1	....	....	3 2/3	2	....	0	....	....	1	....	....	....	....	....	....	....	....	3
Oak Park, Illinois	3	1882	....	1 1/3	2/3	....	....	2	1/3	1/3	....	....	....	2/3	....	2/3	....	....	....	....	....	....	2
Racine, Wisconsin	4	1883	1	1	1	1/3	1/3	3 2/3	2/3	....	1/3	....	....	1	....	2/3	....	....	....	1	....	....	3 2/3
Richmond, Indiana	4	1885	....	1 1/2	1	1/2	....	3	1/2	....	....	....	1/2	....	1/2	....	....	....	....	1	....	....	2 1/2
St. Louis, Missouri	4	1882	1	1	2/5	1	....	3 2/5	....	....	....	....	....	1	....	....	....	....	....	1	....	....	2

x indicates time not specified.

TABLE E—1881–1885, *Continued*

Town or City	Science: Physiology	Physical Geography	Natural Philosophy	Physics	Chemistry	Geology	Botany	Zoölogy	Natural History	Astronomy	Geography	First Book of Science	Biology	Total	Social Studies: Ancient History	Medieval History	Modern History	U. S. History	English History	French History	General History	History of Civilization	Total
Ashland, Nebraska	1/3	2/3	....	1/3	....	....	1/3	1/3	....	....	....	....	....	2	....	....	....	....	....	1/3	2/3	1/3	....
Auburn, Indiana	2/3	2/3	2/3	....	2/3	....	....	....	....	....	....	....	....	2 2/3	....	....	....	2/3	....	....	2/3	....	....
California, Missouri	x	....	x	....	x	x	x	....	....	....	....	....	....	?	....	....	....	x	....	....	x	....	x
Cedar Rapids, Iowa	1/2	1/2	1	....	1/2	1/2	1/2	....	....	1/2	....	....	....	4	....	....	....	1/2	....	....	1	....	....
Chicago, Illinois	1/2	1/2	1	....	1	1/2	1/2	....	1/2	1/2	....	....	....	5	....	....	....	....	....	....	....	....	1
Danville, Illinois	1/2	....	2/3	....	1/2	1/2	....	1/3	....	1/2	....	....	....	3	....	....	....	....	....	....	1	....	....
Dayton, Ohio	1/2	....	....	1	1/2	....	1/2	....	....	1/4	....	....	....	2 3/4	....	....	....	....	....	....	1/2	....	....
Emporia, Kansas	1/2	....	1/2	....	1/2	1/2	1/2	1/2	....	....	....	....	....	3	1/2	....	....	....	1/2	....	....	....	....
Fargo, North Dakota	2/3	2/3	2/3	....	2/3	2/3	2/3	....	2/3	1/3	....	....	....	5	....	....	....	....	2/3	....	2/3	....	....
Fort Scott, Kansas	1/2	1	1/2	....	....	....	....	....	....	....	....	....	....	2	....	....	....	....	....	....	1	....	....
Forrest, Illinois	2/3	1/3	2/3	....	1/3	1/3	1/3	2/3	....	....	1	....	....	4 1/3	....	....	....	1 1/3	....	....	2/3	....	....
Kansas City, Missouri	1/2	1/2	1	....	1/2	1/2	1/2	....	....	1/3	....	....	....	4	....	....	....	....	....	....	....	....	1
Lincoln, Nebraska	1/3	1/3	1/3	....	1/3	1/3	1/3	....	1/3	....	....	....	....	2 1/3	....	....	....	....	1/3	....	1/3	....	....
Lawrence, Kansas	....	1/2	1/2	....	....	....	....	....	....	....	....	....	....	1	....	....	....	1/2	....	....	1	....	....
Laporte, Indiana	1/3	1/3	....	2/3	1/3	1/3	1/3	1/3	....	1/3	....	3	....	6	....	....	....	....	....	....	....	....	1
Monticello, Illinois	1/2	1/3	2/3	....	1/3	....	1/2	2/3	....	2/3	....	....	....	3 2/3	....	....	....	2/3	....	....	1	....	....
Madison, Wisconsin	....	1/3	2/3	....	2/3	....	2/3	....	....	....	....	....	....	2 1/3	1/3	....	....	....	1/3	....	....	....	2/3
Moline, Illinois	1/3	....	2/3	....	2/3	....	5/6	1/3	....	....	....	....	....	2 5/6	1/3	1/3	1/3	....	....	....	....	....	....
Milwaukee, Wisconsin	2/3	....	....	1	2/3	1/3	....	....	....	1/3	....	....	2/3	3 2/3	1/3	....	....	....	1/3	....	1	....	....
Newark, Ohio	1/2	2/3	....	1	2/3	1/3	....	....	....	1/3	....	....	....	3 1/2	....	....	....	....	....	....	....	2/3	....
Oskaloosa, Iowa	1/2	1/2	2/3	....	....	....	1/2	....	....	1/2	....	....	....	2 2/3	....	....	....	1/2	1/2	....	1	....	....
Oak Park, Illinois	1/3	1/3	2/3	....	....	....	1/3	....	....	....	1/3	....	....	2	....	....	....	1/3	....	....	2/3	....	....
Racine, Wisconsin	2/3	....	....	1	2/3	1/3	2/3	1/3	....	1/3	....	....	....	4	1/3	....	....	....	1/3	....	....	....	....
Richmond, Indiana	1/2	1/2	....	1	1	....	1/2	1/2	....	....	....	....	....	4	....	....	....	....	....	....	1	....	....
St. Louis, Missouri	1	....	1	....	1	1/2	....	1/2	....	....	....	....	....	4	....	....	....	....	....	....	1	....	....

x indicates time not specified.

TABLE E—1881–1885, *Continued*

Town or City	Social Studies: Science of Government	Civil Government	United States Constitution	Political Economy	Civil and Literary History	Total	Latin: First year Latin	Caesar	Cicero	Virgil	Sallust	Total	All Foreign Languages: German	French	Greek	Total	Commercial Subjects: Bookkeeping	Business Forms	Commercial Arithmetic	Total	Miscellaneous: Mental Philosophy	Moral Philosophy	Logic	Drawing	Pedagogy	Total
Ashland, Nebraska	....	1/3	....	....	....	1 2/3	1	0	....	....	....	2	....	....	....	2	2/3	....	....	2/3	....	....	....	....	....	....
Auburn, Indiana	....	1/3	....	....	....	1 2/3	1 1/3	2/3	....	1/3	....	2 1/3	....	....	....	2 1/3	1/3	....	....	1/3	....	....	....	....	....	....
California, Missouri	....	....	....	....	....	?	1	0	0	0	....	4	....	....	....	4	....	....	....	....	....	x	....	....	....	?
Cedar Rapids, Iowa	1/2	....	....	1/2	....	2 1/2	1	1	1	1	....	4	....	....	....	4	1/2	....	....	1/2	....	....	....	....	....	....
Chicago, Illinois	....	1/3	....	1/3	....	1 2/3	2/3	2/3	2/3	1	....	3	4	2	3	12	1	....	....	1	....	....	....	x	....	?
Danville, Ill nois	....	1/2	....	1/2	....	2	1	....	1	1	....	4	....	....	....	4	1/3	....	....	1/3	....	....	....	....	....	....
Dayton, Ohio	....	....	1/2	....	....	1	1	1	1/2	1	1/2	4	4	....	3	11	....	....	....	....	1/2	....	....	....	....	1/2
Emporia, Kansas	....	....	....	....	....	1	0	0	0	....	....	3	2	....	....	5	....	....	....	....	....	....	....	....	....	....
Fargo, North Dakota	....	2/3	....	1/3	....	2 1/3	1	1	1	1	....	4	3 2/3	....	....	7 2/3	1/3	....	....	1/3	....	....	....	....	....	....
Fort Scott, Kansas	....	1/2	....	....	....	1 1/2	1	1	1/2	1/2	....	3	....	....	....	3	1	....	....	1	....	....	....	....	....	....
Forrest, Illinois	....	1/3	....	....	....	2 1/2	....	....	....	....	....	....	....	....	....	....	1/3	....	....	1/3	....	....	....	....	....	....
Kansas City, Missouri	....	1/2	....	....	....	1 1/2	1	0	0	0	....	4	4	4	3	15	....	....	....	....	1	....	....	....	....	1
Lincoln, Nebraska	....	....	....	....	....	2/3	1	0	....	....	....	2	2	....	....	4	1/3	....	....	1/3	....	....	1/3	....	....	1/3
Lawrence, Kansas	....	1/2	....	....	....	2	1 1/2	1/2	....	1/2	....	2 1/2	....	....	....	2 1/2	1	....	1/2	1 1/2	....	....	....	....	....	....
LaPorte, Indiana	....	1	....	....	....	2	1	1	1	1	....	4	....	....	....	4	1/3	....	....	1/3	....	....	....	....	....	....
Monticello, Illinois	....	1/3	....	....	....	2	1	1	1/3	2/3	....	3	....	....	....	3	1/3	....	....	1/3	....	....	....	....	....	....
Madison, Wisconsin	....	2/3	....	1/3	....	2 1/3	1 1/3	2/3	0	0	....	4	2	2	3	11	1/3	1	....	1 1/3	1/3	1/3	....	....	....	2/3
Moline, Illinois	....	1	....	....	....	1 1/3	....	....	....	....	....	....	....	....	....	....	1/3	....	....	1/3	....	1/3	....	....	....	1/3
Milwaukee, Wisconsin	....	....	1/3	1/3	1	3 1/3	1	2/3	1	2/3	....	3 1/3	3	2	....	8 1/3	....	....	....	....	2/3	....	....	....	....	2/3
Newark, Ohio	1	....	....	....	....	1 2/3	1	0	0	0	....	4	4	....	....	8	1/2	....	....	1/2	....	....	....	....	....	....
Oskaloosa, Iowa	....	....	....	1/2	....	2 1/2	1	0	0	1	....	3	1	....	....	4	....	....	....	....	....	....	....	....	1	1
Oak Park, Illinois	....	1/3	....	....	....	1 1/3	2/3	2/3	2/3	1	....	3	2	....	....	5	2/3	....	2/3	1 1/3	....	....	....	....	....	....
Racine, Wisconsin	....	....	....	1/3	....	1	1	1	1	1	....	4	3	....	....	7	1/3	....	....	1/3	1/3	....	....	....	....	1/3
Richmond, Indiana	....	....	1/2	....	....	1 1/2	1	1	1/2	....	....	3 1/2	....	....	....	3 1/2	1	....	1/2	1 1/2	....	....	....	....	....	....
St. Louis, Missouri	....	....	1	....	....	2	1	0	0	....	....	3	4	2	3	12	....	....	....	....	1	....	....	....	....	1

x indicates time not specified; o indicates subject was offered but the character of subject matter not given. For example, in the case of second year o merely indicates that Latin was offered but Caesar is not specified.

TABLE F—1886–1890

Town or City	Years in course	Date	Mathematics: Arithmetic	Algebra	Geometry	Trigonometry	Surveying	Plane Geometry	Solid Geometry	Total
Alliance, Nebraska	3	1890	⅔	1⅓				1		3
Appleton, Wisconsin	4	1887		1⅓	1				⅓	2⅔
Baraboo, Wisconsin	4	1887	⅓	1⅔				½	½	3
Columbus, Ohio	4	1889	½	1½	½	½		½		3½
Cincinnati, Ohio	4	1887	½	1½	1	½	½			4
Cresco, Iowa	3	1888		1⅓	1⅓					2⅔
Danville, Illinois	4	1888		x	x			x	x	
Dayton, Ohio	4	1886		1	1	¼				2¼
Evansville, Indiana	4	1888	½	1½	1					3
Fairbury, Nebraska	3	1889	⅓	1⅓	1					2⅔
Greenview, Illinois	4	1887	1	1	1					3
Geneseo, Illinois	4	1887	⅓	1⅓		⅓		⅓	⅓	2⅔
Grand Rapids, Michigan	4	1890	1	1½	1½					4
Kankakee, Illinois	4	1890	⅓	1	1					2⅓
Lafayette, Indiana	4	1887	½	1½	1½	½				4
LeRoy, Minnesota	3	1890	1⅔	1⅓	⅔					3⅔
Lincoln, Nebraska	4	1887		⅓	⅔					1
Monmouth, Illinois	3	1889	⅔	1⅓	1					3
Martinsville, Ohio	3	1889	⅔	1⅓	⅔	x				2⅔
Morrison, Illinois	3	1888	⅔	1	⅔	⅓				2⅔
Moulton, Iowa	4	1890	2	2	1					5
Mount Carroll, Illinois	4	1890	1	1⅓	½					2⅚
Madison, Wisconsin	4	1887	1	1	1					3
Napoleon, Ohio	4	1888	1	1	1	⅔	⅓			4
Neosha, Missouri	3	1890	x	x	x	x				?
Odell, Illinois	4	1889	⅓	1½				1	½	3⅓
Prairie du Chien, Wis.	4	1890	⅔	1	1					2⅔
Springfield, Illinois	4	1890	⅓	1⅓	1⅓	⅙				3⅓
Sandusky, Ohio	4	1889	⅔	1	1	⅙				3
Waverly, Iowa	4	1888	1	1	1¼					3¼

Town or City	English: Gramma	Analysis	Word Analysis	Reading	Composition	Rhetoric	History of English Literature	English Literature	American Literature	Classics	Literature	Orthography	Etymology	Elocution	First year English	Second year English	Third year English	Fourth year English	Total
Alliance, Nebraska	1⅓					1		1											3⅓
Appleton, Wisconsin					⅔			1											1⅔
Baraboo, Wisconsin		⅓	⅓	x	⅓	⅓					⅔	⅓							2⅓
Columbus, Ohio	½				1	x		1							½	1	½		3½
Cincinnati, Ohio	½							2			1			x					2½
Cresco, Iowa															1	⅔			1⅔
Danville, Illinois	x			x	x	x		x	x							0	0		?
Dayton, Ohio						½		1											1½
Evansville, Indiana					x	x					x								?
Fairbury, Nebraska				x		⅔									0	0	0		3
Greenview, Illinois	1			x		1		x							0	0	0		?
Geneseo, Illinois	⅓				⅓	⅓		⅔	⅓										2
Grand Rapids, Michigan	1					1		1											3
Kankakee, Illinois	⅓	½		x	x	1		⅔	⅓										2⅚
Lafayette, Indiana					1	1		1						½	½				4
LeRoy, Minnesota	1		1			½					½								4
Lincoln, Nebraska	⅔		½		½	⅔	⅓		1										3⅔
Monmouth, Illinois	⅓					⅔		⅔		x					0	0	0		?
Martinsville, Ohio	⅓			1		⅓		⅓											2
Morrison, Illinois	⅔			⅓		⅔		⅓	⅓										2⅓
Moulton, Iowa	1			½		½		½					½						3
Mount Carroll, Illinois	1		1			⅔		1											3⅔
Madison, Wisconsin		1				⅓					2								3⅓
Napoleon, Ohio	1			⅔	⅔	1		2			1								6⅓
Neosha, Missouri					x	x		x											?
Odell, Illinois	⅓														0	0	0		3⅓
Prairie du Chien, Wis.	⅓	⅓			⅓	⅔		½	½										2⅔
Springfield, Illinois															0	0	0	0	4
Sandusky, Ohio	⅓					½		⅔											1½
Waverly, Iowa	⅔				⅓	⅔		1											3

x indicates time not specified.

TABLE F—1886–1890, *Continued*

Town or City	Science: Physiology	Physical Geography	Natural Philosophy	Physics	Chemistry	Geology	Botany	Zoölogy	Astronomy	Geography	Entomology	Total	Social Studies: Ancient History	Medieval History	Modern History	United States History	English History	French History	General History	Science of Government	Civil Government	United States Constitution	State Constitution	Political Economy	Historical Reading	Civics	Total
Alliance, Nebraska	1	1	....	1	....	....	2/3	....	....	....	....	3 2/3	....	....	....	1/3	....	....	1/3	....	2/3	....	....	....	....	....	1 1/3
Appleton, Wisconsin	1/3	1/3	....	1/2	....	1/2	2/3	....	....	....	....	2 1/3	1/3	....	1/3	....	....	....	....	....	....	1/3	....	....	....	....	1
Baraboo, Wisconsin	2/3	2/3	....	1	....	....	1/3	1/3	....	....	....	3	1/3	1/3	....	....	1/3	....	....	....	....	1/3	1/3	1/3	....	....	2..
Columbus, Ohio	....	1/3	....	1	1	....	1/2	....	1/2	....	....	3 1/2	1/2	....	1/2	1/2	....	....	....	....	....	....	1/2	....	....	....	2
Cincinnati, Ohio	1/2	....	1	....	1	1/2	1/2	1/2	1/2	....	....	4 1/2	....	....	....	....	....	....	1	....	....	1/4	....	....	....	....	1 1/4
Cresco, Iowa	1/3	1/2	....	2/3	2/3	1/3	1/2	....	....	....	....	3	....	....	....	....	....	....	2/3	....	1	....	....	....	....	....	1 2/3
Danville Illinois	x	x	....	x	....	x	x	....	....	....	x	?	....	x	x	....	x	....	x	....	x	x	....	....	x	....	?
Dayton, Ohio	1/2	....	1	1/2	....	....	1/2	....	1/4	....	....	2 3/4	....	....	....	....	....	....	1/2	1/2	....	1/2	....	....	....	....	1 1/2
Evansville, Indiana	1/2	1/2	....	1	1	....	1/2	1/2	1/2	....	....	4 1/2	....	....	....	....	1	....	1	....	1/2	....	....	....	....	....	2 1/2
Fairbury, Nebraska	1/2	1/2	....	2/3	1/2	....	1/2	....	....	....	....	2 2/3	....	....	....	1/3	....	....	1	....	1/3	....	....	....	....	....	1 2/3
Greenview, Illinois	....	2/3	1	....	....	1	1/3	1	....	1	....	5	1/3	1/3	1/3	1	....	....	....	....	1/3	....	....	1/3	....	....	2 2/3
Geneseo, Illinois	1/3	2/3	1/3	....	1/3	1/3	1/3	2/3	1/3	1/3	....	3 2/3	1/3	1/3	1/3	1/3	2/3	....	....	....	1/3	....	....	1/3	....	....	2 2/3
Grand Rapids, Michigan	....	1/2	....	1	1	1/2	1/2	1	1/2	....	....	5	1/2	....	1/2	1	1/2	....	....	....	1/2	....	....	1/2	....	....	3 1/2
Kankakee, Illinois	1/3	2/3	1	....	1/2	1/2	1/2	2/3	1/3	1/3	....	4 1/6	....	....	....	1/3	....	....	1	....	1/3	....	....	1/3	....	....	2
Lafayette, Indiana	1 1/2	1	....	1	1/2	....	1 1/2	1/2	1/2	....	....	6 1/2	....	....	....	....	....	....	....	....	1/2	....	....	....	....	....	1/2
LeRoy, Minnesota	1/2	1/2	....	2/3	....	....	1/3	1/3	1/3	1	....	3 2/3	....	....	....	1 1/3	....	....	1/3	....	2/3	....	....	1/3	....	....	2 2/3
Lincoln, Nebraska	1/2	1/2	....	2/3	2/3	1/3	1/3	....	1/3	....	....	3 1/3	....	....	....	....	2/3	....	2/3	....	1/3	....	....	....	....	....	1 2/3
Monmouth, Illinois	2/3	1/3	....	1	....	....	1/3	1/3	....	....	....	2 2/3	....	....	....	....	....	....	....	....	1/3	....	....	....	....	....	1/3
Martinsville, Ohio	1/3	2/3	....	2/3	....	1/3	1/3	....	1/3	....	....	2 2/3	....	....	....	2/3	1/3	....	2/3	....	....	....	....	....	....	....	1 2/3
Morrison, Illinois	1/3	....	2/3	....	1/3	1/3	1/3	1/3	1/3	....	....	2 2/3	2/3	....	....	2/3	....	....	....	....	1/3	....	....	....	....	....	1 2/3
Moulton, Iowa	1/2	1	....	1	1/2	1/4	1/4	1/2	1/4	1/4	....	4 1/2	....	....	....	1	1/2	1/2	1 1/2	....	1/2	....	....	1/2	....	....	4 1/2
Mount Carroll, Illinois	2/3	2/3	2/3	....	1/2	2/3	2/3	2/3	1/2	....	....	4 5/6	....	....	....	1	....	....	1	....	....	....	....	1/3	....	1/3	2 2/3
Madison, Wisconsin	2/3	1/3	1/3	....	2/3	1/3	1/3	2/3	....	....	....	2 1/3	1/3	....	....	....	1/3	....	....	....	2/3	....	....	1/3	....	....	1 2/3
Napoleon, Ohio	2/3	1	....	....	....	....	....	....	2/3	1/3	....	2 2/3	....	....	....	1 1/3	....	....	1	....	1/3	....	....	....	....	....	2 2/3
Neosha, Missouri	x	x	....	....	....	x	x	x	....	....	....	?	....	....	....	....	x	....	x	....	x	....	....	....	....	....	?
Odell, Illinois	1/2	1/2	....	1	....	1/2	1/2	1/2	....	....	....	3 1/2	....	....	....	1/2	1/2	....	1	....	1/3	....	....	....	....	....	2 1/3
Prairie du Chien, Wis.	1/3	1/2	....	2/3	....	1/3	1/2	1/3	....	....	....	2 2/3	1/3	1/3	....	2/3	1/3	....	....	....	2/3	....	....	1/3	....	....	2 2/3
Springfield, Illinois	....	1/3	1	....	1	1/2	2/3	1/2	1/2	....	....	4 1/2	....	....	....	....	....	....	....	....	2/3	....	....	2/3	2	....	3 1/3
Sandusky, Ohio	1/3	1/3	1/3	1/2	1/2	1/3	1/3	....	1/3	....	....	3	2/3	....	....	1	1/2	....	1	....	1/3	....	....	....	....	....	3 1/2
Waverly, Iowa	....	1	2/3	....	1/2	....	1/2	....	....	....	....	2 2/3	....	....	....	....	....	....	1	....	2/3	....	....	....	....	....	1 2/3

x indicates time not specified.

TABLE F—1886–1890, *Continued*

Town or City	Latin: First year Latin	Latin: Caesar	Latin: Cicero	Latin: Virgil	Latin: Sallust	Latin: Viri Romae	Latin: Total	All Foreign Languages: German	All Foreign Languages: French	All Foreign Languages: Greek	All Foreign Languages: Total	Commercial: Bookkeeping	Commercial: Business Forms	Commercial: Commercial Arithmetic	Commercial: Business Arithmetic	Commercial: Commercial Law	Commercial: Phonography	Commercial: Total	Miscellaneous: Mental Philosophy	Miscellaneous: Moral Philosophy	Miscellaneous: Drawing	Miscellaneous: Theory and Art of Teaching	Miscellaneous: Psychology and Pedagogy	Miscellaneous: Manual Training	Miscellaneous: Total
Alliance, Nebraska												2/3						2/3							
Appleton, Wisconsin	1	x		x			?	3			5								1/3		2/3	1/3		x	1
Baraboo, Wisconsin	1	0	0	0			4	2			5	1/3						1/3			2/3	2/3			1 1/3
Columbus, Ohio	1	0	0	0			4	4			8	x					x	?							
Cincinnati, Ohio	1	0	0	0			4	4	3	3	14													x	?
Cresco, Iowa												1						1							
Danville, Illinois	1	0	0	0			4					x			x										
Dayton, Ohio	1	0	0	0			4	2		3	9	x						?	1/2		1/2				1
Evansville, Indiana	1	0	0	0			4	4		2	10	1/2						1/2					1		1
Fairbury, Nebraska	2/3	2/3	2/3				2				2	1/3						1/3							
Greenview, Illinois												2/3				2/3		1 1/3							
Geneseo, Illinois	1	0	0				3				3	2/3				1/3		1		1/3					1/3
Grand Rapids, Michigan	1	0	0	0			4	4	3		11	1 1/2						1 1/2							
Kankakee, Illinois	1	0	0				3				3	1/2						1/2	1/3		1/3				2/3
Lafayette, Indiana	2/3	1 1/3	1/2	1			3 1/2	3			6 1/2														
LeRoy, Minnesota	1						1				1	1/3						1/3							
Lincoln, Nebraska	1	0	0				3	3		2 1/3	8 1/3	1/3						1/3							
Monmouth, Illinois	1	0					2				2	2/3						2/3							
Martinsville, Ohio	1	0					2				2														
Morrison, Illinois	1	0					2				2	1/3						1/3							1/3
Moulton, Iowa	1	0					2				2	1/2						1/2					1/4		1/4
Mount Carroll, Illinois												2/3						2/3		1/3	1/3				2/3
Madison, Wisconsin	1	1	0	0			4	2	3		9	1/3	2/3	1/3		1/3		1 2/3	1/3	1/3		1			1 2/3
Napoleon, Ohio	1	1	1	1			4				4	1						1							
Neosha, Missouri																									
Odell, Illinois	2/3	1	1	2/3	1/3	1/3	4				4														
Prairie du Chien, Wis.	1/2	0	0				2 1/2	2			4 1/2	2/3						2/3	1/3			2/3			1
Springfield, Illinois	1	0	0	0			4	4			8	1/2						1/2							
Sandusky, Ohio	1	0	0	0			4	4			8	x				x		?	1/2						1/3
Waverly, Iowa	1	0	0				3	1			4	2/3						2/3				1			1

x indicates time not specified; o indicates subject was offered but the character of subject matter not given. For example, in the case of second year o merely indicates that Latin was offered but Caesar is not specified.

TABLE G—1891–1895

Mathematics

Town or City	Years in course	Date	Arithmetic	Algebra	Plane Geometry	Solid Geometry	Geometry	Trigonometry	Mensuration	Total
Aberdeen, South Dakota	4	1891	1	1			1			3
Adrian, Michigan	4	1895	½	1½			1			3
Addison, Michigan	3	1895	⅔	1½			1			3⅙
Appleton, Wisconsin	4	1892		1			1			2
Aurora, Illinois	4	1894	x	1½			1½			3
Auburn, Indiana	3	1894	1	1⅓			1			3⅓
Attica, Indiana	4	1895	½	2			1			3½
Carson, Minnesota	3	1893		1½	½	½				2½
Chicago, Illinois	4	1892		1			1½	½		3
Cadillac, Michigan	4	1895	½	2			1			3½
Calumet, Michigan	4	1895	½	1½			1			3
Canal Fulton, Ohio	3	1892		1⅓			1			2⅓
Cleveland, Ohio	4	1891	1	1			1	½		3½
Delavan, Wisconsin	4	1894	⅓	1	⅔	⅓				2⅓
Danville, Illinois	4	1895	⅔	1⅔			1			3⅓
Des Moines, Iowa	4	1895	½	1½			1½			3½
Ft. Scott, Kansas	3	1892		1½			1			2½
Flandreau, South Dakota	3	1894	⅓	1⅓			1			2⅔
Fremont, Nebraska	4	1892	½	1½			1½			3½
Harveysburg, Ohio	3	1891	1	1⅓			⅔			3
Hebron, Nebraska	3	1893	½	1½			1			3
Joliet, Illinois	3	1894		1			1	⅔		2⅔
Janesville, Minn	3	1891		1	1	1				3
Keokuk, Iowa	4	1892	½	1½		1			½	3½
Lanark, Illinois	4	1894	⅔	1⅓			1	⅔		3⅔
Lebanon, Indiana	4	1894	½	2			1½			4
Lincoln, Nebraska	4	1893		1⅓	⅔	½		½		3
Minerva, Ohio	4	1894	1½	1½			1			4
Mt. Gilead, Ohio	3	1892	⅓	1⅓			1	⅓		3
Moline, Illinois	4	1891		1½			1½			3
Monroe, Wisconsin	4	1891		1⅓			1			2⅓
Madison, Wisconsin	4	1891	⅓	1			1			2⅓
Magadore, Ohio	3	1892		1½			1			2½
Montello, Illinois	4	1895	1	1⅓			1⅔			4
Oskaloosa, Iowa	4	1894	1	2			1			4
Olney, Illinois	4	1893	2	1½			1			4½
Racine, Wisconsin	4	1891	⅓	1	⅔	⅓		⅓		2⅓
Springfield, Illinois	4	1893	⅓	1⅓			1⅓	⅓		3⅓
Sioux City, Iowa	4	1892		1⅓			1			2⅔
Superior, Nebraska	4	1892	1	1⅓	⅔	⅓				3⅓

English

Town or City	Grammar	Analysis	Word Analysis	Reading	Composition	Rhetoric	History of English Literature	English Literature	American Literature	Literature	Classics	Etymology	Orthography	Elocution	First year English	Second year English	Third year English	Fourth year English	Total
Aberdeen, South Dakota						1		⅔							1				2⅔
Adrian, Michigan					½	½				1			½		1	½	½		4½
Addison, Michigan								⅔										1	⅔
Appleton, Wisconsin																1	1		3
Aurora, Illinois					1	½		1							0	0			2½
Auburn, Indiana															1	1			2
Attica, Indiana					1½			⅗	⅗						⅗				3 3/10
Carson, Minnesota			½		½	½		1											2½
Chicago, Illinois					⅗		1				1								2⅗
Cadillac, Michigan					½			1½	½						½				1½
Calumet, Michigan					½					1	1								2½
Canal Fulton, Ohio					⅓	⅓				⅓				⅓	1	1			3⅓
Cleveland, Ohio	1					½		1	½		1								4
Delavan, Wisconsin	⅓	⅓	⅓		⅔	⅓		1											3
Danville, Illinois	⅓				⅔	⅓		1	1										3⅓
Des Moines, Iowa					1	½				1									2½
Ft. Scott, Kansas	½				x	1	1-5	1	1		x								3 7/10
Flandreau, South Dakota	⅓					⅔		⅔	⅓		⅔								2⅔
Fremont, Nebraska	1		½			1				1				1					4½
Harveysburg, Ohio				1	x												⅔		1⅔
Hebron, Nebraska	x					x				1						1			2
Joliet, Illinois					⅓	⅔		⅔			1								2⅔
Janesville, Minn						½		1											1½
Keokuk, Iowa	½					½		1½		1½									4
Lanark, Illinois					⅔	⅔				⅔	½								2½
Lebanon, Indiana	½				1	1		1½	2										6
Lincoln, Nebraska					x					x				1	1	1	1		4
Minerva, Ohio	1					½		½					½						2½
Mt. Gilead, Ohio										1									1
Moline, Illinois					⅔					2									2⅔
Monroe, Wisconsin														1	1	1			3
Madison, Wisconsin					⅔	⅔				1	⅓	⅓							3
Magadore, Ohio	½					½								½					1½
Montello, Illinois	⅓				⅔	1		1											3
Oskaloosa, Iowa						½				2½				1					4
Olney, Illinois	x		½			⅔		½	x		x								1⅔
Racine, Wisconsin	⅓				⅔	⅓		⅔			1⅓								2
Springfield, Illinois														1	1	1	1		4
Sioux City, Iowa						⅓		⅔	⅓			⅓							1⅔
Superior, Nebraska								⅓						1					1⅓

x indicates time not specified.

TABLE G—1891–1895, *Continued*

Science

Town or City	Physiology	Physical Geography	Natural Philosophy	Physics	Chemistry	Geology	Botany	Zoölogy	Biology	Astronomy	Geography	Meteorology	Total
Aberdeen, S. Dak.	2/3	2/3		2/3	2/3		2/3			1/3			3 2/3
Adrian, Mich.	1/2	1/2		1	2/3		1/2						3 1/6
Addison, Mich.	1/3	2/3		2/3	2/3	1/3	1/3			1/3			3 1/3
Appleton, Wis.	2/3		2/3		2/3	2/3	2/3	2/3					4
Aurora, Ill.	1/2	1		1	1/2	1/2	1/2	1/2		1/2			5
Auburn, Ind.	1/2	1/2		1/2	1/2								2
Attica, Ind.	1/2			1/2	1/2		1/2	1/2					2 1/2
Carson, Minn.		1/2		1			1/2						2
Chicago, Ill.				1	1	1/3			1	2/3			4
Cadillac, Mich.				1	1	1/2			1 1/2				4
Calumet, Mich.	1/2			1	1		1/2						3
Canal Fulton, Ohio	1/3	1/2		1/2		2/3	1/3						2 1/3
Cleveland, Ohio	1/3	2/3		1	1/2					1/2			3
Delavan, Wis.	2/3	2/3		1	1/3		2/3						3 1/3
Danville, Ill.	1/2	1/3		1	1		1/2	1/3		1/3	1/3		4 1/3
Des Moines, Iowa	1/2	1/2		1	1/2	1	1/2	1		1/2			5
Ft. Scott, Kan.	1/2	1/2		1/2	1/2	1/2	1/2						3
Flandreau, S. D.	2/3	1/3		2/3				1/3		1/3			2 1/3
Fremont, Neb.	1/2			1	2/3	1/2	1/2			1/2	1/2		4 1/6
Harveysburg, Ohio	1/3	2/3		1			1/3			2/3			3
Hebron, Neb.		1/2		1/2			1/2						1 1/2
Joliet, Ill.	1/3	2/3					1/3	2/3		1/2			3 1/2
Janesville, Minn.	1/2	1/2		1/2			1/2						2
Keokuk, Iowa	1/2			1	1/2	1/2	1/2	1/2					3 1/2
Lanark, Ill.	1/3	1/3	2/3		1/3	1/3	1/2	2/3		2/3			3 5/6
Lebanon, Ind.		1/2		1	1		1						3 1/2
Lincoln, Neb.	1/2			1	1	1/2				1/2			3 1/2
Minerva, Ohio		1/2		1/2		1/2	1/2			1/2			2 1/2
Mt. Gilead, Ohio		1/3		1/2			1/2			1/3			1 2/3
Moline, Ill.	2/3			1	1	1/2	2/3	1/2					4 1/3
Monroe, Wis.	1			1/3	1/3		2/3						2 1/3
Madison, Wis.	1/3	1/3		1			2/3						2 1/3
Magadore, Ohio	1/2	1		1									2 1/2
Monticello, Ill.	1/3	2/3	2/3		1/3		2/3	1/2					3 1/3
Oskaloosa, Iowa	1	1/2		1	1	1/2	1/2	1/2		1/2			5 1/2
Olney, Ill.	1/2			1	1	1/2	1/3	1/2		1/2			4 1/3
Racine, Wis.	1/3	2/3	1		2/3	1/3	2/3			1/3			4
Springfield, Ill.		1/3	1		1	1/2	2/3	2/3		1/2			4 2/3
Sioux City, Iowa	1/3	1/3		1	1/2	1/3	1/2	1/3		1/3		1/3	4
Superior, Neb.	1	1/3		1	2/3		1						4

Social Studies

Town or City	Ancient History	Modern History	U. S. History	English History	French History	General History	Outlines of History	State Constitution	U. S. Civil Government	State Government	Civics	Political Economy	Political History	Historical Reading	Civil Government	Current Events	Social Science	History	
Aberdeen, S. Dak.				1/3		1/3					1/3								1
Adrian, Mich.			1			1					1								3
Addison, Mich.			1/3			1				2/3									2
Appleton, Wis.												1/3						1	1 1/3
Aurora, Ill.			1/2									1/2			1/2			2	3 1/2
Auburn, Ind.						2/3									1/3				1
Attica, Ind.						4/5					1/2					1 1/2			1 4/5
Carson, Minn.	1/2			1/2											1/2				1 1/2
Chicago, Ill.	1					1							2/3		1/3		1		4
Cadillac, Mich.	1		1/2	1/2	1/2							1/2			1/2				3 1/2
Calumet, Mich.			1/2	1/2		1							1/2						2 1/2
Canal Fulton, Ohio						1						1/3			2/3				2
Cleveland, Ohio												1						1	2
Delavan, Wis.	1/3		1/3					1/3										2/3	1 1/3
Danville, Ill.	2/3		1/3	1/3		1						1/3			1/3				3
Des Moines, Iowa				1/2		1													1 1/2
Ft. Scott, Kan.	1/2		1/2	1/2		1									1/2				3
Flandreau, S. D.			1/3			1 1/3					2/3				1/2				2 1/3
Fremont, Neb.						1													1
Harveysburg, Ohio			2/3			1					1/3								2
Hebron, Neb.															1/3				1/3
Joliet, Ill.						1			2/3						1/3				2
Janesville, Minn.	1					1									1/2				2 1/2
Keokuk, Iowa	1/2			1	1/2										1/2			1	3 1/2
Lanark, Ill.			1/3			2/3						1/3	1/3		2/3				2 1/3
Lebanon, Ind.			1/2			1					1/2	1	1						4
Lincoln, Neb.		1/2	1/2	1/2		1					1/2	1/2							3 1/2
Minerva, Ohio						1/2									1/2				1
Mt. Gilead, Ohio						1									1/3				1 1/3
Moline, Ill.															1			2	3
Monroe, Wis.	1/3			2/3											2/3				1 2/3
Madison, Wis.				2/3		1									1/3				2
Magadore, Ohio						1									1/2				1 1/2
Monticello, Ill.			1/3			1									1/3	1/3			2
Oskaloosa, Iowa				1			1					1/2			1/2			1/2	2 1/2
Olney, Ill.	1/2														1/2				1
Racine, Wis.	1/3			1/3											1/3				1
Springfield, Ill.													2/3	4	2/3				5 1/3
Sioux City, Iowa	2/3			1/3								1/3			1/3				1 2/3
Superior, Neb.			1			1													2

TABLE G—1891–1895, *Continued*

Town or City	Latin: First year Latin	Latin: Caesar	Latin: Cicero	Latin: Virgil	Latin: Sallust	Total	All Foreign Languages: German	All Foreign Languages: French	All Foreign Languages: Greek	All Foreign Languages: Spanish	Total	Commercial Subjects: Business Practice	Commercial Subjects: Bookkeeping	Commercial Subjects: Business Forms	Commercial Subjects: Commercial Arithmetic	Commercial Subjects: Business Arithmetic	Commercial Subjects: Commercial Law	Commercial Subjects: Commercial Geography	Commercial Subjects: Stenography	Commercial Subjects: Typewriting	Total	Miscellaneous: Mental Philosophy	Miscellaneous: Psychology	Miscellaneous: Ethics	Miscellaneous: Pedagogy	Miscellaneous: Manual Training	Miscellaneous: Drawing	Total
Aberdeen, S. Dakota	1	x	x	x		4	1	1			6		1			1					2		⅔		⅓			1
Adrian, Mich	x	x	x	x		4	2	2			8																	
Addison, Michigan													½								½							
Appleton, Wisconsin	1	1	1	1		4	3				7														⅓	2		2⅓
Aurora, Illinois	1	1	1	1		4	2				6																	
Auburn, Indiana	1	½		½		2	1				3																	
Attica, Indiana	x	x	x			3					3		½								½							
Carson, Minnesota	1	1	½	½		3	1	1			5														½			½
Chicago, Illinois	x	x	x	x		4	4	4		4	16		1						1	1	3		1			4	x	5
Cadillac, Michigan	1	1	1	1		4	2		2		8		1								1		½					½
Calumet Michigan	1	1	1	1		4	2				6												½					½
Canal Fulton, Ohio	x	x				2					2					⅓					⅓							
Cleveland, Ohio	1	1	1	x		4	4		3		11		x	x			x											
Delavan, Wisconsin	⅔	x	x	x		3⅔	2				5⅔		⅓								⅓	⅓			⅓			⅔
Danville, Illinois	1	1	1	⅔		3⅔	2				5⅔														⅔			1
Des Moines, Iowa	x	x	x	x		4	2				6												⅓					
Ft. Scott, Kansas	1	½	¾	¾		3					3		½								½	½						1
Flandreau, S. Dakota	1	1				2					2					⅓					⅓		½					
Fremont, Nebraska	⅔	⅔	⅔	½		2½					2½		1		1		1	1	1		5							
Harveysburg, Ohio	1	⅓		⅔		2					2																	
Hebron, Nebraska													½								½							
Joliet, Illinois	1	1	1	1		4	2		2		8																	
Janesville, Minn	x	⅔	⅔	⅔		3					3		1								1	1						1
Keokuk, Iowa	1	1	1	1		4	4				8																	
Lanark, Illinois	1	1		1		3					3		⅓		⅓		⅓				1							
Lebanon, Indiana	1	1	1	1		4					4													½				½
Lincoln, Nebraska	x	x	x	x		4	2	1	2		9																	
Minerva, Ohio	1					1	1				2	x	1	x							2							
Mt. Gilead, Ohio	1	1	1			3					3																	
Moline, Illinois	x	x	x	x		4					4		1								1							
Monroe, Wisconsin	1	1	1	1		4	2				6														⅔			⅔
Madison, Wisconsin	⅔	1⅓	⅔	1	⅓	4	2	1⅓	3		10⅓																	⅓
Magadore, Ohio	x	x	x			3					3												⅓					
Monticello, Illinois	1	⅔	⅔	⅔		3					3		⅔								⅔							
Oskaloosa, Iowa	1	1	½	½		3					3		½				½				1				½			½
Olney, Illinois	1	1				2					2																	
Racine, Wisconsin	1	1	1	1		4					4		⅔								⅔				⅔			⅔
Springfield, Illinois	x	x	x	x		4	4		3		11																	
Sioux City, Iowa	⅔	1	1	1		3⅔	3		2		8⅔		1			1	⅓		1		3⅓							
Superior, Nebraska	?	1⅓	1			3⅓					3⅓		⅓								⅓							

x indicates time not specified.

TABLE H—1896–1900

Town or City	Years in Course	Date	Mathematics: Arithmetic	Algebra	Plane Geometry	Solid Geometry	Geometry	Trigonometry	Total	English: Grammar	Analysis	Word Analysis	Reading	Composition	Rhetoric	History of English Literature	English Literature	American Literature	Literature	Classics	Etymology	Elocution	First year English	Second year English	Third year English	Fourth year English	Authors	Total
Adel, Iowa	4	1896	1	1½	1	⅓			3⅚	⅔		½		⅔	⅔			⅔	1									4⅙
Adrian, Mo.	3	1897	1	2			1		4						½				1									1½
Appleton, Wisconsin	4	1897		1	1				2										2				0	0				4
Attica, Indiana	4	1897		1½			1½	½	3½					1½					2									3½
Boone, Iowa	4	1896	1	1½	1	⅔		⅓	4½	⅓		1							1				⅔	⅓	⅓			3⅔
Columbus, Ohio	4	1897	1	1½			1½		4														0	0	0	0		4
Creston, Iowa	4	1897	½	1½			1½		3½	½				⅘	⅗				2⅗									5
Crookston, Minn.	4	1897		1½	½	½			2½					½	½					1								2
Danville, Illinois	4	1898	⅓	1			1⅓		2⅔	⅓					½	1	½	⅓					0					2⅔
Evansville, Indiana	4	1896		2			1¼	½	3¾					2	⅔				1⅔									4⅓
Evansville, Wisconsin	4	1897		1			1		2						1				1									2
Ft. Wayne, Indiana	4	1896	½	1⅓	⅔	½			3						1				2									3
Fredonia, Kansas	3	1896	1	1½			1½		3						½		1			2								3½
Girard, Illinois	4	1900		1½			1		2½														0	0	0	0		4
Grand Rapids, Michigan	4	1896	½	1½			1		3	1				½	1		1											3½
Indianola, Iowa	4	1899	1	1⅔			1⅓		4	1⅓					⅔		1			1								4
Jacksonville, Illinois	4	1896		1			1⅓	⅓	2⅔														0	0	0	0		4
Jamestown, Ohio	4	1896	½	1⅓	⅔	½			3	¼													0	0	0			3¼
Knoxville, Illinois	3	1900		1			1		2					⅓	⅓	⅓	⅓						½	½				2⅓
Lewiston, Illinois	3	1896		1			1		2					1½	½		1								0			4
Lebanon, Ohio	4	1897	1	2			1	⅓	4⅓										1					0				2
Lexington, Missouri	4	1898	1	1⅔			1⅓		4														0	0	0			3
Lincoln, Nebraska	4	1897		2	⅔	½		½	3⅔	½		½											0	0				3
Madison, Wisconsin	4	1898	⅖	1	1				2⅖										1				⅗	⅗	⅖	⅖		3
Mantua, Ohio	3	1896		2			1		3						½								0		0			2½
Marion, Illinois	4	1899	1	2			1		4								1						0					2
Maumee, Ohio	3	1898	⅓	1⅓			1		2⅔	⅓	⅔						⅓							0				2⅓
Middleville, Michigan	4	1898	⅔	1⅔			1		3⅓	1					1		1	1										4
Monroe, Michigan	4	1896	1	1			1		3			½											0	0	0			3½
Moron, Kansas	3	1896	½	1½			1		3						1		1						0					3
Markle, Indiana	3	1896		1½			1		2½					½	½			1										2
Macomb, Illinois	4	1898	½	1½	1½				3½				⅘	⅘	½					2		3-10					½	4 1/10
Newark, Ohio	4	1898		1	⅔	⅓			2						1		⅔	⅔			1			½				3⅚
Oskaloosa, Iowa	4	1899	½	1½			1½		3½	½					½		1		1				0					4
Pawnee City, Nebraska	4	1898	½	1½	1	½			3½	1½				½	½				2									4½
Prairie du Chien, Wis.	4	1897	⅓	1			⅔		2	⅓				⅔	⅔	1												2⅔
Sioux City, Iowa	4	1900		1⅔			1	⅓	3						⅔						1							1⅔
Stillwater, Minnesota	4	1897	½	1½			1		3	½						1	1											2½
Streator, Illinois	4	1896	⅓	1⅔		⅓	1	⅓	3⅔			1		⅓	⅓			x	⅓									2
Waverly, Iowa	4	1900	½	1⅓			1⅙		3														0	0	0	0		4

x indicates time not specified; o indicates subject was offered but the character of subject matter not given. For example, in the case of second year o merely indicates that Latin was offered but Caesar is not specified.

TABLE H—1896–1900, *Continued*

Science

Town or City	Physiology	Physical Geography	Natural Philosophy	Physics	Chemistry	Geology	Botany	Zoölogy	Biology	Astronomy	Natural History	Geography	Physiography	Mineralogy	Total
Adel, Iowa	⅓	⅓	....	1	....	½	⅔	....	....	....	....	....	....	....	2⅚
Adrian, Mo.	....	....	....	½	....	....	....	½	....	....	....	....	....	....	1
Appleton, Wisconsin	⅓	....	....	1	⅔	⅓	⅔	....	....	....	....	....	....	....	3
Attica, Indiana	½	....	....	½	1	....	½	1	....	....	....	....	....	....	3½
Boone, Iowa	⅓	⅔	....	1	½	⅓	⅔	....	....	½	....	....	....	....	4
Columbus, Ohio	⅓	1	....	1	1	....	⅓	....	⅓	....	....	....	....	....	4
Creston, Iowa	½	½	....	1	½	....	½	½	....	½	....	....	....	....	4
Crookston, Minn.	½	½	....	1	½	....	½	....	⅓	....	....	....	....	....	3⅓
Danville, Illinois	⅓	....	....	1	⅔	....	⅔	⅓	....	⅓	....	....	....	....	3⅓
Evansville, Indiana	....	½	....	1	1	....	1	½	....	....	....	....	....	....	4
Evansville, Wisconsin	½	½	....	1	1	....	½	....	....	....	....	....	....	....	3½
Ft. Wayne, Indiana	....	½	....	1	....	....	½	....	....	....	....	....	....	....	2
Fredonia, Kansas	½	....	....	1	½	....	....	....	....	....	....	....	....	....	1
Girard, Illinois	½	½	....	1	....	....	½	½	....	....	....	....	....	....	3
Grand Rapids, Mich.	....	½	....	1	1	....	½	....	½	½	....	....	....	....	4
Indianola, Iowa	....	⅔	....	1	....	....	⅓	⅓	....	⅓	....	....	....	....	2⅔
Jacksonville, Illinois	½	½	....	1	⅔	....	⅓	⅔	....	....	....	....	....	....	3⅔
Jamestown, Ohio	....	½	....	⅔	....	....	⅓	....	....	....	....	....	....	....	1½
Knoxville, Illinois	⅓	⅔	....	1	....	....	⅔	½	....	....	....	....	....	....	3
Lewiston, Illinois	½	½	....	1	½	....	½	½	....	....	....	....	....	....	3½
Lebanon, Ohio	⅔	....	....	1	½	⅔	½	....	....	....	....	⅓	....	....	3⅔
Lexington, Missouri	½	½	....	1	....	....	....	....	1	....	....	....	....	....	3
Lincoln, Nebraska	½	....	....	1	1	½	½	½	....	½	....	....	....	½	5
Madison, Wisconsin	⅗	1	....	1	....	....	....	....	1	....	....	....	....	....	3⅗
Mantua, Ohio	....	1	1	....	....	....	½	....	....	....	....	....	....	....	2½
Marion, Illinois	½	½	....	1	1	....	½	½	....	....	....	....	....	....	4
Maumee, Ohio	⅓	⅔	....	⅔	....	....	....	....	....	....	....	⅓	....	....	2
Middleville, Mich.	1	½	....	....	1	1	....	½	....	....	....	....	....	....	3
Monroe, Michigan	½	½	....	....	1	1	....	....	....	....	....	....	....	....	3
Moron, Kansas	....	....	....	....	½	....	....	....	....	....	....	....	....	....	½
Markle, Indiana	....	1	....	....	½	....	½	....	....	....	....	....	....	....	2
Macomb, Illinois	½	½	....	1	1	....	½	½	....	½	....	....	....	....	4½
Newark, Ohio	½	⅓	....	1	⅔	....	⅓	⅔	....	⅓	....	....	....	....	3⅚
Oskaloosa, Iowa	....	½	....	1	½	½	½	½	....	....	....	....	....	....	3½
Pawnee City, Nebraska	....	½	....	1	1	....	½	....	....	....	....	....	....	....	3
Prairie du Chien, Wis.	⅔	⅔	....	1	....	....	⅓	....	....	....	....	....	....	....	2⅔
Sioux City, Iowa	....	....	....	1	½	....	⅔	⅓	....	½	⅓	....	....	....	3⅓
Stillwater, Minn.	½	½	....	1	1	½	½	....	....	½	....	....	½	....	5
Streator, Illinois	⅓	....	....	1	⅔	⅓	⅓	⅔	....	⅓	....	....	....	....	3⅔
Waverly, Iowa	½	½	....	1	....	½	½	½	....	....	....	....	....	....	3½

Social Studies

Town or City	Ancient History	Medieval History	Modern History	United States History	English History	French History	General History	United States Constitution	Civil Government	Civics	Political Economy	American Politics	Social Science	History	Economics	Total
Adel, Iowa	....	....	....	⅔	⅓	....	1	....	⅓	....	....	....	....	....	....	2⅓
Adrian, Mo.	....	....	....	....	....	....	1	....	1	....	....	....	....	....	....	2
Appleton, Wisconsin	⅓	....	....	....	⅓	⅔	....	....	⅔	....	⅓	....	....	....	....	2⅓
Attica, Indiana	....	....	....	....	....	....	1	....	....	....	....	....	½	....	....	1½
Boone, Iowa	....	....	....	....	⅓	....	1	....	⅔	....	⅓	....	....	....	....	2⅓
Columbus, Ohio	1	....	....	½	½	½	1	....	....	½	....	....	....	....	....	4
Creston, Iowa	1	....	....	½	1	....	....	....	½	....	½	....	....	....	....	3½
Crookston, Minn.	½	....	....	....	½	....	½	....	....	½	....	....	....	....	....	2
Danville, Illinois	⅓	....	....	⅓	⅔	....	1	....	⅓	....	⅓	⅓	....	....	....	3⅓
Evansville, Indiana	½	....	½	....	....	....	....	....	½	....	....	....	....	....	....	1½
Evansville, Wisconsin	....	....	....	....	1	....	1	....	....	....	....	....	....	....	....	2
Ft. Wayne, Indiana	....	....	....	1	1	½	....	....	½	....	....	....	....	....	....	3
Fredonia, Kansas	....	....	....	....	....	....	1	....	....	....	....	....	....	....	....	1
Girard, Illinois	....	....	....	....	½	....	1	....	....	½	1	....	....	....	....	3
Grand Rapids, Mich.	1	....	....	½	½	....	1	....	½	....	½	....	....	....	....	4
Indianola, Iowa	....	....	....	1	....	1	....	....	⅔	....	⅓	....	....	....	....	3
Jacksonville, Illinois	⅔	....	....	⅓	⅓	⅓	....	....	⅓	....	....	....	....	....	....	2
Jamestown, Ohio	....	....	....	⅓	....	....	⅔	....	½	....	....	....	....	....	....	1½
Knoxville, Illinois	⅓	⅓	⅓	....	....	....	....	....	....	⅔	1	....	....	....	....	2⅔
Lewiston, Illinois	....	....	....	....	....	....	1	....	....	....	....	....	....	....	....	1
Lebanon, Ohio	....	....	....	....	....	....	1	....	....	⅓	⅔	....	....	....	....	2
Lexington, Missouri	....	....	....	....	1	....	1	....	....	½	....	....	....	....	....	2½
Lincoln, Nebraska	1	....	....	1	....	....	....	....	....	½	½	....	....	....	....	3
Madison, Wisconsin	....	....	....	1	....	....	....	....	1	....	....	....	....	1⅕	....	3⅕
Mantua, Ohio	....	....	....	....	....	....	....	....	½	....	....	....	....	1	....	1½
Marion, Illinois	....	....	....	....	....	....	1	....	½	....	....	....	....	....	....	1½
Maumee, Ohio	....	....	....	⅓	....	....	1	....	⅓	....	....	....	....	....	....	1⅔
Middleville, Mich.	....	....	....	....	1	....	1	....	....	⅔	....	....	....	....	....	2⅔
Monroe, Michigan	1	....	....	½	1	....	....	....	½	....	....	....	....	....	....	3
Moron, Kansas	....	....	....	....	....	....	1	....	½	....	....	....	....	....	....	1½
Markle, Indiana	....	....	....	....	....	....	1½	....	½	....	....	....	....	....	....	2
Macomb, Illinois	....	....	....	½	½	....	1	....	½	....	½	....	....	....	....	3
Newark, Ohio	....	....	....	....	⅓	....	⅔	....	⅓	....	....	....	....	....	....	1⅓
Oskaloosa, Iowa	½	....	½	½	½	....	....	....	....	½	½	....	....	....	....	3
Pawnee City, Nebraska	....	....	....	....	....	....	1	....	....	½	....	....	....	....	....	1½
Prairie du Chien, Wis.	....	....	....	½	½	....	½	½	....	....	⅓	....	....	....	....	2⅓
Sioux City, Iowa	⅔	....	....	....	⅓	....	....	....	⅓	....	⅓	....	....	....	....	1⅔
Stillwater, Minn.	1	....	½	....	....	....	....	....	....	½	⅓	....	....	....	....	2⅓
Streator, Illinois	⅔	⅓	⅔	⅓	....	....	....	....	⅓	....	⅓	....	....	....	1	3⅔
Waverly, Iowa	....	....	....	½	½	....	....	....	....	....	....	....	....	....	....	1

TABLE H—1896–1900, *Continued*

Town or City	Latin: First year Latin	Latin: Caesar	Latin: Cicero	Latin: Virgil	Latin: Sallust	Latin: Ovid	Total	All Foreign Languages: German	All Foreign Languages: French	All Foreign Languages: Greek	Total	Commercial: Bookkeeping	Commercial: Business Forms	Commercial: Commercial Arithmetic	Commercial: Banking	Commercial: Commercial Law	Commercial: Commercial Geography	Commercial: Stenography	Commercial: Typewriting	Commercial: Business Composition	Commercial: Phonography	Total	Miscellaneous: Mental Philosophy	Miscellaneous: Moral Philosophy	Miscellaneous: Psychology	Miscellaneous: Ethics	Miscellaneous: Pedagogy	Miscellaneous: Manual Training	Miscellaneous: Domestic Science	Miscellaneous: Drawing	Total
Adel, Iowa	1	⅔	⅔	⅔			3				3	⅔				⅓						1									½
Adrian, Mo	1	½	½				2				2	1										1				½	⅓	4	3		7⅔
Appleton, Wisconsin	1	0	0	0			4	4			8	1		⅔		⅓		2	2			6			⅓						
Attica, Indiana	1	0	0	0			4				4																				⅓
Boone, Iowa	1	0	0	0			4				4	⅓										⅓	⅓							x	?
Columbus, Ohio	1	0	0	0			4	4	2	2	12		1				½				1	2½					½				½
Creston, Iowa	1	1	1	1			4				4	½		½								1									
Crookston, Minn	1	1	1	1			4	2		2	8																⅔				1
Danville, Illinois	1	⅔	1	1			3⅔	4	2		9⅔	1	x	x		x		x	x			?			⅓					x	½
Evansville, Indiana	1	1	⅔	⅔			3⅓	4	2	3	12⅓	x		x		x	x	x	x			?			½		1				1½
Evansville, Wisconsin	1	1	1	1			4	2			6	½										½			½						
Ft. Wayne, Indiana	1	1	1	1			4			2	6																				1
Fredonia, Kansas	1	1	½	½			3	2			5														1						
Girard, Illinois	1	0	0	0			4	2			6	½										½									1
Grand Rapids, Mich	1	1	1	1			4	4	2		10	1										1			1						
Indianola, Iowa	1⅓	1	⅔	1			4	1			5	⅓										⅓									
Jacksonville, Ill	1	0	0	0			4	4			8																			x	?
Jamestown, Ohio	½	1½	1	1			4				4	½										½									
Knoxville, Ill	1	⅔	⅓				2				2	1										1									
Lewiston, Ill	1	1	1				3				3																				
Lebanon, Ohio	1	0	0	0			4				4																				
Lexington, Missouri	1	0	0				3			2	5	⅔				⅓						1									½
Lincoln, Nebraska	1	1	1	1			4	2		2	8	½										½			½		1/5			1/5	⅖
Madison, Wisconsin	1	x	x	x			4	4		4	12																				
Mantua, Ohio	1	x	x				3				3	½										½									
Marion, Illinois	1	1	1	1			4				4																				
Maumee, Ohio												⅔										⅔									
Middleville, Mich	1	0	0	0			4				4																				
Monroe, Mich	1	0	0	0			4	2		2	8	1										1									
Moron, Kansas	1	0	0				3				3	½										½									½
Markle, Indiana	1	1					2				2	½										½			½						?
Macomb, Ill	1	1	1	1			4	1½			5½	½	½	½		½						2		x							
Newark, Ohio	1	0	0	0			4	4			8	½										½									
Oskaloosa, Iowa	1	0	0	0			4	1			5	1		½		½						2					⅓				⅔
Pawnee City, Neb	1	1	1	1			4	2			6	½										½			⅓		½				½
Prairie du Chien, Wis	1⅓	⅔	1	1			4	2			6	⅔										⅔									
Sioux City, Iowa	1	⅔	1	1	⅓	⅓	4⅓	4		2	10⅓	1		1		⅓						2⅓								½	½
Stillwater, Minn	1	1	1	1		½	4½	2		2	8	½							1	1		2½								⅓	⅔
Streator, Ill	1	1	1	1			4	2			6	1	1	1	⅓	⅓	⅔	1⅔	1	1		8			⅓						
Waverly, Iowa	1	0	0	0			4	2			6	½										½									

x indicates time not specified; o indicates subject was offered but the character of subject matter not given. For example, in the case of second year o merely indicates that Latin was offered but Caesar is not specified.

TABLE I—1906–1911

Town or City	Years in Course	Date	Mathematics							English						Science										
			Arithmetic	Algebra	Plane Geometry	Solid Geometry	Trigonometry	College Algebra	Total	Grammar	Rhetoric	Public Speaking	Composition	Literature	Total	Astronomy	Biology	Botany	Chemistry	Geology	General Science	Physics	Physical Geography	Physiology	Zoology	Total
Aberdeen, South Dakota	4	1910	½	1½	1	½	....	....	3½	½	½	....	½	2½	4	....	....	½	1	....	....	1	½	....	½	3½
Akron, Ohio	4	1908	....	2	1	½	....	....	3½	....	....	....	....	....	4	....	....	½	1	....	....	1	½	....	....	3
Ann Arbor, Michigan	4	1909	½	1½	1	....	½	....	3½	....	....	....	....	....	3	....	....	½	1	....	....	1	½	....	½	3½
Appleton, Wisconsin	4	1911	....	1	1	....	....	....	2	....	1½	....	....	2½	4	....	1	....	1	....	....	1	½	....	....	3½
Calumet, Michigan	4	1906	....	1½	1	1	½	....	4	....	....	....	....	....	4	....	1	....	1	....	....	1	½	½	....	4
Cheboygan, Michigan	4	1909	....	1½	1	1	....	....	3½	....	....	....	....	....	4	....	....	½	1	....	....	1	1	½	½	4½
Columbia, Missouri	4	1910	....	2	1	½	½	....	4	....	....	....	....	....	4	....	1	....	....	....	....	1	....	....	....	2
Danville, Illinois	4	1909	....	1½	1	½	....	....	3	....	....	....	....	....	4	....	....	1	1	....	....	1	½	½	1	5
Delavan, Michigan	4	1910	½	1	1	....	....	....	2½	....	....	....	....	....	4	....	....	½	....	....	....	1	1	....	....	2½
Detroit, Michigan	4	1909	½	1½	1	½	1	½	5	....	....	....	....	....	4	....	....	1	2	....	....	1	1	½	1	6½
Elgin, Illinois	4	1910	....	1½	1	½	½	....	3½	....	....	....	....	....	4	....	....	1	1	....	....	1	1	½	1	5½
Elkhart, Indiana	4	1907	½	1½	1	½	½	....	4	....	....	....	....	....	4	½	....	1	1	....	....	1	....	....	1	4½
Evanston, Illinois	4	1908	....	1½	⅔	½	½	½	3½	....	....	....	....	....	4	....	....	1	1	....	....	1	½	¼	1	4¾
Fairbury, Nebraska	4	1908	½	1½	1	½	....	....	3½	....	....	....	....	....	3	....	....	1	1	....	....	1	½	½	....	4
Fort Wayne, Indiana	4	1910	....	1½	1	½	....	....	3	....	....	....	....	....	3	....	....	2	1	....	....	1	1	....	....	5
Hutchinson, Kansas	4	1908	....	1½	1	½	....	....	3	....	....	....	....	....	4	....	....	1	1	....	....	1	1	½	....	4½
Ionia, Michigan	4	1910	....	1½	1	½	....	....	3	....	....	....	....	....	4	....	....	½	1	....	....	1	1	....	½	4
Kankakee, Illinois	4	1906	....	1½	1	½	....	....	3	....	....	....	....	....	4	½	....	½	1	....	....	1	....	½	½	4
Kenilworth, Illinois	4	1911	....	1½	1	½	½	....	3½	....	....	....	....	....	4	....	....	1	1	....	....	1	1	¼	1	5¼
La Crosse, Wisconsin	4	1908	....	1½	1	½	....	....	3	....	....	....	....	....	4	....	....	½	1	....	....	1	½	½	....	3½
Lansing, Michigan	4	1910	½	1½	1	½	½	....	4	....	....	....	....	....	4	....	1	....	1	....	....	1	1	½	....	4½
Laporte, Indiana	4	1910	....	1½	1	½	....	....	3	....	....	....	....	....	4	....	....	1	1	....	....	1	1	....	1	5
La Salle, Illinois	4	1907	....	1½	1	½	½	½	4	....	....	....	....	....	4	....	....	1	2	½	½	1	½	½	1	7
Leavenworth, Kansas	4	1910	½	1½	1	½	½	....	4	....	....	....	....	....	3	....	....	1	1	....	....	1	1	1	....	5
Marinette, Wisconsin	4	1910	½	1½	1	½	....	....	3½	....	....	....	....	....	4	....	....	1	1	....	....	1	1	½	....	4½
Miamisburg, Ohio	4	1909	....	1½	1	½	....	....	3	....	....	....	....	....	3½	....	....	½	....	....	....	1	½	½	....	2½
Mitchell, South Dakota	4	1911	½	1½	1	½	½	....	4	....	....	....	....	....	4	....	....	½	1	....	....	1	½	....	½	3½
Monroe, Wisconsin	4	1908	½	1½	1	....	....	....	3	....	....	....	....	....	4	....	....	1	1	....	....	1	½	½	....	4
Muscatine, Iowa	4	1910	½	1½	1	½	½	....	4	....	....	....	....	....	4	½	....	1	1	½	....	1	½	½	½	5½
Omaha, Nebraska	4	1910	½	1½	1	½	½	....	4	....	....	....	....	....	4	½	....	½	1	½	....	1	½	½	½	5
Oshkosh, Wisconsin	4	1909	....	1½	1	½	½	....	3½	....	....	....	....	....	4	....	....	½	1	....	....	1	½	½	1	4½
Ottawa, Illinois	4	1907	....	1½	1½	½	....	....	3	....	....	....	....	....	3	....	....	⅔	1	....	....	1	....	⅓	1	4
Ottumwa, Iowa	4	1911	½	2	1	½	....	....	4½	....	....	....	....	....	4	....	....	1	1	....	....	1	1	½	1	5½
Pontiac, Illinois	4	1906	1	1½	1	½	....	....	4	....	....	2	....	....	4	....	....	½	1	....	....	1	....	⅔	⅔	3⅚
St. Louis, Missouri	4	1911	....	1½	1	½	½	....	3½	....	....	....	....	....	4	....	1	....	1	....	....	1	....	....	....	3
Saginaw, Michigan	4	1911	....	2	1	½	½	....	4	....	....	....	....	....	4	....	1	....	1	....	....	1	1	....	....	4
Sheboygan, Wisconsin	4	1910	1	1½	1	½	....	....	4	....	....	....	....	....	4	½	....	1	1	....	....	1	½	½	½	5
Sioux Falls, South Dakota	4	1910	....	1½	1	½	½	....	3½	....	....	....	....	....	4	....	1	1	1	....	....	1	1	....	....	5
Yankton, South Dakota	4	1911	½	1½	1	½	1	....	4½	....	....	....	....	....	4	....	....	½	1	....	....	1	½	½	....	3½
Ypsilanti, Michigan	4	1911	½	1½	1	½	½	....	4	....	....	....	....	....	4	....	....	½	1	½	....	1	....	½	½	4

TABLE I—1906–1911, *Continued*

Town or City	Social Studies: Ancient History	Medieval History	English History	American History	Civics	Economics	General History	History	Total	Foreign Languages: Latin	French	German	Greek	Spanish	Total
Aberdeen, South Dakota	1	1	1	½	½				4	4					4
Akron, Ohio				½	½	½			1½	4		4			8
Ann Arbor, Michigan	1	1		1	½				3½	4	2	2	3		11
Appleton, Wisconsin	1	1	½	½	½	1			4½	4		4			8
Calumet, Michigan	1	1		1	½				3½	4		2			6
Cheboygan, Michigan	1	1		½	½				3	4		2			6
Columbia, Missouri	1	1	1	1					4	4		3			7
Danville, Illinois	1	1	1	½	½	½			4½	4	4	4			12
Delavan, Michigan	1	1		½	½				3	4		2			6
Detroit, Michigan	1	1	1	½	½	½			4½	4	4	4	2½	2	16½
Elgin, Illinois	1	2		½	½				4	4		3			7
Elkhart, Indiana	1	1	½	1	½	½			4½	4		2			6
Evanston, Illinois	1	1	½		½				3		3	3	3		9
Fairbury, Nebraska	½		½	½					1½	4					4
Fort Wayne, Indiana	1		1	½	½				3	4		4	2		10
Hutchinson, Kansas		1		2					3	4		2			6
Ionia, Michigan	1	1		½	½				3	4		2			6
Kankakee, Illinois	1	1		½	½				3	4		2			6
Kenilworth, Illinois	1	1	½	½	½	½			4	4	3	3	3	3	16
La Crosse, Wisconsin	1	1		½	½				3	4	2	4	3		13
Lansing, Michigan	1	1	1	½		½			4	4		4	2		10
Laporte, Indiana	1	1	1	½	½	½			4½	4		3			7
La Salle, Illinois	1	1	½	½	½	½			4	4	2	4			10
Leavenworth, Kansas	1	1	1	1	1				5	4	1	3			8
Marinette, Wisconsin	1	1		½	½				3	4		2			6
Miamisburg, Ohio	1	½		½	½				2½	4		2			6
Mitchell, South Dakota	1	1	½	½	½	½			4	4		2			6
Monroe, Wisconsin	1	1		¾	¼	½			3½	4		4			8
Muscatine, Iowa	1	½	½	1					3	4		2			6
Omaha, Nebraska	½	1	½	½	½	½			3½	4	4	4	3		15
Oshkosh, Wisconsin	1	1	½	1	½	½			4½	4		4			8
Ottawa, Illinois	1	1			1				3	4	3	3	3		13
Ottumwa, Iowa	1	1		1					3	4		3			7
Pontiac, Illinois			⅔	1	½	½	1		3⅔	4		2			6
St. Louis, Missouri						½		2	2½	4	4	4	3	4	19
Saginaw, Michigan	1	1	1	1	½	½			5	4	4	4			12
Sheboygan, Wisconsin	1		1	½	½				3	4		4			8
Sioux Falls, South Dakota	1	1	1	½	½				4	4		3			7
Yankton, South Dakota	1	1	1	½	½	½			4½	4		3			7
Ypsilanti, Michigan	1	1	1	½	½	½			4½	4	2	3			9

TABLE I—1906–1911, *Continued*

Town or City	Commercial Subjects: Commercial Arithmetic	Commercial English	Commercial Geography	Commercial Law	Commercial History	Typewriting	Stenography	Bookkeeping	Total	Fine and Practical Arts: Agriculture	Domestic Science	Domestic Art	Domestic Economy	Mechanical Drawing	Manual Training	Art	Total	Miscellaneous: Pedagogy	Psychology	Ethics	Total
Aberdeen, S. Dak.	......	......	½	½	......	......	......	......	1	......	......	......	......	......	......	......	......	......	......	......	......
Akron, Ohio	½	......	½	......	......	1	2	1	5	......	......	......	......	......	4	......	4	......	......	......	......
Ann Arbor, Michigan	½	......	½	½	½	......	3	1½	6½	......	......	......	......	......	......	......	......	......	......	......	......
Appleton, Wisconsin	1	......	......	......	......	2	2	1	6	......	4	......	......	......	3	......	7	......	......	......	......
Calumet, Michigan	......	......	½	......	......	2	2	2	6½	......	3	......	......	......	4	......	7	......	......	......	......
Cheboygan, Michigan	½	......	½	½	......	1½	1½	1½	6	......	2	......	......	......	2	......	4	......	......	......	......
Columbia, Missouri	......	......	......	......	......	......	......	......	......	......	4	......	......	......	1	......	5	......	......	......	......
Danville, Illinois	1	......	......	½	½	2	2	2	8	......	1	......	......	......	......	......	1	......	......	......	......
Delavan, Michigan	......	......	......	......	......	......	......	½	½	......	......	......	......	......	......	......	......	½	......	......	½
Detroit, Michigan	½	......	½	½	......	2	3	2	8½	......	4	3	......	......	4	......	11	......	......	......	......
Elgin, Illinois	½	......	½	½	......	1	1	½	4	......	1	......	......	......	1	......	2	......	......	......	......
Elkhart, Indiana	1	......	½	½	......	1	1	1	5	......	......	......	......	......	......	......	......	......	......	......	......
Evanston, Illinois	......	......	......	......	......	......	......	......	......	......	......	......	......	......	2	......	2	......	......	......	......
Fairbury, Nebraska	½	......	½	½	......	......	......	......	1½	½	......	......	......	......	......	......	½	......	......	......	......
Fort Wayne, Indiana	½	......	......	......	......	......	......	......	½	......	......	......	......	......	......	......	......	......	......	......	......
Hutchinson, Kansas	......	......	......	½	......	1	1	½	3	......	1	1	......	......	2	......	4	......	½	......	½
Ionia, Michigan	1	½	½	½	......	2	2	4	10½	......	......	......	......	......	......	......	......	......	......	......	......
Kankakee, Illinois	½	½	½	½	......	1	1	½	4½	......	......	......	......	......	......	......	......	......	......	......	......
Kenilworth, Illinois	......	......	½	½	½	2	2	2	7½	......	......	......	4	......	4	......	8	......	......	......	......
La Crosse, Wisconsin	½	......	½	½	......	2	2	1	6½	......	......	......	......	......	......	......	......	......	......	......	......
Lansing, Michigan	½	½	......	......	......	2	2	1½	6½	......	......	......	......	......	......	......	......	......	......	......	......
Laporte, Indiana	1	½	......	½	......	......	......	1½	3½	......	1	......	......	......	4	......	5	......	......	......	......
La Salle, Illinois	......	......	......	1	......	......	3	1	5	......	4	......	......	......	4	4	12	¼	......	......	¼
Leavenworth, Kansas	1	......	1	1	......	2	2	1	8	......	......	......	......	½	......	......	½	½	½	......	1
Marinette, Wisconsin	½	½	½	½	......	1½	1½	1	6	......	2	......	......	......	2	......	4	¼	¼	......	½
Miamisburg, Ohio	......	......	......	......	......	......	......	......	......	......	......	......	......	......	......	......	......	......	......	......	......
Mitchell, S. Dak.	......	......	......	......	......	......	......	......	......	½	2	......	......	......	2½	......	5	......	......	......	......
Monroe, Wisconsin	......	½	......	......	......	2½	2	1	6	......	......	......	......	......	......	......	......	......	......	......	......
Muscatine, Iowa	......	......	½	½	......	2	2	2	7	......	......	......	......	......	2	......	2	......	......	......	......
Omaha, Nebraska	......	......	......	......	......	......	......	......	......	½	2	......	......	......	2	......	4½	½	......	......	½
Oshkosh, Wisconsin	¼	¼	½	½	......	1½	1½	1½	6	......	4	......	......	......	4	......	8	......	......	......	......
Ottawa, Illinois	......	......	......	......	......	2	2	1	5	......	1	......	......	......	2	......	3	......	......	......	......
Ottumwa, Iowa	......	......	......	......	......	2	2	1	5	......	......	......	......	......	2	......	2	½	½	......	1
Pontiac, Illinois	......	......	1	......	......	......	......	2	3	......	......	......	......	......	......	......	......	1	......	......	1
St. Louis, Missouri	1	½	½	......	......	2	2	2	8	......	......	......	......	......	4	......	4	......	1	1	2
Saginaw, Michigan	½	½	1	½	......	2	2	2	8½	......	1	1	......	......	2	......	4	......	......	......	......
Sheboygan, Wisconsin	1	......	½	½	......	2	2	1½	7½	......	......	......	......	......	......	......	......	½	......	......	½
Sioux Falls, S. Dakota	½	......	½	½	......	2	2	2	7½	......	......	......	......	......	4	......	4	......	......	......	......
Yankton, S. Dakota	......	......	½	½	......	......	......	......	1	½	......	......	......	......	......	......	½	......	......	......	......
Ypsilanti, Michigan	......	......	......	......	......	......	......	½	½	......	1	......	......	......	1	......	2	......	......	......	......

TABLE J—1915–1918

Town or City	Years in Course	Date	Mathematics: Arithmetic	Algebra	Plane Geometry	Solid Geometry	Trigonometry	College Algebra	Total	Total English	Science: Biology	Botany	Chemistry	Geology	General Science	Physics	Physical Geography	Physiology	Zoology	Total	Social Studies: Ancient History	Medieval and Modern History	English History	American History	Civics	Economics	State History	Citizenship	Contemporary Life	Total
Aberdeen, S. Dakota	4	1915	....	1½	1	½	½	....	3½	4	....	1	1	....	....	1	....	½	1	4½	1	1	½	½	½	½	....	....	....	4
Akron, Ohio	4	1917	....	2	1	½	....	....	3½	4	....	½	1	....	....	1	½	....	....	3	½	½	½	....	½	....	....	....	....	2
Albert Lea, Minnesota	4	1916	....	1½	1	½	....	....	3	4	....	1	1	....	....	1	1	½	½	5	1	1	½	½	½	½	....	....	....	4
Ann Arbor, Michigan	4	1915	....	1½	1	½	½	....	3½	4	1	....	1	....	½	1	....	....	....	3½	1	1	1	1	....	½	....	....	....	4½
Appleton, Wisconsin	4	1916	1	1½	1	½	....	....	4	4	1	....	1	....	....	1	....	½	....	3½	1	1	....	½	½	½	....	....	....	3½
Burlington, Iowa	4	1917	....	1½	1	½	....	....	3	4	1	....	1	....	....	1	1	....	....	4	1	1	1	....	½	½	....	....	....	4
Calumet, Michigan	4	1916	½	1½	1	½	½	½	4½	4	1	....	1	....	....	1	½	½	....	4	1	1	....	1	....	....	....	....	....	3
Cheboygan, Michigan	4	1916	½	1½	1	½	....	....	3½	4	1	....	1	....	....	1	1	....	....	4	1	1	....	1	....	....	....	....	....	3
Columbia, Missouri	4	1916	....	1½	1	½	½	....	3½	4	1	....	....	....	....	1	....	....	....	2	1	1	....	....	....	....	....	....	....	2
Danville, Illinois	4	1916	....	1½	1	½	....	....	3	4	....	1	1	....	....	1	½	½	1	5	1	....	1	1	½	....	....	....	....	3½
Delavan, Wisconsin	4	1916	½	1½	1	½	....	....	3½	4	....	....	....	....	1	1	....	½	....	2½	1	1	....	1	½	½	....	....	....	4
Detroit, Michigan	4	1918	½	1½	1	½	½	....	4	4	....	1	2	....	....	1	....	....	1	5	1	1	1	1	½	....	....	....	....	4½
Elgin, Illinois	4	1916	....	1½	1	½	½	....	3½	4	....	1	1	....	1	1	½	½	1	6	1	1	....	½	½	½	....	....	....	3½
Elkhart, Indiana	4	1918	....	1½	1	½	½	....	3½	4	....	1	1	....	1	1	....	....	1	5	1	1	½	1	½	½	....	....	....	4½
Evanston, Illinois	4	1917	....	1½	1	½	½	....	3½	4	....	1	1	....	1	1	....	....	1	5	1	1	1	1	½	1	....	....	....	5½
Fort Wayne, Indiana	4	1916	....	2	1	½	½	....	4	4	....	1	1	....	....	1	1	....	....	4	1	....	1	½	½	....	....	....	....	3
Hutchinson, Kansas	4	1917	½	1½	1	½	½	....	4	4	....	1	1	....	1	1	....	½	....	4½	1	1	....	1	....	½	½	....	....	4
Ionia, Michigan	4	1918	....	1½	1	½	....	....	3	4	1	½	1	....	1	1	....	....	....	4½	1	1	....	½	½	....	....	....	....	3
Kankakee, Illinois	4	1916	....	1½	1	½	....	....	3	4	1	1	1	....	....	1	½	....	1	5½	1	1	½	½	½	....	....	....	....	3½
Kenilworth, Illinois	4	1916	....	1½	1	½	½	....	3½	4	....	½	1	....	....	1	½	....	½	3½	1	1	1	1	½	½	....	....	....	5
Lansing, Michigan	4	1917	....	1½	1	½	½	....	3½	4	....	½	1	....	....	1	1	1	½	5	1	1	....	1	....	½	....	....	....	3½
La Salle, Illinois	4	1916	....	1½	1	½	....	....	3	4	1	½	1	½	½	1	½	½	½	6	1	½	½	½	½	1	....	....	....	4
Leavenworth, Kansas	4	1918	....	2	1	½	½	....	4	4	1	....	2	....	1	1	....	1	....	6	1	1	....	1	1	1	....	1	1	7
Marinette, Wisconsin	4	1917	⅓	1½	1	½	....	....	3⅓	4	....	1	1	....	1	1	....	½	....	4½	1	1	....	½	½	½	....	....	....	3½
Miamisburg, Ohio	4	1916	....	1½	1	½	....	....	3	4	1	....	....	....	....	1	....	....	....	2	½	1½	....	½	½	....	....	....	....	3
Mitchell, S. Dak.	4	1917	....	1½	1	½	½	....	3½	4	1	....	1	....	½	1	½	....	....	4	1	....	....	....	½	½	....	....	....	2½
Monroe, Wisconsin	6	1917	2	1½	1	½	....	....	5	6	....	½	1	....	....	1	½	....	....	3	1	1	....	2	½	....	....	....	....	4½
Muscatine, Iowa	4	1917	....	1½	1	....	....	....	2½	4	....	1	1	....	1	1	....	½	1	5½	1	½	....	1	½	½	....	....	....	3½
Norwalk, Ohio	4	1915	....	1½	1	1	½	....	4	4	1	....	1	....	1	1	....	....	....	4	1	1	....	½	½	½	....	....	....	3½
Omaha, Nebraska	4	1915	½	1½	1	½	½	....	4	4	1	....	1	½	1	1	....	....	....	4½	1	1	½	1	½	1	....	....	....	5
Oshkosh, Wisconsin	4	1816	....	1½	1	½	½	....	3½	4	1	½	1	....	½	1	½	½	....	5	1	1	½	½	½	½	....	....	....	4
Ottumwa, Iowa	4	1918	½	1½	1	½	....	....	3½	4	....	1	1	½	....	½	1	½	....	4½	....	1	½	½	½	½	....	....	....	3
Pontiac, Illinois	4	1916	....	1½	1	½	....	....	3	4	½	½	1	....	....	1	½	....	½	4	1	....	1	1	½	....	....	....	....	3½
St. Louis, Missouri	4	1918	½	1½	1	½	½	....	4	4	....	½	1	....	....	1	½	½	....	3½	½	½	½	½	½	....	....	....	....	2½
Saginaw, Michigan	4	1917	....	1½	1	½	....	....	3	4	....	1	1	....	1	1	....	½	....	4½	1	....	1	1	½	½	....	....	....	4
Sheboygan, Wisconsin	4	1917	....	1½	1	½	....	....	3	4	1	....	1	....	1	1	....	½	....	4½	1	1	1	½	½	½	....	....	....	4½
Sioux Falls, S. Dak.	4	1917	....	1½	1	½	½	½	4	4	....	1	1	....	....	1	1	1	½	5½	1	1	1	½	½	½	....	....	....	4½
Watertown, S. Dak.	4	1915	....	1½	1	½	....	....	3	4	....	½	1	....	....	1	½	½	½	4	1	1	....	½	½	....	....	....	....	3
Yankton, S. Dak.	4	1918	½	1½	1	½	....	....	3½	4	1	....	1	....	½	1	½	½	....	4½	1	....	....	½	½	½	....	....	....	2½
Ypsilanti, Michigan	4	1915	....	1½	1	½	½	½	4	4	....	½	1	....	1	1	....	....	½	4	1	1	....	½	1½	....	....	....	....	4

TABLE J—1915–1918, *Continued*

Town or City	Foreign Languages							Commercial Subjects														
	Latin	French	German	Greek	Spanish	Swedish	Total	Commercial Arithmetic	Commercial English	Commercial Geography	Commercial Law	Commercial History	Typewriting	Stenography	Bookkeeping	Accounting	Business Methods	Banking	Salesmanship	Office Practise	Advertising	Total
Aberdeen, South Dakota	4		3				7	½					2	2	1		½					6
Akron, Ohio	4		4				8	½		½	½		1	2	1							5½
Albert Lea, Minnesota	2		4				6			½												½
Ann Arbor, Michigan	4	3	4	2	2		15	1	½	½	½		1	1½	2				½			7½
Appleton, Wisconsin	4		2				6		½		½		2	2	1		½					6½
Burlington, Iowa	4	2	4		3		13	½	½	1	1		2	2	1							8
Calumet, Michigan	4	2	3				9		½	½	½		½	2	1½							5½
Cheboygan, Michigan	4		2				6			½	½	½	1	1	1							4½
Columbia, Missouri	4		3				7						½	½	1							2
Danville, Illinois								1		½	½		2	2	2							8
Delavan, Wisconsin	4		2				6						1	1	1					½		3½
Detroit, Michigan	4	4	4	3	4		19		½	½	½	½	2	3	2					½		9½
Elgin, Illinois	4		3		2		9	1	½	½	½		1	2	2							7½
Elkhart, Indiana	3½						3½		1	1	½		1	2	1				½			7
Evanston, Illinois	4	3	3	3	2		15	1	½	½	½		2	2	1	½						8
Fort Wayne, Indiana	4	4	4		2		14						1	1	1½							3½
Hutchinson, Kansas	4		3				7	½		1	½	½	2	1	2	½	½					8½
Ionia, Michigan	4		2				6	½					2	1½	2		½					6½
Kankakee, Illinois	4		2				6	1		½	½		2	2	1							7
Kenilworth, Illinois	4	3	3	3	3		16	½		1	½		2		1		1					6
Lansing, Michigan	4	2	4				10		1	½	½	½	½	3	1		½					7½
La Salle, Illinois	4	2	2				8	½	½	1	½		1½		2			½				6½
Leavenworth, Kansas	4		3		2		9	1			½		1	2	1							5½
Marinette, Wisconsin	4		2			2	8		½		½		1	1	1½				½			5
Miamisburg, Ohio	4		2				6	1	1	½	1		1	2	2							8½
Mitchell, South Dakota	4		2				6	1		½	½		2	1	1							6
Monroe, Wisconsin	6		6				12	1		½	½		2	2	1					½		7½
Muscatine, Iowa	4		4				8	½	½	½		½	2	2	½							6½
Norwalk, Ohio	4	1	2		2		9	1		½				1½	1½							4½
Omaha, Nebraska	4	4	4	3	2		17				½	½	2	2		1			½	½	½	7½
Oshkosh, Wisconsin	4		4				8	¼	¼	½	½		1	1	1½			½				5½
Ottumwa, Iowa	3	1			4		8	½	½				1½	1	1		½					5
Pontiac, Illinois	4		2				6	1		½	½	1	1	2	1½		½					8
St. Louis, Missouri	4	4	4	3	4		19	1		½	½	½	2	2	2	½	2		½			11½
Saginaw, Michigan	4	2	2		2		10			1	½		1	2	2						½	7
Sheboygan, Wisconsin	4		4				8		½		½	½	2	2		½						6
Sioux Falls, South Dakota	4	2	4		2		12	1		½	½	½	2	2	2			½			½	4½
Watertown, South Dakota	4		3				7	½			½		1	1	1							4
Yankton, South Dakota	4		2		2		8	½		½	½		2	½	1							5
Ypsilanti, Michigan	4	2	4				10	½			½		1½	1½	2							6

TABLE J—1915-1918, *Continued*

Town or City	Fine and Practical Arts																															Miscellaneous			
	Agriculture	Domestic Science	Domestic Art	Domestic Economy	Mechanical Drawing	Manual Training	Pattern Making	Machine Shop	Metal Work	Pottery	Household Chemistry	Camp Cooking	Forging	Machine Fitting	Printing	First Aid	Electricity and Applied Mechanics	Building Construction	Carpentry	Concrete Work	Home Decorations	Home Management	Form Mechanics	Design	Telegraphy	Home Nursing	Millinery	Art and Needlework	Laundry and Sanitation	Household Physics	Total	Pedagogy	Psychology	Biblical Literature	Total
Aberdeen, S. Dak.	3	2				2																									7				
Akron, Ohio				4			1	1					1						1												8				
Albert Lea, Minn.	4	4				4																									12				
Ann Arbor, Mich.		3				3					1																				7				
Appleton, Wis.		3½		3½		4		½	½		½		½					½													13½		½		½
Burlington, Iowa	1	3				3																									9			1	1
Calumet, Mich.		4				4																									8				
Cheboygan, Mich.																																			
Columbia, Mo.	1	1			1	1																									4	1	1		2
Danville, Ill.		2				2																									4				
Delavan, Wis.		1																													1				
Detroit, Mich.	½	4	4		4								2																		14½				
Elgin, Ill.		4				4																									8				
Elkhart, Ind.		2				4							1		4																11				
Evanston, Ill.						3																									3				
Fort Wayne, Ind.		2			1½	1	½						½	½																	6				
Hutchinson, Kansas	1½	4				4																									9½		½		½
Ionia, Mich.	3	2				2																									7				
Kankakee, Ill.				2		4																									6	½			½
Kenilworth, Ill.		4				4																									8				
Lansing, Mich.			1	1			1	2	1								¼	1													7¼				
La Salle, Ill.	3	2				2																									7	½			½
Leavenworth, Kan.	1	2	2			3																									8	½	½		1
Marinette, Wis.		4				4																									8				
Miamisburg, Ohio	½	1																													½				
Mitchell, S. Dak.	3	2				2					1																				9				
Monroe, Wisconsin		6				4																									10				
Muscatine, Iowa	1																														1				
Norwalk, Ohio	1										1																				2				
Omaha, Neb.	½	4	4			2																			½						11	½			½
Oshkosh, Wisconsin		4				4																									8				
Ottumwa, Iowa	½	4				4																									8½	½	½		1
Pontiac, Ill.	2	4				4																									10	½			½
St. Louis, Mo.			4			4																									8				
Saginaw, Mich.	4	2	2		4	2		1			1	1/5	½																		16 7/10				
Sheboygan, Wis.	4	4				4																½					½			½	13½	½			½
Sioux Falls, S. Dak.	2	1			2	4	½	2							2							½		½				4	½		19	½	½		1
Watertown, S. Dak.	1			2		2																									5				
Yankton, S. Dak.	2	2		4				4		1																					13	½	½		1
Ypsilanti, Mich.	2	1				4																1					1	2			11				

BIBLIOGRAPHY

Authorities and Sources

I

Aurner, Clarence Ray. *History of Education in Iowa*, 1915. Chapters xix–xxii. A good account of secondary education in Iowa. Curricula in considerable detail.

Barnard, Henry. *American Journal of Education*, XIX (1870), 465–576. Contains curricula, both elementary and secondary, for the late 60's.

Bennett, Charles E., and Bristol, George P. *The Teaching of Latin and Greek in the Secondary School*, 1899, pp. 50–54, 111–24. Some historical material.

Education in Indiana. Information concerning the establishment of high schools.

Bourne, Henry E. *The Teaching of History and Civics*, 1912. Chapter iv. General treatment of the development of subject-matter.

Brown, Elmer E. *The Making of Our Middle Schools: An Account of the Development of Secondary Education in the United States*, 1902. Chapter xiv. Good account of the early high schools.

Carpenter, G. R., Baker, F. T., and Scott, F. N. *The Teaching of English in the Elementary and the Secondary School*, 1903. Chapter iv. Discussion of the development of subject-matter in secondary English.

Dexter, Edwin G. *A History of Education in the United States*, 1904. Chapter xii. A brief treatment of secondary education.

Handschin, C. H. *The Teaching of Modern Languages in the United States*, 1913. Some good material on subject-matter.

Mann, C. R. *The Teaching of Physics*, 1912. Chapters ii, iii, and iv. Some historical material.

Monroe, Paul. *A Cyclopedia of Education*, 1911. I, 92; III, 51. Brief historical accounts of subject-matter.

Report of the United States Commissioner of Education, 1886–87, pp. 534–50, 631–41; 1896–97, II, 1886–94; 1916, II, 447. Good material dealing with high-school subjects in first two citations. Statement of the number of secondary schools, public and private, in the last one.

Smith, David E. *The Teaching of Geometry*, 1911. Chapters vi–vii. Some discussion of the development of subject-matter.

Woodhull, John F. "The Teaching of Physical Science," *Teachers College Record*, XI (January, 1910), 5–26. Good historical sketch of the development of subject-matter.

II

The following are the sources for data used in Appendix, Tables A–J. They contain high-school courses of study and are valuable in furnishing details concerning the subjects offered. Considerable material is also included dealing with subject-matter.

Central High School, Aberdeen, South Dakota: Announcement and Course of Study, 1915. Leaflet.

Course of Study of the Public Schools, Aberdeen, South Dakota, 1891, pp. 20–21.
Manual of the Aberdeen (South Dakota) City Schools, 1910–11, pp. 27–38.
Announcement of the Public Schools, Addison, Michigan, 1895–96, p. 8.
Rules and Regulations and Course of Study, Adel, Iowa, 1896, p. 16.
Course of Study and Rules and Regulations, Adrian, Missouri, 1896–97, p. 15.
Report of the Officers and Pupils of the Adrian, Michigan, Public Schools, 1856–57, p. 34.
Report of the Superintendent of Public Instruction of the State of Michigan, 1875. Adrian, p. 301. Ann Arbor, p. 311.
Rules and Regulations and Course of Study, Adrian, Michigan, 1895, p. 58.
Course of Instruction for the Akron, Ohio, High School, 1917. Leaflet.
Course of Study and Manual of Instruction for the Public Schools of Akron, Ohio, 1908, pp. 191–216.
Public School Bulletin, Albert Lea, Minnesota, 1916, pp. 10–25.
Course of Study and Rules and Regulations of the Public Schools, Alliance, Nebraska, 1890, p. 14.
American Journal of Education, XIX, 535-36.
Catalog of the Ann Arbor (Michigan) High School for the Academic Year, 1908–09, pp. 30–31.
Catalog of the Ann Arbor (Michigan) High School for the Year 1915, pp. 24–36.
Report of the Superintendent of Public Instruction of the State of Michigan, 1855–56–57. Ann Arbor. Report of Union Schools, pp. 440–41.
Annual Catalog District Schools, Appleton, Wisconsin, 1891–92, pp. 15–18.
Annual Catalog of the Public Schools, Appleton, Wisconsin, 1886–87, pp. 17–19.
Appleton (Wisconsin) Public Schools: Course of Study, 1911, pp. 32–36.
Ibid., 1916, pp. 38–43.
Catalog of Public Schools, Appleton, Wisconsin, 1897, pp. 57–62.
Rules and Regulations and Revised Course of Study, Appleton, Wisconsin, 1876, p. 18.
Outline of Course of Study and Rules and Regulations, Ashland, Nebraska, 1881, p. 8.
Manual of Public Schools, Attica, Indiana, 1897, p. 64.
Report and Manual of the Public Schools, Attica, Indiana, 1895, p. 45.
Manual of the Public Schools, Auburn, Indiana, 1894–95, p. 9.
Rules and Regulations of the Public Schools, Auburn, Indiana, 1882–83, pp. 9–10.
Annual Report Board of Education, Aurora, Illinois, 1894, pp. 25–26.

Course of Study and Rules and Regulations, Baraboo, Wisconsin, 1887, p. 20.
Report of Superintendent of Public Instruction of the State of Michigan (Battle Creek), 1859, p. 254.
Bedford (Indiana) Graded Schools, 1875, p. 2.
Report of the Superintendent of Public Instruction of the State of Wisconsin (Beloit), 1869, p. 104.
Rules and Regulations and Graded Course of Study, Boone, Iowa, 1896, pp. 103–6.
Course of Study, Burlington, Iowa, 1917. Leaflet.

Course of Study of City Schools, Cadillac, Michigan, 1895–96, p. 12.
Public Schools of City of California, Missouri, 1883–84, p. 38.
Course of Study and Rules and Regulations, Calumet, Michigan, 1895–96, p. 78.

General Rules and Course of Study of the Public Schools of Calumet, Michigan, 1916, pp. 18–26.
Public Schools, Calumet, Michigan, 1906, pp. 76–88.
Course of Study and Rules and Regulations, Canal Fulton, Ohio, 1892, p. 12.
Rules, Regulations and Course of Study, Casson, Minnesota, 1893, p. 33.
Report Board of Education, Cedar Rapids, Iowa, p. 14.
Catalog of the Public Schools, Cheboygan, Michigan, 1909–10, pp. 14–15.
Course of Study of the Cheboygan (Michigan) High School, 1916. Leaflet.
Annual Report Board of Education, Chicago, Illinois, 1872, p. 220.
Ibid., 1883, p. 21.
Report Board of Education, Chicago, Illinois, 1862.
Ibid., August, 1892.
Annual Report Board of Education, Cincinnati, Ohio, 1868, p. 153.
Ibid., 1879, pp. 304–6.
Annual Report of Public Schools, Cincinnati, Ohio, 1887, II, 145–47.
Annual School Report, Cincinnati, Ohio, 1857, pp. 123–24.
Annual Report Board of Education, Cleveland, Ohio, 1875, pp. 18–27.
Ibid., 1876, pp. 69–73.
Ibid., 1891.
Annual School Report, Cleveland, Ohio, 1869, pp. 62–64.
Report of Superintendent of Public Instruction, Coldwater, Michigan, 1859, p. 260.
Thirty-eighth Annual Report of the Columbia (Missouri) Public Schools, 1910–11, pp. 18–26.
Forty-fourth Annual Report of the Public Schools, Columbia, Missouri, 1916, pp. 40–50.
Annual Report Board of Education, Columbus, Ohio, 1873, pp. 84–91.
Ibid., 1878, II, 45–46.
Ibid., 1889, pp. 222–23.
Ibid., 1897, pp. 228–29.
Rules and Regulations and Course of Study, Cresco, Iowa, 1888, p. 11.
Catalog and Manual of Public Schools, Crookston, Minnesota, 1896–97, pp. 71–75.

Annual Report Board of Education, Danville, Illinois, 1895, p. 35.
Annual Report of the Public Schools, Danville, Illinois, 1871, pp. 26–27.
Ibid., 1881, p. 14.
Ibid., 1888, p. 14.
Course of Study and Requirements for Graduation, Danville (Illinois) High School, 1916. Leaflet.
Courses of Study and Plan of Work, Danville, Illinois, 1898, pp. 4–5.
Danville (Illinois) High School Announcement and Course of Study, 1909–10, pp. 7–15.
Annual Report Board of Education, Dayton, Ohio, 1875, pp. 248–50.
Ibid., 1878, pp. 235–37.
Ibid., 1883–84, pp. 169–70.
Ibid., 1886, pp. 169–70.
Ibid., 1886, pp. 169–70.
Report of the Public Schools, Decatur, Illinois, 1870, pp. 22–27.
Announcement of the Delavan (Wisconsin) High School, 1917. Leaflet.

Catalog of the Public Schools, Delavan, Wisconsin, 1893, pp. 26–28.
Course of Study of the Delavan High School, Delavan, Wisconsin, 1910–11. Leaflet.
Regulations and Course of Study (North) Des Moines, Iowa, 1895–96, p. 30.
Annual Report of Board of Education, Detroit, Michigan, 1868, p. 57.
Catalog of the Detroit (Michigan) High Schools, 1909–11, pp. 42–47.
Hand-Book of the Detroit (Michigan) High Schools, 1917–18, pp. 34–81.
Report of President Board of Education, Detroit, Michigan, 1859, pp. 23–24.

Annual Report of the Board of Education and Course of Study, City of Elgin, Illinois, 1916, pp. 74–114.
Annual Report of the Board of Education, City of Elgin, Illinois, 1910, pp. 114–32.
Elkhart (Indiana) High School, 1915–16. Leaflet.
Elkhart (Indiana) Public Schools; With Suggestions and Directions to Teachers, 1907, pp. 117–39.
Annual Report City of Emporia, Kansas, 1885, p. 42.
Evanston (Illinois) Township High School, 1907–8, pp. 7–19.
Ibid., 1917, pp. 23–46.
Annual Report of the Public Schools, Evansville, Indiana, 1888, p. 54.
Revised Course of Study, Evansville, Indiana, 1896, pp. 6–7.
Regulations and Course of Study, Evansville, Wisconsin, 1897, p. 45.

City Schools of Fairbury, Nebraska, 1907. Leaflet.
Manual of Public Schools, Fairbury, Nebraska, 1889–90, pp. 19–21.
Manual of Public Schools, Fargo, North Dakota, 1885, pp. 39–40.
Course of Study and Rules and Regulations, Flandreau, South Dakota, 1894, p. 12.

Rules, Regulations and Course of Study, Forrest, Illinois, 1885, p. 17.
Annual Report of City Schools, Fort Scott, Kansas, 1892, pp. 59–61.
Manual of Board of Education and Course of Study, Fort Scott, Kansas, 1883, p. 3.
Course of Study in the High School, Fort Wayne, Indiana, 1895, p. 10.
Program of Studies of the Fort Wayne (Indiana) High and Manual Training School, 1910. Leaflet
Ibid., 1916. Leaflet.
Rules, Regulations and Course of Study, Fredonia, Kansas, 1896, p. 33.
Rules and Regulations and Course of Study, Fremont, Nebraska, 1892, pp. 61–66.

Course of Study and Catalog of Pupils, Galena, Illinois, 1879, p. 23.
Annual Report Public Schools, Galesburg, Illinois, 1865, p. 9.
Outline of Course of Study and Regulations for the Government of the Schools, Geneseo, Illinois, 1887, p. 14.
Catalog of the Public Schools, Girard, Illinois, 1900, p. 5.
Annual Report Board of Education, Grand Rapids, Michigan, 1880, pp. 67–73.
Ibid., 1891, p. 118.
Ibid., 1896, p. 166.
Course of Study and Rules and Regulations, Greenview, Illinois, 1887, pp. 18–19.

Rules and Regulations and Course of Study, Harveysburg, Ohio, 1891, pp. 12–13.
Course of Study and Rules and Regulations, Hebron, Nebraska, 1893, p. 13.
Annual Report and Course of Study of the Public Schools of Hutchinson, Kansas, 1908, p. 98.
Course of Study, Hutchinson (Kansas) High School. Typewritten copy.

Rules and Regulations and Course of Study, Indianola, Iowa, 1899, pp. 30–31.
Announcement and Course of Study, Ionia (Michigan) High School, 1917. Leaflet.
Manual of the Ionia (Michigan) Public Schools, 1910–11, pp. 30–40.
History of Education in Iowa, III, 345–47. (Creston, Iowa.)
History of Education in Iowa, III, 282–84.
History of Education in Iowa, III, 295–96.
History of Education in Iowa, III, 316.
History of Education in Iowa, III, 235.
History of Education in Iowa, III, 286–87.
History of Education in Iowa, III, 301–2.
History of Education in Iowa, III, 304.
History of Education in Iowa, III, 299.
History of Education in Iowa, III, 314–15.

Annual Report of the Public Schools, Jacksonville, Illinois, 1878–79, p. 76.
Ibid., 1896–97, p. 43.
Annual Report of the Superintendent of Schools, Jacksonville, Illinois, 1869, p. 50.
Rules and Regulations and Course of Study, Jamestown, Ohio, 1896, pp. 19–20.
Rules and Regulations, Janesville, Minnesota, 1891, p. 13.
Annual Report, Rules and Regulations, and Course of Study, Joliet, Illinois, 1894–95, p. 78.
Report of Superintendent, Joliet, Illinois, 1873, pp. 51–52.

Catalog of Officers and Teachers of the Public Schools, Kalamazoo, Michigan, 1864–65, pp. 14–16.
Annual Report of the Public Schools, Kankakee, Illinois, 1890, pp. 37–38.
Ibid., 1906, pp. 34–37.
Ibid., 1916.
Rules and Regulations of the Public School, Kankakee, Illinois, 1875, p. 10.
Annual Report of the City Schools, Kansas City, Missouri, 1883–84, pp. 119–20.
New Trier (Kenilworth, Illinois) Township High School Year Book, 1910, pp. 13–61.
Ibid., 1915–16, pp. 23–66.
Revised Course of Study and General Regulations, Keokuk, Iowa, 1892–93, pp. 5–7.
Superintendent's Report and Rules and Regulations, Knoxville, Illinois, 1900, pp. 20–21.

Rules and Regulations of the Public Schools, Lacon, Illinois, 1856, p. 4.
Public Schools, La Crosse, Wisconsin: Course of Study, Rules and Regulations, 1908, pp. 91–104.
Report and Manual of the Public Schools, Lafayette, Indiana, 1887, pp. 46–48.
Graded Course of Study, Lanark, Illinois, 1894, p. 15.
Course of Study and Text-Books for the Lansing, Michigan, High School, 1917. Leaflet.
Lansing, Michigan, Public Schools Course of Study, 1910, pp. 71–88.
Calendar, Laporte, Indiana, Public Schools, 1875, pp. 30–31.
Ibid., 1879, 1885, p. 36.
Calendar Public Schools, Laporte, Indiana, 1883, p. 32.
Public Schools, Laporte, Indiana, 1910, pp. 39–57.

Circular of Information, Township High School, La Salle-Peru, Illinois, 1915–16. Leaflet.
Eighth Annual Catalog of the Township High School, La Salle and Peru, Illinois, 1906–7, pp. 15–53.
Annual Report Board of Education, Lawrence, Kansas, 1884, p. 48.
Annual Report Superintendent of Schools, Leavenworth, Kansas, 1867, pp. 43–44.
Course of Study Leavenworth, Kansas, High School, 1910. Typewritten copy.
Ibid., 1918. Leaflet.
Manual of Public Schools, Lebanon, Ohio, 1897, p. 63.
Report, Courses of Study, and Rules and Regulations, Lebanon, Indiana, 1894, p. 29.
Rules and Regulations and Courses of Study, Le Roy, Minnesota, 1890.
Ibid., 1859, p. 294.
Course of Study and Rules and Regulations, Lewiston, Illinois, 1896, p. 24.
Manual of Public Schools, Lexington, Missouri, 1897–98.
Annual Report of Board of Education, Lincoln, Nebraska, 1896–97, pp. 50–51.
Annual Report Superintendent of Public Schools, Lincoln, Nebraska, 1882, pp. 14–15.
Course of Study and General Regulations, Lincoln, Nebraska, 1893, p. 8.
Manual of Public Schools, Lincoln, Nebraska, 1888, pp. 52–54.
Rules of the Board of Education, Lincoln, Nebraska, 1877, p. 34.

Rules and Regulations, Macomb, Illinois, 1875, p. 11.
Rules and Regulations and Course of Study, Macomb, Illinois, 1898–99, p. 38.
Annual Report Board of Education, Madison, Wisconsin, 1876, p. 32.
Ibid., 1883, pp. 52–53.
Ibid., 1898, pp. 56–57.
Report Board of Education, Madison, Wisconsin, 1863.
Ibid., 1867.
Ibid., 1892, pp. 39–41.
Rules and Regulations and Course of Study, Mantua, Ohio, 1896, p. 13.
Manual and Course of Study and General Information of the Marinette (Wisconsin) High School, 1916, pp. 16–35.
Marinette Free High School, Marinette, Wisconsin: A Manual of the Course of Study and General Information, 1910, pp. 3–16.
Manual of Public Schools, Marion, Illinois, 1899, p. 61.
Report of the Public Schools, Markle, Indiana, 1896, p. 19.
Rules and Regulations and Course of Study, Mattoon, Illinois, 1877, p. 5.
Regulations and Courses of Study, Maumee, Ohio, 1898, p. 14.
Course of Study of the Miamisburg (Ohio) High School, 1909. Leaflet.
Rules Governing the Choosing of Courses of Study and Courses of Study of the Miamisburg (Ohio) High School, 1916. Leaflet.
Report Superintendent of Public Instruction, Michigan, 1855–56–57, p. 465.
Catalog Containing Course of Study, etc., Middleville, Michigan.
Annual Report of School Board, Milwaukee, Wisconsin, 1874, p. lx.
Ibid., 1884, p. 54.
Rules and Regulations, Minerva, Ohio, 1894, p. 14.
Annual Report and Course of Study of the Public Schools of Mitchell, South Dakota, 1916–17, pp. 14–51.

Annual Report of the Public Schools of Mitchell, South Dakota, 1911–12, pp. 10–12.
Annual Report of Moline, Illinois, Public Schools, 1881, p. 24.
Annual Report of Public Schools, Moline, Illinois, 1891, p. 38.
Announcement of the Public Schools, Monroe, Michigan, 1896, p. 29.
Catalog of the Public Schools of Monroe, Wisconsin, 1907–8, pp. 75–78. *Course of Study of the Monroe, Wisconsin, High School* (Junior-Senior), 1917. Leaflet.
Manual of Graded Course of Study, Monroe, Wisconsin, 1891, pp. 27–28.
Catalog and Report of the Public Schools, Monticello, Illinois, 1895, p. 42.
Course of Study and Second Annual Catalog, Monticello, Illinois, 1881, p. 21.
Course of Study and Rules and Regulations, Moron, Kansas, 1896, p. 11.
Manual of High School, Mount Gilead, Ohio, 1892, pp. 20–21.
Announcement of the Public Schools of Muscatine, Iowa, 1910–11, pp. 14–17.
Course of Study High School, Muscatine, Iowa 1917. Leaflet.

Annual Report of the Public Schools, Napoleon, Ohio, 1888, p. 29.
Annual Report of the Public Schools, Neosha, Missouri, 1889–90, p. 50.
Annual Report Board of Education, Newark, Ohio, 1896–97–98, p. 53.
Bi-Annual Report of Superintendent of Schools, Newark, Ohio, 1881–82, p. 57.
Annual Report Board of Education, New Haven, Conn. 1859, p. 31.
Proceedings Board of Education, Normal, Illinois, June, 1870. A list of subjects taught in the high school arranged according to years and terms.
Course of Study, Norwalk, Ohio, 1915. Leaflet.

Revised Regulations and Course of Study, Oak Park, Illinois, 1882, pp. 27–29.
Annual Report and Manual of Public Schools, Oberlin, Ohio, 1873, pp. 7–9.
Ibid., 1877, p. 22.
Course of Study and Rules and Regulations of Public Schools, Odell, Illinois, 1889, p. 9.
Annual Report Public Schools, Olney, Illinois, 1893, pp. 29–30.
Course of Study of the Omaha (Nebraska) High School, 1910. Leaflet.
Ibid., 1915. Leaflet.
Manual of the Public Schools of Oshkosh, Wisconsin, 1908–9, pp. 27–29.
Ibid., 1918, pp. 33–38.
Annual Report Public Schools, Oskaloosa, Iowa, 1899, p. 105.
Manual and Annual Report of the City Schools, Oskaloosa, Iowa, 1892–93–94, pp. 67–68.
Rules and Regulations and Course of Study, Oskaloosa, Iowa, 1873, p. 13.
Ibid., 1878, p. 37.
Rules, Regulations and Course of Study, Oskaloosa, Iowa, 1884, p. 41.
Catalog of the Officers, Teachers, and Students of the Ottawa (Illinois) Township High School, 1907–1907, pp. 5–13.
Public Schools, Ottumwa, Iowa, 1918, pp. 42–67.
Rules and Regulations and Course of Study of the Public Schools of Ottumwa, Iowa, 1911, pp. 40–49.

Rules and Regulations and Course of Study, Pawnee City, Nebraska, 1897–98, p. 17.
Pontiac (Illinois) Township High School, 1905–6, pp. 12–22.
Pontiac (Illinois) Township High School Catalog, 1917, pp. 12–21.

Catalog of the Public Schools, Prairie du Chien, Wisconsin, 1890, p. 7.
Rules and Regulations and Course of Study, Prairie du Chien, Wisconsin, 1897, p. 9.

Manual Board of Education, Racine, Wisconsin, 1891, p. 60.
Public Schools of the City of Racine, Wisconsin, 1883, pp. 49–50.
Report Board of Education, Racine, Wisconsin, 1857–58, p. 73.
Annual Report Public Schools, Richmond, Indiana, 1875, p. 31.
Ibid., 1877, p. 15.
Ibid., 1885, pp. 68–69.
Proceedings Board of Education, Rock Island, Illinois, May, 1856.

Saginaw, Michigan, High School Circular of Information and Curriculum of Study, 1917, pp. 6–14.
Saginaw, Michigan, High School Course of Study, 1911. Leaflet.
Annual Report of Public Schools, Sandusky, Ohio, 1889, pp. 80–82.
Courses of Study of the Sheboygan (Wisconsin) High School, 1910. Leaflet.
Ibid., 1917. Leaflet.
Public Schools of Sioux City, Iowa, 1891–92, pp. 49–51.
Report of Public Schools, Sioux City, Iowa, 1900, pp. 46–47.
Course of Study of the Sioux Falls (South Dakota) High School, 1910. Leaflet.
Ibid., 1917. Leaflet.
Annual Report of Public Schools, Springfield, Illinois, 1890, p. 54.
Ibid., 1893, p. 65.
Annual Report Superintendent of Schools, Springfield, Illinois, 1867, pp. 26–27.
Ibid., 1880, pp. 72–73.
Course of Study, Stillwater, Minnesota, 1897–98, pp. 84–91.
Annual Report Board of Directors, St. Louis, Missouri, 1871, p. 59.
Ibid., 1878, pp. 49–50.
Annual Report of the President and Board of Directors, St. Louis, Missouri, 1882, p. 11.
High School Courses of Study, St. Louis, Missouri, 1911. Leaflet.
Ibid., 1918. Leaflet.
Streator Township High School, Streator, Illinois, 1896–97, pp. 6–8.
School Calendar, Superior, Nebraska, 1892, p. 26.

Rules and Regulations of the Public Schools, Waterloo, Iowa, 1870, p. 19.
Course of Study of the Watertown, South Dakota, High School, 1918. Typewritten copy.
Manual of the Public Schools, Waverly, Iowa, 1900, pp. 52–53.
Rules and Regulations of the Public Schools, Waverly, Iowa, 1888, p. 22.
Rules and Regulations and Course of Study, Wilton, Iowa, 1880, p. 8.

Course of Study of the Yankton (South Dakota) City Schools, 1911, pp. 55–63.
Ibid., 1917–18, pp. 63–94.
The High School, Ypsilanti, Michigan: Annual Announcement, 1917, pp. 15–20.
The Public Schools, Ypsilanti, Michigan: Course of Study and Rules and Regulations, 1911, pp. 119–29.

III

Other sources used as supplementary to Section II.

Students' Manual, Aberdeen City Schools, Aberdeen, South Dakota, 1903–4.

Adrian Public Schools, Adrian, Michigan. *Report of the Board of Education (1890–95)*, 1895. Details of work in English.

Announcement of the Adrian High School, Adrian, Michigan, 1898. Contains outline of work in English.

Catalog of the Officers, Teachers and Students of the Alton (Illinois) Township High School, 1903–4.

Catalog of the Public Schools of the City of Appleton, Wisconsin, 1893. List of textbooks.

Ibid., 1900. List of textbooks.

Course of Study for the Attica, Indiana, Public Schools for the Year 1893–94. Some details of work in literature.

Report and Manual of the Attica, Indiana, Public Schools, 1895. List of textbooks.

Course of Study and Rules and Regulations of Augusta, Illinois, Public Schools, 1886.

Annual Report Board of Education, Aurora (Illinois) Public Schools, East Side, 1907.

Ibid., 1917.

Aurora Public Schools, West Side, Aurora, Illinois, 1907.

Organization of the Board of Education, Enrollment of Pupils and Teachers and Course of Study of the Public Schools of District No. 5, Aurora, Illinois, 1887.

Report of the Board of Education, Baltimore, Maryland, 1851.

Ibid., 1855.

Manual of the Public Schools, Batavia, Illinois, 1902.

Course of Study and Rules and Regulations of the Public Schools of Belvidere, Illinois, 1888–89.

Rules and Regulations and Course of Study of the Public Schools of Boone, Iowa, 1910.

Annual Report of the School Committee Together with the Annual Report of the Superintendent of the Public Schools of Boston (Massachusetts). 1858.

Ibid., 1859.

Ibid., 1880.

Regulations of the School Committee, Boston, Massachusetts, 1823.

Ibid., 1827.

Ibid., 1829.

Ibid., 1830.

Ibid., 1833.

Ibid., 1838.

Rules of the Schools Committee and Regulations of the Public Schools of the City of Boston (Massachusetts), 1839.

Ibid., 1841.

Ibid., 1844.

Ibid., 1849.

Ibid., 1851.

Ibid., 1853.

Course of Study of Burlington, Iowa, 1910. Typewritten copy.

Ibid., 1855.

Course of Study in High and District Schools of Burlington, Iowa, and Rules and Regulations for the same. Adopted by the board of education, 1888–89. List of textbooks.

Public Schools, Calumet, Michigan, 1906.

Revised Course of Study of the City of Camden, Illinois, 1890.

Course of Study with Rules and Regulations of the Public Schools of Canal Fulton, Ohio. Adopted November, 1892.

Course of Study, Carthage, Illinois, 1909–10. Leaflet.

Sixth Annual Report, 1860. Department of Public Instruction. City of Chicago. Discusses the relative value of modern languages. Recommendation that more time be devoted to natural sciences.

Twelfth Annual Report Board of Education for the Year Ending July 31, 1866. Department of Public Instruction of City of Chicago. Defense of the high school by the superintendent, pp. 46–65. He also advocates reorganization of the course of study to meet the demands of the community. The German Realschule commended as meeting the demands of modern life.

Ibid., Sixteenth Annual Report, 1869.

Ibid., Seventeenth Annual Report, 1871. In this report the president of the board urges the necessity of meeting the educational need of the industrial classes; also comments on the service rendered by the high school as a training school for teachers. List of textbooks.

Ibid., Twenty-first Annual Report, 1874. An interesting statement concerning the work done in the high school as compared with the average college course, p. 18.

Ibid., Twenty-first Annual Report, 1875. Discussion in the report of the two-year high schools.

Ibid., Twenty-second Annual Report, 1876. Historical sketch, pp. 50–60. List of textbooks.

Ibid., Twenty-fourth Annual Report, 1878. Industrial education discussed in the report.

Twenty-seventh Annual Report, 1881. President in his report urges the necessity of a law authorizing a tax levy for the support of industrial education.

Ibid., Twenty-eighth Annual Report, 1882. President in his report comments on the demand for industrial education.

Ibid., Twenty-ninth Annual Report, 1883. Both the president and the superintendent in their reports urge the introduction of manual training.

Ibid., Thirtieth Annual Report, 1884. Discussion of relative merits of academies and high schools. President in his report discusses the influence of higher institutions upon the high schools.

Ibid., Thirty-second Annual Report, 1886. Interesting discussion of manual training. The president in his report opposes the introduction while the superintendent in his report advocates it.

Ibid., Thirty-third Annual Report, 1887. A new president of the board urges the importance of manual training.

Ibid., Thirty-fifth Annual Report, 1889. Discussion of the overcrowded condition of the curriculum. List of textbooks.

Ibid., Thirty-seventh Annual Report, 1891.

Ibid., Thirty-eighth Annual Report, 1892. Discussion of work in manual training and physical culture.

Ibid., Thirty-ninth Annual Report, 1893. Discussion of the plan of industrial education in the public schools.

Ibid., Fortieth Annual Report, 1894. President of the board discussed the report of the Committee of Ten.

Ibid., Forty-second Annual Report, June 26, 1896. Discussion of commercial education by president of the board.

Ibid., Forty-third Annual Report, 1897. Discussion of commercial education by president of the board.

Austin Public Schools. Report of Board of Education. School District No. 2. Town of Cicero, Cook County, Illinois, 1895.

Common Schools of Cincinnati (Ohio). Part First: Forty-second Annual Report for the School Year Ending June 30, 1872. Part Second: A Handbook for the School Year Ending June 30, 1873.

Ibid., 1878. *Part First: Forty-ninth Annual Report. Part Second: A handbook for 1879.*

Twenty-ninth Annual Report of the Cleveland, Ohio, Public Schools for the Year Ending August, 1865. Various supplementary documents dealing with school conditions.

Sixteenth Annual Report of the Board of Managers for the Year Ending 1852. Public Schools of the city of Cleveland, Ohio. List of textbooks.

Thirty-fourth Annual Report of the Board of Education of Cleveland, Ohio, for the Year Ending August 31, 1870.

Ibid., Thirty-fifith Annual Report, 1871.

Ibid., Thirty-ninth Annual Report, 1875.

Ibid., Forty-seventh Annual Report, 1883. Percentages shown of pupils enrolled in each grade from 1873 to 1883. Also number of pupils enrolled in the various high school courses.

Ibid., Forty-ninth Annual Report, 1885. This report shows the number of pupils enrolled in each of the high-school courses.

Ibid., Fiftieth Annual Report, 1886. List of textbooks.

Ibid., Fifty-third Annual Report, 1889. Explanation of work in manual training.

Annual Report of the Board of Education of the Columbus (Ohio) Public Schools for the Year Ending August 1, 1879.

Ibid., 1880.

Ibid., 1892.

Ibid., 1893.

Ibid., 1894.

Annual Report of the Board of Education, of the School Commissioners and Superintendent, with the Laws Pertaining to the Public Schools of Columbus, Ohio, 1851.

Manual of the Public Schools of Connersville, Indiana, 1907.

Annual Report Board of Education, Danville, Illinois, and Rules and Course of Study, 1895.

Annual Report of the Board of Education, Danville (Illinois), 1902.

Course of Study and Requirements for Graduation, Danville (Illinois) High School, 1913. Leaflet.

Fifth Annual Catalog of Danville (Illinois) Union Schools and Circular of Information, 1889.

Annual Report of the Board of Education for the School Year Ending August 31, 1875. Dayton, Ohio, Public Schools. List of textbooks.

Ibid., 1876. List of textbooks.

Ninth Annual Report of the Board of Education of Decatur, Illinois, with Rules and Course of Study, 1874.

Ibid., Twenty-seventh Annual Report, 1891.

Catalog of the Delavan Public Schools, Delavan, Wisconsin, 1894. Courses of Study. List of Alumni. Catalog of library. Contains discussion of aims and purposes of the high school. List of textbooks.

Delavan Public Schools, Delavan, Illinois, 1891. Some details of work in English.

Bi-Annual Report of the Public Schools of (West) Des Moines, Iowa, 1892–94.

Annual Report of the Board of Education of the City of Detroit, Michigan, with Reports of Committees and Teachers, 1853. In the report the president discusses the legal status of the high school.

Eighteenth Annual Report of the Detroit (Michigan) Public Schools, with Accompanying Documents for the Year 1860. Brief historical account of the high school. Causes of opposition to the high school discussed.

Official Report of D. Bethune, President of the Board of Education, Detroit, Michigan, for the Year 1858. Reports of teachers of Union Schools and the reports from the Committee on Schools and Committee on Teachers. In this report the president discusses the "Free Academy or High School" as the "Academic link between the Free School and the University."

Report of the Public Schools of the City of Detroit, Michigan, for the Year 1855.

Twenty-first Annual Report of the Board of Education of Detroit, Michigan, for the Year Ending December 31, 1863.

Annual Report of the Board of Education of the City of Duluth, Minnesota, July 31, 1893.

Junior High Schools, Duluth, Minnesota, 1917. Leaflet.

Annual Report of the Board of Education and Course of Study of the City of Elgin Illinois, 1910.

Course of Study in the Elgin, Illinois, High School, 1891. Four-page pamphlet. List of textbooks.

Course of Study with Rules and Regulations of the Public Schools of the East Side Schools of El Paso, Illinois, 1892.

Ibid., 1895. Some details of work in English.

First Annual Announcement with Course of Study and Rules and Regulations of the West Side Public Schools. El Paso, Illinois, 1895. Some details of work in English.

Annual Report of the Board of Education of the City of Emporia, Kansas, for the Year Ending June 30, 1900.

Fifth Annual Report of the Board of Education of the Emporia (Kansas) City Schools for the Year Ending July 31, 1889. List of Textbooks.

Evanston (Illinois) Township High School, 1905–6. Leaflet.

Evanston Township High School, 1894–95. Four-page pamphlet.

Revised Course of Study of the Evansville, Indiana, High School, 1897. Some details of work in English.

Course of Study of the Public Schools of Exeter, Nebraska, 1893.

Rules and Regulations of the School Board and Course of Study of the Schools of Fairfield, Ohio, 1889. List of classics given.

City Schools of Flint, Michigan, 1897–98.

Course of Study with Rules and Regulations for the Public Schools, Forrest, Illinois, 1894.

Annual Report of the Fort Scott, (Kansas) City Schools for the Year Ending July 31, 1892, and Announcement for 1892–93. List of textbooks. Some details of work in English.

Course of Study of the Public Schools of Fort Wayne, Indiana, 1899. List of textbooks.

Course of Study and the First Annual Catalog of Pupils of the Galena, Illinois, City Schools Together with Rules and Regulations, 1879.

Course of Study of the Galena, Illinois, High School, 1896. Two-page pamphlet. List of textbooks.

General Rules and Course of Studies, Graduates, etc., Galena Public Schools, Galena, Illinois. 1894.

Rules for the Government of the Galena, Illinois, Public Schools with Course of Study and a List of Graduates of the High School.

Course of Study of the Geneseo, Illinois, High School. Four-page pamphlet.

Outline of the Course of Study and Rules and Regulations of the Public Schools of Geneseo, Illinois. Pamphlet.

Course of Study and Rules and Regulations of the Gibson City Schools, Gibson City, Illinois, With the Superintendent's Report, 1895. Details of work in English.

Course of Study for the Public Schools of Gibson City, Illinois, 1889. List of textbook.

Catalog of the Girard, Illinois, Public Schools, 1900. List of textbooks.

Annual Catalog of the Officers, Inspectors, and Students of the Grand Rapids, Michigan, Public Schools, 1860.

Fourteenth Annual Report of the Board of Education of the City of Grand Rapids, Michigan, Together with the School Law and Rules and Regulations of the Schools and the Public Library, 1886. List of classics given.

Course of Study and Rules and Regulations of the South Side Public Schools of Grayville, Illinois, 1893.

Course of Study and Rules and Regulations of the Public Schools of Greenview, Illinois, 1894.

Course of Study in the Hannibal (Missouri) High School, 1912–13.

Rules and Regulations and Course of Study of the Public Schools of Harveysburg, Ohio, 1891.

Rules and Regulations, Manual of Instruction, and Graded Courses of Study of the Public Schools of Hinsdale, Illinois, 1891. Some details of work in English.

Thirteenth Annual Report of the Board of Education, District No. 1, Hyde Park, Illinois, 1886.

Ionia (Michigan) Public Schools. Manual and Report of the Board of Education, 1912.

Circular Containing Courses of Study, Programs, Rules and Regulations of the Public Schools of Independence, Iowa, 1891.

Annual Report of the Kankakee (Illinois) Public Schools, 1909.

Seventeenth Annual Report of the Kansas City (Missouri) Public Schools for the Year 1887–88.

A Manual of the Public Schools of Keithsburg, Illinois, 1893–94.

New Trier (Kenilworth, Illinois) Township High School, 1910.

Course of Study of the Knoxville, Illinois, Public Schools with Rules and Regulations of the Board of Education, 1892. Outline of work in English.

Superintendent's Report and Rules and Regulations of the Knoxville, Illinois, Public Schools Together with Courses of Study, 1900.

Courses of Study of the Public Schools of Lacon, Illinois, 1894.

Third Annual Report of the Board of Education of the Lyons Township High School (La Grange) Cook County, Illinois, 1891.

Ibid., Fourth Annual Report, 1892.

Ibid., Eighth Annual Report, 1896.

Ibid., Ninth Annual Report, 1897.

Ibid., Eleventh Annual Report, 1899.

Fourth Annual Report of the Lakeview (Illinois) High School, 1878.

Second Annual Report of the Trustees of the Lakeview (Illinois) High School, 1876.

A Graded Course of Study of the Lanark, Illinois, Public Schools, 1894.

Calendar of the Laporte (Indiana) Public Schools for 1880–81.

Ibid., 1882–83.

Report of the Public Schools of Laporte (Indiana) for the Year Ending June 24, 1889. List of textbooks.

Ibid., 1891–92. Some details of work in English. Outline of high-school work in some detail.

Sixth Annual Report of the Board of Education of the City of Lawrence, Kansas, 1873.

Ibid., Eighth Annual Report, 1875.

Ibid., Ninth Annual Report, 1876.

Ibid., Eleventh Annual Report, 1878.

Ibid., Twelfth Annual Report, 1879.

Ibid., Thirteenth Annual Report, 1880.

Ibid., Fourteenth Annual Report, 1881.

Ibid., Fifteenth Annual Report, 1882.

Ibid., Twentieth Annual Report, 1887. List of classics given.

Ibid., Twenty-first Annual Report, 1888.

Ibid., Twenty-second Annual Report, 1889.

Ibid., Twenty-third Annual Report, 1890.

Manual of the Lebanon (Indiana) High School, 1909.

Report of the Lebanon, Indiana, Public Schools for 1894–95 and Course of Study Together with Rules and Regulations for the Government of the Schools.

Course of Study with Rules and Regulations of the Public Schools of Le Roy, Illinois, Together with the Names of Alumni and other Items of Interest Concerning the Le Roy Public Schools, 1889.

Public Schools of Le Roy, Illinois, 1894–95, Rules and Regulations, Course of Study and Manual of Information.

Course of Study and Rules and Regulations of the Lewiston, Illinois, Public Schools, 1896.

Course of Study with Rules and Regulations of the Public Schools of Lexington, Illinois, Together with Names of Alumni, 1892.

Annual Report of the Board of Education of the Public Schools of Lincoln, Nebraska, for the Year 1896–97.

Course of Study and Rules and Regulations of the Lincoln, Nebraska, Public Schools, 1900.

Eighth Annual Report of the Board of Education by the Superintendent of Public Schools of the School District of Lincoln (Nebraska) for the School Year Ending June 11, 1880.

Third Annual Report of the Board of Education of the School District of Lincoln (Nebraska) for the School Year Ending June 25, 1875.

Rules, Regulations and Course of Study of the Public Schools of Lodi, Wisconsin, Adopted August 30, 1895.

Report of the School Committee of Lowell, Massachusetts, 1839.

Ibid., 1840.

Ibid., 1843.

Ibid., 1851.

Ibid., 1852.

Ibid., 1857.

First Annual Catalog of the Public Schools of Mackinaw, Illinois, for the Session 1895.

Rules and Regulations and Course of Study of the Public Schools of Macomb, Illinois, 1902–3.

Annual Report of the Board of Education and Superintendent of Schools for the Year 1864–65. Department of Public Instruction, City of Madison, Wisconsin.

Annual Report of the Board of Education of Madison (Wisconsin), 1870. List of textbooks.

Ibid., 1869.

Ibid., 1872.

Ibid., 1867.

Ibid., 1884. List of textbooks.

Ibid., 1885. Historical sketch, 1838–85.

Annual Report of the City of Madison (Wisconsin), 1895. History from 1858 to 1895. Historical material.

Annual Report of the Public Schools of the City of Madison (Wisconsin) for the Year 1889–90. List of textbooks.

Course of Study of the Public Schools of Maquoketa, Iowa, 1896.

County, Illinois, 1878. List of textbooks.

Manual and Course of Study of the Public Schools of Marinette, Wisconsin, 1905–6.

Announcement and Catalog of the Marlette, Michigan, Public Schools, Containing Organization, Course of Study and Rules and Regulations for the School Year 1900–1901.

Rules and Regulations and Course of Study of the Marseilles, Illinois, Public Schools.

Mason City, Illinois, Public Schools, 1891.

Annual Report of the Public Schools, Mattoon, Illinois, 1891. Meager details of work in composition.

Course of Studies, Public Schools of McLeansboro, Illinois, 1897. List of textbooks.

An Announcement and Course of Study of the Mendon High School at Mendon, Adams County, Illinois, 1895.

Course of Study for the Public Schools of Metropolis, Illinois, 1896–97.

Twenty-fourth Annual Report of the Superintendent of Public Instruction of the State of Michigan with Accompanying Documents for the Year 1860. Union School Reports.

Ibid., 1874. Report of City Union Schools. An interesting discussion in this report of the decision of the Supreme Court establishing the legal status of the high school.

Ibid., *Thirty-ninth Annual Report*, 1875. Contains reports of city graded and high schools.

Ibid., *Fortieth Annual Report*, 1876. Report of city and graded and high schools.

Ibid., *Forty-fourth Annual Report*, 1880. Historical sketch relating to secondary education.

Course of Studies, Rules and Regulations of the Miles Public Schools, Miles, Iowa, 1893.

Annual Report of the School Board of the City of Milwaukee (Wisconsin) for the Year Ending August 31, 1877.

Ibid., 1878.

Ibid., 1879.

Course of Study of the Public Schools of the City of Milwaukee, Wisconsin, 1909.

Regulations and Rules of the Studies of the Mohomet Graded Schools, Champaign County, Illinois, 1878. List of textbooks.

Course of Study of the Moline (Illinois) High School, 1910–11. Leaflet.

Twenty-third Annual Report of the Public Schools of Moline, Illinois, 1896. Outline of work in some detail. Manual training discussed.

Ibid., *Twenty-fourth Annual Report*, 1897.

Ibid., *Twenty-fifth Annual Report*, 1898.

Sixty-eighth Annual Report of the Public Schools of Monmouth (Illinois), 1912.

Catalog and Report of the Public Schools of the City of Monticello, Illinois, for the Year Ending June 30, 1895.

Course of Study and Rules and Regulations of the Public Schools of Monticello, Illinois, 1898.

Rules and Regulations of the Public Schools of Monticello, Illinois, 1905.

Course of Study of the Morris (Illinois) High School for the Year 1899–1900. Four-page leaflet.

Morrison Public Schools, Morrison, Illinois. Rules and Regulations and Course of Study, 1898.

Course of Study of the Public Schools of Mount Carroll, Illinois, 1900.

Manual of the Mount Gilead, Ohio, High School, Containing Rules and Regulations, the Revised Course of Study, Catalog of the Graduates and General Information, 1892. List of textbooks.

Rules and Regulations and Course of Study of the Public Schools of Mount Pulaski, Illinois, 1900–1901.

Rules and Regulations and Course of Study, Including a List of Graduates of the Mount Sterling (Illinois) Public Schools, 1896.

Manual of the Mount Vernon Public Schools, Mount Vernon, Illinois. Course of Study, Rules and Regulations, 1895. Some details of the work in literature.

Annual Report of the Board of Education of the City of Murphysboro, Illinois, 1899. List of textbooks.

Eighth Year Book of the Murphysboro (Illinois) Township High School, 1909–10.

Second Annual Catalog Murphysboro (Illinois) Township High School, 1902–3.

Course of Study and Rules and Regulations of the Navarre Union Schools, Navarre, Ohio, 1896.

Course of Study of the Nebraska City-Public Schools, Nebraska City, Nebraska, 1894.

Ibid., 1895. Contains details of work in English.

Course of Study and Rules and Regulations of the Neola Public Schools, Neola, Iowa, 1898.

Annual Report of the Board of Education with Course of Study, etc. Oakland, Illinois, 1897.

Revised Course of Study with Rules and Regulations of the Odell (Illinois) Public Schools, 1889.

Twenty-sixth Annual Report of the Public Schools of Olney, Illinois, for the Year Ending July 1, 1893. Financial and statistical report and course of study.

Ibid., Twenty-eighth Annual Report, 1895. List of textbooks.

Ibid., Tenth Annual Report, 1897.

Manual and Annual Report of the Oskaloosa, Iowa, Schools, 1896.

Rules and Regulations and Course of Study of the Public Schools of Oskaloosa, Iowa, 1876.

Ibid., 1880. Contains list of textbooks.

Annual Report of the Controllers of the Public Schools of the City of Philadelphia (Pennsylvania), 1837.

Ibid., 1840.

Regulations and Course of Study of the Public Schools of Piper City, Illinois, 1894.

Annual Report of the Public Schools of Richmond (Indiana) for the School Year Ending May 28, 1875 with Courses of Study and General Rules and Regulations.

Annual Report of the Superintendent of the Public Schools of Richmond, Indiana, to the Board of Education for the Year Ending June 7, 1882. List of textbooks.

Annual Report of the Superintendent of the Richmond (Indiana) Public Schools for the Year Ending June 20, 1879, with Course of Study and Rules and Regulations.

Ibid., 1880.

Biennial Report of the Public Schools of Richmond, Indiana, for the Years Ending July 31, 1890 and July 31, 1891 with Announcements for 1891–92 and Rules and Regulations and Course of Study.

Ibid., 1886–88.

Ibid., 1888–89. List of classics given. List of textbooks. Historical sketch of the schools.

Catalog of the Officers and Teachers of the Public Schools of the City of Richmond, Indiana, and the Pupils of the High School and Grammar Schools. Rules and Regulations for the Organization and Government of the Schools; and the Superintendent's Report for the Year Ending August 31, 1870. Aims and purposes of the high school discussed.

Rules and Regulations for the Government of the Public Schools of Shenandoah, Iowa, with Course of Study and Announcements for 1894–95. List of text-textbooks.

Report Board of Education, Springfield, Massachusetts, 1853.

Ibid., 1855.

Twenty-ninth Annual Report of the Public Schools of Springfield (Illinois) for the Year Ending August 31, 1887.

Ibid., *Thirty-fourth Annual Report*, 1892. Aims and purposes of the high school discussed. Outline of work in English.

Ibid., *Thirty-sixth Annual Report.* Outline of work in English. Manual training discussed. Discussion of influence of report of Committee of Ten.

Thirteenth Annual Report of the Superintendent of Public Schools of Springfield (Illinois) to the Board of Education, 1871.

Ibid., *Fourteenth Annual Report*, 1872. List of textbooks.

Ibid., 1873. List of textbooks.

Ibid., 1874.

Ibid., 1876.

Ibid., 1877.

Ibid., 1878.

Ibid., 1879.

Fifty-ninth Annual Report Springfield (Missouri) Public Schools, 1906–7.

Sterling (Illinois) Township High School, 1909–10.

Thirteenth Annual Report of the Board of Directors of the St. Louis (Missouri) Public Schools for the Year Ending August 1, 1867. Historical sketch, pp. 98–114. An interesting review of the controversy regarding the establishment of a high school.

Ibid., *Twenty-fourth Annual Report*, 1878.

Fifteenth Annual Report of the Board of Education of the St. Louis (Missouri) Public Schools for the Year Ending August 1, 1869.

Fifty-third Annual Report of the Board of Education, St. Louis, Missouri, 1917.

Twenty-seventh Annual Report of the President and Board of Directors of the St. Louis (Missouri) Public Schools for the Year Ending August 31, 1881.

Ibid., *Twenty-ninth Annual Report*, 1883.

Ibid., *Thirty-first Annual Report*, 1885.

Thirty-second Annual Report, St. Louis, June 30, 1886.

Thirty-third Annual Report, St. Louis, June 30, 1887.

Thirty-fourth Annual Report, St. Louis, June 30, 1888.

The Streator Township High School, Streator, Illinois, 1896–97.

Ibid., 1899–1900.

Streator (Illinois) Township High School, 1906–7.

Announcement of the Taylorville (Illinois) Township High School, 1891. Leaflet.

Catalog and Annual Announcement of the Taylorville (Illinois) Township High School, 1896.

Catalog and Fourth Annual Announcement of the Taylorville (Illinois) Township High School, 1894.

Regulations and Course of Instruction of the Tipton, Ohio, Public Schools. Adopted August 9, 1892. List of textbooks.

Course of Study of the Watertown, South Dakota High School, 1911. Typewritten copy.

Rules and Regulations and Course of Study for Use in the Public Schools of Wheaton, Illinois, 1895. List of textbooks.

Course of Study of the Wilmette, Illinois, Public Schools, 1898.

Rules and Regulations and Course of Study of the Public Schools of Wilton, Iowa, 1880.

Ypsilanti High School Annual Catalog, Ypsilanti, Michigan, 1905.

COLLEGE AND UNIVERSITY CATALOGS

The *Catalogs* of the following universities and colleges furnish information concerning entrance requirements.

Butler University (Indiana), 1892–94.
Cornell College (Iowa), 1860–1900.
DePauw University (Indiana), 1890–1900.
Earlham College (Indiana), 1891–94.
University of Illinois, 1867–90.
University of Indiana, 1890–1900.
University of Wooster (Ohio), 1870–75, 1880, 1885–87, 1890, 1894.

IV

Textbooks constitute the chief source of information for discussions and conclusions in Part II and in the section of Part III devoted to subject-matter.

1. MATHEMATICS

Breslich, Ernst R. *First-Year Mathematics for Secondary Schools*, 1915 (1906-1909); *Second-Year Mathematics for Secondary Schools*, 1916 (1910); *Third, Year Mathematics for Secondary Schools*, 1917.

Davies, Charles. *Elementary Algebra, Embracing the First Principles of the Science*, 1853.

Davies, Charles. *Elements of Geometry*, 1862, 1875.

Davies, Charles. *Elements of Geometry and Trigonometry from the Works of A. M. Le Gendre*, 1862.

Evans, G. W., and Marsh, J. A. *First Year Mathematics*, 1916.

Fish, Daniel W. *The Complete Arithmetic*, 1874.

Greenleaf, Benjamin. *Introduction to the National Arithmetic on the Inductive System*, 1868.

Loomis, Elias. *A Treatise on Arithmetic, Theoretical and Practical*, 1856.

Loomis, Elias. *Elements of Algebra, Designed for Beginners*, 1856.

Milne, William J. *A Practical Arithmetic on the Inductive Plan, Including Oral and Written Exercises*, 1877.

Ray, Joseph. *Ray's Higher Arithmetic: The Principles of Arithmetic Analyzed and Practically Applied.* 1858. For advanced students.

Robinson, H. W. *New Elementary Algebra, Containing the Rudiments of the Science for Schools and Colleges*, 1859.

Robinson, H. W. *The Practical High Arithmetic for Schools, Academies and Mercantile Colleges Combining the Analytic and Synthetic Methods and Forming a Complete Treatise on Arithmetical Science and Application and Its Commercial and Business Application*, 1863.

Schuyler, A. *A Complete Algebra for High Schools and Colleges*, 1870, 1883.

Stoddard, J. F. *Stoddard's Complete Arithmetic Being the New and Practical Arithmetic of the Series, with Editions for a Full and Practical Course in High Schools and Academies: Embracing an Explanation and Application of the Metric System of Weights and Measures, Forms of Bills, Notes, Accounts, etc.*, 1868.

Tappin, Eli T. *Treatise of Geometry and Trigonometry. Written for the Mathematical Course of Joseph Ray*, 1868.

Wells, Webster. *Essentials of Algebra*, 1897.

Wells, Webster. *Essentials of Plane and Solid Geometry*, 1898.

Wentworth, G. A. *New School Algebra*, 1898.

Wentworth, G. A. *Plane and Solid Geometry*, 1899.

Wentworth, G. A., Smith, D. E., and Brown, J. C. *Junior High School Mathematics.* Books I, II, III, 1917, 1918.

2. ENGLISH

Appleton's Fifth Reader.

Bachus, F. J. *Shaw's New History of English and American Literature.* Revised and rewritten, 1875.

Bain, Alexander. *English Composition and Rhetoric.* 1866.

Brubaker, A. R., and Snyder, Dorothy. *High School English. Books I and II*, 1910.

Buhlig, Rose. *Business English*, 1914.

Carpenter, G. R., Baker, F. J., and Scott, F. N. *The Teaching of English*, in the Elementary and the Secondary School, 1903.

Cathcart, G. R. *Literary Reader: Typical Selections from Some of the Best English and American Authors from Shakespeare to the Present Time*, 1875.

Clark, Stephen W. *A Normal Grammar Analytic and Synthetic, Illustrated by diagrams*, 1870.

Cleveland, Charles D. *A Compendium of American Literature Chronologically Arranged with Biographical Sketches of the Authors and Selections from Their Works*, 1859. (Stereotyped edition, 1879.)

Cleveland, Charles D. *A Compendium of English Literature Characterized and Arranged from Sir John Mondeville to William Cowper Consisting of Biographical Sketches of the Authors, Selections from Their Works with Notes, etc.*, 1848. (Stereotyped edition, 1874.)

Frank, Maude M. *Elements of High School English*, 1915.

Greene, Samuel S. *A Grammar of the English Language Adapted to the Use of Schools and Academies*, 1860.

Halleck, Rueben Post. *A History of English Literature*, 1913.

Halleck, Reuben Post. *New English Literature*, 1913.

Hart, John S. *A Manual of English Literature: A Textbook for Schools and Colleges*, 1872.

Herrick and Damon. *Composition and Rhetoric for Schools*, 1899.

Hill, Adam S. *Principles of Rhetoric and Their Application*, 1879.

Hill, David J. *Elements of Rhetoric and Composition*, 1878.

Kellogg, Brainerd. *A Textbook on Rhetoric Supplementing and Developing All the Senses with Exhaustive Practice*, 1880, 1892.

Martin, Benjamin. *Choice Specimens of American Literature and Literary Reader*, 1874.

McGuffey's Sixth Elective Reader, Revised Edition, 1879.

Moody, W. V., and Lovett, R. M. *A History of English Literature*. 1913.

National Speaker, 1853.

Newcomer, Alfonso. *A Practical Course in English Composition*, 1893.

Newcomer, Alfonso. *English Literature*, 1905.

Pancoast, H. S. and Shelly, P. V. D. *First Book in English Literature*, 1910.

Parker's Exercises in Rhetorical Readings, 1852.

Proceedings North Central Association of Colleges and Secondary Schools: Report of the Commission on Units and Curricula, 1917.

Progressive Speaker and School Reader, 1858.

Rankin, T. E., and Aiken, W. A. *English Literature*, 1917.

Reed, Alonso, and Kellogg, Brainerd. *Higher Lessons in English—A Work of English Grammar in which the Science of the Language is Made Tributary to the Art of Expression*, 1877, 1885, 1896.

Saunders, Charles W. *Saunder's Rhetorical and Union Sixth Reader Embracing Full Exposition of the Principles of Rhetorical Reading with Numerous Specimens Both in Prose and Poetry from the Best Writers, English and American, as Exercises for Practice, and with Notes and Sketches, Literary and Biographical, Forming a Brief Though Comprehensive Course in English Literature*, 1862.

Scott, F. N., and Denney, Joseph. *New Composition and Rhetoric*, 1911.

Spaulding, William. *The History of English Literature with an Outline of the Origin and Growth of the English Language, Illustrated by Extracts. For Use of School and Private Students*, 1853.

Standard Fifth Reader, 1857.

Swinton, William. *A General Etymology and Syntax of the English Language*, 1874.

The Student's Reader, 1877.

Webster, W. F. *English for Secondary Schools*, 1910.

Welch, A. S. *Analysis of the English Sentence, Designed for Advanced Classes in English Grammar*, 1862.

Whateley, Richard, *Elements of Rhetorical Composition*.

3. GENERAL SCIENCE

Barber, F. D., Fuller, M. L., Prosser, J. L., and Adonis, H. W. *First Book in General Science*, 1916.

Caldwell, O. W., and Eikenberry, W. L. *Elements of General Science*, 1914.

Clark, Bertha M. *An Introduction to Science*, 1915.

Elhuff, Lewis. *General Science. First Course*, 1916.
Hessler, John C. *The First Year of Science*, 1914.
Pease, Clara A. *A First Year Course in General Science*, 1915.
Snyder, William H. *First Year Science*, 1914.
Weckell, Ada L. and Thalman, Joseph L. *A Year in Science: A Textbook for First Year in High Schools*, 1916.

4. THE BIOLOGICAL SCIENCES

Bergen, J. Y. *Elements of Botany*, 1896.
Bergen, J. Y. and Caldwell, O. W. *Practical Botany*, 1913.
Boyer, E. R. *A Laboratory Manual in Elementary Biology. An Inductive Study in Animal and Plant Morphology Designed for Preparatory and High Schools*, 1894.
Brown, Eli. *The Eclectic Physiology*, 1884.
Colton, B. P. *An Elementary Course in Practical Zoölogy*, 1886.
Cutter, John S. *Comprehensive Physiology, Anatomy and Hygiene*, 1885.
Gray, Asa. *How Plants Grow. A Simple Introduction to Structural Botany with Popular Flora; or an Arrangement and Description of Common Plants both Wild and Cultivated*, 1858.
Higner, R. W. *Practical Zoölogy*, 1915.
Hitchcock, Edward, and Hitchcock, Edward Jr., *Elementary Physiology*, 1866.
Hooker, Washington. *Natural History for the Use of Schools and Families*, 1860.
Hunter, G. W. *Laboratory Problems in Civic Biology*, 1916.
Hutchinson, J. C. *A Treatise on Physiology and Hygiene. For Educational Institutions and General Readers*, 1875, 1895.
Kellogg, V. L., and Doane, R. W. *Elementary Textbook of Economical Zoölogy and Entomology*, 1915.
Martin, H. N. *The Human Body. A Text-Book of Anatomy, Physiology and Hygiene, Including a Special Account of the Action upon the Body of Alcoholic and Other Stimulants and Narcotics*, 1884.
McBride, T. H. *Lessons in Elementary Botany for Secondary Schools*, 1895.
Packard, A. S. *Zoölogy, Sixth Revised Edition*, 1883.
Steele, J. Dorman. *Hygienic Physiology with Special Reference to the Use of Alcoholic Drinks and Narcotics, Being a Revised Edition of the Fourteen Works in Human Physiology*, 1868. Abridged editions, 1872, 1884.
Steele, J. Dorman, and Jenks, J. W. P. *A Popular Zoölogy*, 1887.
Ware, John. *Philosophy of Natural History*, 1860.
Youmons, Eliza A. *The First Book of Botany. Designed to Cultivate the Observing Powers of Children*, 1870.

5. THE PHYSICAL SCIENCES

Allyn, Lewis B. *Elements of Applied Chemistry*, 1912.
Appleton's School Physics, 1891.
Block, Henry, and Davis, H. B. *Practical Physics for Secondary Schools*, 1913.
Bowman, John. *An Introduction to Practical Chemistry Including Analysis*, 1873.
Carhart, H. C. and Chute, H. N. *Physics for High School Students*, 1901.
Carhart, H. C. and Chute, H. N. *Principles of Physics*, 1912.
Comstock, J. L. *A System of Natural Philosophy*, 1840.

Comstock, J. L. *Elements of Chemistry: Designed for the Use of Schools and Academies*, 1861.
Cook, C. G. *Practical Chemistry for High School Students*, 1913.
Cooley, LeRoy C. *A Text-Book of Chemistry. A Modern and Systematic Explanation of the Elementary Principles of the Science. Adopted to Use in High Schools and Academies*, 1869.
Cooley, LeRoy C. *Natural Philosophy for Common and High Schools*, 1872.
Gage, A. P. *Introduction to Physical Science*, 1887.
Greene, William H. *Lessons in Chemistry*, 1884.
Hooker's Chemistry, 1863.
Irwin, F. C., Rivett, B. J. and Tatlock, O. *Elementary and Applied Chemistry*, 1915.
Lynde, C. J. *Physics for the Household*, 1914.
Mann, C. R. and Twiss, G. R. *Physics*. Revised Edition, 1910.
McPherson, William, and Henderson, W. E. *First Course in Chemistry*, 1915.
Plympton, G. W. *Parker's Philosophy*. Revised, 1871.
Reed, J. O. and Henderson, W. B. *High School Physics*, 1913.
Remsen, Ira. *Elements of Chemistry. A Text-Book for Beginners*, 1887.
Rolfe and Gillette. *A Text-Book of Natural Philosophy*, 1868.
Snell, J. F. *Elements of Household Chemistry*, 1914.
Steele, J. Dorman. *A Fourteen Weeks Course in Chemistry*, 1867.
Steele, J. Dorman. *Fourteen Weeks in Natural Philosophy*, 1878.
Steele, J. Dorman. *Popular Physics*.

6. THE EARTH SCIENCES

Appleton's Physical Geography. Prepared on a New and Original Plan, 1887.
Brocklesby, John. *Elements of Physical Geography with a Treatise on the Physical Phenomena of the United States. Mitchell's Series*, 1867.
Dana, J. D. *A Text-Book of Geology Designed for Schools and Academies. Revised Edition*, 1874.
Dana, J. D. *Revised Text-Book of Geology, Fourth Edition. Revised and Enlarged. Edited by William N. Rice*, 1897.
Davis, W. M. and Snyder W. H. *Physical Geography*, 1898.
Geike, Archibald. *Class-Book of Geology*, 1890.
Guyat, Arnold. *Physical Geography*, 1873.
Hinman, Russell, *Eclectic Physical Geography*, 1888.
Hitchcock, Edward, and Hitchcock, Edward H. *Elementary Geology. New edition*. 1860.
Houston, Edwin J. *Elements of Physical Geography for the Use of of Schools, Academies and Colleges*, 1875.
Nicholson, H. A. *Text-Book of Geology for Schools and Colleges*, 1871.
Norton, William H. *Elements of Geology*, 1905.

THE SOCIAL STUDIES

Alden, Joseph. *The Science of Government in Connection with American Institutions*, 1866.
Allen, W. F., and Myers, P. V. N. *Ancient History for Colleges and High Schools*, 1888.

Anderson, John J. *New Manual of General History with Particular Attention to Ancient and Modern Civilization with Numerous Maps and Engravings. For the Use of Colleges, High Schools, Academies, etc.*, 1882.

Andrews, Israel W. *Manual of the Constitution of the United States Designed for the Instruction of the American Youth in the Duties, Rights and Obligations of Citizenship*, 1864.

Ashley, Roscoe L. *Ancient Civilization*, 1915. *Medieval Civilization*, 1915. *Modern European Civilization*, 1918. *American Government for Use in Secondary Schools*, 1910. *The New Civics*, 1918.

Barnes' One Term History. A Brief History of the United States, 1871, 1880, 1881.

Beard, Charles A., and Beard, Mary R. *American Citizenship*, 1914.

Bullock, Charles J. *Introduction to the Study of Economics*, 1897.

Burch, Henry R., and Patterson, S. H. *American Social Problems: An Introduction to the Study of Society*, 1918.

Champlin, J. T. *Lessons on Political Economy Designed as a Basis for Instruction in that Science in Schools and Colleges*, 1868.

Chorning, Edward. *A Student's History of the United States.* Third revised edition, 1913.

Clark, S. S. *The Government. What It Is. What It Does*, 1902.

Dale, Charles F. *The American Citizen*, 1891.

Eggleston, Edward. *A History of the United States and Its People for the Use of Schools*, 1884.

Ely, Richard T. *Outlines of Economics*, 1893.

Fish, George P. *A Brief History of the Nations and Their Progress and Civilization*, 1896.

Goodrich, S. C. *Ancient History from the Creation to the Fall of Rome*, 1848.

Guitteau, William B. *Preparation for Citizenship*, 1914.

Herrick, C. A. *History of Commerce and Industry*, 1917.

Jones, J. A. and Sanford, A. H. *American History*, 1909. *Government in State and Nation*, 1910.

Knowlton, D. C. and Howe, S. B. *Essentials in Modern European History*, 1917.

Martin, G. H. *A Text-Book on the Civil Government in the United States*, 1875.

McCleary, J. T. *Studies in Civics*, 1888.

McLaughlin, A. C. *History of the American Nation*, 1913. *Readings in the History of the American Nation*, 1914.

Montgomery, D. H. *The Student's American History*, 1897.

Montgomery, D. H. *The Student's American History.* Revised edition, 1913.

Morey, W. C. *Ancient Peoples: A Revision of Morey's "Outlines of Ancient History,"* 1915.

Mussey, D. M. *American History*, 1911.

Myers, P. V. N. *Outlines of Medieval and Modern History for High Schools, Seminaries, and Colleges*, 1885. *A General History for High Schools and Colleges*, 1889. *Ancient History.* Second revised edition, 1916.

Quackenbos, J. D. *Illustrated School History of the World from the Earliest Ages to the Present Time Accompanied with Numerous Maps and Engravings*, 1879.

Ridpath, J. C. *History of the United States Prepared on a New and Comprehensive Plan Embracing the Features of Lyman's Historical Chart.*

Scott, Edward B. *A School History of the United States from the Discovery of America to the Year 1870*, 1870.

Scudder, Horace E. *A History of the United States of America with an Introduction Narrating the Discovery and Settlement of North America*, 1897.

Sheldon, Mary D. *Studies in General History. Student's Edition.* 1885.

Smith, J. R. *Commerce and Industry*, 1916.

Steele, J. Dorman, and Steele, Esther B. *A Brief History of Ancient, Medieval and Modern Peoples with Some Account of Their Movements, Institutions, Arts, Manners and Customs*, 1883.

Swinton, William. *Outlines of the World's History, Ancient, Medieval and Modern with Special Reference to the History of Civilization and the Progress of Mankind*, 1874.

Thalheimer, B. M. E. *The Eclectic History of the United States*, 1881.

Thompson, J. M. *History of the United States: Political, Industrial, Social*, 1915.

Thurston, Henry W. *Economic and Industrial History for Secondary Schools*, 1899.

Towne, Ezra T. *Social Problems: A Study of Present Day Social Conditions*, 1916.

Townsend, Calvin. *Analysis of Civil Government, Including a Topical and Tabular Arrangement of the Constitution of the United States. Designed as a Class-Book for the Use of Grammar, High and Normal Schools, and Other Institu ions of Learning*, 1869.

Walker, F. A. *Political Economy*, 1884.

Wayland, Francis. *The Elements of Political Economy*, 1841. *The Elements of Political Economy*, Recast by A. L. Chapin, 1878.

Webster, W. C. *A General History of Commerce*, 1903.

Webster, Hutton. *Ancient History*, 1913.

West, William M. *The Ancient World from the Earliest Time to 800 A.D.* Revised edition, 1917.

Willard, Emma. *Universal History in Perspective. Divided into Three Parts—Ancient, Middle and Modern*, 1865.

8. LATIN

Allen, W. Ford, Allen J. H. *Allen's Latin Lessons.*

Andrews, E. A. *First Lessons in Latin, or an Introduction to Andrews and Stoddard's Latin Grammar*, 1853.

Collar, W. C. and Daniell, M. G. *First Year Latin*, 1901.

Collar, W. C. and Daniell, M. G. *The Beginner's Latin Book*, 1886.

Jones, Elisha. *First Lessons in Latin; Adapted to the Latin Grammars of Allen and Greenough, Andrews and Stoddard, Bartholomew, Buillow and Morris, Gildersleeve and Harkness, and Prepared as an Introduction to Caesar's Commentaries on the Gallic War*, 1877.

Pearson, Henry C. *Essentials of Latin*, 1905. *Revised 1911, 1912, 1915.*

Scott, Harry F. *First Latin Book for Junior High Schools*, 1918.

Smith, M. L. *Latin Lessons*, 1913.

INDEX

INDEX

TABLES